A Short History of Stupidity

Stuart Jeffries

A Short History of Stupidity

polity

Copyright © Stuart Jeffries, 2025.

The right of Stuart Jeffries to be identified as author of this Work has been asserted by him in accordance with Sections 77 and 78 of the Copyright, Designs and Patents Act 1988.

First published by Polity Press in 2025.

Polity Press
65 Bridge Street
Cambridge CB2 1UR, UK

Polity Press
111 River Street
Hoboken, NJ 07030, USA

All rights reserved. Except for the quotation of short passages for the purpose of criticism and review, no part of this publication may be reproduced, stored in a retrieval system or transmitted, in any form or by any means, electronic, mechanical, photocopying, recording or otherwise, without the prior permission of the publisher.

ISBN-13: 978-1-5095-6349-4 – hardback

A catalogue record for this book is available from the British Library.

Library of Congress Control Number: 2024952568

Typeset in 11.5 on 14 Adobe Garamond
by Fakenham Prepress Solutions, Fakenham, Norfolk NR21 8NL
Printed and bound in Great Britain by CPI Group (UK) Ltd, Croydon

The publisher has used its best endeavours to ensure that the URLs for external websites referred to in this book are correct and active at the time of going to press. However, the publisher has no responsibility for the websites and can make no guarantee that a site will remain live or that the content is or will remain appropriate.

Every effort has been made to trace all copyright holders, but if any have been overlooked the publisher will be pleased to include any necessary credits in any subsequent reprint or edition.

For further information on Polity, visit our website:
politybooks.com

Contents

Acknowledgements · vi

Introduction · 1
1 What Is Stupidity? · 11
2 Ancient Stupidity · 22
3 Eastern Stupidity · 56
4 The Value of Folly · 91
5 Modern Stupidity · 117
6 Stupid Eugenics · 143
7 Stupid Intelligence · 174
8 Mass Stupidity · 217
9 Structural Stupidity · 235
10 Digital Stupidity · 261
Conclusion · 281

Notes · 288
Index · 311

Acknowledgements

Many people, not all of them stupid, but here unnamed to protect them from what might be career-ruining association with a book about cognitive deficiency, have helped me at various stages. Thank you to the otherwise unsung heroes behind this book: librarians, neighbours, academics, and long-suffering commissioning editors. I think it's nonetheless right to name Elise Heslinga at Polity, who saw a gap in the market and imagined that I might be able to fill it with intelligent reflections on stupidity. She shouldn't be blamed for any shortcomings in style and substance that you're about to encounter. Nor should my agent Philip Gwyn Jones, who inspired me with brilliant ideas on how to help the book appeal to a wider readership. Nor should Justin Dyer, who worked with surprising good grace to meticulously exorcize the demons of gibberish and misinformation from the manuscript at a late stage. I particularly want to thank Professor Jin Li of Brown University, whose notes on an earlier draft of chapter 3 spared me from provoking the understandable outrage of everybody currently residing in Asia, not to mention those of Asian heritage and indeed anyone who knows more than me about eastern philosophical traditions – which, as you might guess, is most of humanity. Those who remain outraged shouldn't hold the deficiencies of that chapter against Jin Li, but against me. The book was chiefly written with the help of my wife Kay and daughter Juliet, who, thanks to their brilliance, daily provided correctives to my dimwittedness. Whether their examples helped this book become less stupid than it would otherwise have been is a question for cleverer persons than me to decide.

Introduction

The rise of the dunces

Dumb, slow, simple, thick, foolish, silly, unintelligent, dopey, gormless, oafish, irrational, unreasonable, ignorant, bone-headed, dense, moronic, brain-dead, air-headed, unintelligent, asinine, imbecilic, loony, and boobyish. But enough about me. The list of synonyms for stupid is long, but each term, be it more or less scientific or more or less abusive, is crucially different in use and meaning from stupidity. Not every imbecile is stupid; gormlessness may conceal deeply intelligent thought; boobs can be clever; and while being brain-dead may disqualify you from membership of Mensa, calling someone who is literally brain-dead stupid is absurd, almost a comic understatement. The lunatics who take over the asylum are not on that account stupid. Ignorance is bliss, but no one suggested stupidity is.

It's a good time to write about stupidity. If I had a pound for every time I've read that we are living in a golden age of stupidity and that not just the five horsemen of the stupid apocalypse (Donald Trump, Elon Musk, Vladimir Putin, and – if you'll indulge a little British parochialism – the politically cataclysmic clown shows of Nigel Farage and Boris Johnson) but plenty of others are riding roughshod over humanity's intellectual achievements, replacing truth with post-truth, enthroning lies, and deposing scientific reason, I would be as rich as those horsemen. The seductions of stupidity from which these geniuses have benefited are not entirely new. The Viennese satirist Karl Kraus had Hitler in his crosshairs when he wrote nearly a century ago: 'The secret of the demagogue is to appear as dumb as his audience so that these people can believe themselves as smart as he.'[1] Nonetheless, that doesn't help us understand why Trump said about Puerto Rico: 'This is an island, surrounded by water, big water, ocean water.'[2] Or why Sarah Palin called on 'peaceful Muslims' to 'refudiate' plans to build a mosque near Ground Zero in New York.[3] Nor does it explain why Palin later claimed she had mistakenly typed an f rather than a p, which, given how far the f is from the p on a QWERTY keyboard, seems pancipul. D, of course, is much closer to f than p on the keyboard and so the possibility remains she was trying to write 'redudiate'. At the time of writing, no Muslims have apparently 'refudiated' anything.[4]

If we are to fight back against stupidity – and I'm going to go out on a limb and suggest that would be a good idea – we need first to know the nature of our enemy. To do that we need to clarify what the term means and trace its genealogy from ancient times, when stupidity was seen as intrinsically linked to human evil, to today, when you might be forgiven for thinking it has become a desirable commodity, a must-have, with stupid celebrities venerated more than those who have at least two brain cells to rub together. In this book, then, we will trace how stupidity first became associated with evil, then became detached from evil, and finally became the phenomenon that we know today – one that many pride themselves on being able to exploit in other people, with, to put it mildly, calamitous consequences for such rival phenomena of human civilization as democracy, wisdom, and excellence. I will take you for a journey, then, from stupid to stupid and back again, passing by those very clever thinkers who have reflected on what stupidity is, detouring via the counter-intuitive possibility that stupidity might be desirable and the more intuitive possibility that it is a character flaw.

But first things first.

What is stupidity?

Is it a failure of knowledge or of understanding? Is it as incorrigible as Kant thought? Is it eliminable, as Galton and other eugenicists hoped? Are we reaching Peak Stupidity? Or have we passed it? Or, worst-case scenario, are we too stupid to realize where we are in relation to Peak Stupidity, not to mention its opposite, Trough Stupidity? Or is stupidity a constant, and, if so, would it be stupid to be complacent about its existence?

INTRODUCTION

In his short story 'The Quantity Theory of Insanity', Will Self contended, with no scientific evidence but much imaginative flair, that there is 'only a fixed proportion of sanity available to any given society at any given time'.[5] In that respect, stupidity is very much like insanity: it is an ineradicable fact about human civilization, or a vast unconquerable realm whose borders change but little, if ever, like Switzerland.

That at least was the perspective of two of the cleverest – and gloomiest – thinkers to tackle the subject. 'In general, indeed,' wrote Schopenhauer, 'the wise in all ages have always said the same thing, and the fools, who at all times form the immense majority, have in their way, too, acted alike, and done just the opposite; and so it will continue.'[6] Voltaire wrote: 'We shall leave this world as foolish and as wicked as we found it on our arrival.'[7] The stupid, like the poor, are always with us.

Stupidity is almost always somebody else's quality, not ours. The French saying 'Les absents ont toujours tort' (those who are absent are always wrong) has its parallel in the world of stupidity judgements. Stupidity is someone else's curse. If we describe ourselves as stupid, we can only be at most half-serious: really, recognizing our failings takes a great deal of intelligence. As Sartre wrote about self-deception: in order to be self-deceiving, 'I have to know this truth very precisely in order to hide it from myself the more carefully.'[8] To recognize one's stupidity, one has to be clever, which would, you'd think, mean that you'd never be able to recognize your stupidity because in principle there would be none to find. If you are stupid, you probably won't realize you are. If you are stupid or clever, you will be able to designate, fairly or otherwise, other people as suffering from this most baffling of ailments. Stupidity, like beauty, is in the eye of the beholder.

If so, then perhaps stupidity is not really amenable to scientific study: it is a pejorative term, a subjective judgement, and, as David Barker argues in his essay 'The Biology of Stupidity: Genetics, Eugenics and Mental Deficiency in the Inter-War Years',[9] whenever science has been harnessed to remove the burden of stupidity from human society, that science has been overwhelmingly bogus. From craniology and Galtonian eugenics to today's renascent race science, such dodgy disciplines have been used to support a more-or-less racist socio-political doctrine, itself devoid of scientific justification and indeed arguably stupid, which treats social inequalities as rooted in biology. Such biological determinism,

INTRODUCTION

as we will see, has taken stupidity to be eradicable only by the most extraordinary and cruel means, from castration to educational apartheid policies.

Science fiction has long imagined future societies both utopian and dystopian in which stupidity along with other presumed defects has not been eradicated but exists in bracing juxtaposition to human excellence. In Aldous Huxley's *Brave New World*, drawing in part on the eugenicist inclinations of his scientist brother Julian, society is divided into five classes with the Alphas at the top and the Epsilons, the lowest caste which performs the most menial of tasks and lacks intellectual capacity, at the bottom.

If Schopenhauer and Voltaire are right, stupidity might shadow wisdom, but it is by no means its opposite. Intelligence can be measured by means of IQ tests, or so some scientists suppose. But there is no measure for stupidity, unless negatively by deficiency of intelligence, as measured by low IQ test scores. Yet self-respecting scientists are reluctant to suggest stupidity is the functional opposite of intelligence and might be measured by poor performances in IQ tests. Not because, as I will argue, IQ tests are dubious measures of an ill-conceived phenomenon, namely intelligence, but because stupidity is an even more slippery term. Science can't measure stupidity. Stupidity is a judgement rather than a measurable fact.

There are already two contrary narratives about stupidity: one where stupidity is always with us, another where we are moving towards a blissful time when stupidity is a thing of the past. Neither, it seems to me, considers the most plausible option, which is the story that I will be telling in this book: that stupidity evolves, that it mutates and thereby eludes extinction.

Stupidity is big business. By making us feel stupid and making us do stupid things, corporations can earn big bucks. I shall therefore also consider how stupidity may otherwise be valuable to enterprises who find that workers serve shareholders better by being stupid; and to individuals who find, not least in our technologically complex, information-overloaded world, that a kind of learned witlessness serves them well. This last kind of stupidity – a self-preserving, strategically intelligent stupidity – seems on the face of it a contradiction in terms, but I hope to show it is not. At times, stupidity might be the best choice.

INTRODUCTION

Finally, let us consider how stupidity has been, is, and will continue to be cultivated by politicians who subvert democracy by making their electors weapons of their own stupidity. It's not just such masters of post-truth stupefaction as Donald Trump or Boris Johnson who surfed to power deftly on swelling tides of popular stupidity, but all are exemplars of a trend that threatens to undo democracy. We are, many commentators suggest, in an age in which knowledge is more or less willingly disregarded, while ignorance and stupidity are prized as fool's gold. Stupidity should therefore be thought of as a global phenomenon, defined by the British philosopher Sacha Golob as 'a distinct form of failure; separate from, but likely aiding and abetting, political, ethical and other shortcomings'.[10] Thus conceived, it is having not so much a golden age as a global chokehold.

My own stupidity

In the early 2000s, I made a stupid mistake. I suggested that a British TV celebrity, in her own words famous for nothing, might do well to spend some of her fortune on a remedial education rather than on breast surgery and liposuction.[11] I was suggesting, in a sense, that personal stupidity could be overcome. For that modest proposal – made at a time when stupidity and ignorance, far from being excoriated, were becoming economically valuable, and the stupidity or ignorance of others was becoming something that one could not indict without being oneself indicted for insensitivity, classism, privilege, or some other offence – I was attacked.

At the time, the British dental nurse-turned-reality show celebrity Jade Goody typified for me the rise of shameless stupidity that was sweeping the new millennium. Her story is in fact an exemplary parable, demonstrating not just the difference between ignorance and stupidity, but also that ignorance can be, and often very deliberately is, cultivated and monetized, and that there is nothing stupid about that.

Even a TV quiz show such as *University Challenge*, long predicated, you might reasonably suppose, on showcasing the brightest and best of young British intellect, has occasionally been sucked into the stupefying vortex. 'What was Gandhi's first name?' asked long-time host Bamber Gascoigne. 'Goosey?' replied the contestant. The fact that one can trace the respondents' chain of reasoning here – Gandhi sounds like Gander, the male of a goose solemnized in the nursery rhyme 'Goosey Goosey Gander/Whither shall I wander?' – only makes the stupidity more evident. A later presenter of the programme, Jeremy Paxman, asked ostensibly clever students this question: 'Timothy Dalton, Orson Welles, Toby Stephens, and Michael Fassbender are among the actors who have played which romantic figure, the creation of Charlotte Brontë?' The response: 'Inspector Clouseau.'[12]

To be fair, both *University Challenge* contestants did look ashamed, which is the right response to having one's ignorance exposed, certainly if ancient philosophers (whose perspectives on stupidity we will consider in chapter 2) are reliable guides to the matter. Ignorance is not just a fault, but *the* fault – at least according to Socrates. In *Lives and Opinions of the Eminent Philosophers*, Diogenes Laertius says that Socrates 'declared that there was only one good, knowledge, and only one evil, ignorance.'[13] Viewed through that Socratic lens, Jade Goody was not just ignorant but evil. But then Socrates didn't live in a culture where ignorance could be ingeniously parlayed into a fortune by means of reality show dominance.

In her short life, Jade Goody never appeared on *University Challenge*. Instead, in 2002 she became a star on the British reality show *Big Brother*. She regaled millions with her ignorance. She thought a ferret was a bird, that an abscess was a green French drink, that Pistachio painted the *Mona Lisa*, that there was a part of England called East Angular, that Parada was a fashion designer, and that there's a language called Portuganese.[14]

But, for all the laughing, it was I who was stupid rather than Goody. She fully realized, even if unconsciously, that there is a difference between stupidity and ignorance.

Goody's intelligence came from using her very ignorance to make her fortune – which, as we shall see, is the opposite of stupidity. She was hardly the last person to do so: indeed, arguably, since her death in 2009 and the subsequent rise of social media, the opportunities to deploy ignorance and what might be taken as stupidity as elements of a lucrative personal brand have multiplied exponentially. Jade Goody is dead but today her spiritual descendants are legion – damned by elite gatekeepers as stupid, cultivating ignorance, and thereby helping spread what the Austrian novelist Robert Musil, who was spared *Big Brother* in his lifetime, called the spiritual malaise of stupidity.[15]

INTRODUCTION

When she went into the Big Brother house with her fellow contestants on the Channel 4 (un)reality show, Goody had just been evicted from a council flat over £3,000 of unpaid rent and was facing jail over an unpaid council tax bill. She quickly became famous for her apparent stupidity, and was written up in the tabloids as a 'witch' or 'public enemy'. The *News of the World* called her 'a lazy lump of lard'.

Writing in the *Guardian*,[16] I tried to defend Goody, if not for her racism, then as a woman who, I felt, was vulnerable to attack. The *Sunday People* called her Miss Piggy on account of her appearance and proffered hate-filled headlines such as 'Ditch the Witch. Gobby Jade is public enemy no. 1'. I suggested that she was in for 'the most horrible time of her life'. For a moment, it seemed that a vulnerable and evidently poorly educated woman was going to be figuratively lynched for the 21st-century crime of being dim, mouthy, and libidinous on a reality show.

I was wrong. After her eviction, Goody became a success, a multi-platform brand astutely making the best of her assets. A few years after her eviction, she was still in the public eye, having amassed a £2 million fortune that included proceeds from her fitness videos and a property portfolio. By 24, she had launched a Living TV show called *Jade's Salon*, retailed a perfume, and published *Jade: My Autobiography*, which became a bestseller in part because it detailed the awful circumstances of her childhood.[17] When I interviewed her to publicize that book, she told me she went into the Big Brother house 'to get a bit of peace and quiet . . . I thought it was going to be a hotel where I could be a kid. I've never been a kid.'[18] Goody's home life sounds like something anyone would want to escape. There's a photograph in her autobiography of Goody aged four wearing a vest and knickers, standing in a living room between two men, one of whom is smiling for the camera and the other looking mildly interested in what the girl is doing. It would be an everyday intimate family snap but for the fact that Goody is taking her first puff on a joint. Her eyes are closed as she imitates a stoner's toke. The caption reads: 'One for the family album, eh?'

Aged 26, Goody appeared in a follow-up TV series called *Celebrity Big Brother*. There she fell to racially abusing Bollywood star and fellow housemate Shilpa Shetty, calling her 'Shilpa Fuckawallah, Shilpa Durupa, Shilpa Poppadom'. She was summoned before the Big Brother authorities to account for herself. Suddenly the woman who had been merely a captivatingly thick celebrity became something more sinister: a racist in a presumed multicultural society.

She seemed to typify how low Britain had fallen, her apparent stupidity at one with her racism. Gordon Brown, then Chancellor of the Exchequer, publicly condemned the show during a visit to India, fearing an Anglo-Indian diplomatic row. 'It's not in me to be racial about anybody,' Goody explained. 'If it's offended Indians out there, I apologize.'

After leaving the house, Goody went to India to atone. In August 2008, she went on *Bigg Boss*, India's answer to *Big Brother*. While in the house, she was told she had cervical cancer and left the show. She underwent months of chemotherapy and radiotherapy, later learning her cancer had spread and that she had only months to live. Brown now mutated into Goody's unlikely champion, telling reporters we should 'applaud her determination to help her family' by selling the media rights to her wedding, while the UK tabloids could no longer find a bad word to say about her. The pig who deserved burning had become our sacrificial lamb.

I had made a stupid mistake, then, in not realizing Goody's intelligence in monetizing her ignorance.

In any event, nothing became her more in life than how she left it. Aged 27, she died of cervical cancer. Her final days as a cancer sufferer transformed her into a serious figure whose frankness about her illness was seen as widely beneficial. Her decision to live out those days in public earned her large sums of money from the media, but she insisted that her motive for this was to assure the future of her two young sons. That, in itself, was astute, the very opposite of stupidity.

The bigger point is that in our world where ignorance sells – in which it's not so much the economy, stupid, as the stupid economy – Goody did well not to spend any money on a remedial education. In an age where we monetize ourselves, we brand ourselves on social media, we perform simulacra of ourselves, Goody astutely realized that her ignorance was her fortune, and indeed if she lost that ignorance by means of education she would lose her USP.

One reason I wanted to write this book is because there is a second truth that Jade Goody realized about our society and from which she made a fortune in a rather brilliant way. The pleasure we take in others' misfortunes and even their stupidity is something that can be exploited. Like a karate black belt, Goody took all the force of the condemnations thrown at her, pivoted, and used them to help herself land safely. We live in a Spitegeist where joy in others' misfortunes and in others' displays of ignorance is addictive. In *Schadenfreude: The Joy of Another's Misfortune*, Tiffany Watt Smith contended that 'If there was ever an environment that would leave us jonesing for a new hit of justice, it is our digital age.'[19] Goody died just as social media was coming to prominence. Stupidity, both the performance of it and the attribution of it to others, has since become big business.

Why stupidity persists

In this book, I am going to trace both the history of an idea and how it has mutated to survive despite the not unreasonable thought that, in evolutionary terms at least, humans, if they were really so very concerned about not being stupid, might have used their intelligence to deselect for it. Jade Goody's rise and fall is emblematic of how we are comfortable in damning people for their presumed stupidity and how much we want stupidity to remain part of our lives while, paradoxically, energetically and repeatedly disdaining it. Humans have not just sought to sustain stupidity but also to eradicate it in ways that are crueller, more self-defeating, self-deluded, and thereby stupid – as we will see – than one would have supposed our species, particularly after the Holocaust, was capable of.

Such attempts thrived during the 20th century in misbegotten, witless, and cruel social policies, prominent not just in Nazi Germany but also in the United States, that ruined the lives of some of the most vulnerable in the name of eradicating stupidity. And yet, if experience of living in the 21st century indicates anything, it is that stupidity is alive and well and, in any culture war or intellectual smackdown, ready to defend its throne against its cognitive betters. Stupidity has eluded attempts to make it extinct, as suggested by the very titles of two films, Mike Judge's 2006 *Idiocracy* and Fanny Armstrong's 2009 *The Age of Stupid*, not to mention the lucrative spate of books analysing the problem, such as *The Psychology of Stupidity*, *The Stupidity Paradox*, and the disappointingly titled *The*

INTRODUCTION

Little Book of Stupid Questions. Indeed, stupidity is not so much a scar on humanity as a business opportunity: hence the spate of self-help books aimed at inoculating readers from this virulent virus, such as *How to Deal with Idiots (And Stop Being One Yourself)*, *Surrounded by Idiots: The Four Types of Human Behaviour (or, How to Understand Those Who Cannot Be Understood)*, and, most helpful of all, *Why Your Cat Thinks You're An Idiot*.[20] In that sense, the present volume isn't so much a brilliant and timely analysis of our age's leading pathology (though if you could say as much in any reviews I'd be grateful) as key to my retirement plan.

The book will ask these questions: If IQ tests measure intelligence, do they also measure stupidity, and if not, why not? Can animals be stupid, or is it a particularly human quality? Why did the Nazi leaders prosecuted at Nuremberg have such high IQs? Who linked IQ to race and how? Why were so many boys and girls of colour in Britain diagnosed as being educationally sub-normal and sent to special schools? And what were the consequences of doing so, for them and for society? Are there other kinds of intelligence than those measured by intelligence tests? If there truly is emotional intelligence, is there also emotional stupidity, and if so, what does it look like? Were the much-derided Neanderthals really so stupid or were they merely projections of humanity's fear of its own stupidity? If we are so clever, why did we give such sciences as eugenics and phrenology credence for so long? Is stupidity valuable? Has stupidity functional value for post-truth populists? Is artificial intelligence stupid? Can and should genetic engineering eliminate stupidity? Or is stupidity too valuable to be rendered extinct? Was Schopenhauer right that stupidity will and should always be a feature of human life?

But before we answer these questions, we need to define our terms. Stupidity is not ignorance, nor is it witlessness, nor is it insanity. Each is different from the other in important respects. I will try to account for those differences in the next chapter.

1

What Is Stupidity?

The clever professor's foolishness

'"Basically," said the American mathematician John Allen Paulos, looking a little sheepish, "I was motivated by exuberance, greed and arrogance. I became infatuated. Or demented."'[1]

Paulos, a stereotypically wild-haired mathematics professor at Temple University in Philadelphia, was recalling how he nearly lost all his savings by doing something very stupid. 'It was early 2000, the market was booming, and my investments in various index funds were doing well but not generating much excitement.' He received an unexpected windfall. 'It entrained a series of ill-fated investment decisions that, even now, are excruciating to recall.'[2] He invested in WorldCom, 'the pre-eminent global communications company for the digital generation,' as its ads boasted, at $47 per share. Today, WorldCom is remembered as a telecoms company that imploded in a carnival of cooked books and executive extravagance, its shares made worthless in the biggest accountancy fraud of its time, but Professor Paulos did not have the benefit of hindsight. He continued:

> After buying the shares, I found myself idly wondering, why not buy more? I don't think of myself as a gambler, but I willed myself not to think, willed myself simply to act, willed myself to buy more shares of WCOM, shares that cost considerably more than the few I'd already bought. Nor were these the last shares I would buy. Usually a hard-headed fellow, I was nevertheless falling disastrously in love.[3]

Paulos had fallen victim, he said, to several cognitive delusions. For example, there was the phenomenon of confirmation bias: the mental trick whereby, having made his purchases, he cast about looking for reasons to show that he'd made a brilliant decision, while ignoring evidence against this. And he bought more and more shares even as the price fell, demonstrating another truth: that people will take a greater risk to protect money they already have invested than to gain money they don't yet have, aka the sunk cost fallacy.

Paulos fell for another delusion, namely that with enough intelligence and the right method of analysis, you've got a good chance of predicting which shares will do well. He was wrong: WorldCom went spectacularly bust and filed for bankruptcy in 2002. It lost $180bn (£110bn), and its shares were rendered worthless.

The case of Paulos's disastrous investment is held up, not least by the professor himself in his book *A Mathematician Plays the Stock Market*, as an example of a very clever man doing something very stupid. It might, however, be better understood as showing something different: had Paulos not been so clever, he might not have done something so stupid. In his career, he had become very astute at pointing out the intellectual failures of others. His book *Innumeracy*, with its retrospectively ironic subtitle *Mathematical Innumeracy and Its Consequences*,[4] looks at real-world examples of stupid people gulled into believing in such phenomena as psychics, astrology, UFOs, and insurance and – of course – stock market scams.

For our purposes, Paulos's story shows something else too, namely the problem of understanding stupidity and of distinguishing it from a host of other very nearly similar terms.

'Stupidity is a lack of intelligence, understanding, reason, or wit. It may be innate, assumed or reactive. The word stupid comes from the Latin word *stupere*.' That, at least, is Wikipedia's definition of stupidity. But are matters so simple? Ignorance is not stupidity. Being wrong is not necessarily stupid. Folly, error, self-deception, are not stupidity. Non-English terms such as the Greek *amathia* or the German *Dummheit* do not map very closely onto stupidity. Clever professors do dumb things. What, then, is stupidity?

One problem is that stupidity is predicated not just of persons but also of actions. Which makes matters confusing. Worse yet, although

WHAT IS STUPIDITY?

we call a person or a person's action stupid, at least for some philosophers of stupidity, individuals become stupid chiefly because of the groups or traditions of which they are members. This is what makes stupidity a uniquely dangerous character flaw. Many other human flaws – drunkenness, tardiness, shortcomings in personal daintiness – are merely personal ones and so can be more readily eradicated, but, as the philosopher Sacha Golob puts it, stupidity is the product of the groups and societies in which we are raised. He writes: 'We get most of our concepts, our mental tools, from the society we are raised in. . . . Once stupidity has taken hold of a group or society, it is thus particularly hard to eradicate – inventing, distributing and normalising new concepts is tough work.'[5]

That's one theory. Consider the Conservative Party.

John Stuart Mill, the Victorian English philosopher and Liberal MP, claimed the Conservatives were the 'stupidest party'.[6] If stupidity is the preserve of groups and traditions, then that would suggest that all the Conservative Party's members are stupid insofar as their mental tools were forged in the stupidest party's intellectual crucible. But that seems a stretch: surely, there have been and are Conservative Party members who are not stupid. (Either that, or the clever ones left for fear of feeling out of place.)

But what of the stupidity of clever Professor Paulos? Clearly he did something stupid, but that didn't make him stupid. But what is it to do something stupid? One possibility, again set out by Golob,[7] is that stupidity is a failure to optimally use one's cognitive capacities. This seems promising because that failure is not equivalent to simply having weak cognitive capacities. For Golob, having weak cognitive capacities is something different. Dumbness for him is synonymous with unintelligence. And unintelligence, clearly, is the inverse of intelligence, which, if it is anything, is that which is measured by intelligence tests. Clearly, it would be folly to call the professor of mathematics unintelligent, or dumb, though describing his investment choices as such does not seem far-fetched.

In doing something stupid, Paulos arguably revealed something about the nature of stupidity. It is domain-specific. Just as there are footballers who might be described as having high football IQs but are functionally illiterate, or persons of high emotional intelligence incapable of tying their shoelaces, so perhaps Paulos's stupidity was only relative to a field beyond his competence. In Golob's terms, he failed to use his cognitive faculties optimally.

There's another term that could be useful here: folly. 'Much seeming stupidity [*Dummheit*] is really folly [*Narrheit*],' argued Friedrich Schlegel in 1797.[8] The problem with this term is that the waters of folly have been muddied by the long history of performance of folly. Shakespeare's many fools – from Malvolio in *Twelfth Night* to *King Lear*'s Fool – often suggest that folly is in fact truth-telling. When Erasmus wrote *In Praise of Folly*, as we shall see, he wasn't providing an endorsement for clever professors who come intellectually and financially unstuck by gambling on the stock market.

We could also use the term 'foolish'. Paulos was foolish in the sense defined by the Canadian psychologist Keith Stanovich: 'Foolishness is a domain-specific failure to act prudently, for example due to poor risk assessment.'[9] Perhaps Paulos's actions would be better conceived of in this way: losing vast sums of money in increasingly ill-judged stock market wagers seems rather different from a lack of cognitive ability, and hence dumbness or unintelligence. A failure to optimally use one's cognitive capacities is not the same as having weak cognitive capacities.

Neither, though, is quite the same as stupidity, certainly not if we follow Golob, who defines stupidity in these terms:

> An individual or group A is stupid with respect to goal G and concept C if (i) A's use of C in pursuit of G is self-hampering & (ii) where the reason for the use of C is that A's conceptual inventory either does not include a non-self-hampering concept capable of playing the same explanatory role or where such a concept is present in that inventory but A has only limited cognitive access to it.[10]

Golob cites the example of General Haig, Commander of British forces on the Western Front from December 1915 through to the end of World War I, to demonstrate his point. Haig was a man embodying the adage that British troops were lions led by (those ostensibly stupid animals) donkeys. Sir Ian Hamilton, leader of the Gallipoli campaign, suggested that Haig thought of the Western Front as 'mobile operations at the halt', that is, that infantry forces could be understood as merely stationary cavalry forces and that High Command's strategy could proceed accordingly. Haig did not literally think that infantry regiments were cavalry. Rather, the charge is that the basic conceptual framework he used to make sense of what was happening was one taken from the cavalry warfare in which he had trained – the trenches were analysed in the language of 'mobile operations', albeit with the caveat that nothing was in fact moving.

This, for Golob, is an exemplary case of stupidity. 'For Kant stupidity is a disease of determinative judgement, an inability to go *from* universal *to* particular.' Golob argues the opposite: 'Stupidity is rather an inability to go *from* particular *to* universal and a resultant inability to develop the required concepts' (original emphases).[11] In that sense, a million men died from Haig's stupidity.

If Golob is right about this, then Paulos is off the hook. He was foolish not stupid in his investments. His problem in investing foolishly was not that he didn't develop the required concepts, which is what a stupid person would have done, but that he got suckered by a range of confirmation biases and other illusions. 'When people allow themselves to be taken in by treasure seekers, alchemists, and lottery agents, [this] is not to be attributed to their stupidity,' as Immanuel Kant had it.[12]

Not of course that such fine-grained taxonomic clarification would stop that terrible burning sensation the professor even now often feels on his face when he thinks of how much he lost by buying WorldCom stock. How much did he lose playing the stock market, one interviewer asked him. He declined to say. 'Substantial,' he replied. 'Leave it at substantial.'[13]

That said, the shame of being a brilliant academic exposed for some of the intellectual failings he diagnosed in others does have its compensations. He managed to defray his losses by writing a lucrative book about becoming a dot.com dupe. This shows a truth about stupidity. Stupid people are different from unintelligent ones: the former can learn from their stupid mistakes; the latter not so much.

The strait-jacket of conventional thinking

Perhaps the above discussion, though, is stupid about stupidity. It doesn't really take into account the normative character of the use of the term.

Worse, it risks missing altogether forms of intelligence that don't fit into society's social norms. That's not to say there is anything wrong with Golob's definition of stupidity, but that it is insufficient to give a rich account of the very phenomenon it defines. It fails to consider the possibility that some behaviours considered as stupid are actually intelligent. Perhaps the IQ test we use to sort the intelligent from the stupid and the stigmatizing of some groups of humans – not just races, but those suffering or otherwise living with various deficits, disorders, and impairments – is itself a stupid perspective, one failing to appreciate different ways of being intelligent, insightful, clever, or many other human cognitive qualities.

Consider, for instance, the case of Pete Wharmby. Diagnosed as autistic at the age of 34 in 2017 and with attention deficit hyperactivity disorder (ADHD) in 2024, he has dedicated himself to improving the lot of fellow autistic people, who disproportionally suffer from depression, anxiety, and reduced life expectancy and, importantly, are more likely to be unemployed than non-autistic people. His writings celebrate neurodiversity, a neologism coined in the late 1990s by an Australian sociologist named Judy Singer as an umbrella term to describe conditions like autism, dyslexia, and ADHD. Singer's aim was to call attention to the fact that many atypical forms of brain wiring also convey unusual skills and aptitudes. Her aim was political: she wanted to do for neurodivergent people what previous movements have done for other stigmatized groups, or, as she put it in one interview, 'to do for neurologically different people what feminism and gay rights had done for their constituencies'.[14]

Certainly there is something cognitively deranging and perhaps liberating for a non-neurodiverse person such as me to read about the weird, perhaps even stupid, practices common in our neurotypical societies. This is just what I experienced reading Pete Wharmby's 2023 book *Untypical: How the World Isn't Built for Autistic People and What We Should Do About It*. There he describes himself as akin to the boy Mowgli in Rudyard Kipling's *Jungle Book*, learning the ways of a strange alien world, though in Wharmby's case without a Baloo or Bagheera to guide him. Gradually, Wharmby writes, he figured out the laws of the neurotypical world, but they scarcely seemed sensible to him, Indeed, one of the pleasures of reading his book is to see for the first time how stupid many neurotypical practices are. He writes:

> Our brains work in ways that appear to be so alien to the neurotypical population, that sometimes I'm left absolutely bewildered by the discrepancy. How can it be, for instance, that *implying* something in a weird passive-aggressive way is the default technique when trying to get something done for you? How is it in any way possible that one of the best ways to nurture and feed a friendship is to ask a person incessantly 'How are you doing' without properly listening to the answer? How is it that isolation – being left with only one's thoughts – is a widespread trope for *unhappiness*, of all things? From my point of view – the point of view of a slightly pissed-off autistic person – all of this is beyond reason.[15]

I read this alternately laughing and wincing: laughing at the funny analysis of stupid social norms and wincing at how true this account of the stupid counter-productive functioning of neurotypical society is. That phrase 'beyond reason' is especially resonant: perhaps what the straight neurotypical world is structurally unreasonable, that's to say, predicated on unwitting stupidity. Why don't neurotypicals simply ask for what they want? Why do we ask meaningless questions? Why are we so anxious about solitary behaviours that we stigmatize them? Are we stupid or something? Wharmby's askew perspective reminds me a little of Craig Raine's 1979 poem 'A Martian Sends a Postcard Home', in which a discombobulated visiting alien details strange human practices: 'At night, when all the colours die, they hide in pairs / and read about themselves – in colour, with their eyelids shut.'[16] What seems normal when viewed from one perspective becomes, when seen from another, strange, weird, charming, or, on occasion, stupid.

All this pertains to the definition of stupidity we are considering here since what neurotypical norms may regard as perfectly intelligent and reasonable are, seen from another perspective, completely potty. If we are to define stupidity in a way that conveys not just the necessary and sufficient conditions of the term but also how it is used normatively and on occasion to abuse or stigmatize, we need to recognize that what is regarded as stupid or intelligent depends substantially on one's perspective. A neurodivergent person, say, with what is diagnosed as slow auditory processing may take a while to digest what someone is saying, but that does not mean they are thick, dim, or stupid. Someone we take to be a disabled person may have intellectual skills and aptitudes scarcely dreamt of by neurotypical authority figures in all their limited cognitive powers. 'Autistic people, for instance, have prodigious memories for facts, are often highly intelligent in ways that don't register on verbal IQ tests, and are capable of focusing for long periods on tasks that take advantage of their natural gift for detecting flaws in visual patterns,' writes *Wired* editor Steve Silberman in his article 'Neurodiversity Rewires Conventional Thinking About Human Brains'. 'By autistic standards, the "normal" human brain is easily distractible, is obsessively social, and suffers from a deficit of attention to detail.'[17]

This is not just a semantic issue but a practical one with consequences for how human society flourishes or degenerates. How witless of conventional society to allow unemployment rates of neurodivergent persons to be high or to marginalize them in jobs that don't harness their potential superpowers. 'One reason,' writes Silberman, 'that the vast majority of autistic adults are chronically unemployed or underemployed, consigned to make-work jobs like assembling keychains in sheltered workshops, is because HR departments are hesitant to hire workers who look, act, or communicate in non-neurotypical ways – say, by using a keyboard and text-to-speech software to express themselves, rather than by chattering around the water cooler.'

But such hesitancy is folly, even stupid. Already, Silberman argues, neurodivergent people have made huge contributions to human society thanks to being brilliant in non-neurotypical ways. Consider, for instance, three dyslexic geniuses: Carver Mead was the father of very large-scale integrated circuits; William Dreyer designed one of the first protein sequencers; while Herman Hollerith, who helped launch the age of computing by inventing a machine to tabulate and sort punch cards, once leaped out of a school window to escape his spelling lessons because he was dyslexic.

Silberman has a piece of intelligent advice for those who struggle to appreciate the value of non-neurotypical intelligence Strikingly, he couches it in a computer metaphor. 'One way to understand neurodiversity is to remember that just because a PC is not running Windows doesn't mean that it's broken. Not all the features of atypical human operating systems are bugs.' The corollary is that different forms of intelligence should be welcomed (and, by implication, different forms of stupidity eliminated) and that social norms can sometimes be unhelpful constraints. What one sees as a disability needing treatment, another might take as a sign of intelligence. 'Trying to make someone "normal" isn't always the best way to improve their life,' says American disability rights activist Ari Ne'eman, co-founder of the Autistic Self-Advocacy Network.[18]

This is particularly stupid when one considers that some neurodivergent people (particularly so-called high-functioning autistic people among them) not only communicate better using computer screens rather than face to face but also thrive online and with high-tech – often more so than their neurotypical peers. In a breakthrough 1998 paper called 'Neurodiversity: On the Neurological Underpinnings of Geekdom', Harvey Blume argued that neurotypical is only one form of brain wiring, and arguably an inferior one. Blume wrote: 'The common assumption in cognitive studies these days is that the human brain is the most complicated two-and-a-half pounds of matter in the known universe. With so much going on in a brain, the argument goes, the occasional bug is inevitable: hence autism and other departures from the neurological norm.' But that is stupid, he argued. 'Who can say what form of wiring will prove best at any given moment? Cybernetics and computer culture, for example, may favour a somewhat autistic cast of mind.'[19]

But only one form of wiring has been traditionally favoured by employers. In the US, the Stanford Diversity Project estimated in 2019 that 80% of people on the autism spectrum are unemployed or underemployed, which, you'd think, is folly, since many of those people have untapped potential. Indeed, that potential is being increasingly recognized by firms changing hiring practices to accommodate neurodivergent people. Microsoft, for instance, from 2012 onwards, specifically targeted neurodivergent people by changing the tech giant's hitherto forbidding interview process. Many of the normative behaviours required in a job interview – making eye contact, delivering a firm handshake, and selling yourself – are things that many autistic people might have difficulty doing. As Gwen Moran of *Fortune* magazine reported in 2019: 'People with autism, anxiety disorders, and some other cognitive differences may struggle with intense interviewing processes spanning weeks and [which] may include four or five interviews in a single day.'[20]

While researching his 2015 book *Neurotribes: The Legacy of Autism and the Future of Neurodiversity*,[21] Steve Silberman found some employers changing their recruitment processes to accommodate neurodiverse applicants. One company, he related, even had applicants solve problems with Lego instead of explaining what a good employee they could be. This was not necessarily virtuous behaviour, but certainly good business: in a tight labour market, companies pragmatically look for new talent. Or as the headline for Gwen Moran's 2019 *Forbes* article put it: 'As workers become hard to find, Microsoft and Goldman Sachs hope neurodiverse talent can be the missing piece.'

Perhaps, Silberman argues, there is a parallel between biological diversity and neurodiversity: 'In forests and tide pools, the value of biological diversity is resilience: the ability to withstand shifting conditions and resist attacks from predators. In a world changing faster than ever, honoring and nurturing neurodiversity is civilization's best chance to thrive in an uncertain future.'[22] It would be stupid for human society to set that chance aside.

But to be open to doing so requires quite a lot of thinking, not least about what we consider to be a disability and what an ability, about what is a squish-worthy bug and what is a desirable feature, what is folly and what is wise, and, ultimately, what is stupid and what intelligent. The deranging, helpful suggestion of the above neurodivergent writers and thinkers is that the boundaries between these pairs are not necessarily where society has put them. IQ tests and narrow-minded hiring practices may sharpen these boundaries, but at a considerable cost. Perhaps in fact there is no line but only a vague boundary between stupidity and intelligence, just as there may be no defensible way in some cases of deciding whether stupidity is a form of madness or disability. Certainly, as we will see, stupidity and folly have at times in history been taken as synonymous; at others stupidity has been taken as a cognitive deficiency that amounts to a disability that, by means of brutal breeding policies, is to be exterminated from human society.

In the Sorites paradox, a heap of sand is reduced by a single grain at a time. When does it cease to be heap? Arguably, there is no precise moment when the reducing of a pile of sand by one single grain transforms it from heap into non-heap. Perhaps stupidity is a similarly fuzzy concept which, paradoxically, we make into a non-fuzzy concept by bogusly imposing on it non-fuzzy characteristics. For instance, we use IQ tests to sharply delimit, perhaps foolishly, the intelligent from the stupid; by not hiring dyslexics, HR companies define those they take to be intelligent and employable from those who are not. Both are ways of forcing on a fuzzy concept a sharply normative character that can and, as we will see later, does have disastrous consequences for human flourishing. Both human practices were surely devised to help society function better, but in fact may only help make it stagnate or at least function at sub-optimal levels. Now that, one might think, is really stupid.

2

Ancient Stupidity

A meeting with a strange woman

More than two millennia ago, an impetuous youth called Chaerephon set off on a quixotic quest. He travelled 250 miles or so from Athens to a chasm near Delphi that the Greeks called the Omphalos, or navel of the world. Chaerephon wanted to ask a simple question of a sage sitting on a stool next to this chasm, a woman who was, most likely, inspired by mind-altering hallucinogens.

Today the Omphalos is handily located near the EO 48, but that road hadn't been built in 440 BCE. Chaerephon was obliged to climb foothills, purify himself with holy water from the Castilian Spring, then, having arrived at Delphi, walk along its Sacred Way that was flanked by grand statues, murals, and temples left by the oracle's grateful clients. Among these treasures was a colossal sphinx on top of a 40-foot column, a temple of the Athenians built to commemorate victory at the Battle of Marathon, and a solid gold lion rampant on 117 blocks of white gold.

At the end of the Sacred Way, Chaerephon may well have paused in front of the Temple of Apollo to take in the improving maxims carved onto its walls, namely 'Know Thyself' and 'Nothing in Excess'. Then he entered. Most likely his nose was filled with the smell of roasting flesh from nearby sacrificial offerings and his ears rang with the chatter of pilgrims who had come to seek answers to great questions such as whether a crop would fail, a marriage be happy, or a battle victorious. Hexameters were published of priestesses' often confoundingly enigmatic prophecies that were the products of *enthousiasma* or divine inspiration, such as this one quoted by Pausanias:

> But one day, when a Tithorean man pours libations
> and offerings of prayer on the earth to Amphion and Zethus;
> when Taurus is warmed by the might of the glorious sun;
> at that time, beware of disaster for the city, no small one.
> For the fruit of the harvest wastes away in it
> when people divide the earth and bring it to Phocus' grave.[1]

Which, you might think, has minimal usefulness for public officials striving to fend off disaster and food shortages.

Then Chaerephon pressed on to the temple's inner sanctum, or *adyton*, where a peasant woman, reputedly chosen for having led a blameless life (whatever that means), sat alone on a tripod seat over an opening in the earth, imbibing its emissions. She was called Pythia, though that was most likely the job title. Several women held the post as the oracle at Delphi. She was the god Apollo's spokeswoman, a prophetess or sibyl. Whether divinely inspired by the deity, out of her mind on consciousness-altering gases, or both, is uncertain.

Geologists have recently suggested that vapours from the chasm were hallucinogenic hydrocarbons such as ethane or ethylene. Ancient sources contended rather that the priestess's prophetic trances were induced by the effects of inhaling fumes from a sacred fire of laurel (which may have been cannabis), or from gas caused by the decomposing corpse of the python that Apollo had killed and thrown into the pit, though that last idea seems far-fetched. Only idiots believe that roasted python fumes have hallucinogenic properties.

In any event, Chaerephon, probably sweaty from his trek, dazzled by the treasures and other glories he had just witnessed, awed by the holy of holies he had just entered, and, you'd think, starting to hallucinate a little himself, asked the question he had been nurturing in his bosom since Athens.

'Is there anybody wiser than Socrates?'

'No,' Pythia replied, pithily.[2]

Whatever you think of the judgement, it was certainly more straightforward than her gnomic warnings about looming poor harvests.

Then, as far as we know, Chaerephon trotted back to Athens to tell his friend and mentor the good news before leaving the historical record. Socrates, though, was not pleased to learn he was the least stupid of mortals, but baffled. Years later, in 399 BCE, when he was tried by an estimated 500 Athenian men on accusations of impiety and corrupting Athenian youth, he said: 'Whatever does the god mean? For I know I am not wise, not extremely wise, not even moderately wise. So whatever does he mean by saying I am the wisest?'[3]

Such at least are the words that Plato puts into Socrates' mouth in his unsuccessful self-defence speech. It's a good question: his trial, after all, took place in the late Bronze Age, so long before the Stanford–Binet Intelligence Scale or any other IQ test. On what grounds could Apollo or his Pythian mouthpiece decide who was the wisest of humans?

Socrates was baffled in part because he believed the oracle could not lie but also because he knew he was not wise. From the latter point, we may extrapolate two paradoxes: first, that only the wise know they are not wise, and, second, that only the stupid imagine they aren't stupid. Socrates' claim that he knew he wasn't wise is founded on the virtue of humility and is, to followers of Socratic wisdom, a necessary condition for wisdom. But it is not a sufficient one: some ignorant people, notably the stupid ones, don't have it. 'Humility is not a particular habit of self-effacement,' wrote the Irish-English philosopher Iris Murdoch, 'rather like having an inaudible voice, it is selfless respect for reality and one of the most difficult and central of all the virtues.'[4] It is not a virtue one should brag of possessing. When Donald Trump told a reporter, 'I think I'm much more humble than you would understand,'[5] he demonstrated he wasn't. If only he had read more Plato. But then cultivating humility, which Socrates takes as essential for overcoming one's stupidity, is hard work; it is not something one boasts about, though without it one cannot know oneself, and without knowing oneself one can never become virtuous.

Socrates went on to tell his judges that, after hearing this report of his unparalleled wisdom, he decided to question everyone he could find who claimed to be wise or appeared so. His quest was for the truth about what is wisdom, and who has it. Indeed, the dialogues that Plato wrote are the only record we have of Socrates testing the minds of those who suppose themselves wise and/or erroneously believe they know things that, on close questioning by Socrates, they are compelled to admit they do not. They are not just ignorant but ignorant about their ignorance, which, as we shall see, is one leading form of stupidity.

Who, then, is wise? Socrates, at the end of his life, found the truth and told it to his judges. 'The truth is, my fellow Athenians, that only God is wise. What the oracle meant was that what we know is little or nothing. Apollo didn't just mean me; I am just an example. What God means is, "The wise know their own wisdom is worth no more than anyone's."'[6]

Each Socratic dialogue, then, or at least those that are not burdened with Plato's positive metaphysical, cosmological, or other dubious positive views (such as the insane hypothesis in *The Republic* that philosophers should be the ruler-kings of any sensible polity), is a piece of intellectual therapy in which, through painstaking cross-examination by Socrates, a man who thought he was wise at the outset realizes by the end the truth that he is not. Plato's translator Benjamin Jowett puts it well:

> Self-humiliation is the first step to knowledge, even of the commonest things. No man knows how ignorant he is, and no man can arrive at virtue and wisdom who has not once in his life, at least, been convicted of error. The process by which the soul is elevated is not unlike that which religious writers describe under the name of 'conversion', if we substitute the sense of ignorance for the consciousness of sin.[7]

The conversion is not from ignorance to knowledge, but from unwitting ignorance to knowledge that one has been ignorant, by means of which one becomes wiser about one's lack of wisdom and, most pertinently, realizes the extent of one's stupidity. Without that spiritual journey from ignorance about one's shortcomings to knowledge of one's shortcomings, one can never lead the good life. Plato and Socrates, in common with many ancient Greek thinkers, believed that the good life involves overcoming one's ignorance about some things and realizing that one's ignorance about others may well be insurmountable. Being knowledgeable about that latter ignorance is a feature of wisdom. It is not, really, that ignorance is evil or bad per se, but rather that the unwillingness or inability to overcome ignorance is evil.

Stupidity, then, is not just a fault, but an evil – perhaps even the greatest evil. Centuries later, the German Enlightenment philosopher

Immanuel Kant held that one can be both good and stupid, which seems to be a common enough belief today; ancient Greek philosophers believed otherwise. In *The Nicomachean Ethics*, for instance, based on notes made by his son 60 or so years after Socrates' death, Aristotle wrote: 'It is not possible to be good without practical wisdom, or practically wise without moral virtue.'[8] The Greek term *eudaimonia*, often mistranslated as happiness, captures this: for Aristotle, *eudaimonia* is the proper goal of human life but it is not, like happiness, a subjective state. Rather, *eudaimonia* is an objective feature of the person who leads a good life – a combination of well-being and flourishing. True, such well-being may be accompanied by a subjective sense of happiness that comes from knowing one is living virtuously, but that is not essential to the matter. Pigs can be happy wallowing in mud, stupidly blissful in their ignorance of higher activities. Stupidity is not thereby a virtue. That stupid bliss might even be part of their function, as Aristotle sees it, by means of which they flourish. A pig that did not stupidly wallow in mud would not only be missing out on filthy good times but also betraying its function as a flourishing mud wallower.

For humans, matters are different. Happy wallowing in mud is not for us. It would be wicked for us to wallow in mud, be that mud literal or the metaphorical mud that is the multi-form stupefaction of our current age of stupidity: consumerism, low-grade entertainment, and finessing one's fatuous image on social media. One can be happy and stupid, but not virtuous and stupid. John Stuart Mill, whose photographs make him look quite the stranger to mud baths, wrote: 'It is better to be a human being dissatisfied than a pig satisfied; better to be Socrates dissatisfied than a fool satisfied. And if the fool, or the pig, is of a different opinion, it is only because they only know their own side of the question.'[9]

This pig–human distinction was a problem for Mill, officially the defender of utilitarianism, which proposes that the ultimate goal of human life, its *summum bonum*, should be to maximize the happiness of the greatest number and, in principle, cannot object if all humanity is happily wallowing pig-like in mud. But it is not a problem for Aristotle or Socrates: stupidly wallowing in mud in misplaced self-satisfaction is a betrayal of what it is to flourish as a human, and therefore evil. Stupidity is an evil we can and must overcome.

But why bother? Who wants to know that they are stupid? If ignorance is bliss, isn't stupidity, which involves ignorance about one's ignorance, bliss squared? That realization of one's pig-like immersion in unworthy pleasures is a good thing because only when one knows one is stupid can one become less so. But that is paradoxical: if you are stupid, how do you stop being so? Doesn't one's very stupidity preclude one from making that ostensibly desirable lifestyle change? Hold that thought.

In the *Apology*, Socrates sought to irritate those filled with puffed-up delusions about their wisdom. But not only individuals: Socrates acted, he told his judges, 'as upon a great noble horse which was somewhat sluggish because of its size and needed to be stirred up'.[10] He imagined himself as 'that gadfly which God has attached to the state' and Athens as a sluggish horse that had become not just ignorant but stupid. Moreover, his task was to bring this ancient age of stupidity to an end. 'All day long and in all places [I] am always fastening upon you, arousing and persuading and reproaching you,' he told his judges, and by extension the Athenian people. 'You will not easily find another like me, and therefore I would advise you to spare me.'[11] His judges' decision to find him guilty demonstrated something that Socrates, being wise, suspected, namely their stupidity. By sentencing him to death, they were voting to continue unchecked by his wisdom.

Like Jade Goody, Socrates wore his ignorance proudly. Just before he was sentenced to death, he told his judges, 'And this is the point in which, as I think, I am superior to men in general, and in which I might perhaps fancy myself wiser than other men – that whereas I know but little of the world below, I do not suppose that I know.'[12] Note that here Socrates does not say that he knows 'nothing'. Instead, he says that he knows 'little'. The main point is not that he wants to glorify ignorance, but that he wants to expose those who pretend to know things that they don't. The enemy of knowledge, according to Socrates (and Plato), is not ignorance. Not to know is not shameful. Someone who does not know, and is aware of their ignorance, can do something about their lack of knowledge and start to study and learn and improve themselves.

This, especially for those who seek the truth, may seem disappointing. After all, the pursuit of wisdom and knowledge should, ideally, lead one to more than realizing the potentially alarming extent of one's own ignorance and/or stupidity. But Socrates, in all his appealing humility, realized that wisdom consists not in possessing the truth but in implacably pursuing it. That pursuit is a difficult business, like hunting a grey fox through twilit woods, unlikely to end in success. One may well never catch one's prey but its pursuit is the thing, the means by which one overcomes one's ignorance and does virtuous battle with the demon stupidity. In a sense, this battle is Socrates' interpretation of the maxims found on the walls of the Temple of Apollo: not just know thyself but know thy shortcomings the better to overcome them. The other maxim, 'Nothing in Excess', is pertinent too: we might dream of hunting down the truth, but it would be excessive to expect that this protean prey can be caught. Viewed from another perspective, this pursuit is absurd: Socrates, if he was wise, would have been foolish to pursue something that can't be, or at least is unlikely to be, captured. Not so: wisdom consists first and foremost of disabusing oneself of one's prideful attachment to ignorance or, which seems less of a moral fault, one's ignorance about how ignorant one is. Wearing ignorance as a badge of honour is more shameful than not knowing one is ignorant, and thus being incapable of wearing such a badge.

What is stupidity for Socrates? Two Greek terms are key, *agnoia* and *amathia*. *Agnoia* means 'not-knowing', ignorance, and *amathia* takes several forms but essentially means 'not-learning'. Worse than the type of *amathia* that is an *inability to learn*, there is another form that is the *unwillingness to learn*. That is the most shameful of what we would call stupidity and the fault that Socrates wants to indict.

Bracing words for a stupid boy

This becomes clear in the *First Alcibiades*, a celebrated dialogue ascribed to Plato in which Socrates is in conversation with his sometime lover Alcibiades. It's an absolutely scintillating exchange, juxtaposing two opposites, an ageing, ugly, wise spurned lover and a gorgeous, ambitious 19-year-old Athenian, in which the former counsels the latter to overcome the self-delusion that leads many a self-regarding twit into politics before they have the requisite skills, humility, or acumen.

This is a vital text for future thinkers about stupidity in particular and philosophy in general. For the postmodern French philosopher Michel Foucault, the *First Alcibiades* is the foundational document of a new philosophy wherein, by following the Delphic oracle's call to know thyself, we learn to care for the self. For the German philosopher Friedrich Nietzsche, it typified how Socrates, that 'mystagogue of science', is 'the vortex and turning point of Western civilization'.[13] Socrates seduced not just Alcibiades but the rest of us to his personal folly, namely his obsessive pursuit, by means of rational inquiry, of the truth.

Those who find it hard to envisage the meeting between these two very different ancient Greek men might enjoy consulting François-André Vincent's 1776 painting *Alcibiades Being Taught by Socrates*.[14] In it, Alcibiades is wearing a magnificent plumed helmet and a frankly ill-advised blush pink robe cinched at the shoulder over an equally marvellous verdigris and gold breastplate as he listens to the gnarly old sage in dull robes set him straight. For the dandified narcissist Alcibiades is stupid, and not just because he is, stupidly, unable or unwilling to realize that blush pink is just the thing to wear in battle only if you want to make yourself into an archery target.

The dialogue is gripping in part because it showcases two devices characteristic of the Socratic method, both of which can be seen as a form of cross-examination that leads the master's interlocutor to realize that they do not know what they supposed they knew, that they were ignorant about their ignorance. Socrates describes himself as a midwife, since he regards his role in these dialogues as to help his interlocutors develop their understanding. The first device, the *elenchus*, is a method for getting to the truth by a process of questioning and answering that serves to refute an interlocutor's argument or to undermine a rhetorical position. In this dialogue, for instance, Alcibiades asserts: 'There is a difference between justice and expediency. Many persons have done great wrong and profited by their injustice; others have done rightly and come to no good.'[15] Here the *elenchus* involves Socrates doubting the assertion, inducing Alcibiades to agree to other assertions that contradict his original assertion and thereby showing the original thesis is false and the opposite true.

Second, there is Socratic irony, which is the pose of ignorance to induce the interlocutor into making statements that can then be challenged. Here the irony is that Socrates feigns his own ignorance, the better to expose Alcibiades' real ignorance. This was a live issue for Socrates as he worried that Athens teemed with statesmen who through their ignorance and unwillingness to learn were tarnishing the golden age of his beloved city state. In the *First Alcibiades*, then, Plato, through Socrates, is offering a critique of politics as usual. He is trying to shake not just Alcibiades but also Athens out of their stupidity.

Down the millennia, this ancient dialogue resonates for us. Like Donald Trump or Boris Johnson before they took top posts in their respective polities, though more beautiful than either, Alcibiades was poised to enter public service without the necessary competence and, worse, filled with the complacent self-regard and pride that led him to believe he needn't overcome those shortcomings. The *First Alcibiades* is a warning of what calamities are likely to ensue when stupidity, filled with misplaced self-esteem, lust for power and pride, enters politics.

Socrates' complaints to his lover, then, are remarkably pertinent to more recent politics. It is not just that the likes of Johnson or Trump are ignorant about what it takes to be good rulers but also that, in their failure to follow the Delphic oracle's injunction 'Know Thyself', they are ignorant of their ignorance. As a result, they risk becoming dangerous not just to themselves but also to those whom they are supposed to serve. In 2020, for instance, President Trump took to the White House briefing room and encouraged his top health officials to study the injection of bleach into the human body as a means of fighting Covid.[16] His prideful ignorance about the question of how we should inoculate ourselves against a particularly virulent virus led him to propose a dangerous remedy rather than following the Socratic path via self-humiliation to wisdom, recognizing how little he knew about such matters, and deferring to his scientific advisers. In the same year, Boris Johnson attended a birthday party in 10 Downing Street, for which he later received a police fine, one of six such boozy gatherings that took place during the Covid lockdown in the UK when he frequently appeared on television, urging people to stick to strict social distancing rules.[17] Trump, one might say, was stupid for being so filled with self-regard as to imagine not just that he was not ignorant about how to treat the coronavirus, but also that he knew more than his scientific advisers; Johnson was so filled with stupid pride as to imagine that the rules he asked his electors to adhere to did not apply to him.

At one point in the dialogue, Socrates asks Alcibiades if it is true that those who are ignorant of some matter, such as shipbuilding, should defer to the expertise of those who are not, thereby, sensibly, setting out to sea in boats that are less liable to sink. Alcibiades agrees to this and accepts the point that the only people who make mistakes are not those who have expertise in a field, nor those who are aware of their ignorance of that field and so defer to experts in it, but rather those who do not know, while thinking that they do. It's this last bunch who are the real liabilities, those who have misplaced confidence in their own expertise, forever setting out to sea in self-made boats that sink shortly after leaving harbour in a fine cosmic comeuppance.

'Then this is ignorance of the disgraceful sort which is mischievous?' asks Socrates. Alcibiades agrees. 'And most mischievous and most disgraceful when having to do with the greatest matters?' 'By far,' replies Alcibiades.[18] This idea that ignorance and stupidity are not just faults but evils, which to us moderns does not seem plausible (just because you don't know, say, Pi to at least five decimal places doesn't mean you're a bad person), is commonplace among the greatest ancient Greek thinkers.

Neither Trump nor Johnson was properly aware of his shortcomings, which, if Socrates is right, made them evil, base, and stupid. Socrates insists that such self-knowledge, along with what Jowett calls self-humiliation, is necessary for an aspiring politician.

But what does Alcibiades know better than the multitude that would justify offering advice and becoming their ruler? A shoemaker has a certain expertise – that's why we take our shoes to them to be repaired rather than to philosophers, notwithstanding the latter's allegedly unparalleled wisdom. What is the parallel in the case of Alcibiades, the would-be statesman? The cobbler, one might think, learned how to mend shoes from a master or taught himself. What was Alcibiades' route to expertise in statecraft, Socrates wonders. If you are to be a good statesman, you must know the difference between the just and the unjust, he suggests; otherwise, you would have no business recommending when to go to war. For only just wars should be prosecuted. But Alcibiades says he never learned the difference between justice and injustice from a master, nor did he inquire into the matter himself.[19]

Here, Socrates is leading Alcibiades down a shady path to personal enlightenment that the stupid boy never imagined he would take. It is the path of self-humiliation from deluded pride to the necessary illumination if one is to realize not just how little one knows, but also that one has been ignorant about one's ignorance.

But there is a fascinating twist in that path. Socrates recalls watching Alcibiades as a little boy playing dice with friends. The little Alcibiades called out those who cheated, which suggests to Socrates that he did know the difference between the just and the unjust.

This is a key moment in the dialogue for psychologists of stupidity since here Socrates demonstrates, or rather gets Alcibiades to demonstrate, a counter-intuitive fact about himself, namely that he is ignorant that he knows, or at least knew, something. At an abstract level, this sounds like a contradiction. It sounds counter-intuitive that one could be ignorant that one knows something. But, as we will see, it is only an apparent contradiction. Stupid people can be ignorant about what they know. Or, as Sacha Golob puts it, a 'concept is present in that inventory but A only has limited cognitive access to it'. [20] It is one of the leading forms of stupidity. And what's more, as we will see, stupid people can be ignorant not just about what they know but also about how they acquired that knowledge.

The little Alcibiades, then, seeing his friend cheating and realizing that to do so was unjust, was ignorant that he knew the nature of justice from such a recollection. The mature Alcibiades, in a sense, is even more ignorant than his childhood self, since he supposed he did not know because he had not learned from a reliable authority or bothered to find out for himself what justice was. But, as Socrates induces Alcibiades to realize, he at least instinctively recognized injustice when he saw it. Alcibiades is too stupid, effectively, to realize that the cure for his own stupidity is latent within him. In this, Socrates is a midwife, assisting at the birth of Alcibiades' wisdom.

Alcibiades is so filled with unbecoming presumption that he imagines he will be a boon to the Athenian people. He thinks that he should lead because he's handsome, wealthy, and born of a good family. Alcibiades was the nephew of the great Athenian statesman Pericles, who was the boy's guardian. This is the same Pericles regarded as largely responsible for the full development of Athenian democracy and who restored Athens to its former grandeur by commissioning the building of the Acropolis. If Athens had a golden age, it was thanks in no little measure to Pericles' statesmanship. None of this Periclean wisdom has rubbed off on his nephew, Socrates notes, nor on his sons.

Socrates insists that Pericles, though a great and wise statesman, and to that extent a role model for Alcibiades, was a hopeless mentor or teacher of wisdom to the boys in his charge. Those who have overcome their own stupidity, Socrates seems to suggest, need not be good remedial teachers of wisdom. According to Alcibiades, Pericles' two sons were simpletons and Alcibiades' own brother, Cleinias, also raised under Pericles' guardianship, 'is a madman; there is no use in talking of him'. [21]

It's ironic here that Socrates' insistence on the value of humility is undone by his suggestion that only he can provide the remedial instruction that the stupid Alcibiades needs to overcome his shortcomings. There is an erotic tenor to this: the spurned lover, Socrates, is asserting that he, and he alone, is capable of intimately schooling Alcibiades. The know-nothing philosopher at least knows more than anyone else about the ignorance of others. The dialogue is replete with such paradoxes, no more than this one: to overcome one's humility, one needs help from one who has learned humility and, thereby, become self-satisfyingly better than those who have not. Humility in Socrates' philosophy is a personal quality of which he can be, paradoxically, proud.

Alcibiades, understandably though self-deludingly, sought to bask in the reflected glory of his uncle Pericles. Later aspirants to high office have attempted to do the same. During a vice-presidential debate in 1988, the Republican candidate Senator Dan Quayle mentioned the late President John F. Kennedy, as if aiming to gain lustre by the association, perhaps even to be taken as a latter-day JFK. 'I knew Jack Kennedy,' snapped his rival, the Democratic vice-presidential candidate Lloyd Bentsen, who served in Congress at the same time as JFK. 'Senator, you're no Jack Kennedy.'[22] Socrates, in the *First Alcibiades*, is Lloyd Bentsen, not so much a gadfly nipping at Alcibiades as an old man armed with a sharp needle with which he satisfyingly punctures a stupid boy's inflated idea that he is fit to govern.

'Before many days have elapsed, you think that you will come before the Athenian assembly and will prove to them that you are more worthy of honour than Pericles, or any other man that ever lived, and having proved this, you will have the greatest power in the state,' Socrates tells Alcibiades.

> When you have gained the greatest power among us, you will go on to other Hellenic states, and not only to Hellenes, but to all the barbarians who inhabit the same continent with us . . . the world, as I may say, must be filled

with your power and name – no man less than Cyrus and Xerxes is of any account with you.[23]

This is a worrying moment, then, not just for Athenian democracy, but also for the fate of the ancient world: a puffed-up, deluded dimwit teen thinks he has what it takes to rival Cyrus and Xerxes, the Persian kings both of whom had the honorific 'the great' imposed upon them.

But really, Socrates wonders, what use will Alcibiades be to the Athenian people if he does enter public life? As far as Socrates knows, Alcibiades' list of accomplishments is short.

> You learned the arts of writing, of playing on the lyre, and of wrestling; the flute you never would learn; this is the sum of your accomplishments, unless there were some which you acquired in secret; and I think that secrecy was hardly possible, as you could not have come out of your door, either by day or night, without my seeing you.[24]

So, is Alcibiades going to advise Athenians about what he knows, namely writing, playing the lyre, or wrestling? Hardly, replies Alcibiades. But then what? After all, if the Athenians wanted advice about their health, they would consult a physician; or if about shipbuilding, they would visit a shipbuilder. Why would they seek leadership on affairs of state from someone so devoid of accomplishments that, quite possibly, he may not even be Athens' go-to guy for tips on playing the flute? Alcibiades suggests he will advise Athenians about matters that he knows better than they, and when pressed he says that he means when it is better to go to war and when better to choose peace.

Here Socrates exposes Alcibiades' witlessness by taking the ironic stance of affecting ignorance. It is clear, for instance, when an expert adviser on food tells another that some dish is better than another, he knows why. (Perhaps it's more wholesome, tastier, or won't go straight to one's thighs.) In those cases, we have a clear idea of what the criteria are for one thing being better than another. But what's the parallel in the case of peace and war, asks Socrates, in his pose of ignorance? What decides whether war is better than peace, or vice versa? Alcibiades has claimed he knows this difference and indeed that, if he is to be a worthwhile statesman to the Athenians, it is just such specialist discrimination he will need. But, on humiliating questioning from Socrates, he admits he is ignorant of what criteria could be used to decide that peace is better than war, or vice versa. This, to Socrates, is scandalous in someone imagining that they are already fitted to be a political leader: 'When the subject is one of which you profess to have knowledge, and about which you are ready to get up and advise as if you knew, are you not ashamed, when you are asked, not to be able to answer the question? Is it not disgraceful?' 'Very,' replies the chastened Alcibiades.[25]

This is the first of a series of humiliations that Socrates induces the stupid boy to visit upon himself. But that self-humiliation, it is essential to realize, is not an end in itself: rather, it is part of the self-care of the soul that arises from self-knowledge, in particular self-knowledge about one's shortcomings.

But perhaps, Socrates suggests, there is a way of avoiding this disgraceful corollary he and Alcibiades have just reached whereby his young ex-lover is forced to admit that he knows no better than anyone else when it is better to go to war or choose peace. He invites Alcibiades to have another go at demonstrating his fitness for office. 'Well, then, consider and try to explain what is the meaning of "better", in the matter of making peace and going to war with those against whom you ought to go to war?' urges Socrates. 'To what does the word refer?'[26] Here, the mask of Socratic irony, whereby he affects ignorance, slips: Socrates clearly has a notion of justice being central to good statesmanship, and indeed has an agenda that he wants Alcibiades to share.

Alcibiades suggests that what the Athenian people want to know from their rulers is not the just course of action, but what is expedient. That is, what is useful or convenient. He clearly has an idea that justice is different from expediency and, indeed, may in some circumstances be opposed to it. Socrates here helps Alcibiades realize he is wrong in that belief and helps him give birth to the truth, namely that justice and expediency are one and the same. This is the *elenchus* at work.

Initially, Socrates' attempt to induce Alcibiades to agree he is wrong in supposing the just and the expedient coincide seems fanciful: might politicians not justify a course of action that is expedient rather than one that is just? Consider this possibility. If a council leader, Veronica, orders the filling of some potholes shortly before election day, to capture the votes of the anti-pothole majority in the motoring lobby, that might well seem politically expedient but hardly just, particularly if the works are funded from, for the sake of argument, closing care homes. Indeed, here expediency does not just look like political pragmatism but also veers close to cynicism: the electors are to be bought off by something that is in their interests, but not – we are to suppose – because filling in potholes is a good thing in itself. Here, the expedient and the just are very different phenomena, despite what Socrates says. Why is he so convinced these are the same thing?

Socrates doesn't explain. Instead, he induces Alcibiades, as part of his crypto-Maoist self-improvement project, to demonstrate that justice and expediency coincide. Some honourable things are evil and some dishonourable ones good, suggests Alcibiades. For example, those who die or are wounded in rescuing a companion or kinsman from the battlefield act honourably, while those who neglect that duty of rescuing them but escape to safety are dishonourable. And yet there is evil in the case of the former and good in the case of the latter. Socrates here invites Alcibiades to agree that those who act courageously in the above example act well and thereby do good. Alcibiades does indeed agree, and so Socrates presses on with his cross-examination of the stupid boy.

The dialogue here, as happens in many such exchanges, is unwittingly funny and ironic, since Socrates fires off volley after volley of questions to an interlocutor who is reduced to one-word answers – as if they were stupefied rather than edified by his reasoning. Even though Socrates is, by his own lights, leading Alcibiades through his chain of reasoning to release from his shameful state of ignorance, the text seems to suggest that Alcibiades increasingly agrees to any old thing his teacher says just to shut the old man up.

Thus we have the following rather slippery chain of reasoning:

Socrates: And happiness is a good?
Alcibiades: Yes.
Socrates: Then the good and the honourable are again identified.
Alcibiades: Manifestly.
Socrates: Then, if the argument holds, what we find to be honourable we shall also find to be good?
Alcibiades: Certainly.

Socrates: And is the good expedient or not?
Alcibiades: Expedient.[27]

It's very much as if the old man's zest for argument is met by a grumpy teenager shrugging agreement in the hope that the Socratic third degree will soon be over and he can go back to what he does best, prancing about looking gorgeous in his marvellous robes.

And yet the chain of reasoning that Socrates induces Alcibiades to accept is hardly plausible: his example does seem to show that behaving justly is closely, perhaps even intrinsically, connected with behaving honourably and doing good actions, but not that acting expediently or doing expedient things is just. Nonetheless, Socrates, mutating from gadfly to human steamroller, presses on, crushing his interlocutor with questions, if not with logic. The dialogue continues:

Socrates: And the honourable is the good?
Alcibiades: Yes.
Socrates: And the good is expedient?
Alcibiades: Yes.
Socrates: Then, Alcibiades, the just is expedient?
Alcibiades: I should infer so.
Socrates: And all this I prove out of your own mouth, for I ask and you answer?
Alcibiades: I must acknowledge it to be true.[28]

There is no 'must' to it and no logical inference by Alcibiades. Socrates hasn't proved his point, nor has he led Alcibiades from his native stupidity to enlightenment. He hasn't demonstrated that the just and the expedient coincide. I read this dialogue against the rhetorical grain: what I hear in Alcibiades' replies is not agreement born of irrefutable logic but the words of someone who remains just as stupid about the nature of justice and expediency at the end of the argument as he was at the start.

But that's only my interpretation. Alcibiades, for his part, is willing to concede defeat and admit that he was, but is no longer, stupid. 'But indeed, Socrates,' he says, 'I do not know what I am saying; and I have long been, unconsciously to myself, in a most disgraceful state.'

Socrates, with the magnanimity of the winner of an argument, says kindly: 'Nevertheless, cheer up; at fifty, if you had discovered your deficiency, you would have been too old, and the time for taking care of yourself would have passed away, but yours is just the age at which the discovery should be made.' Trump and Johnson, even in later life, did not take such pains. But then neither of them had Socrates nipping at their heels, urging them to realize their shortcomings. Alcibiades, meanwhile, when thus nipped and realizing his stupidity, asks Socrates what he should do. 'Answer questions, Alcibiades; and that is a process which, by the grace of God, if I may put any faith in my oracle, will be very improving to both of us.'[29]

But hold on. What about potholes? Earlier we suggested if potholes are filled in just before an election using funds deployed by Veronica, an electioneering council leader who wants to court the motorists' vote, even if doing so involves closing care homes, that might be expedient (in the sense of being useful to Veronica's chances of being re-elected) but not at all just since knowingly and cynically making care home residents' lives worse to do so is not just. It seems rather a perfect instance of acting dishonourably. Or perhaps that assertion shows how stupid I am in not understanding the true nature of justice. Perhaps, for instance, Veronica and her advisers deem it essential to ensure their re-election by these dubious means and so continue their rule, which, quite possibly, is much more just than their rivals would behave were they to get into power. Once returned to power, for instance, Veronica might impose wealth taxes on yacht owners and other disgusting plutocrats to increase the number and excellence of local care homes, some existing examples of which, admittedly, have had to be temporarily closed during the election campaign to bankroll the potholing repairs deemed necessary for polling success. But, in hindsight, we can see what Veronica and her advisers realized in advance: that temporarily closing care homes was not just only expedient but also just as it would safeguard their residents' well-being. But that, to put it mildly, would be a stretch: the equivalence of justice and expediency that Socrates incites Alcibiades to assert here is by no means evident. And yet this is key to the Socratic struggle to overcome stupidity: we do the right thing because we have knowledge and often do the wrong thing because of insufficient knowledge. When we thought it was merely expedient and not just to close care homes in order to pay for potholes to be filled, we had insufficient knowledge. Morality is always like this for Socrates: doing the right thing intrinsically is for him associated with knowledge.

Perhaps, then, Alcibiades has not relieved himself of his stupidity, but rather added to it by agreeing to Socrates' suggestion that the just and the expedient coincide. And Socrates, for all his wisdom, shows himself to be stupid too for not recognizing his ignorance about the true nature of justice. Equally, it is possible that by making his student agree to something that is false, he fails to recognize his unsuitability as a teacher.

Let a thousand stupids flourish!

Why should we read (or perform) Socrates' dialogues 2,500 years after these conversations took place? What do they have to tell us in the 21st century? Here's a thought. Our world is one in which power-crazed and ignorant latter-day Alcibiadeses thrive and the wise are erased from public discourse. It's as if we are living through what Yeats wrote in 'The Second Coming': 'The best lack all conviction, while the worst / Are full of passionate intensity.'[30] If we are to overcome our 21st-century shortcomings, we need Socratic wisdom more than ever.

In *The Socratic Method: A Practitioner's Handbook*,[31] Ward Farnsworth argues that in our times of thriving political demagoguery and social media pile-ons, the Socratic virtues of humility, reflection, and wisdom are rarely in evidence. Our culture disdains the cool, calm, reasonable pursuit of the truth through dialogue that treats one's interlocutor, if not their views, with friendly respect. Instead, our culture increasingly encourages arguments to be won and lost through displays of fury, ostracism, and abuse. Social media in particular monetizes the principle of 'engagement through enragement', an engagement measured by analytic tools that results effectively in the commodification of stupidity, making performed rage and witlessness the must-have commodities to attract advertisers and thereby enrich shareholders, but that is inimical to Socratic wisdom. These may be tactics for winning arguments but not for the pursuit of truth, nor the overcoming of stupidity. Farnsworth, a University of Texas legal scholar, sets out rules for Socratic engagement that we would do well to adhere to as if they were the 12 Commandments in the Struggle against Stupidity.

1 Everything is open for inquiry and no view should be immune from questioning. Just because my views hurt your feelings doesn't mean I should refrain from airing them. Indeed, the very publicity of my idiotic views could be one of the best ways of reducing the amount of idiocy in the world, since only in airing them can they be challenged.
2 The purpose of inquiry is to get as close to the truth as possible, not to win arguments or make someone feel good.
3 Questioning is good and admitting error even better. As Farnsworth puts it, 'Being shown that you've erred or been imprecise is a favour. Comfort in confessing error is a sign of health.'[32] The desire to remain ignorant and the prideful unwillingness to admit one is wrong are signs of mental sickness.
4 Arguments are met with arguments. Not with smears, character assassinations, or claims to be offended by what the other has just said. If you disagree with someone's view, you must demonstrate why with compelling argument. 'You smell' is not an argument.
5 You don't defer to someone's view because of the number of letters after their name or the volume with which they yell their views but are only moved to change your position by the quality of their reasoning. Claims that anyone's perspective is entitled to deference (or scepticism) are themselves judged on evidence and reasons. It is possible that, for instance, Trump was right about bleach as a possible Covid cure and his nation's leading infectious disease expert, Dr Nicholas Fauci, wrong in contradicting that view, but, you'd think, unlikely – not least because Fauci could give a reasoned account against Trump's view while Trump could not give a plausible one of how he came to propose the suggestion.
6 Argument starts from common ground of agreement. 'Then,' as Farnsworth puts it, 'each side does the favor of trying to help the other see inconsistencies between that point of agreement and their position on whatever else is under discussion.'[33] This is the *elenchus* in action, or what Farnsworth calls elenctic reasoning.
7 One distrusts one's own partisanship in order not to bend reasoning to suit prior favoured views. This is a salutary rule of engagement for our times: when you are away from the echo chamber of your Instagram or the intellectual silo of your Twitter, you are unlikely to adhere to it.

8 Popular opinion and easy consensus are distrusted.
9 Good manners are necessary. Shouting down and name calling are out of order. Irony and sarcasm are tolerable principally if directed at oneself or at know-it-alls. But they should be using sparingly. Tickling is frowned upon.
10 Interlocutors say what they really think. Least of all should they say what their audience wants to hear. Leave that to populist politicians.
11 The giving or taking of offence undermines rational inquiry. See the 'You smell' problem earlier.
12 My favourite, because it is so rare: one should always maintain, Farnsworth writes, 'a reserve of doubt, an awareness of one's own ignorance and blind spots, and a recollection that others have been equally sure and have been wrong, over and over again'.[34] This is the Socratic virtue of humility.

At the outset of the book, we came across the view, shared by Schopenhauer and Voltaire, that stupidity is an immovable rock in human life, an insurmountable block to the human race's hopes of achieving intellectual and spiritual perfection. Stupidity is ineradicable. This looks very much like Farnsworth's perspective when he writes: 'These problems cannot be solved. They are embedded in human nature; social media is merely an accelerant, though a powerful one.'[35]

Here's a consoling thought. Our age of stupidity is no worse than that of earlier times; rather, humans have always been stupid and, one might reasonably argue, will continue to be so. 'There is no Socratic age for which nostalgia is in order,' writes Farnsworth. 'The Socratic ethic has never been the dominant force in the world, or in the academy, just as and just because it is never the dominant force in the psyche. It's always the resistance.'[36] Stupidity rules.

Happier the person who wallows in the mire of stupidity, tweeting without reflection or self-interrogation their toxic views; better the person who seeks power without having the requisite skills to satisfy their passionate yet unedifying desires. The oracle at Delphi may have enjoined each of us to know ourselves, and Socrates is recorded as having told his judges 'the unexamined life is not worth living', but maybe the former is a stupid piece of advice and the latter false. Perhaps the assertion that the unexamined life is not worth living could be demonstrated to be false through elenchic reasoning and its opposite, the proposition that the unexamined life is worth living. Socrates is stupid for encouraging others to undertake the work of self-examination and they are stupid for accepting his encouragement.

One critic of Socrates argues that the rigorous examination of life for which he proselytized can have negative effects on those taking part and, by extension, on society. The pursuit of the truth, the obsessive absorption in argumentation, dialectical reasons, and cross-examination, become as addictive and mind-bending as the hallucinogenic fumes that fuelled Pythia's predictions. Socrates, argues philosopher William S. Jamison, aimed to encourage young interlocutors such as Alcibiades how to think critically by 'showing them how to examine others and themselves by questioning the definitions of the virtues. This becomes an infinite loop since one definition is defined by others, which in turn need to be defined. You eventually end up drawing a circle that may show the use of a word or idea, but not the justification for using it.' Philosophical inquiry, as practised by Socrates, Jamison suggests, becomes a self-absorbed, perhaps even futile, pursuit, an addiction masquerading as wisdom. For Jamison, when Socrates proclaims that the 'unexamined life is not worth living', he is ' not only voicing an unwillingness to stop his way of life, but cannot imagine giving up the ecstasy he has come to feel living that way'.[37]

If so, the judges who found Socrates guilty of corrupting the young had a point. He supplied his Athenian lovers and students, effectively, with an entry-level drug that left them jonesing for more. By inspiring them to examine their lives and shortcomings, he turned them on to the intellectual life for which he has for 2,500 years been the poster boy. Philosophy is not or not only the pursuit of wisdom, but a dangerous addiction that can ruin young minds.

Indeed, in Book VII of Plato's *Republic*, Socrates is alive to the dangers of indulging in philosophy too soon.

> There is a danger lest they should taste the dear delight too early; for youngsters, as you may have observed, when they first get the taste in their mouths, argue for amusement, and are always contradicting and refuting others in imitation of those who refute them; like puppy-dogs, they rejoice in pulling and tearing at all who come near them. [. . .] And when they have made

many conquests and received defeats at the hands of many, they violently and speedily get into a way of not believing anything which they believed before, and hence, not only they, but philosophy and all that relates to it is apt to have a bad name with the rest of the world.[38]

Socrates was certainly alive to the idea that too much philosophy too early could corrupt a person and prevent them understanding that the task of philosophy is to pursue the truth. This becomes clear in *The Republic* when he says: 'When a man begins to get older, he will no longer be guilty of such insanity; he will imitate the dialectician who is seeking for truth, and not the eristic, who is contradicting for the sake of amusement; and the greater moderation of his character will increase instead of diminishing the honour of the pursuit.'[39] 'Eristic' here means someone given to argument for argument's sake.

This suggests not that the pleasure of Socratic reasoning is that it induces a kind of ecstasy, as Jamison proposes; rather, that youthful ecstasy is itself a kind of stupefaction preventing one from doing philosophy correctly, that is, in the moderate, truth-seeking method of the mature, ideally bearded, philosopher. Jamison says of philosophy as praised by Socrates: 'Once you get a taste of this kind of thing, you do not want to give it up.'[40]

But that's presumptuous. We don't know if Socrates was addicted to the experience of philosophizing, nor if he practised philosophy as a means of seeking ecstasy. Rather, we know that he implacably pursued the truth, while paradoxically not expecting to find it.

But even that hunt for the truth – seemingly the royal road from stupidity to the little wisdom of which humans may be capable – is folly for some later thinkers. For Nietzsche, Socrates' folly casts a long shadow over Western civilization. But what is that folly? In *The Birth of Tragedy*, Nietzsche defines it thus: 'The illusion that thought, guided by the thread of causation, might plumb the farthest abysses of being and even correct it.'[41] Here he asks the question that has been gnawing away at us during this chapter: why should stupidity be overcome? What is so worthwhile about the life of wisdom and reason? And one of his answers seems to be that, for Socrates, it helps us overcome death.

Nietzsche writes: 'For this reason, the image of the dying Socrates – mortal man freed by knowledge and argument from the fear of death – is the emblem which, hanging above the portal of every science, reminds the adept that his mission is to make existence appear intelligible and thereby justified.'[42]

For Nietzsche, there are two basic drives: the Dionysian and the Apollonian. Both dramatically clash, for him, in the greatest of ancient Greek tragedies (namely those by Sophocles; Euripides' tragedies are too infused with Socratic rationalism for his taste) in which the protagonist struggles to make Apollonian order against Dionysian chaos. The god Dionysus personifies rapture, ecstasy, transport, disorder, intoxication, emotion, ecstasy; the Dionysian reveller is in wild thrall to music and dance, trances, and the loss of the individual ego. The Dionysian spirit may be the primal force of life, the ultimate force at the heart of a universe that is cruel, creative, and thoroughly beyond good and evil. Dionysus may not have been stupid, but he was no intellectual, and incapable of following the Delphic oracle's injunction 'Know Thyself' because he was temperamentally incapable of seeing himself from without. There is no 'he' since, succumbing to his intoxication, Dionysus is not just gender fluid but every kind of fluid, endlessly mutable, and resistant to being pinned like a butterfly on the board of philosophical reason. Dionysus would deny the principle of individuation if he could stop dancing long enough to make any kind of argument.

Socrates was no Dionysian. In so far as he is the philosopher who launched the war against stupidity, he is Apollonian. Apollo represents harmony, progress, clarity, logic. But that makes Socrates sound utterly cool headed. Not so, he enjoys his enthusiasm, but unlike the Dionysian, he is not carried off by his ecstasies. Philosophy isn't like that, nor is the work of overcoming stupidity an ecstatic labour.

The programme of self-improvement Socrates counsels for Alcibiades requires that he is capable of coolly reflecting on his own shortcomings. That programme also requires a principle of individuation: it is necessary for Alcibiades to appreciate that there is a 'he' who is not just ignorant but also stupid. Without that principle, Socrates would not have been able to present himself to his judges as very different from them, not least in having overcome death's sting.

Socrates effectively told his judges that they had no power over him since, even though he was a philosopher of very little brain, he knew that death's tragic power could be overcome. But while later Stoic philosophers, for whom he was a mentor, went uncomplaining to their deaths buoyed by the conviction that it was good to serenely accept what one cannot change, Socrates baulked against that acceptance. He was inspired by the myth that death is not the end, that rather it is a liberation from our mere bodies and involves returning to our eternal dwelling places, our immaterial souls. This is why he says to his judges: 'It is not difficult to avoid death, gentlemen of the jury; it is much more difficult to avoid wickedness, for it runs faster than death.'[43] That wickedness, which includes stupidity, since stupidity is not just evil but the leading evil, is an eternal scar on one's very soul unless we follow the Socratic method.

In his last moments, sentenced to death and ready to raise the fatal cup of hemlock to his lips, indeed choosing to die rather than accept the help of friends who had arranged for him to flee, Socrates founded a new secular religion devoted to reason and knowledge. But even at its birth, that religion was very different from the one honoured by every philosopher since. For modern scientists, after all, belief in an eternal soul that transcends death, though perhaps an appealing notion, is something that we cannot know. Just as Socrates (rightly) argues we cannot know of the nature of death before we die since we have no means of perceiving what, if anything, the afterlife consists in, so we cannot know what we will become when we leave our confining bodies. We are ignorant of what comes after our death and stupid if we believe that it consists in what we cannot know. If so, then Socrates, for all his wisdom, is stupid.

Nietzsche calls Socrates a mystagogue of science, since he believed in the immortality of the soul and that, ultimately, our souls give us access to the true nature of being. Our physical senses are prone to illusion, for Socrates, but beyond those senses, for those wise enough to overcome their stupidity, there are other means of perception not tied to our human bodies. These give us access to an eternal realm of forms wherein the true reality of justice, human beings and dogs, the good and the beautiful, exist unchanging. The contrast between our ephemeral world and the eternal realm of the forms is made plain by Socrates in Book VII of *The Republic*. Imagine a group of people living in a cave, never seeing the light of day, bound so they can only look straight ahead. Behind them is a fire, and behind that fire a wall on top of which are statues that are manipulated by other people unseen behind that wall.

The fire projects shadows onto another wall facing the prisoners, and it is these shadows that the chained cave dwellers take for reality. But it is not reality: an escapee sees the fire, the statues, and supposes that they rather than the shadows are reality. But he is wrong: taken out of the cave, he finally sees real objects: real trees, flowers, houses, human beings, and animals. He realizes that the shadows were copies of the statues, which in turn were copies of the real things.

Instead of a dance of the seven veils, the low-budget Socratic dance of the two veils ultimately reveals reality. Finally, the escapee's eyes, which have been used to the darkness of the cave, become adjusted to the light, so much so that he can bear to look up into the sun, which is the cause of everything he sees around him: the light, his capacity for sight, the existence of flowers, trees, and other objects. The sun is the emblem of the Form of the Good. Returning to the cave, the escapee's visions are treated by the chained prisoners as those of a madman. And yet he knows his mission: to lead as many as possible from the cave to the light. When Socrates invites Alcibiades to overcome his shameful stupidity, the former is like the enlightened former prisoner returning to the cave, not to instil knowledge, but to encourage the young man to perform his own examination and self-examination, thereby turning Alcibiades' soul towards the right desires that will enable him to lead the good life. The only cause of darkness and obscurity would be a cognitive deficiency. That is stupidity.

For Nietzsche, though, this whole project, this journey from the dark cave of stupidity to the blazing sun of enlightenment, is based on an illusion. Perhaps, he counters, the light of reason cannot penetrate into the darkest corners. Socrates was not aware of the point at which knowledge has its 'gaze fixed on what is still hidden'.[44] For Socrates, everything can be illuminated, can be known, and be shown to be good. But this supposed knowledge that everything is good is a metaphysical presumption. Just what we would expect from a card-carrying Apollonian: unlike Dionysus, Apollo is always dreaming, and so full of illusions. The will to knowledge and the pursuit of the truth that enthuse Socrates are predicated on metaphysical illusions, namely that the world is good and that everything is knowable.

The Socratic project was devised to resist the harrowing conclusions of Socrates' philosophical predecessor Democritus, who came to the conclusion that we live in a meaningless universe onto which we impose meaning and value. Hamlet supposed as much when he told Rosencrantz and Guildenstern: 'There is nothing either good or bad, but thinking makes it so.'[45] Democritus realized this long before the Prince of Denmark, writing: 'Only in opinions do sweetness, coldness and colour exist; in truth, nothing exists besides atoms and empty space.'[46] It would be stupid to believe otherwise. There is no Form of Good, but rather an infinite number of eternally moving atoms. It is the task of science to account for their movements but not to impose values on these physically indivisible entities. Humans are just atoms without purpose or meaning.

Socrates' battle against stupidity needs to be seen in the context of Democritus' cold vision of a meaningless universe, whose basic materials can be understood, and their motions plotted, but with regard to which any sense of purpose must be an illegitimate imposition. As Nietzsche put it, Democritus' universe is meaningless: 'The world is entirely without reason and instinct, shaken together. All the gods and myths are useless.'[47]

This was intolerable to Plato, who burned the works of Democritus. None of them survive and so we know of his philosophy only second hand. Plato's Theory of Forms amounts to a metaphysical reply to Democritus' nihilism, effectively arguing that supra-sensible reality consists of general concepts that are themselves substances inhering in a transcendental realm where they are steadily perceived by enlightened souls with powers very different from our untrustworthy bodily senses.

Socrates' battle against stupidity is part of a spiritual ascension up a cognitive ladder that, as we rise, gives new perspectives, revealing to us our previous ignorance about ourselves and ultimately revealing the world as a regulated good. In this, the Alcibiades of this dialogue is poised to place his foot on the first rung.

This battle against stupidity is, at least for Nietzsche, principally motivated not by a quest for the truth and the overcoming of illusions, but by fear. 'Fear about oneself,' Nietzsche writes, 'becomes the soul of philosophy.'[48] And the struggle against that fear involves the creation, rather than the elimination, of illusions. Knowledge is a panacea in the sense it offers a cure for the disenchantment of Democritus and the cosmic despair, you'd think, it might well engender. As Nietzsche's biographer puts it: 'A person who has awakened to consciousness simply cannot tolerate existence in a cold atomistic universe but instead longs for the feeling of being at home. Philosophy is nothing but a longing to get home.'[49]

So there is a bitter irony at the heart of the battle against stupidity, this will to knowledge. Socrates aims at overcoming illusions. The ignorant, like Alcibiades, or those prisoners shackled in the dark cave, are to be enlightened, shown their shortcomings, and be led to the light, where they can live the good life without illusions. But, in truth, so Nietzsche suggests, they are led from one set of illusions to others. Socrates may seem a hard-headed rationalist, hunting for the truth without fear or favour, but for Nietzsche he is a fear-driven romantic, someone all too human in that he cannot bear much reality, if that reality is properly understood in the way Democritus did as utterly meaningless and devoid of inherent worth. Socrates' triumph over death by shedding his mortal self and merging with his eternal immaterial soul is, in part, escape from this reality, which is the reality of what science tells us about the nature of the world. That reality is intolerable, hence the Socratic insistence towards the end of his last conversations with his friends before he takes the fatal poison not just that the myth of the afterlife and the soul surviving bodily death is a 'noble risk', but also that the truth of the world is that it is illuminated by the light of the sun, the Form of the Good.

For Nietzsche, these are not truths but illusions, consolatory myths. We might go further: they are signs of our stupidity, our unwillingness to confront the truth about the human condition or the nature of the universe. And yet, for Nietzsche, this Socratic vision of life, death, and the universe persisted for millennia: Christianity, for instance, insists that good and evil are true aspects of the objective world, that death is not the end of life, and that as a result it is not to be feared, perhaps it is even to be welcomed. Instead of living in truth and enlightenment at the end of our Socratic project of self-improvement, then, we live in deeper folly, more profound stupidity than existed before.

Alcibiades would have done well to flee the corruption of his teacher and disdain the strange brew of reason and myth in Socrates' hemlock cup.

The slavery of stupidity

There is a more charitable interpretation of Socrates' battle against stupidity. Michel Foucault, in the French intellectual's last lectures before his death from AIDS in 1984, reflected on what Socrates' mission was in exhorting his fellow Athenians in general and Alcibiades in particular to follow the injunction of the Delphic oracle's injunction to 'Know Thyself'. 'Socrates appears as the person whose essential, fundamental, and original function, job, and position is to encourage others to attend to themselves, take care of themselves, and not neglect themselves.'[50] We have taken Socrates' mission to be a chiefly intellectual or cognitive makeover, transforming Alcibiades into someone fitted for political leadership. For Foucault, though, Socrates is proposing something more radical, a transformation that enables the student of Socrates to escape a kind of slavery.

Alcibiades at the start of the dialogue is, despite his pomp and breeding, a slave, in thrall to his stupidity and ignorance. The poignancy and drama of the dialogue is that Socrates makes Alcibiades aware of the extent of that stupidity, a necessary step to overcoming it.

At one point, Socrates asks: 'And are you, Alcibiades, a freeman?' to which Alcibiades replies: 'I feel that I am not; but I hope, Socrates, that by your aid I may become free, and from this day forward I will never leave you.'[51] It is heartening that, thanks to Socrates, Alcibiades comes at this moment to recognize his lack of freedom, his stupidity and ignorance; for only through recognizing them can he obliterate their power. Perhaps, we might think, Alcibiades is on the right path to becoming a mature and wise public servant. It gives me no pleasure to point out that would be a stupid inference.

In Foucault's earlier work – which involved studies of modern discourses on madness, clinics, prisons, and government – the forces of domination are everywhere. To become a subject is to be subjected to dominant external forces. One is assigned a race, a sex, a nation; one is allocated resources on the basis of others' assessments of one's health, academic performance, abilities and disabilities. Or so Foucault supposes. Even those of us who imagine ourselves to be free are constituted by such definitions and assessments; you internalize these discourses about yourself and become a subject as a result. These discourses create subjects and at the same time involve amassing vast amounts of data and knowledge that can be used not just to define you, but also to control you, to subject you to the will of outside forces.

The rise of the confessional in medieval Catholic Europe is the leading example for Foucault of what it is to become a subject. By confessing our sins to an unseen priest, we enter a nexus of power relations from which there is, seemingly, no escape: we become comprehensible to ourselves as individuals only in terms that have been imposed on us by authoritarian forces, be they those of the church or the state. It is an utterly grim, if plausible, worldview.

In his last works, though, Foucault imagines a different way of becoming a subject, one that amounts to a psychic rebellion against such subjectified conformism. It is one that draws heavily on Socrates' wisdom in the *First Alcibiades*. Indeed, the care of the self that Foucault recognizes in Socrates' exhortations to Alcibiades and others involves not just overcoming stupidity, but also radically changing what seems fixed and immutable, namely oneself. Foucault had long supposed that the self was not a fixed thing but an immanent creation. One of the reasons he was attracted to Socrates' dialogue with Alcibiades is that it involves just such care of self, a self-critical process in which one is invited to feel shame for what one is, to recognize one's ignorance and stupidity, and cast them off.

Consider Socrates' reproof to his judges in the *Apology*: 'Are you not ashamed for devoting all your care to increasing your wealth, reputation and honours, while not caring for or even considering your reason, truth and the constant improvement of your soul?'[52] Here Socrates is charging his judges with not caring for themselves properly. They should not cultivate frivolous ephemeral things, but attend to the care of their souls. This is not just a personal but also a political matter. Only those who have looked their own stupidity in the face and tried to overcome it are fit to govern. Only those who do not neglect themselves and are involved in lifelong projects of self-care should be considered for political office – or indeed be considered to be capable of living a good life.

To know thyself in the way the Delphic oracle suggests, then, involves more than knowing facts, nor is education out of ignorance and stupidity something that ends when one leaves school. When, in Jane Austen's 1814 novel *Mansfield Park*, the poor relation Fanny Price arrives at her aunt's country estate to live, she feels stupid because she is ignorant of foreign languages and geography and has no musical accomplishments, unlike her proud, disdainful cousins Maria and Julia Bertram. But Fanny is not stupid, just ignorant. She knows her shortcomings and sets about improving herself. In this, she is akin to what Socrates wants Alcibiades to become. Education, improvement, and care of the self are habits to be developed throughout one's life.

For Fanny's rich relatives, by contrast, education's leading purpose, at least for girls, is to give them the decorous accomplishments that make them attractive to suitors. Education is not intrinsically valuable but instrumentally so; moreover, it does not involve care for one's soul, as Socrates suggests, nor does it involve moral growth, the expansion of one's worldview, but rather amounts to the mastery of a checklist of more or less marketable accomplishments.

Education's lease on Maria and Julia Bertram has too short a date. When their aunt Mrs Norris reminds the two young sisters that there is more for them to learn, 13-year-old Maria replies: 'Yes, I know there is, till I am seventeen.' But Maria's education consists mostly of rote learning. 'How long ago it is, aunt, since we used to repeat the chronological order of the kings of England, with the dates of their accession, and most of the principal events of their reigns!' says Maria. 'Yes,' adds Julia; 'and of the Roman emperors as low as Severus.'[53]

Fanny's self-improvement is very different: we see her aged 18 reading Lord Macaulay's accounts of China, and when Sir Thomas Bertram returns from his Antiguan plantations to his country estate, she asks him about the slave trade. Such curiosity, one would have thought, isn't what a girl in Regency England needed to snare a rich husband. And yet her continued self-improvement shows up something important about the relationship between ignorance and stupidity. One can remain ever so stupid no matter how many facts one learns. To learn facts by rote may give the appearance of overcoming ignorance but most likely enables one to become more smugly ignorant about one's shortcomings – just the kind of pride Socrates warned against. Maria may know, for instance, that King Charles I died on 30 January 1649, but not why, and may well be ignorant that his execution came at the end of a long and bloody English Civil War.

To know historical facts without appreciating their causes seems on the face of it stupid, and Maria's façade of knowledge is one that conceals under-development. Moreover, neither of the Bertram sisters, still less their father, consider moral improvement to be part of their education. This is precisely the improvement that Socrates counsels for that earlier puffed-up teen, Alcibiades: the path of self-humiliation, that honest assessment of the extent of one's own ignorance, is necessary to overcome one's stupidity. But Maria and Julia Bertram have no Socrates to guide them, only a dim mother and an aloof father, and hence, as Jane Austen puts it, 'it is not very wonderful that, with all their promising talents and early information, they should be entirely deficient in the less common acquirements of self-knowledge, generosity and humility. In everything but disposition they were admirably taught.'[54] Like many of the English upper classes, they were meticulously prepared by their expensive educations for lifetimes of being stupid.

In terms of *Mansfield Park*'s leading teenage girls, both Socrates and Foucault were more akin to Fanny Price than to the stupid Bertram sisters. Care for the self is a lifelong project, not one that involves amassing data and learning dainty skills in order to snare a husband.

The notion of 'the care of the self', to quote the title of the third volume of Foucault's *History of Sexuality*, published in the year of his death,[55] involves awakening from such material concerns to care of one's soul through practices 'which permit individuals to effect by their own means or with the help of others a certain number of operations on their own bodies and souls, thoughts, conduct, and way of being, so as to transform themselves in order to attain a certain state of happiness, purity, wisdom, perfection, or immortality'. For Foucault, care of the self means the 'search, practice, and experience by which the subject carries out on himself the necessary transformations to have access to the truth'. And then once you pursue the truth, as Socrates did, and as he recommended Alcibiades should, there is a rebound effect: 'The truth enlightens the subject; the truth gives beatitude to the subject; the truth gives the subject tranquility of the soul.' This effect 'transfigures his very being'.[56] For Socrates, his self-humiliation and subsequent wisdom work like a superpower, a shield making him impervious to attack by his foes. Even death loses its sting as he realizes both the Stoic truth that what one cannot control should be of no concern to us and, more questionably, that death is not the end.

This notion of self-care was taken by Stoic thinkers, who were much influenced by Socrates, such as Seneca and Epictetus, as a solitary affair by which one masters, as Foucault puts it, how to dwell within yourself, the types of relationships you can have with yourself.

In his *Hermeneutics of the Subject*, published only in 2005 and based on his final lectures at the Collège de France and Berkeley, Foucault identified three techniques of self-care. They are all to be found in the *First Alcibiades*. First, one must unlearn bad habits. Second, the care of the self is a struggle, a never-ending battle, or, as Foucault puts it, 'The soul must be deployed like an army that is always liable to be attacked by an enemy.' Third, self-care is therapeutic and philosophy is too, since it aims to 'cure the diseases of the soul'.[57]

For Socrates, such a radical self-transformation was hardly the solitary affair it was for the Stoics. We learn to care for ourselves in public, by entering dialogue (not least with the likes of Socrates), in family relationships and erotic ones too. What's more, care of the self has a desirable outcome not just for oneself but also for society. Socrates tells Alcibiades:

> If we do not know ourselves, we cannot know what belongs to ourselves or belongs to others, and are unfit to take a part in political affairs. Both for the sake of the individual and of the state, we ought to aim at justice and temperance, not at wealth or power. The evil and unjust should have no power, – they should be the slaves of better men than themselves. None but the virtuous are deserving of freedom.[58]

The corollary of Socrates' speech is that those who are evil, unjust, in thrall to the gimcrack temptations of wealth and power, in short the stupid, should be not just excluded from power but also enslaved. Alcibiades' later career suggests that he was one of those stupid people who should, for the sake of the public good, be kept as far from public office as possible.

Alcibiades, such a disappointment

What happened to Alcibiades after his dialogue with Socrates? Did he fulfil his Socratic mission, overcome his stupidity, and rule wisely? Sadly not. For a while, at least, he was a close follower of his master. In 432 BCE, Socrates aided Alcibiades when he was wounded during the Battle of Potidea. In 442, Alcibiades protected Socrates during the Athenian flight after the Battle of Delium. Any teacher would be proud of such a pupil.

After that, though, his political and military career became a model for everything that Socrates despised in Athenian politics. Alcibiades became a frequent speaker at the Ecclesia, or assembly, and as a general steered Athens into an ill-fated alliance with three Peloponnesian city states that was defeated by the Spartans at the Battle of Mantinea in 418 BCE.

He succeeded in restoring his reputation with Athenians by entering seven chariots at the Olympic Games and taking first, second, and fourth places – which, true, is not in the Socratic playbook, but still a bravura move. Thereafter, though, he changed sides more often than he changed his sumptuous robes, which was quite a feat, but one that showed him to be unscrupulous, fixated on power and wealth, and so not the kind of ruler Socrates hoped he would become.

Alcibiades' subsequent life reads like a case study of how not to live in Socratic terms. At one point, he shared the command of a military expedition to Syracuse but, after setting sail, was sentenced to death in absentia for allegedly mutilating busts of Hermes and equally sacrilegiously profaning the Eleusinian Mysteries. He jumped ship to elude execution and went to Sparta, advising the Spartans to help the Syracusans and promoting other policies aimed at crushing Athens. While in Sparta, he also found time to seduce the wife of the king while the latter was out of town – a stupid move, not least because it helped predispose his new allies against him. He fled Sparta for Sardis, hoping to charm the Persian governor, and while there learned of a plot by Athenian captains of the fleet to stage an anti-democratic coup. Alcibiades, far from defending democracy, hoped – contrary to his Socratic schooling – that he might benefit from this overthrow of democracy. Incredibly, after this coup failed, he was sought out by the Athenian fleet to help defeat Sparta. This he duly did, helping the Athenians achieve victory at Abydos in 411 BCE and Cyzicus the following year, later returning to Athens in triumph. But he remained a divisive figure, undermining Athenian self-confidence and cultivating bitter foes.

He retired to his castle in Thrace, but that was not the end of the story. When the Athenians lost their fleet in a surprise attack by the Spartan admiral Lysander, Alcibiades realized he was no longer safe in his castle and so fled to Phrygia, where he was murdered by Persian soldiers.

The entry on Alcibiades in the *Encyclopaedia Britannia* concludes with this assessment: 'Perhaps the most gifted Athenian of his generation, Alcibiades possessed great charm and brilliant political and military abilities but was absolutely unscrupulous. His advice, whether to Athens or Sparta, oligarchs or democrats, was dictated by selfish motives, and the Athenians could never trust him enough to take advantage of his talents.' Alcibiades was incapable of practising his master's virtues but instead became an example of the consequences of undisciplined and restless ambition. Ironically, when Socrates was charged with corrupting the youth of Athens, the case for the prosecution was strengthened by citing what had become of Alcibiades. That seems terribly unfair on Socrates, who had counselled Alcibiades precisely not to be corrupted by power and wealth, and to overcome his native stupidity. Alcibiades, however, despite Socrates' mentoring, did not examine his life sufficiently, remaining trapped, perhaps unwittingly, on the stupid treadmill, pursuing wealth and power until his unedifying death.

3

Eastern Stupidity

The stupidity of cleverness

'Look,' said Siddhartha softly to Govinda, 'there is the Buddha.'[1] An unassuming man in a yellow cowl bearing an alms bowl is walking through a grove along with hundreds of monks from whom he can scarcely be distinguished. The scene unfolds in a grove near an unnamed river in India during the lifetime of the Buddha, so sometime between 563 and 483 BCE – a century or more before Socrates was coaching Alcibiades on how not to be stupid.

Siddhartha and Govinda, two childhood friends, have become *samanas*, ascetics who, starving and nearly naked, wander India, begging for food and questing for enlightenment. The former, the beautiful, respected son of a member of India's priestly Brahmin caste who is preoccupied with finding liberation from suffering, or nirvana, has followed his father and other elders in performing religious rites, but, like them, still has not achieved enlightenment.

Siddhartha has chosen another path. For two years, he and Govinda have followed the *samanas* in self-denial, abjuring property, sex, and all sustenance except that required to live, hoping thereby to achieve enlightenment. But they have not achieved that end. And so, hearing of a monk who has achieved true nirvana, they travel to this grove.

What makes the Buddha stand out? First, Siddhartha notices that he seems 'to be smiling inwardly'. And then he notices more. 'His face and his step, his peaceful downward glance, his peaceful downward-hanging hand, and every finger of his hand spoke of peace, spoke of completeness, sought nothing, imitated nothing, reflected a continual quiet, an unfading light, an invulnerable peace.'[2]

Siddhartha, as he gazes transfixed, falls in love. He has found what he has never encountered before: someone who has attained nirvana, the liberation from self and enlightenment that guarantees an end to suffering. He realizes all this in what is little more than a glance. Suddenly, he is confronted by what he has long wanted to become, a serene, gently smiling monk untroubled by what the first Noble Truth of Buddhism calls *dukka*, the innate suffering of humans bound in an endless cycle of craving, desire, and rebirth called *samsara*.

Arthur Schopenhauer, the 19th-century German philosopher much attracted to Buddhism, wrote of the human condition as akin to the fate of Ixion.[3] Ixion was bound for all eternity to a wheel of fire that span across the heavens as punishment for some affront to Zeus. Unenlightened humans in our unremitting cupidity and stupidity are like Ixion. We are bound not to a wheel of fire, but to a cycle of desire. We are habituated to endless desiring, momentary satisfaction, and then renewed striving. The goal of the enlightenment Siddhartha hopes to achieve is to break this cycle and, what's more, end the tragedy of endless reincarnation that dooms us to repeats of that recurring torture.

Siddhartha sees that the Buddha has reached this goal. 'He looked attentively at Gotama's head, at his shoulders, at his feet, at his still downward-hanging hand, and it seemed to him that in every joint of every finger of his hand there was knowledge; they spoke, breathed, radiated truth. Never had Siddhartha esteemed a man so much, never had he loved a man so much.'[4]

There are lots of depictions in literature of falling in love at first sight, but none quite as profound in their significance as this scene from Hermann Hesse's 1922 novel *Siddhartha*. Even though the book was written by a western novelist, this scene in particular and the rest of the novel in general tell us a great deal about the differences between western and eastern conceptions of wisdom. Often, as we will see, eastern philosophy and religion – be it Vedic, Hindu, Buddhist, Jainist, Confucian, or Daoist – departs from western pursuits of knowledge, wisdom, and intelligence in very marked ways. One corollary of this difference is that the pursuit of intelligence may sometimes be stupid and get in the way of the true enlightenment that Buddhists call nirvana.

This becomes clear a few pages later when the young ascetic meets the Buddha as he wanders through a grove. In the interim, the impetuous youth has heard the Buddha preach. Life, the Illustrious One tells his followers, is pain, but the path to release from suffering has been found. He patiently sets out his teachings, all the while speaking in a perfect, quiet voice full of peace.

The first truth is that life is suffering. We suffer, like Ixion, because we fail to recognize this truth. We delude ourselves about the true character of life. Everything is impermanent. Things and selves are unstable, always changing and, despite what we suppose, have no essences. Unenlightened stupidity or folly consists in our desire to retain our identity as enduring selves and to seek fulfilment in the satisfaction of desires. In truth, neither is possible. Identities are fleeting; desires can only be momentarily satisfied and the brief experience of desire satisfaction leaves us jonesing for more. Wisdom consists in overcoming such stupid delusions. The second noble truth follows from this. Called the Truth of Arising, it contends that the craving or *taṇhā* that gives rise to the rebirth (we crave rebirth, sensual pleasures, existence, and – oddly, too – non-existence) needs to be stilled if suffering is to end. The third truth, the Truth of Cessation, involves liberation from attachment to the world and to our cravings. The fourth truth is the Truth of the Path which leads to the cessation of suffering, and here the Buddha details in what this so-called Noble Eightfold Path consists.

The Buddha expounds all this in the grove to his followers. But Siddhartha is not satisfied. He thinks he spots a flaw in Buddha's reasoning, a loose thread that, if pulled, might unravel the whole system. When he meets the Buddha wandering in the grove, he sets out his worry.

> According to your teachings, this unity and logical consequence of all things is broken in one place. Through a small gap there streams into the world of unity something strange, something new, something that was not there before and cannot be demonstrated and proved: that is your doctrine of rising above the world, of salvation. With this small gap, through this small break, however, the eternal and single work law breaks down again. Forgive me if I raise this objection.[5]

There is a parallel here with the sage old philosopher and the beautiful young man in the previous chapter. Like Socrates, the Buddha wants to put his followers on the right path; like Alcibiades, Siddhartha is young, handsome, and presumptuous. Unlike Alcibiades, though, Siddhartha's problem is not that he is stupid, but that he is too clever. He has listened well, thought intelligently, and found a flaw in the Buddha's system. That is a credit to him, says the Buddha. But it misses the point of his teachings. 'Let me warn you, you who are thirsty for knowledge against the thicket of opinions and the conflict of words,' says the Buddha.

> Opinions mean nothing; they may be beautiful or ugly, clever or foolish, anyone can embrace or reject them. The teaching which you have heard, however, is not my opinion, and its goal is not to explain the world to those who are thirsty for knowledge. Its goal is quite different; its goal is quite different; its goal is salvation from suffering. That is what Gotama teaches, nothing else.[6]

Although there are many differences between Socrates, as representative of western wisdom, and the Buddha, as representative of eastern wisdom, they share this much in common: each has, through his own philosophical reflections, inoculated himself against fate. The Buddha has found a way of eluding suffering; Socrates tells his judges after his death sentence that they have no power over him. The ancient Greek tells his judges with grand audacity to

> face death with a good hope and know for certain that no evil can happen to a good man, either in life or after death. He and his are not neglected by the gods; nor has my own approaching end happened by mere chance; I see clearly that that time had arrived when it was better for me to die and be released from trouble.[7]

Equally, the Buddha is beyond evil, and even his painful death a few years later could be borne. The wise, be they Socrates or the Buddha, have devised intellectual and spiritual *cordons sanitaires* so that they elude suffering and meet their fates with cheerful miens. The stupid, namely those who ignore their teachings, are not so fortunate; they are fortune's playthings and bound to suffer.

The purpose of the Buddha's teachings is not to produce an unassailably consistent intellectual fortress nor to make his followers clever, but to encourage his followers to overcome the self and reject the life of the world and desires. Siddhartha accepts all this but, unlike his friend Govinda, who has decided to join Buddha's followers, does not think he is able to achieve salvation from suffering in this way. He explains to the Buddha:

> We Samanas seek release from the self, O Illustrious One. If I were one of your followers, I fear that it would only be on the surface, that I would deceive myself that I was at peace and had attained salvation, while in Truth the Self would continue to live and grow, for it would have been transformed into your teachings, into my allegiance and love for you and for the community of the monks.[8]

In that sense, Siddhartha is nothing like Alcibiades. He needs not a sage like Socrates at his side counselling wisdom, but to find his own path from stupidity to spiritual awakening. Wisdom, that antidote to stupidity, is not something that can always be taught. Sometimes pupils must find their own paths to it. Govinda may learn from instruction; Siddhartha, though, must learn from his own experience. Each has set out on different paths to the same goal, that of enlightenment, or nirvana.

At this point, it's worth announcing something that probably requires a spoiler alert. The name Siddhartha means in Sanskrit He Who Achieves His Goal. This was also the name of the young Buddha before, aged 35, he achieved enlightenment under a pipal tree. Thereafter, Siddhartha Gautam became known as the 'Buddha', meaning enlightened one.

The Buddha, like Siddhartha, had spent several years as a young man living as an ascetic in order to overcome desire for food, sex, and comfort, but the yogic disciplines and fasting this path required led him nearly to starve to death. Only after he accepted a bowl of rice from a young girl and ate did he have the realization that these self-denials were not the way to achieve spiritual enlightenment. In a sense, then, the tale that Hermann Hesse tells is a reworking of the Buddha's story: our eponymous hero Siddhartha is emulating his master's path to the same goal.

Seven weeks after his enlightenment, the Buddha left his place under the tree and decided to teach others what he had learned. One key lesson for his followers is that the enlightened person, freed from desire and the cycle of rebirth, unites wisdom and virtue. In the *Digha Nakaya*, one of the first collections of Buddhist sutras or discourses, wisdom and virtue are described as two hands that wash and purify the other: both wisdom and virtue are necessary to enlightenment, but neither is alone sufficient. This view chimes with that of the ancient Greeks, for whom virtue and knowledge were one. In both the *Meno* and *Euthydemus* dialogues, Socrates argues that virtues are in themselves neither beneficial not harmful, but are only beneficial when accompanied by wisdom and harmful when accompanied by folly.

The difficult marriage of wisdom and virtue

This association of wisdom with virtue – and, by corollary, wisdom's opposite, stupidity – is a key difference between western and eastern philosophies. In Zhen-Dong Wang et al.'s paper 'The Comparison of the Wisdom view in Chinese and Western Cultures', for instance, the authors write: 'Wisdom views in different cultural contexts are closely connected with the corresponding culture's worldview.' Western culture, for these authors, regards wisdom as a tool. 'The wisdom is used to solve to the contradiction between individuals and the external world. . . . The western wisdom view attaches great weight to the exploration of the world, which is one of the reasons for the discovery of the new world and the first industrial revolution.' The tendency is to use 'wisdom to understand and change the world'.[9] This may be a tendentious analysis of what western wisdom amounts to, and yet if there is such a thing as western stupidity, and I am going to go out on a limb and suggest that there is, the implication of Wang et al.'s argument is that modern western thinking can be taken as stupid since it fails to realize the interconnectedness of wisdom and virtue.

Once these two have been decoupled, as they have been in western cultures since Socrates' time (as we will see in later chapters), anything is possible – not least imperial projects, slavery, and the despoliation of the earth. And yet, the authors argue, wisdom and virtue are indivisible in the great intellectual systems of eastern thought they consider:

Buddhism, Daoism, and Confucianism. This might suggest that Chinese and other eastern cultures are temperamentally incapable of imperialism, enslaving others, or ruining the planet, because, unlike the West, wisdom and virtue are inseparable. That, though, would be a fanciful inference.

But the point remains that being virtuous, for those persuaded by the great eastern philosophies, is necessary for wisdom. Not so, arguably, for those in the West. Jin Li, Professor of Education and Human Development at Brown University, argues in her book *The Self in the West and East Asia: Being or Becoming* that rising individualism in the West destroyed the marriage of wisdom and virtue. She writes:

> In the West, the overarching and continuously predominant view is that humans are discrete beings, that is, individuals that are bounded by their skin separate from other human beings. . . . The most important consequence of such a view is that the individual is the basic unit in society that is believed to possess his/her cognitive capacity, moral power, political power, social privileges and responsibility.[10]

Such western individualism may well seem like folly to eastern eyes. And not just foolish, but lacking that leading virtue that the great Chinese sage Confucius (551–479 BCE) thought we should cultivate, namely benevolence or humaneness. Such, for Confucius, was the way to wisdom. He didn't quite put it this way, but the implication of his philosophy is this: cultivating virtue is not just its own reward but the royal road out of stupidity.

Does that mean that western individualism, mired, as Jin Li argues it is, in selfish ambition, rootless pursuit of individual desires, and other amoral asocial activities, is stupid? It is possible. Think of it this way. In the West, the human self is like an avocado. So at least argues Gish Jen in *The Girl at the Baggage Claim: Explaining the East–West Culture Gap*. In the individualistic West, she claims, the self is 'a kind of avocado, replete with a big pit on which it is focused'. In the collectivist East, by contrast, the 'flexi-self' is interdependent, 'a context-focused self, oriented toward serving something larger than itself'.[11] The flexi-self, Jen supposes, 'starts with debt' to parents, teachers, and community. The big pit, by contrast is relatively debt free, beholden to no one but itself and ambitious for personal success.

Rather disappointingly, Jen doesn't say which kind of fruit best characterizes this flexi-self. Quite possibly, though, it is like a seedless grape, utterly selfless; or, perhaps even like a blackberry, a group of drupes with little pips inside each cell of the collective that is, paradoxically, a single fruit. Whatever the truth of this diverting matter, I suspect the flexi-self is more likely to be a little pip than a big pit. No matter: this big pit/flexi-self distinction is so profound, Jen suggests, that it helps account for different western and eastern attitudes in personal relationships, teaching, storytelling, architecture, and even 'our ideas about law, rehabilitation, religion, freedom, and choice'. She goes so far as to suggest that big-pit western individualism produces individual geniuses scarcely imaginable in the East. This may be one reason why China has produced no Nikolai Tesla, J. Robert Oppenheimer, Steve Jobs, or Bill Gates, and wins much fewer Nobel Prizes than a nation, you'd think, teeming with clever people. Jen isn't suggesting that the eastern mindset produces lumpen populations stupidly incapable of innovation or genius, but rather that eastern innovation is different from that of the West. The flexi-self, she writes, is more attuned to patterns than to 'the strange and novel'; the Chinese, she argues, are not 'divergent thinkers – thinkers who can easily generate novel uses for a brick, say, or a tree branch'. She adds that 'the Chinese themselves are aware that their style of innovation differs from that of the West, and that, however exuberant and successful, it is not the sort that wins Nobel Prizes'.[12] The relative dearth of Nobel Prizes on East Asian mantelpieces indicates that there is more to human excellence than the individual achievement annually celebrated in Stockholm.

All that said, I confess when I first encountered Jen's distinctions, I rebelled against them. Surely it is simplistic to contrast western big-pit selves who selfishly disregard their debts to others and disdain connections with society, and who are 'assertive and full of self-esteem and yet anxiously protective of self-image and obsessed with self-definition',[13] with Eastern flexi-selves who, for their part, are modest, care for their parents, and hardworking, if lacking in ambition and drive. These read like stereotypes that do both those of East and West few favours. Aren't there flexi-selves in the West and big-pit individuals in the East? The welfare states of western Europe, to take one example, are hardly products of big-pit individualism. I'll bet, what's more, there are

Shanghai entrepreneurs even now disregarding their debts to others as they narcissistically strive to become boring masters of the universe just like their coevals on the other side of the Pacific. What's more, Jen's taxonomy is hardly exhaustive. Instead of positing an East–West cultural gap, she could have written about a North–South one. Are populations of the global South more like flexi-selves or big-pit ones? What would be an appropriate fruit to capture those of us living in the global North? These are questions, I suspect, that indicate, if not the stupidity, then the shortcomings of Jen's distinctions and, to my mind, are quite harmful to avocados' self images (if they have them).

Read more closely, though. Jen's book sidesteps such shortcomings but only by being perhaps cunningly nebulous about whether, in positing an East–West cultural gap, she's describing defined geographical areas or non-localized mindsets. In any event, Jen is an American novelist born to Chinese parents so, you'd think, like Joni Mitchell, can look at life from both sides now, seeing the virtues and vices of big-pit and flexi-selves. Indeed, towards the end of her book she argues that 'Asian Americans tend to test in the middle of the flexi-self-to-big-pit-self spectrum' and advocates blending independence and interdependence in what she calls 'ambidependence'.[14] Like some latter-day Confucius, she imagines that the cultivation of this virtue of ambidependence – if it is a virtue – might help us improve our performances in such vital activities as childrearing, sports, and playing video games. Such ambidependents are not, you'd think, stupid.

For all my misgivings, though, this East–West cultural divide, if it exists, is of long standing and has great consequences for the way in which East and West conceive of wisdom and, by extension, stupidity. Jin Li notes that Aristotle asked one of the key western philosophical questions in his text the *Categories*, namely 'What is a man?' This, Li suggests, typifies the differences in western and eastern mindsets. He could have asked another question such as 'How does a man grow from infancy to adulthood?' 'Does an infant grow by him/herself or does he/she require others' nurturance?' Aristotle, writes Jin Li, 'does not ask the questions that a mother in either ancient or current times would ask'.[15] That's a good point: if more ancient Greek philosophers had been women, perhaps western philosophy would have been less trapped in a constraining mindset that has made so many of us, one might suppose, big pits when we could have been little pips. As a result of being ensnared in what Li calls Aristotelian ontology, western civilization has been since ancient times trapped in a 'being-way of thinking'. Hence, she suggests, the obsession in western philosophy of seeking necessary and sufficient conditions to define particular terms; hence, too, the character of scientific inquiry in the West; and the veneration of individual genius. Aristotle's contemporary, Confucius, sought wisdom in a very different way: instead of seeking necessary and sufficient conditions to answer the question 'What is a man?' (Aristotle's answer, by the way, was 'the rational animal'), he forswore such ontological speculation, regarding it as unhelpful to the essential task, namely the cultivation of wisdom and virtue, and, thereby, presumably, nimbly eluding the temptations of stupidity. In *The Analects*, the collection of sayings assembled by his followers after his death in 497 BCE, we are told 'there were four things the Master abstained from entirely: he did not speculate, he did not claim or demand certainty, he was not inflexible, and he was not self-absorbed'.[16] These four things, Li suggests, are precisely what result from what she calls Aristotelian ontology. That's to say, seeking certainty, being rigid in the face of change, and being big-pittedly self-absorbed are foolish in that they are predicated on misconstruing what the world is like. Worse, each is a distraction from the path of Confucian self-cultivation.

Learning wisdom from idiots

There are many droll proverbs in Chinese culture that give examples of stupidity from which, ideally, we can learn from other people's stupidity to be wise. For example, the expression 'carving a mark on the boat to search for a sword' draws on the ancient tale of a man who dropped his sword in the water while crossing a river. Instead of retrieving it from the water, he carved a mark on the side of his boat where it fell. His folly – not realizing that the boat had moved while the sword remained at the same spot in the river – exemplifies a greater stupidity, that of ignoring changing situations. You don't need to be Chinese to recognize this wisdom: if the boatman had appreciated pre-Socratic ancient Greek philosopher Heraclitus's insistence that the world is ever-changing, encoded in his remark 'You can't step in the same river twice,' he might not have behaved so foolishly.

EASTERN STUPIDITY

Another story told by Mencius (372–289 BCE), the ancient philosopher known as the Second Sage (the first being Confucius), tells of a different kind of stupidity. A farmer, eager to make his seedlings grow quickly, pulled them up slightly in the ground. Doing so, though, damaged the seedlings so they withered and died. Hence the saying 'pulling up seedlings to help them grow'. Moral? Impatience and disrespecting natural processes to achieve quick results is often folly.

One day, another parable of stupidity tells us, a man from Yan admired the elegant way people from Handan walked, so he tried to imitate them. Instead of mastering their graceful walk, though, he became so immersed in imitation that he forgot how to walk at all and was compelled to crawl home. Hence the expression 'Learning to walk in Handan.' Moral? Blindly copying without sensitively appreciating the essence of that which one is trying to emulate is folly. This, you might think, is a moral that the sage Chinese entrepreneurs behind such successful knock-off brands as Hi-Phone, iPad, and Gooje have virtuosically taken to heart.

Consider, too, the story of the man who decides to steal a bell. Sensibly worried that he would be heard nicking the bell, he decides to take action. Unfortunately, he is an idiot. He covers his own ears, thinking that will make his getaway with the bell unheard. Moral? Solipsism is folly. When the bell tolls, it doesn't only toll for thee.

These are all fabulous stories for connoisseurs of stupidity. My favourite, though, concerns a man who one day saw a rabbit run into a tree and accidentally break its neck. Delighted that the universe had apparently provided him with free dinner and supposing this would be a regular phenomenon, he gave up his usual work as a farmer and sat by the tree stump waiting for another rabbit to suffer a fatal accident. A kinder person would have put pillows around the stump to cushion blows likely to be experienced by scurrying wildlife, but not this guy. Of course, no rabbit came. Not then, nor on any subsequent day. Perhaps, for all we know, the farmer is still there keeping fatuous vigil and his farm gone to ruin. Hence the expression 'Waiting for a rabbit by a tree stump.' Moral? One must astutely consider situations carefully, not be beguiled by deluding and self-serving inferences from past events to future ones, take appropriate action, and not neglect one's duties.

Jin Li reckons that this last story has a particular resonance for Chinese people. It does not just indict a particular kind of stupidity, but encodes an implicit critique of Daoism, in many ways the rival philosophy to Confucianism in ancient China, and whose leading tenet, namely *wu-wei*, she thinks, has been misconstrued to suggest that taking no action is wise and by means of doing nothing one might well expect the universe to provide. In the West, she points out, we have the saying that there is no such thing as a free lunch; in the East, there is an expression 'There is no such thing as pies that fall from the sky.' Nor are the woods filled with rabbits reliably racing to their deaths to be collected by workshy farmers. Chinese people both ancient and modern disapprove of such indolent free-riders, Li tells me, and still less appreciate such free-riders justifying their folly by referring to, yet misunderstanding, the fundamental philosophical principle of Daoism articulated by its founder, Laozi (who flourished in the 6th century BCE). Daoist thinking does not advocate 'no action', Li insists: that would be stupid, as the foolish farmer example shows. Rather, it advocates something harder and much more relevant to overcoming stupidity, namely 'effortless action'.

The wisdom of doing nothing

But what on earth could 'effortless action' mean? Isn't the very notion self-contradictory? 'No action', after all, is something that even the most witless slacker can – and probably does – adopt as a lifestyle philosophy as they sit rolling in their underwear surrounded by pizza boxes. 'Effortless action', or what Daoists call *wu-wei*, by contrast, is a fundamental philosophical principle or lifestyle goal championed by ancient and modern eastern sages that, nonetheless, is apt to leave even the most committed and clever of the rest us scratching our proverbial heads uncomprehendingly. In his book *Trying Not to Try: Ancient China, Modern Science, and the Power of Spontaneity*, Edward Slingerland attempts to explain what *wu-wei* is and why we would do well – somehow – to cultivate it. We often stupidly act with too much conscious striving to be happy or achieve goals and in so doing sabotage ourselves. Worse yet, if we attempt to act spontaneously, we also fail: willed spontaneity, after all, is a self-contradiction. What we need instead is 'effortless action'. 'People in *wu-wei* feel they are doing nothing, while at the same time they might be creating a brilliant work of art, smoothly negotiating a complex social situation, or even bringing the entire world into harmonious order,' writes Slingerland.[17] He cites the great jazz saxophonist Charlie Parker who advised aspiring musicians 'Don't play the saxophone. Let it play you.' Parker's playing was seemingly effortless, apparently spontaneous. It was, if you'll forgive the expression, bebop *wu-wei*. He also cites the actor Michael Caine, who said that the way to play a role authentically is not to memorize a script but rather not to try to memorise it. 'You must be able to stand there *not* thinking of that line. You take it off the other actor's face. . . . Otherwise, for your next line, you're not listening and not free to respond naturally, to act spontaneously.'[18]

Charlie Parker and Michael Caine are, in their different ways, describing a familiar and desirable psychological state, captured in the terms 'being in the zone' or 'going with the flow'. But how do we get in the zone, how do we go with the flow and acquire what Slingerland calls the 'dynamic, effortless and unselfconscious taste of mind of a person who is optimally active and effective?' Frankly, I am too stupid to know but am happy to learn that even the greatest Chinese sages themselves spent a long time figuring out how to get there. They note that those fortunate people in *wu-wei* additionally have something called *de* (pronounced, amusingly, for followers of the western sage Homer Simpson, as *duh*). *De* is a virtue or radiance that others can detect, and serves as an outward sign that you have *wu-wei*. 'If you have *de*,' writes Slingerland, 'people like you, trust you and are relaxed around you. Even wild animals leave you alone.' Especially in troubled political times, to have *de* as the manifestation of *wu-wei* is very desirable. 'For rulers and others involved in political life, *de* has a powerful, seemingly magical effect on those around them, allowing them to spread political order in an instantaneous fashion. They don't have to issue threats or offer rewards, because people simply want to obey them,' adds Slingerland.[19] Fascinating, though for my part I've never come across such a ruler: lots of them (Boris Johnson, Liz Truss, Donald Trump – add your own favourites) have had what might be called the *duh* factor, involving alienating witlessness and stupid narcissism, but none in my lifetime has manifested *de*. None of them has been virtuosic in the effortless action that Jin Li suggests harmonizes with the Dao, or the Way. 'Those who fail to discern the Dao,' she tells me, 'are indeed cast as foolish, even stupid, as they are likely to fail, often resulting in disastrous outcomes.' I have certainly encountered politicians who fit *that* bill.

Western civilization and other oxymorons

Before we go much further, it is probably helpful to explain how and why Confucianism and Daoism arose in ancient China and also how both reacted to, revolted against, and ultimately merged with the Buddhist philosophy we considered at the start of this chapter that Indian sages brought to China across the Himalayas. During the so-called Warring States period between the 5th and 3rd centuries BCE, China suffered great social chaos and political upheaval. Slingerland tells us that during this time huge conscript armies roamed the land, devastating crops and making life miserable for common people. It was also, probably not coincidentally, a time of great philosophical creativity during which Confucius, Laozi, and other sages flourished. Confucianism, in particular, might be thought of as a philosophy that provided an antidote to uncertain, chaotic times, stressing the perils of failure to exercise balance and harmony in human affairs and extolling patience, perseverance, discipline, and hard work.

'If we were to choose just one word to characterise the Chinese ideal way of life, that word would be harmony,' writes Chenyang Li in *The Confucian Philosophy of Harmony*. But, argues Li, that Confucian harmony has been often misconstrued: it doesn't mean human adjustment to a fixed cosmic order but instead 'a dynamic, generative process, which seeks to balance and reconcile differences and conflicts through creativity and mutual transformation'.[21] That sounds like hard work and not, it might be added, the kind of labour self-obsessed big-pit western selves are temperamentally adapted to undertake. When asked what perfect virtue consisted in, Confucius replied,

> To be able to practice five things everywhere under heaven constitutes perfect virtue. Gravity, generosity of soul, sincerity, earnestness, and kindness. If you are grave, you will not be treated with disrespect. If you are generous, you will win all. If you are sincere, people will repose trust in you. If you are earnest, you will accomplish much. If you are kind, this will enable you to employ the services of others.[21]

Such perfect virtue, one might well think, is worth cultivating particularly as a bulwark against the chaos of the Warring States era or, indeed, in our own no less violent, chaotic times.

But even for Confucius, the desirable lifestyle task of developing both wisdom and virtue together is not easy. In *The Analects*, he admits to struggling to develop both. ' Quietly to store up knowledge in my mind to learn without flagging, to teach without growing weary, these present me with no difficulties,' he says, but in the next paragraph adds: 'It is these things that cause me concern: failure to cultivate virtue, failure to go more deeply into what I have learned, to move to where it is, and inability to reform myself when I have defects.'[22] The well-lived life, for Confucius, involves constant attention to those inabilities in a personal struggle to overcome them. Wisdom and knowledge without virtue, while thinkable, is shameful for him. The key virtue of Confucian thought is benevolence, or what others more recently have called humaneness. For Confucius, acting benevolently confers one particularly desirable advantage on the person who does so: the benevolent person is free from worries. 'If, on examining himself, a man finds nothing to reproach himself for, what worries and fears can he have?'[23] That's a good point, though a sceptic might suggest that the stupid person, unskilled at investigating their shortcomings, might similarly have no worries and fears; moreover, if they were less stupid, they would have the personal insight to discover that they have a great deal to reproach themselves for and so become worried and afraid.

Clearly, though, Confucius is addressing the wise and virtuous man or, as he terms it in D.C. Lau's translation, the gentleman. 'But what is benevolence?' asked his student Chung-kung in one of the *Analects*. Confucius's answer is curious, but suggests that imperial subjugation, at least, is shamefully devoid of benevolence. 'When abroad behave as though you were receiving an important guest. When employing the services of the common people behave as though you were officiating at an important sacrifice. Do not impose on others what you yourself do not desire.'[24] Measured against this test of benevolence, western civilization comes up short.

Confucius also stressed strict adherence to social roles, emphasizing that the five main relationships – ruler–subject, father–son, husband–wife, elder brother–younger brother, and friend–friend – impose mutual bonds. We can see in this the germ of the flexi-self hailed by Gish Jen, but also a social conservatism and valorization of tradition that, in uncertain times such as the Warring States era, may well be very desirable.

Adherence to Confucian tenets does, though, sound like an enormous fuss. They enjoin us to lead laborious lives governed by duty and marked by constant self-critical examination to ensure that we are properly cultivating virtue and thereby wisdom. No wonder that Daoist contemporaries were implicitly critical of Confucianism. 'A man of the highest virtue does not keep virtue and that is why he has virtue. A man of the lowest virtue never strays from virtue and that is why he is without virtue. The former never acts and leaves nothing undone. The latter acts but there are things left undone,' wrote Laozi in the *Daodejing*, the classic anthology of his wise sayings about personal conduct and how to govern, compiled in about the 4th century BCE.[25] Confucianism, thus conceived, is a try-hard philosophy inimical to real *wu-wei* let alone *de*. Charlie Parker was not a Confucian, more of a go-with-the-flow Daoist kind of guy.

And yet it's important to stress how much these two philosophies have in common. Just as Confucianism might be thought of as a desirable corrective to the chaos of war and political instability, so might Daoism be considered as a different, but no less appealing way of achieving harmony in disharmonious times. In stressing living in harmony with the Dao, which is taken to signify the source, pattern, and substance of all matter, Laozi produced a life philosophy that, like Confucianism, emphasized balance and harmony. Both drew on the ancient Chinese yinyang principle which asserts that opposing yet complementary forces interact to form a dynamic system in which the whole is greater than the assembled parts. This metaphysical principle stresses something about the nature of the world that big-pit westerners quite possibly miss: that change is incessant and everything interrelated. 'In reality,' writes Robin R. Wang in *Yinyang: The Way of Heaven and Earth in Chinese Thought and Culture,* 'we not only find that opposites exist through interaction with and in dependence on each other, but also that the same thing can be considered to have opposite qualities depending on the context.' Think, Wang suggests, of a door. It can open and it can close, otherwise it would be a wall that does not move or an open space that does not close. Or consider the seasons: 'In the cycle of four seasons, summer is the most yang of the seasons, yet it contains a yin force, which will begin to emerge in the summer, extend through the fall, and reach its culmination in the winter.'[26]

All this may seem to be abstruse metaphysics with no connection to the question of how to avoid the clutches of stupidity. Not so. Wisdom, for Confucians as much as Daoists, involves appreciating the ramifications of this yin and yang principle. 'Mutual inclusion has important consequences in terms of strategy because it indicates that, when one thing appears to you as present, that thing entails opposite forces that are hidden and in motion but that have not yet appeared,' writes Wang.[27] Failing to have the wisdom to tell your yin from your yang and, moreover, that the pair are in profitably dialectical cosmological relationship would indicate for Confucians and Daoists alike that you are quite the chump, devoid of wisdom and therefore virtue.

That said, Daoists sought balance and harmony in ways that may well have made more socially conservative Confucians raise sceptical eyebrows. Daoists were, writes Edward Slingerland, 'the original hippies, dropping out, turning on, and stickin' it to the Man more than 2,000 years before the invention of tie-dye and the Grateful Dead'.[28] Instead of fulfilling their duties and adhering to rigid training to become virtuous and wise, as Confucius counselled, early Daoists in the 5th century BCE fled to the countryside to live in harmony with nature and, Slingerland tells us, practised a form of agriculture so basic that they often pulled ploughs themselves.[29] Incidentally, what with gormless ex-farmers staring at rabbits all day long and Daoists pulling ploughs rather than sensibly harnessing oxen to do the heavy work, it is, incidentally, quite surprising that anybody ate a decent meal in ancient China.

But here's the problem. If Daoists have a point in criticizing Confucianism for striving for and thereby not attaining virtue, surely Daoism might be criticized for the opposite problem, namely its counsel that one should not strive to achieve virtue, or indeed anything but rather go with the natural flow. Or, to put it another way, this whole idea of *wu-wei* or effortless action seems puzzling. How can one become virtuous without striving to be virtuous? How can one try without trying? What Slingerland recommends is quite helpful. He proposes a kind of marriage of Confucianism and Daoism by means of which one can become the kind of harmonious and otherwise excellent person who can try without trying. What he proposes, in a way, is to take the yin of Confucianism and the yang of Daoism and let them interrelate fruitfully.

It works like this. Conscious effort, of the kind recommended by Confucius, is necessary to learn a skill (even Charlie Parker had to learn which end of the sax to blow down); moreover, learning a skill often requires not willed learning but following rules blindly in the ritualistic manner typical of Confucianism. Training oneself to follow rules automatically liberates cognitive energy for other tasks and, what's more, speeds up one's acquisition of skills or desirable traits. What is true of learning to become a good saxophonist is true, too, of cultivating virtue, though the former requires more embouchure and the latter more empathetic consideration of others' well-being.

But that is by no means all that is necessary to be either a saxophone legend or a perfectly virtuous and wise gentleman. Trying can become counter-productive, as Daoists recognize. Non-Daoists, too, recognize this truth: we have all been in meetings where the effort to solve a problem was in inverse ratio to the practical outcome, a phenomenon captured by the expression 'analysis is paralysis'. We are familiar, too, with testimonies from sports people, musicians, and others that their best performances came about almost automatically. Slingerland puts it this way: 'Our [western] culture is very good at pushing people to work hard or acquire particular technical skills. But in many domains actual success requires the ability to transcend our training and relax completely into what we are doing, or simply forget ourselves as agents.'[30] This is what 'going with the flow' or 'being in the zone' amounts to. These are manifestations of *wu-wei*. And, one might well think, those accomplished at such effortless action, or what Slingerland calls cultured spontaneity – be they Charlie Parker or Michael Caine – manifest *de*.

For all the apparent incompatibilities of Confucianism and Daoism, then, elements of both might be useful to elude stupidity and arrive at virtue and wisdom. Indeed, the evolution of Chinese culture from ancient times shows that Chinese people, quite astutely, have taken on board teachings from both. But a third great philosophical system challenged the yin of Confucianism and the yang of Daoism: Buddhism. According to Jin Li, many Confucians were initially very critical of Buddhism, and no wonder.[31] While Confucius had counselled five great virtues – *ren* (humaneness), *yi* (righteousness), *li* (propriety/etiquette), *zhong* (loyalty), and *xiao* (filial piety) – along with strict adherence to social roles, Buddhism involved jettisoning at least some of these virtues since they entailed basic human responsibility for family and social relationships. The idea of abandoning one's parents and children counselled in early Buddhist thought scandalized Confucians. The early life of the Buddha outraged their morals: Prince Siddhartha, the Buddha-to-be, left his family in search of liberation on the day his son, Rahula, was born. And yet Buddhism proved attractive to many Chinese people because it considered matters that neither Confucianism nor Daoism reflected upon, not least the nature of the afterlife and the possibility or otherwise of reincarnation. As Confucianism and Daoism both became part of the eastern mindset, so Buddhism was integrated too, but this was hardly a one-way process. In China, at least, what became known as Zen Buddhism integrated elements of Confucian and Daoist thought. These mutual, multiple, ceaseless integrations and evolutions of already complex belief systems are, one might think, manifestations of the yin and yang principle in action. The complex, syncretic eastern wisdom that resulted, Li suggests, became an everyday spiritual part of life not just in China but also in Korea, Japan, and Vietnam.

One corollary of historical changes in these belief systems and religions is that, whatever eastern wisdom amounts to as a result, it contrasts sharply with the manifold follies of western civilization. When Mahatma Gandhi was asked what he thought of western civilization and drolly replied, 'I think it would be a very good idea,'[32] he meant something like this: the west, in separating wisdom from virtue, and in using its technological prowess without compassion but only to acquire territory and subjugate peoples for profit and to plunder nature with the same aim, was, from the perspective of an eastern wisdom predicated on compassion, passivity, and serenity, barbarically stupid. Not only was western civilization oxymoronic, but what passed for western wisdom was moronic.

When Gandhi attended the Round Table Conference in London to discuss the future of India in the early 1930s, he wore a homespun loincloth in solidarity with the poor of his colonized land. After meeting George V at Buckingham Palace, he was asked if he felt such clothes were proper. Gandhi replied: 'He [the king] had enough for both of us.'[33] The gimcrack allure of royal bling was, for a Hindu such as Gandhi, based on a conception of what was valuable in human life that was false. Or, if you prefer, stupid.

Air travel and other imbecilities

Of course, the great eastern civilizations are not strangers to inflicting conquest, slavery, and despoliation on the world, nor are they innocent of royal bling, but at least two of the great philosophical and religious traditions – Buddhism and Daoism – prize the wisdoms of inaction, passivity, and serenity over the follies of travel, subjugation, material acquisition, desiring, and amassing knowledge through effort. Such, as we have seen, is *wu-wei*. In the *Daodejing*, for instance, we find this:

> Without stirring abroad
> One can know the whole world;
> Without looking out of the window
> One can see the way of heaven.
> The further one goes
> The less one knows.
> Therefore the sage knows without having to stir
> Identifies without having to see
> Accomplishes without having to act.[34]

Instead of racking up air miles, stay home. What sage advice to a world gone stupid. This remark is, you hardly need telling, not to be confused with the business model of Britain's East India Company, nor could it be part of British imperialist Cecil Rhodes' rapacious acquisitive racist mindset. And yet it echoes western wisdom. 'All of humanity's problems,' French philosopher Blaise Pascal said in 1654, 'stem from man's inability to sit quietly in a room alone.'[35] Across the centuries and from one side of the world to another, Laozi and Pascal are united in indicting the folly of action. Only stupid people travel, especially those selfie narcissists on the hunt for Insta-worthy locales. Laozi and Pascal didn't write the last sentence, but I feel sure they would have endorsed its sense that travel is the very emblem of humanity's spirit-crushing, self-frustrating pursuit of desire satisfaction as set out in the Buddha's Four Noble Truths. Neither would have been frequent flyers.

Eastern philosophy and religion prize not travel and changing the world, but remaining inactive and adapting to the world. So, at least, argues Korean-German philosopher Byung-Chul Han in his 2023 book

Absence: On the Culture and Philosophy of the Far East. There, following Daoist thought, he suggests we become like water, passive yet thereby powerful. He writes that in both Daoism and Zen Buddhism, illumination – what the Zen masters call *satori* – is a transition from limited conceptions to limitless ones, to what he calls an 'oceanic feeling'. He quotes from the Chinese Zen text *The Ox and His Herdsman* to help us understand that feeling:

> With one blow the vast sky suddenly breaks into pieces.
> Holy, worldly, vanished without a trace . . .
> The bright moon shines and the wind rustles in front of the temple
> All waters of all rivers flow into the great sea.[36]

Han explains this puzzling verse as follows: 'For the Chinese [he means Chinese Zen and Daoist thinkers], water, or the sea, is the symbol for a thinking or behaviour that adapts or snuggles up to the transforming world and changing things.' The western wisdom mindset is nothing like that, Han claims. 'Opposed to this re-active and re-active thinking, Western thinking is active and acting: it tackles the world from a fixed point, *even sets sail to conquer it* [Han's italics].' For Han, western thinking is like a nautical adventure, overcoming ignorance and amassing knowledge, facing down stupidity – a temperament alien to eastern sages. 'The Chinese sages do not tackle or conquer the world like those adventurous seafarers; they snuggle up to it. Thinking has to stay as supple as possible, so that it opens itself up to the manifold possibilities that exist. Far Eastern thinking is friendly in the sense that it does not insist on set axioms and principles.'[37] Both of the systems of eastern thought Han considers – the Chinese folk religion of Daoism and Zen, a Mahayana Buddhist tradition that arose in what Han calls the Far East stressing non-conceptual awareness and that delightful relief to the weary of limb, the practice of *zazen* (or just sitting) – are heavily influenced by the teachings of the Buddha.

But how can we acquire this eastern wisdom, this snuggly friendliness that Han eulogizes? Without logic, axioms, principles, remedial lessons, or a restless spirit of inquiry, how can we emulate Buddhist sages or Daoist ones? This, perhaps, is just what a stupid westerner innocent of the desirable virtue of *wu-wei* would say. We can't set out to conquer the citadels of eastern thought; nor really can we learn them from masters; we have to find our own path – like the Buddha, like Siddhartha – to enlightenment.

Daoism goes further than western wisdom in this. Don't stay home, it proposes. Instead, give away your possessions, escape the mental prison of having a fixed home, embrace impermanence and live on the road. Or, as Han, might put it, snuggle up to the world rather than attempt to conquer it.

Daoism, as we have seen, is inimical to the pursuit of knowledge that western philosophy occupies itself with in order to avoid stupidity. There's a lovely, deeply paradoxical story about the poet and politician Tao Yuanming (365–427 CE) that captures this. Tao reportedly had a *qin*, a stringless zither. Unconstrained by such matters as virtuosity and dexterity, or indeed making sounds, he did not master his instrument or even play it. Byung-Chul Han, who relates this story, draws the moral: Tao does not exert himself, does not do anything, does not try to master anything.[38] Virtuosity, after all, is based on maximizing activity. Tao preferred to be a virtuoso of doing nothing. If this is *wu-wei* in action, it sounds much more radical than that practised by Charlie Parker. Or, rather, it sounds like nothing at all.

Indeed, Tao's story and many of the sayings included in the *Daodejing* make the phenomenon of *wu-wei* seem much more radically strange and unattainable than Edward Slingerland's account of it. Instead of what Slingerland sometimes seems to be offering, namely practical advice on how to master skills, become virtuous, and get in the zone, Daoist thought suggests that the Way is unattainable and *wu-wei* unteachable.

Certainly, the wisdom of doing nothing against the folly of endless striving and doing is recommended repeatedly in the *Daodejing*, where the primary counsel is to be like water: unresisting, flowing, submissive. 'The most submissive thing in the world,' says Laozi, 'can ride roughshod over the hardest in the world – that which is without substance entering that which has no crevices.' Like a judo black belt using their opponent's weight and motion to the former's advantage, inaction and insubstantiality can be decisively beneficial. 'That is why I know the benefit of resorting to no action. The teaching that uses no words, the benefit of resorting to no action, these are beyond the understanding of all but a very few in the world.'[39]

This is a little disappointing for those who want to become as sage as Laozi or indeed as serene as the Buddha. For Laozi, the Way cannot be taught. Or not very easily. But what is the Way? Clearly, it is very important to Daoism since, as D.C. Lau remarks in his translation of the *Tao Te Ching* (now more commonly translated as *Daodejing*), the Way is conceived of as responsible for the creation of, as well as upholding, the universe. But it is unknowable, argues Lau, who cites several sayings by Laozi to clinch this point, such as: 'The way conceals itself by being nameless.'[40] That makes sense if, as Lau suggests, language is inadequate to the purpose of describing the Way (*dao*). And yet, in another saying, Laozi seems to attempt just that:

> As a thing the way is
> Shadowy, indistinct.
> Indistinct and shadowy,
> Yet within it is an image;
> Shadowy and indistinct,
> Yet within it is a substance.
> Dim and dark,
> Yet within it is an essence.
> This essence is quite genuine
> And within it is something that can be tested.[41]

My science-venerating western sensibility yearns to test this 'something', to expose the essence of the *dao* to view and define it; to overcome my ignorance with the application of reason and thereby become less stupid. But that, most likely, would be a stupid mistake, typical of a western sensibility that has no place here. As Byung-Chul Han puts it, for far eastern philosophy and religion,

> The relationship with the world is not dominated by the decisiveness of doing and acting, nor by the clarity of consciousness and reflection. Rather, one lets the world happen, lets oneself be filled by it by retreating into absence, by being oblivious of self, or emptying oneself like a chamber whose emptiness means it can be filled with light and become bright.[42]

Viewed thus, the far eastern philosophy that Han eulogizes is akin to renowned Japanese tidying expert Marie Kondo, whose philosophy of domestic decluttering, effectively, is aimed at producing joy and serenity in domestic spaces that have become stupefyingly full, perhaps even stupidity enhancing.

Decluttering is not a small matter for eastern wisdom. While western thinking has long been dominated by notions of essence and substance, far eastern thought is, if Han is right, centred on absence. Both Daoism and Buddhism, especially Zen Buddhism, involve a material, intellectual, and spiritual decluttering. 'A Zen monk should be without fixed abode, like the clouds, and without fixed support, like water,' said the Japanese Zen master Dōgen.[43] For the Zen master, there should be no home, no desires, nor any other attachment to get in his way. Similarly, in the *Daodejing* we find this verse:

> In the pursuit of learning, one learns more every day;
> in the pursuit of the way one learns less every day.
> One does less and less until one does nothing at all,
> and when one does nothing at all, there is nothing undone.[44]

The parallel with Marie Kondo is not exact since Laozi sounds, at least in this verse, too much of a feckless slacker to tidy his room. The cynic in me suspects that Laozi is essentially a grown-up adolescent waited on hand and foot by his mother, or some other exploited woman, and that the philosophy of inaction depends on others – cleaners, cooks, workers – scurrying around in the sage's wake. Similarly, the cynic in me suggests that when Dōgen recommends living like the clouds, and without fixed support, like water, somebody who is not a Zen master is offering alms and shelter, preparing the meals and doing the dishes. Perhaps that's unfair on Laozi, who may well not have been an exploitative idler and whose wise counsel on how to live goes well beyond an endorsement of the wisdom of being workshy. Immediately after the verse eulogizing inaction in the *Daodejing*, Laozi offers this advice:

> It is always through not meddling that the empire is won
> Should you meddle, then you are not equal to the task of winning the empire.[45]

It's a very good point and yet one that Socrates, in all his wise words for the stupid Alcibiades as the latter stood on the brink of public office, was not capable of giving. For those of us who have observed the stupid micromanagement of public services, this call to stop meddling and embrace the virtue of inaction is appealing indeed. This may be sage advice on how to govern: rather than micromanaging everything within one's political ambit, the sage leader does less. Of course, it may also be compatible with a neo-liberal rolling back of the state in line with Friedrich Hayek's anti-government philosophy. And yet the main point is this: to do is often a mistake, and to do too much always a mistake. How this might be converted into a manual for rulers, along the lines of Machiavelli's *The Prince*, is beyond me. Rather, it suggests that the wisdom of Laozi, and the counsel he advises for how to conduct one's life and government, can only be grasped intuitively, or through experience. Certainly, words or manuals are not up to the task of inculcating in a person how to follow the Way.

For a book on stupidity, this is disappointing. Stupidity, as we have supposed, is something we would like to overcome. And yet the wisdom of the Buddha and of Laozi suggests that learning and acquiring knowledge may be impediments to doing so.

Touching the void

None of the foregoing should be taken as suggesting that intelligence or the pursuit of knowledge has no place in eastern thinking: that would be patronizing and racist. The Dalai Lama, for instance, writes in his book *The Middle Way: Faith Grounded in Reason*:

> Many centuries ago, humans realised the importance of harnessing the intellect. From that evolved writing and, eventually, formal education. These days, it is a truism to say that education is vital, but it is important to remind ourselves of the larger purpose of education. After all, what good is the accumulation of knowledge if it does not lead to a happier life? . . . You might think that the goal of education is merely to augment one's ability to increase one's wealth, possessions, or power. But just as mere knowledge in and of itself is not sufficient to make us happy, material things or power alone also cannot overcome worry and frustration. There must be some other factor in our minds that creates the foundation for a happy life, something that allows us to handle life's difficulties effectively.[46]

And yet Mādhyamaka, the tradition of Buddhist philosophy and practice to which the Dalai Lama adheres, is antipathetic to reason. Those who have studied Sextus Empiricus's scepticism, Theodor W. Adorno's negative dialectics, or Jacques Derrida's deconstructive method will find much that is familiar in this tradition since it is predicated on arguing that the pursuit of knowledge, the deployment of reason, and any other conceptual attempt to comprehend or master the mysteries of the universe are doomed. The tradition hardly counsels the cultivation of stupidity in denying the power of rational thought; but it does imply that failing to appreciate the shortcomings of rational thought is folly, or indeed stupid.

Founded by the Indian Buddhist monk and philosopher Nāgārjuna (c. 150–c. 250 CE) a couple of centuries after the Buddha's death, the Mādhyamaka school contends that argument and rationality are self-contradictory. Nāgārjuna wrote in the classic statement of his philosophy *Vigrahavyāvartanī* (which has been translated as 'The Refutation of Objections'):

> If your objects are well established through valid cognitions, tell us how you establish these valid cognitions. If you think they are established through other valid cognitions, there is an infinite regress. Then, the first one is not established, nor are the middle ones, nor the last. If these [valid cognitions] are established even without valid cognition, what you say is ruined. In that case, there is an inconsistency. And you ought to provide an argument for this distinction.[47]

To put it another way, rational thinking is always groundless and therefore a manifestation not so much of intelligence as of stupidity. That said, there is no criterion of rationality for Nāgārjuna and so, by western lights at least, no scope for deciding if rational argumentation is intelligent or stupid, nor whether his claim just quoted is sense or nonsense. His philosophy has been called Voidism, involving the thesis that the world is unreal in some sense. The world is called unreal because it is temporary. Things change, and whatever disappears cannot be called real in the ultimate sense of the word. Voidism, for some, is the height of stupidity. It is self-contradictory to propose the philosophy of Voidism since asserting it requires that at least one thing, namely the speaker, be real. Equally, if there is no rational thinking, then the thought expressed in this Voidist argument can be ignored since it is, by definition, not worth considering.

More sympathetically, Nāgārjuna's philosophy draws on the development of early Buddhist thinking. After the Great Schism that followed the Buddha's death, reportedly aged 80 sometime between 486 and 483 BCE, a host of sub-schools arose that produced rival interpretations of his many sutras, or aphorisms. Two influential schools remain, the rival Theravada and Mahayana traditions. The two traditions differ on many things, but for our purposes the most contentious matter is their rival interpretation of remarks the Buddha made in asserting the second of the Four Noble Truths, namely the Truth of Arising. The Buddha taught that human craving is a seemingly unstoppable force powered by three evil forces: greed, hatred, and delusion. In Buddhist imagery, these powers are depicted as a cock, a pig, and a snake, chasing each other in a small circle, each with the tail of another in their mouths. The image suggests an eternity of craving, death and rebirth.

In later philosophical disputes, though, the Theravada and Mahayana traditions differed on how to interpret this notion of origination-in-dependence, roughly the suggestion that everything is connected and dependent, just as the cock, pig, and snake chase each other in an eternal cycle of folly. For those in the Theravada tradition, this notion suggests that all phenomena, or *dharma*, are impermanent but nonetheless real. Take, for example, a chair. As Damien Keown suggests in *Buddhism: A Very Short introduction*,[48] for those in the Theravada tradition, a chair might consist of various parts – legs, seat, back, etc. but there is no chair over and above these parts. The task of Buddhist meditation, for those in the Theravada tradition, is to overcome one's habitual perceptual stupidity and experience the world as it is. 'Our human perceptual habits are remarkably stupid,' wrote the Sri Lankan Theravada Buddhist Bhante Henepola Gunaratana in his 1994 book *Mindfulness in Plain English*. 'We tune out 99% of perceptual stimuli we actually receive, we solidify the remainder into discrete mental objects. Then we react to those objects in programmed habitual ways.'[49] In this, Gunaratana is playing Hamlet to the rest of humanity's Horatio: there are more things in heaven and earth than are dreamed of in our habit-ruined sensibilities; this Hamlet, though, unlike Shakespeare's, proposes how we might rise above such stupid shortcomings. His bestselling book is a guide to how, through meditation and mindfulness, we might overcome our stupidity and change our habits.

For Mahayana Buddhists, however, matters are different. For them, the truth is that *dharma* are not just impermanent but also not real. All phenomena – chairs, trees, you, me – are empty of any real being. To think otherwise is stupid, delusory. As Keown points out, this Mahayana thinking has one very important corollary that upends all we have been discussing so far about the Buddhist pursuit of enlightenment, or nirvana. For, if nothing is real, there can be no difference between nirvana and *samsara* (the path of cyclical rebirth). If nothing is real, there is no distinction to be made between reality and illusion. The corollaries of this way of thinking are astonishing, even though they are, to an extent, mere embellishments of the Buddha's thought. For instance, in Hindu thought, expressed in the *Upanishads* and the *Bhagavad Gita*, it is commonplace that there exists an individual self (*atman*) and a supreme self (or *brahman*) within each being. The Buddha doubted this view: for him there was no self or soul, no immutable spiritual essence behind the individual. Voidism, effectively, elaborates this teaching, contending that such distinctions are in name only: they are empty of real significance.

Think of the matter this way. It is dusk and you see a snake. Terrified, you run away. But it turns out what you saw was a coiled rope. Your mistake, for Nāgārjuna, was to run away. Similarly, fleeing from the world of *samsara* to the calm of nirvana is delusive. 'It follows that nirvana is here and now if we could but see it,' writes Keown.[50] Nirvana – a term found in all the major religions that have arisen in India, including Hinduism, Jainism, Buddhism, and Sikhism – means the profound peace of mind that is acquired with *moksha*, which is the liberation from *samsara*. *Samsara*, in turn, is the endless cyclical suffering of death and rebirth to which we and the rest of the material world are bound. For most of these religions, the escape from *samsara* to nirvana is achieved through ego-transcending disciplines known as *sādhanā*, including, but not limited to, meditation. Such practices are aimed at eliminating worldliness and attachments.

Nāgārjuna, by contrast and rather heretically, suggests that nirvana is immanent rather than transcendental. This, to my mind, is an absolutely scintillating life philosophy, a bravura account that moves from the non-reality of the universe and the self-contradictoriness of rational thought to the opposite position, suggesting that the removal of spiritual ignorance consists in accommodating ourselves to this vale of tears we call life. But, in fact, the Voidist position is consistent: it suggests that everything is void of real existence and has no significance in itself. No difference can be found in things in themselves because they are all ultimately empty; the difference must lie in our perceptions of them.

Nit pickers will point out that if nothing is real, there is nothing that is capable of making a perception, nor of deciding that nirvana and *samsara* are ontologically distinct, nor one more desirable than the other. That's true, no doubt, but it misses the liberating power of this doctrine of emptiness. If conceptual thought is a sham and material objects – including the thinking part of my body – have no real existence, then it would be folly, stupid really, not to attempt other ways of living and other means of accessing the true nature of the world. For many Buddhists, that way involves meditation. That rather than rational contemplation is the path from ignorance to wisdom. For others, perhaps, it is self-indulgent stupidity.

It's an extremist philosophy, no doubt, but one that has an honourable pedigree in eastern philosophy. Since the beginnings of philosophical speculation in India with an ancient body of oral literature called the *Vedas*, eastern philosophers, just like those in the West, have both indulged in metaphysical speculation and, as we see from the example of Voidist thought, counselled that such speculation is futile. For instance, the *Rig Veda*, the oldest known Vedic Sanskrit text, muses on what existed before the universe:

> There was not then what is nor what is not. There was no sky and no heaven beyond the sky. What power was there? Who was that power? Was there an abyss of fathomless waters? . . . Who knows the truth? Who can tell whence and how arose the universe? The gods are later than its beginning: who knows therefore whence came this creation?[51]

From the start of eastern philosophy, one might infer, we are confronted by our own shortcomings, our ignorance and inability to answer the most basic questions about the origin of the universe. But the greatest stupidity of all, perhaps, is to fail to appreciate one's shortcomings and to imagine that all questions have answers, and that knowledge is a mighty enough force to overcome the serried ranks of human stupidity. 'Whereof one cannot speak, thereof one must be silent.' wrote Ludwig Wittgenstein in the last sentence of his *Tractatus Logico-Philosophicus*, published in 1921.[52] The Vedic sages realized this truth millennia earlier.

The ferryman

One day, towards the end of his life, Govinda arrived at a river and asked the old ferryman to take him across. In between now and the time we last saw him, Govinda has become a Buddhist monk, respected by his younger peers for his modesty, but is still unsatisfied, still restlessly questing. For a few minutes, he does not realize that the old ferryman is his childhood friend Siddhartha. Perhaps Siddhartha, by contrast, does recognize that the traveller is Govinda: certainly, in a glance, he seems to know a great deal about the monk, to the extent that he diagnoses why the aged Govinda is still a restless soul. Perhaps, Siddhartha suggests, you seek too much and as a result cannot find what you are seeking. This chimes with the saying quoted above from Gunaratana, who reckoned that in our stupidity, in our habit-hobbled sensibilities, we ignore 99% of reality. Govinda is prone to a similar malady, a kind of tunnel vision. 'When someone is seeking,' Siddhartha explains, 'it happens quite easily that he only sees the thing he is seeking; that he is unable to find anything, unable to absorb anything, because he is only thinking of the thing he is seeking, because he is obsessed with his goal.'[53] Again, this chimes with Byung Chul-Han's critique of western thinking: 'Western thinking has long been dominated by essence, by a preoccupation with that which dwells in itself and delimits itself from the other. Western science, equally, might be understood as penetrating those essences, acquiring knowledge through experiment and action. Far Eastern thinking is different.' Eastern thinking is not like that, Han argues. 'The fundamental topos of Far Eastern thinking is not being but "the way" (dao), which lacks the solidity and fixedness of essence. The difference between essence and absence is the difference between being and path, between dwelling and wandering.'[54]

Siddhartha, since we last saw him talking to the Buddha in the grove, has led a life of unceasing wandering. When Govinda asks him if he has a doctrine, belief, or knowledge that guides him on how to live and do right, he replies that he does not. 'Even as a young man, I came to distrust doctrines and teachings and to turn my back on them.'[55] This rejection of the efficacy of teaching in general and learning from a sage old master in particular is one of the great bracing heresies of Buddhism. Both eastern and western traditions teem with examples of young men seeking out wise teachings from elders and betters: we see it in Alcibiades' relationship with Socrates; we see it, too, in the 700-page verse scripture the *Bhagavad Gita*, part of the epic *Mahabharata*, which consists of a dialogue between a confused youth (the Pandava prince Arjuna) who seeks advice from his sage charioteer guide Krishna (an avatar of Lord Vishnu) on the moral propriety of war and other ethical matters.

Siddhartha rebelled against this venerable means of acquiring wisdom. Instead of being taught by a wise man, he left the grove after talking to the Buddha and began a life of spiritual vagabondage during which he immersed himself not in renouncing the world but in learning its ways. To become wise, to end his suffering, to go beyond everyday stupidity, he needed not to be taught by a wise man, but rather to multiply and to learn from his own experiences.

Nor was the Buddha insistent that Siddhartha needed his teachings to become wise. As we saw in the previous chapter, Socrates has just this belief; he argues that he and only he has the right pedagogic stuff to enlighten. The Buddha, by contrast, had offered only one piece of advice before leaving the young Siddhartha. 'You are clever, O Samana; you know how to speak cleverly, my friend. Be on your guard against too much cleverness.' And with that he leaves, and again Siddhartha notes how the Illustrious One walks and smiles in a way that strikes him as 'So worthy, so candid, so restrained, so childlike and mysterious. A man only walks like that,' reflects Siddhartha, 'when he has conquered his Self. I will also conquer my Self.'[56]

The rest of the novel, indeed, shows how Siddhartha conquers his Self, becoming humble, useful, compassionate, and wise. He relates his teachers were not wise men but a beautiful courtesan, a wise merchant and dice player, and an illiterate ferryman called Vasudeva. 'He was not a thinker, but he realised the essential as well as Gotama,' says Siddhartha of Vasudeva. 'He was a holy man, a saint.'[57] And when Vasudeva died, Siddhartha became the ferryman and, he tells Govinda, it was from his proximity to the river – that emblem of the eternal cycle of change – that he learned most.

Here Siddhartha is challenging the usual means of knowledge acquisition by means of which we arise from ignorance and stupidity. He needed no Socrates, no Buddha. Now an old man, he relates: 'This one thought has impressed me, Govinda. Wisdom is not communicable. Knowledge can be communicated, but not wisdom. One can find it, be fortified by it, do wonders through it, but one cannot communicate and teach it.' Like Nāgārjuna, he is sceptical of the power of conceptual thought and, like much eastern thinking, doubtful of the efficacy of language: 'Everything that is thought and expressed in words is one sided, only half the truth; it lacks all totality, completeness, unity.'[58]

Even the Buddha, for Siddhartha, made that mistake. He divided the world into nirvana and *samsara*, into illusion and truth, suffering and salvation, but this, he suggests, is the fate of all teachers and, by extension, all conceptual thought: both involve a systematic distortion, both are necessarily partial perspectives. 'But the world itself, being in and around us, is never one-sided. Never is a man or a deed wholly Sansara [i.e. *samsara*] or wholly Nirvana; never is a man wholly a saint or a sinner.'[59]

And then, bafflingly to Govinda, Siddhartha argues that this is so because time is unreal. And if time is unreal, then the dividing line that seems to lie between this world and eternity, between suffering and bliss, between good and evil, is also an illusion. This resonates with the central tenet of Voidism, that if nothing is real, there can be no essential difference between nirvana and *samsara*. The pursuit of the former is misguided since nirvana is really here and now rather than in some transcendent realm. Siddhartha, following this thought, suggests that meditation may help us overcome our shortcomings: 'During deep meditation it is possible to dispel time, to see simultaneously all past, present and future, and then everything is good, everything is perfect, everything is Brahman.' Brahman, explains Hesse's glossary to his novel, is 'the unchanging, infinite, immanent and transcendent reality which is the Divine Ground of all matter, energy, time, space, being and everything beyond in this universe'.[60] Which, in itself, is a discombobulating definition, at least to those of us mired in the binary thinking of western metaphysics who, thanks to our stupid limitations, suppose, in our folly, that the transcendent and immanent are, by definition, mutually exclusive. Once more here, eastern wisdom chimes with Jacques Derrida's deconstructive method, since what Siddhartha says here foreshadows the French philosopher's suggestion that western metaphysics creates dualistic oppositions that unfortunately privilege one term of each dichotomy: presence before absence, speech before written word, and (no doubt) reality over unreality.

But if time is unreal, then there is no temporal path to redemption, no narrative to be told of rising above the world's folly. As Siddhartha puts it: 'The sinner is not on the way to a Buddha-like state; he is not evolving, although our thinking cannot conceive otherwise.'[61] It is not just that western metaphysics is constrained by binary thinking; all thinking, by its very nature, is predicated on illusion. In truth (if that is not too binary a conception), everything is everything else, nothing (particularly the human self) is permanently self-identical, and the world is not evolving towards perfection in some Hegelian march of history towards absolute knowledge, nor, more surprisingly, is there a Buddhist journey towards transcendent nirvana. Any such stories, any such progressivist fantasies, are rather stupid since they miss what, for Siddhartha at least, is the very thing the wise notice. Nirvana is here and now; to be enlightened requires a perspectival shift rather than elevation to a transcendental realm. For Siddhartha, the world 'is perfect at every moment; every sin already carries grace within it, all small children are potential old men, all sucklings have death within then, all dying people eternal life. . . . Therefore it seems to me that everything that exists is good, death as well as life, sin as well as holiness, wisdom as well as folly.'[62]

Siddhartha learned this wisdom not through conceptual thought or teaching from a sage but from his own life experiences of lust, desire, despair, and sin. These experiences, one might have thought, should have led him to hate the world in all its bogus allure and potential for bottomless craving. On the contrary: for Siddhartha, those experiences helped him accept the world, assent to it rather like the great ringing 'Yes' that is the last word of Molly Bloom's soliloquy in James Joyce's *Ulysses*. Instead of renouncing the world, instead of comparing it with some imagined realm, he accepts the world as it is. And in so doing, he concludes, 'All is well and nothing can harm me.'[63] He has arrived through a kind of philosophical wisdom akin to Socrates when, on the brink of taking the fatal hemlock, he speaks of being beyond the powers of his judges; he has achieved the *ataraxia*, or imperturbability and equanimity, sought by Stoic and Epicurean philosophers.

Govinda, by contrast, has not found such equanimity. To make his point, Siddhartha picks up a stone. At one point, in his folly, he thought the stone was just a stone; it had no value but might acquire value in the world of change by becoming a man and a spirit. That was what he used to think. Now, though, wisdom consists in seeing that the stone is animal, God, and Buddha. But he doesn't love the stone because it is also God and Buddha or any of the other infinite things that a stone is for him; rather, he loves it because it is a particular stone, worthy of worship. 'But I will say no more about it. Words do not express thoughts very well. They always become a little different the moment they are expressed, a little distorted, a little foolish.'[64] Wisdom can sound like folly just as much, no doubt, as folly can sound like wisdom.

Finally, Govinda asks if everything is an illusion of Maya, only image and appearance, then what is the status of this stone or of that tree – are they real? The question does not matter to Siddhartha. 'If they are illusion, then I also am illusion and so they are of the same nature as me.'[65]

Wisdom for Siddhartha, then, consists in setting aside futile distinctions. In this sense, he is a maverick Buddhist since Buddhism maintains a sharp distinction between appearance and reality. Instead, at least to me, he resembles William James, the philosopher who argued that philosophical debate was useless if the outcome of the debate had no practical consequences. 'There can be no difference anywhere that doesn't make a difference elsewhere,' wrote James.[66] For Siddhartha, with the wisdom of the pragmatist, what is called illusory may well be called real. There is no real difference between the two.

This chimes with ancient Daoist wisdom. The poet Chuang-Tzu, who lived in the 4th century BCE, described a lovely dream.

> Once upon a time, I dreamt I was a butterfly, fluttering hither and thither, to all intents and purposes a butterfly. I was conscious only of my happiness as a butterfly, unaware that I was myself. Soon I awaked, and there I was, veritably myself again. Now I do not know whether I was then a man dreaming I was a butterfly, or whether I am now a butterfly, dreaming I am a man.

Buddhists seek to awaken from their dream, to disabuse themselves of their illusions. That seems to be wisdom. Maybe, though, it is stupid. 'If "Life is a dream" implies that no achievement is lasting,' argued Chuang-Tzu, 'it also implies that life can be charged with the wonder of dreams, that we drift spontaneously through events that follow a logic different from that of everyday intelligence, that fears and regrets are as unreal as hopes and desires.'[67] The implication of such thoughts is perhaps that wisdom and intelligence are as unreal as folly and stupidity.

For the British philosopher John Gray, who was much taken with Daoist thought, it is folly to try to disabuse ourselves of illusions. Daoism, if it teaches anything that might help us become other than stupid, counsels suppleness and non-resistance to that which cannot be resisted. 'We cannot be rid of illusions,' wrote Gray in *Straw Dogs*. 'Illusion is our natural condition. Why not accept it?'[68]

We should, as we will see in the next chapter, learn from the wisdom of Don Quixote. His folly perhaps was unwitting wisdom. He was happy tilting at windmills; perhaps, then, it would have been folly to tell him he was being stupid.

4
The Value of Folly

Fools' paradises

Perhaps ignorance is bliss and stupidity the precondition of happiness. 'Countless studies have shown that people who suffer from depression have more accurate world views than non-depressed people,' writes Kathryn Schulz in *Being Wrong: Adventures in the Margin of Error*.[1] In Miguel de Cervantes's *Don Quixote*, first published in 1605, his eponymous protagonist was many things: myopic, deluded, violent, wounded, impoverished, but depressed? Unlikely. Maybe the wise should envy the deluded, ignorant or stupid? Not so, countered Bertrand Russell, who, in 1951 offered Ten Commandments to capture the essence of his liberal outlook. 'Do not feel envious of the happiness of those who live in a fool's paradise,' went the last of them, 'for only a fool will think that it is happiness.'[2]

But Russell's commandment is itself folly, its dubious premises suppressed so we can't see the weakness of the argument behind the flourish of rhetoric. It supposes that happiness requires the happy person to live in truth and reality. Happiness isn't like that: if you are happy, then you can't really be wrong if you additionally think you are happy. And yet for Russell, there is clearly a wrong way to be happy. If you are happy only because you enjoy torturing children, clearly your happiness is wrong. But that isn't Russell's point. Rather, he is suggesting that anyone whose happiness proceeds from stupidity, madness, folly, or ignorance cannot properly be happy. He thinks there is a normative element to happiness. In this he was following his godfather, John Stuart

Mill, for whom there were higher and lower pleasures. Higher pleasures (reading poetry) are better than lower pleasures (watching daytime TV). But even that distinction doesn't help Russell: in either case of pleasure, be it ever so highbrow or ever so vulgar, one is feeling pleasure, just not of the right kind; but here he is denying that foolish happiness is happiness, not that it is the wrong kind of happiness. And that seems a terrible slur on happiness as experienced by fools, or any of the mad, deluded persons living contentedly in illusory paradises. It is at least possible that Quixote was happy wearing a barber's bowl, thinking it was a golden helmet he had rightly seized from his foe, and that he would have been unhappy to have been disabused of his folly and banished from his fool's paradise.

That said, Cervantes imagined his knight errant as not especially happy, which makes sense given all the beatings and enchantments to which the novelist subjects his hero and his servant during their adventures. Cervantes repeatedly describes Quixote the 'Knight of the Rueful Countenance'.[3] So, if the Don really was happy in his deluded, potentially stupid lifestyle, he would have done well to tell his face.

It is equally possible that we, deprived of the illusions that sustained his lifestyle, are unhappy – either because reality offers a poor soil for happiness to flourish in; or because, as John Gray put it in the previous chapter, illusions are inescapable and our task is to accept them. For Gray at least, we are destined to be fools; the only question is whether we choose to live happily in a fool's paradise or to be miserable in our folly. Gray, sensibly, prefers the former option. Of course, there is another option: we may unwittingly live in a fool's paradise, unaware that others are eyeing us narrowly and thinking we are mad. Indeed, in several scenes, Cervantes presents many of those whom Don Quixote encounters as recognizing something about himself that he never really grasps: that he is living, not necessarily happily, in a land of make-believe. Nonetheless, it is possible that Quixote's folly, paradoxically, may be the most stupid of lifestyles and yet the most desirable. Those of us who envy Don Quixote in his lifestyle cannot aim to emulate him in his delusions since being stupid or deluded is not something one can will into being. Stupidity is like the quality of greatness described by Quixote's near contemporary, the foolish Malvolio in Shakespeare's *Twelfth Night*: some are born stupid, some achieve stupidity, and some have stupidity thrust upon them. Make no mistake, though, even if stupidity is achieved, it is not because one aspires to it; rather, it is achieved despite one's aspirations.

The notion that folly, and perhaps even stupidity, are desirable is incendiary and yet goes to the heart of the topsy-turvy world we are going to explore in this chapter. As the scientific method arose in the early modern world and the claims of reason were pressed as never before, it was shadowed by a kind of anti-philosophy of folly. This foolosophy, if you will, is associated with great Renaissance essays such as the humanist scholar Desiderius Erasmus's *In Praise of Folly*, written in 1509,[4] of which more below, and several by Michel de Montaigne, especially his 'Apology for Raymond Sebond', written between 1575 and 1580.[5] With Don Quixote, Cervantes created the anti-hero of this reason-venerating age, capitalizing on a yearning among the literate for imaginative, fantastical writing beyond the strait-jacket of rationality with newly freed heroes and rogues who became foolish, mad, passionate or anything else frowned upon through reason's chilly lorgnettes.

But foolosophy was developed most sustainedly in Shakespeare's plays in the late 1590s and early 1600s, most notably *A Midsummer Night's Dream*, *As You Like It*, and *King Lear*. For Shakespeare, at least, fools and foolishness are desirable not in themselves but as portals to wisdom. In *A Midsummer Night's Dream*, Nick Bottom the weaver becomes literally asinine with a donkey's head to set off his braying mulishness, and yet, courted by the drug-addled and thereby deluded queen of the fairies, Titania, he couldn't be happier.[6] Nor indeed could Titania, having stumbled across the most desirable of lovers. Their tryst dramatizes how wrong Bertrand Russell was to suppose that those of us living in fool's paradises can't really be happy.

In Act One of *King Lear*, the Fool tells his eponymous master, who has, through his witless hubristic folly, given away his kingdom to two ungrateful daughters and left nothing to his third loving daughter: 'I had rather be any kind o'thing than a fool. And yet I would not be thee, nuncle: thou hast pared thy wits o'both sides and left nothing i'the middle.'[7] Lear's folly is especially striking to us since at this early stage of the play he has no self-understanding, relying on the Fool to point out his witlessness.

The trope of courtly folly being diagnosed from the sidelines by foolish wisdom figures in several of Shakespeare's plays. Often, he portrays those in power as so blinded by self-regard to have become complacently stupid, even to the point of not knowing the best for themselves. In Shakespeare's oeuvre, it is axiomatic that courtly decadence and regal pomp dull the senses and thwart acuity. As the Fool puts it a few lines earlier:

> For wise men are grown foppish
> And know not how their wits to wear.

Such barbs came readily to the playwright, possibly because he observed such foppish folly as a member of theatrical troupes that performed at the courts of Elizabeth I and James I.

Folly, then, assembles subversive forces against a new power at the very moment when reason is seeking to establish its dominance and seal its borders from infection from without. In *A Midsummer Night's Dream*, folly and madness are antidotes to reason's dearth of humanizing imagination. Theseus tells Hippolyta in Act Five that he disbelieves the fantastic noises and fairy stories that have beguiled the audience for the previous four acts, thinking them products of deranged minds:

> Lovers and madmen have such seething brains,
> Such shaping fantasies, that apprehend
> More than cool reason ever comprehends.[8]

That distinction between apprehension and comprehension is key: folly is an affair of the imagination, not the understanding. And, contrary to the notion of reason developed contemporaneously by Britain's leading philosopher, Francis Bacon, folly harnesses the imagination, puts the passionate heart to work, and even mobilizes delusive ravings, and in so doing shows a better means of reaching wisdom than 'cool reason'.

The rest of Theseus's speech, though ostensibly disdainful of the anti-rational militant tendency of humanity, makes folly seem attractive. Reading the following, one yearns to become a lover, a poet, or, just possibly, a lunatic:

> The lunatic, the lover and the poet
> Are of imagination all compact.

> One sees more devils than vast hell can hold:
> That is, the madman. The lover, all as frantic,
> Sees Helen's beauty in a brow of Egypt.
> The poet's eye, in fine frenzy rolling,
> Doth glance from heaven to earth, from earth to heaven,
> And as imagination bodies forth
> The forms of things unknown, the poet's pen
> Turns them to shapes and gives to airy nothing
> A local habitation and a name.
> Such tricks hath strong imagination,
> That if it would but apprehend some joy,
> It comprehends some bringer of that joy;
> Or in the night, imagining some fear,
> How easy is a bush supposed a bear!

Or, indeed, how easy is it to suppose, like Quixote, that windmills are warriors! Or how blissful it is to be ignorant of the truth that you in your delusions are being made fun of by others, again like Quixote. Who would want to be rational or be told the disappointing truth if one might miraculously take an ugly woman as a beautiful one, pen fabulously fantastical verses that to others seem doggerel, or lead an imaginative if deluded life beyond the dreary constraints of good sense? For those who come to praise folly rather than bury it, these questions are rhetorical.

In *As You Like It*, folly is depicted as a mask behind which true wisdom conceals itself, yet another garment in the cross-dressing wardrobe that Shakespeare's characters are apt to explore at the drop of a codpiece. Folly cannot reveal itself on pain of being found telling truth to power and getting whipped for breaching court etiquette. 'Is this not a rare fellow, my Lord?' asks Jaques, impressed at the fool Touchstone's witty barbs. 'He's as good at anything and yet a fool.' To which the Duke replies: 'He uses his folly like a stalking-horse and under the presentation of that he shoots his wit.'[9] In a world of foppish flatterers, folly snarks from the wings, presenting its wisdom as foolishness.

In *King Lear*, Edgar disguises himself in rags and tatters as Poor Tom, and, feigning madness, sees better into the world's folly than those who persist in the allegedly sane straight world of kings and sickeningly immoral power grabs. The Fool's role is to tell wittily encoded truth to power, just as Touchstone does in *As You Like It*, but the tragedy also does something more existentially destabilizing: it depicts folly as the dramatically revealed truth about the human condition, the irredeemable way of the world. King Lear was not a Daoist, not even towards the end of his tragic wanderings from courtly pomp to impoverished vagabondage, though his sense of the omnipresence of human folly and delusion surely shares features with that wisdom. 'When we are born we cry that we are come to this great stage of fools,' he says towards the end of the play,[10] insightful as never before now that he has been stripped of regal trappings and become, as he puts it, 'a very foolish, silly old man'. He is, he reflects, 'more than eighty years old, not an hour more or less. And to put it plainly, I fear I am not in my perfect mind.' Lear, in his very madness, apprehends more than cold reason can ever do.

The folly of definitions

But before we tell this topsy-turvy history, let's get one thing straight. What is folly and how does it differ from stupidity? *The American Heritage Dictionary of the English Language*, not alone in its folly, suggests that a person who is 'stupid' is '1. Slow to learn or understand; obtuse; 2. Lacking or marked by lack of intelligence,' while a person who is 'foolish' is '1. Lacking or exhibiting a lack of good sense or judgment; silly. 2. Resulting from stupidity or misinformation; unwise.'[11]

Stupidity, thus defined, may impel one to do foolish things but is by no means an essential precondition for doing so: Quixote may not be stupid even while charging a field of sheep mistaking them for two battling armies; American mathematician John Allen Paulos was not stupid but did foolish things when he loosened his purse and supposed he could beat the market and the chumps less financially astute than he. But matters aren't so simple: Paulos, after all, may have been said to do stupid things – stupidity and foolishness are often synonymous in our usage, rather than the former being a necessary condition for producing the latter. The American psychologist Robert J. Sternberg, in *Smart People Are Not Stupid, But They Sure Can Be Foolish*,[12] argues otherwise. Stupidity and folly are different; indeed, the paradox Sternberg is interested in is why smart people – that is, those who aren't stupid (where stupid is defined as lack of intelligence) – do foolish things. But again, that distinction doesn't hold very well in normal usage: what Professor Paulos did when he played the stock market ineptly was both stupid and foolish.

Folly is held by some philosophers, notably Nathan Rotenstreich, in his 1985 paper 'Prudence and Folly', to be the opposite of prudence.[13] We can understand that distinction if we consider Lear or Paulos: the former had a kingdom and, suckered by oleaginous speeches of praise from his daughters Goneril and Regan, gave it to them and thereby ensured nothing so certain than that his dotage would be miserable; while Paulos had money and gambled it away, showing that this smart guy is capable of foolishness. But to argue that folly is the opposite of prudence itself seems folly: when Quixote couches his lance and rides into battle against what one can only imagine are quite surprised sheep, the better to win the love of the peasant girl Duclinea del Tobosco, we would want to call him not imprudent, but (adorably) foolish. Prudence has nothing to do with folly here. Rather, Quixote's folly is beyond prudential considerations. Indeed, one way of thinking about it is that it involves a surfeit of imagination that goes beyond the rational calculus of prudence. That said, the Don's imagination is stupidly constrained by his obeisance before convention, not least when he deludedly imagines Dulcinea as a rather identikit glamorous princess with golden hair, eyes like suns, rosy cheeks, coral lips, pearly teeth, alabaster neck, marble bosom, ivory hands, and so on. In his very folly, the quality of his romantic imagination is hardly impressive.

There's an additional problem in separating stupidity from folly. In the language of Shakespeare from the turn of the 17th century, to which we in the 21st century are still beholden, folly can also mean madness. To call the mad imprudent, then, seems silly. To make matters worse, in French, both in the 16th century and now, *folie* means both folly and madness. In Shakespeare's plays, the two terms are sometimes used indifferently. In the opening scene of *King Lear*, Kent says, 'be Kent unmannerly, when Lear is mad', and later in the same scene repeats the sentiment with: 'To plainness honour's bound, when majesty falls to folly.' But Lear's folly might be better seen as neither are neither synonymous nor synchronous with his madness. His folly is amply demonstrated in the same scene when he gives away his kingdom to two ungrateful daughters. By Act Two, he is not mad, but has the presence of mind to predict his mental collapse, saying: 'Oh Fool, I shall go mad.'[14] It is only in the following act that this heartbreaking prediction comes true.

A different way of exploring the difference between folly and stupidity might be to consider how, from Shakespeare onwards, and in particular during the Romantic era, folly was seen as a good thing, a precondition for wisdom. Stupidity has never been accorded such laurels. William Blake writes in one of his 'Proverbs of Hell': 'If the fool would persist in his folly he would become wise.'[15] In other words, wisdom can be achieved only through folly – which here seems rather like the useful cognitive uncertainty of negative capability captured by one of Blake's contemporaries, John Keats. By contrast, wisdom may not be attained by actively pursuing it. In *Twelfth Night*, Viola sees what others do not in Feste the fool, namely that his biting commentary on the folly of his masters feels unassuming and passes by without eliciting offence from those in power. 'This fellow's wise enough to play the fool, and to do that well craves a kind of wit.'[16] His folly is the royal road to wisdom.

Francis Bacon's advice to the queen

Such an upside-down world, so familiar to Shakespeare's audiences when the plays were first performed and indeed today, was not part of Francis Bacon's thinking when, in 1592, he wrote an entertaining speech in praise of knowledge to celebrate the anniversary of Queen Elizabeth I's coronation. Bacon told the queen:

> My praise shall be dedicated to the mind itself. The mind is the man and the knowledge of the mind. A man is but what he knoweth. The mind itself is but an accident to knowledge; for knowledge is a double of that which is; the truth of being and the truth of knowing is all one.[17]

Like Bertrand Russell, Bacon here reckons the pleasure and happiness we take in knowledge to be superior to any caused by delusion, stupidity, folly, or ignorance. Living in a fool's paradise is not for him. But the happiness to be derived from the pursuits of knowledge has a better justification: it is as free as the air and in endless supply, and so very unlike, say, the pleasures of food, wine, drugs, beauty, or sex. He elaborated these thoughts in his 1605 book *The Advancement of Learning*:

The pleasure and delight of knowledge and learning far surpasseth all other in nature; for, shall the pleasures of the affections so exceed the senses, as much as the obtaining of desire or victory exceedeth a song or a dinner; and must not, of consequence, the pleasures of the intellect or understanding exceed the pleasures of the affections! We see in all other pleasures there is a satiety, and after they be used, their verdure departeth; which sheweth well they be but deceits of pleasure, and not pleasures; and that it was the novelty which pleased, and not the quality: and therefore we see that voluptuous men turn friars, and ambitious princes turn melancholy. But of knowledge there is no satiety, but satisfaction and appetite are perpetually interchangeable.[18]

But there is a clear objection here to Bacon's panegyric to knowledge. Why should knowledge have cornered the market in endless delight? In principle, one would have thought that folly is equally devoid of satiety. If so, paradoxically, not even the wisest of us happiness seekers would have a reason to leave a fool's paradise. In any case, folly is proverbially incorrigible, proverbially limited. 'As a dog returns to his vomit, so a fool repeats his folly,' says Proverbs 26:11, and one reason for that eternal return, one might hypothesize, is not just the fool's stupidity, but because those who pursue it anticipate pleasure. This is so even if the proverbially wise King Solomon, who is credited with writing the Book of Proverbs, may not appreciate its truth and, rather, assume, perhaps wrongly, and certainly boringly, that folly is bent on the wrong kind of pleasure. That's the corollary of this proverb: comparing dog vomit to folly, with its implication that both are poisonous, devoid of nutrition, and so pleasurable only to those who are, with all due respect, a bit thick.

Pleasures aside, Bacon's aim was to found human knowledge on a systematic basis. To that end, this early modern overachiever (he was not only legal counsel to Elizabeth I and lord chancellor to James I, but was also described as the father of modern philosophy, even though he seems to have practised the latter only in his spare time) championed induction in his account of scientific method. If we want to experience the pleasurable pursuit of knowledge, that endlessly rewarding activity, he argued, we must set aside the manifold fatuities and aridities of much previous philosophy, particularly logical argument. 'Of induction the logicians seem hardly to have taken any serious thought,' wrote Bacon, 'but they pass it by with a slight notice, and hasten to the formulae of disputation. I on the contrary reject demonstration by syllogism.'[19] That, to put it mildly, was a ballsy move. Demonstration by syllogism seems a watertight method of getting to the truth, being an operation of deduction, which typically proceeds from the general to the specific, from idea ('All men are mortal') to observation ('Socrates is a man') to inescapable conclusion ('Therefore Socrates is mortal').

The hero of that last argument, Socrates, was no stranger to the syllogism, though he preferred, as we have seen, to cross-examine an interlocutor dialectically, the better to expose the latter's stupidity rather than to extend the domain of knowledge. Deductive syllogisms, by contrast, extend the domain of certain knowledge while, no doubt, confirming the stupidity of those who cannot follow such simple chains of reasoning.

Induction is less obviously a secure method of knowledge acquisition than deduction since it involves inference from the particular to the general. An inductive inference is one that doesn't follow deductively from premises but is supported by them in some way. For instance, I note that whenever I eat my favourite food – which happens to be oysters – I feel sick. I infer that I am allergic to oysters, which is a bit of a blow but I will rise above it. Induction here is not a foolproof method: my sickness might have been caused by downing yards of Muscadet every time I eat oysters, but, following Bacon's method, one might do an experiment (I say 'one might', but personally I would rather not) in which I eat oysters but drink no Muscadet to check the original hypothesis. And by such means one converges, ideally, on the truth. It's hardly an infallible method of reasoning, but Bacon nonetheless championed this method of interrogating nature, the better to understand its workings. He proposed that we tabulate the circumstances under which a phenomenon under investigation is present and when it is not as the starting point for a scientific project whose ostensible aim was the secure comprehension of God's creation. For instance, he found that heat was present in the sun's rays, flames, and boiling liquids, but not in the moon's rays, phosphorescence, or natural liquids. He not only was the father of modern empiricism, then, but also anticipated the spreadsheet. And yet this amassing of tabulated systematic observations ideally yielded axioms that were generalized from those facts. Those initial axioms would be tested against additional data, with negative or exceptional instances being particularly important in confirming or disconfirming them.

Bacon's inductive method went on in this patient, frankly unexciting methodical manner, with the process being repeated systematically until secure knowledge was established, always ultimately supported by observed facts, or what we call data. ('This is supposed to be where we find bottomless pleasure, Francis?' one feels like asking. 'Really?') This process was, for him, not just the pleasurable pursuit of knowledge, but also the means to understand God's creation in a way that had not been possible since Adam and Eve were expelled from the Garden of Eden. 'For man, by the fall, fell at the same time from his state of innocence and from his dominion over creation', wrote Bacon in the *Novum Organum* (*New Organon*), the title of the book he published in Latin in 1620. 'Both of these losses, however, can even in this life be in some part repaired; the former by religion and faith, the latter by arts and sciences.'[20] Instead of doubt, foolishness, stupidity, and darkness, Bacon's scientific method offered intellectual redemption for Adam's folly; it offered humanity, mired in the Dark Ages, enlightenment.

Bacon's scientific revolution, nonetheless, has been seen as folly by later philosophers. In the 18th century, the Scottish philosopher David Hume argued that just because the sun has risen every morning for millennia can provide no justification for the inference that it will do so tomorrow. 'It is impossible therefore that any arguments from experience can prove this resemblance from past to future; since all these arguments are found on the supposition of that resemblance.'[21] Just because every time you've hit a white billiard ball into a red one the latter has ended up in the pocket does not mean that the next time you do it the latter will not become a bouquet of flowers or explode, destroying the world and everything in it. And yet the inductive method, even if in significant respects different from that proposed by Bacon, still dominates what scientists do in the laboratory and beyond.

For our purposes, though, it is a second takedown of Baconian scientific method that is more compelling. For this critique, Bacon's pursuit of knowledge sent us on the wrong path towards folly rather than away from it. In *Dialectic of Enlightenment*,[22] written during World War II by two exiled German Jewish Marxist refugees who had fled Hitler and the Holocaust for the American Pacific coast, Bacon is seized on as the father of our woes, the progenitor of folly, something like the midwife of modern stupidity.

Theodor W. Adorno and Max Horkheimer were writing in sunny California, but what they wrote there lay under the lengthening shadows of the Nazi death camps. True, there is no direct path from James I's lord chancellor to Auschwitz, but the pursuit of reason and knowledge, and the manner in which Bacon counselled their pursuit, suggested to Adorno and Horkheimer that the positivist era he catalysed, whereby we overcome mythical superstition and arrive in perfect control of knowledge, establishing ourselves as autonomous masters of the natural world, had that corollary. Where Bacon explicitly saw his scientific revolution as aiding us to understand God's creation, Adorno and Horkheimer maintained that Baconian positivism involves submitting the world not to our awed comprehension, but to human domination.

They had a good point. For Bacon, the pursuit of knowledge is not just intrinsically pleasurable, but indulged in for reasons to do with human control and exploitation of the observable world. Indeed, for him, if the pursuit of knowledge was undertaken merely because it were pleasurable, it would be unworthy. 'Knowledge which tendeth but to satisfaction, is but a courtesan, which is for pleasure, and not for fruit or generation,' he wrote in his essay 'Valerius Terminus: On the Interpretation of Nature'.[23] Rather, the pursuit of knowledge is valuable because it helps us better understand God's creation.

But in a dialectical inversion that Adorno and Horkheimer diagnose, Bacon's mask of humility, kin to Shakespearean motley that hides the fool's wisdom, conceals his darker motivations. Even as Bacon pursues knowledge the better to understand God, he sets up scientific man, seeking to become sovereign over the creation. Viewed thus, his overt piety conceals blasphemous hubris. The sovereignty of God is, thanks to science, to be challenged by His upstart spawn, the latter having come to maturity with the intellectual tools of Bacon's *Novum Organum* and with the conquering imperial spirit that had become Europe's ever since Christopher Columbus crossed the Atlantic on his first voyage a century earlier in 1492. Bacon, for Adorno and Horkheimer, condemns himself from his own mouth, telling Queen Elizabeth in his hymn to knowledge:

> Therefore, no doubt, the sovereignty of man lieth hid in knowledge; wherein many things are reserved, which kings with their treasure cannot buy, nor with their force command; their spials and intelligencers can give no news of them, their seamen and discoverers cannot sail where they grow: now we govern nature in opinions, but we are thrall unto her in necessity: but if we would be led by her in invention, we should command her by action.[24]

This was a perhaps stupid, certainly imprudent, message for Bacon to have put before a queen. After all, it suggests that the pomp of divine succession is scarcely secure in this new age of science: the masters and mistresses of the world in the glowing future he eulogizes will be not those who've inherited their titles from more or less demented fathers (in Elizabeth I's case, Henry VIII), but those who, through their wit and judgement, have implemented his inductive method. The appliance of science rather than the claims of heredity is where real power will lie in the future. Happy birthday, Your Majesty!

It is as though Bacon did something with philosophy that Karl Marx centuries later also sought to do. 'Philosophers have only interpreted the world, in various ways,' wrote Marx in 1845 in his *Theses on Feuerbach*. 'The point, however, is to change it.'[25] Bacon was similarly exasperated, seeing philosophy as a fatuous activity. Bacon's new inductive method, set out in his *Novum Organum*, was aimed at changing the world, and indeed at pinning it under Man's stern heel. Knowledge was not contemplative, as philosophy had historically been; rather, it had a purpose: domination. Adorno and Horkheimer gloss this revolution thus: 'Knowledge, which is power, knows no obstacles: either in the enslavement of men nor in compliance with the world's rulers.' For them, the birth of Bacon's philosophy produces monsters: imperial acquisition, slavery on a hitherto unimagined industrial scale, and, most importantly, the use of technology to establish a new social order. They write: 'Technology is the essence of this knowledge. It does not work by concepts and images, by the fortunate insight, but refers to method, the exploitation of others' work, and capital.'[26]

This is a serious charge, though how Adorno and Horkheimer feel justified in making it is another matter. For them, Bacon's scientific method is the fount and wellspring of the enlightenment in all its darkness. But what justifies this inference? Not deductive syllogism, nor the inductive method Bacon eulogized. Rather, Adorno and Horkheimer arrive at this conclusion through a species of dialectical reasoning and rhetorical flourish that might also be called folly on stilts. The modern dialectical method they rely on, after all, relies on the great German idealist philosopher George Wilhelm Friedrich Hegel, whose philosophy in its entirety was damned as a magnificent folly by Bertrand Russell: 'This [Hegel's philosophy] illustrates an important truth, namely, that the worse your logic, the more interesting the consequences to which it gives rise.'[27] Russell wasn't saying Hegel was stupid, nor were Adorno and Horkheimer arguing that Bacon was, but both takedowns, like those of the Shakespearean fool indicting his master, were indictments of folly. For Adorno and Horkheimer, Bacon's folly extends its remit from England to the world and from the 17th century until the present day.

Indeed, the only thing that is unacceptable in the enlightened age that Bacon ushers in is stupidity. 'The spirit of enlightenment replaced the fire and the rack by the stigma it attached to all irrationality,' Adorno and Horkheimer wrote.[28] This indicates how little these men knew about early modern England: the fire and the rack carried on regardless through this age of supposed enlightenment. But that enlightenment spirit paved the way for the bourgeois society that Adorno and Horkheimer, being (in name if not action) Marxists, deride: 'Bourgeois society is ruled by equivalence. It makes the dissimilar comparable by reducing it to abstract quantities.' This abstraction from observable fact was, for them, Bacon's folly and the results were catastrophic for those who lived thereafter. Adorno and Horkheimer wrote: 'To the Enlightenment, that which does not reduce to numbers, and ultimately to the one, becomes illusion; modern positivism writes it off as literature. Unity is the slogan from Parmenides to Russell. The destruction of gods and qualities is insisted upon.'[29]

Adorno and Horkheimer write of the Enlightenment as a disenchantment, but the opposite is also true: for them, Bacon and his successors are enchanters, filling tables with observed facts and numbers, believing in the power of the scientific method to rule the world. Folly is the result of this enchantment: it leads not to understanding God's creation but to empowering the twin devils that dominated these Marxists' nightmares: a working class so stupefied by technology and consumer products as to desire their own domination; and Auschwitz, the industrialized slaughter of millions of innocent humans. For Adorno and Horkheimer, both these deeply irrational phenomena are consequences of the folly of the enlightenment reason Bacon set in motion.

The title page of Bacon's *Novum Organum*[30] depicts a galleon passing between the Pillars of Hercules that stood either side of the Strait of Gibraltar. As the tide of science rises, the image seems to suggest, so the spirit of domination and conquest sets sail from the well-charted waters of the Mediterranean into the Atlantic, to the New World, to pastures new, to foreign fields destined to be subjugated by Europeans. This galleon might be seen as a ship of fools, Europe's poisoned gift to the world.

What is exported from Europe on Columbus's and succeeding galleons are hideous paradoxes: the darkness of enlightenment; folly masquerading as wisdom; Europeans dressed in martial uniforms the better to conceal their caps and bells. The sheer stupidity of treating nature as something to exploit and other humans as objects to facilitate that exploitation is indicted by Adorno and Horkheimer: 'Myth turns to enlightenment, and nature into mere objectivity. Men pay for the increase of their power with alienation from that over which they exercise their power. Enlightenment behaves toward things as a dictator toward men. He knows them in so far as he can manipulate them.'[31]

Ships of fools, ancient and modern

Before Bacon's galleon set sail, there existed a strange European phenomenon called the Ship of Fools, or *stultifera navis*. Madmen, expelled from European cities, drifted homeless and stateless along Rheinish rivers and Flemish canals. Not yet interred as they would be in the great asylums from the 1600s onwards, they were excluded from society on ships away from population centres, just as lepers were held in lazar houses, or leper colonies, beyond city walls to prevent infection. As Michel Foucault wrote in *Madness and Civilization*, some of the madmen populating and crewing these ships of fools had been publicly whipped and 'in the course of a kind of game . . . were chased in a mock race and driven out of the city with quarterstaff blows'.[32] If these unfortunates were not mad before they were beaten out of the city, you'd think, then their experience on board these ships would have made them so. 'Confined on the ship, from which there is no escape, the madman is delivered to the river with its thousand arms, to the sea with its thousand roads. He is prisoner in the midst of what is the freest, the openest of routes: bound fast at the infinite crossroads.'[33]

This exclusionary social policy in all its folly was revived in 2023 by Britain's Conservative government when Home Secretary Suella Braverman arranged for asylum seekers to be housed on an engineless barge the *Bibby Stockholm*, moored in Portland Port. At least the medieval ships of fools journeyed the rivers and canals. This boat remained stationary, its inmates bound more tightly fast at the infinite crossroads than their forebears. When Leonard Farruku, an Albanian asylum seeker, committed suicide aboard this latter-day ship of folly, which had cost the British taxpayer more than £22 million to fail to solve the problems of cruel human trafficking and rising illegal immigration, his family organized a crowdfunder to pay for the cost of repatriating his body.[34] Medieval folly may not have spawned modern stupidity, but you don't have to look hard to spot a family resemblance.

The ship of fools became an abiding image of the late 15th century, rising on the tide of humanist scholarship and commanding mass appeal. In 1494, the Swiss humanist scholar Sebastian Brant published a bestselling satire called *Narrenschiff* (ship of fools) that was rapidly translated into Latin and leading European languages. Its popularity is in part explained by comic woodcuts depicting its ostensibly idiotic inmates. Brant's work describes a ship laden with fools setting sail for the 'fool's paradise' of Narragonia. This is a departure from the real-life ships of fools, which wandered like precursors of Parisian *flâneurs* without purpose or destination. Moreover, the passengers on Brant's ship of fools were not mad. They were, rather, exemplars of folly and included a corrupt judge, a drunkard, and an untrained physician. Folly, for Brant, meant not the crazy or deluded but the immoral. Folly, that is to say, was harnessed to indict corrupt society in a manner that, a century later, Shakespearean fools would echo. In Hieronymous Bosch's contemporary painting *Ship of Fools* (today held in the Louvre in Paris), a bunch of obvious nitwits are doing stupid things on a boat heading nowhere, not least because its tiller is a long-handled wooden spoon wielded by a chump who clearly knows nothing of navigation and is not paying attention to the direction in which the boat is headed.[35]

But folly is not, for another contemporary humanist scholar, a moral failing, nor an antisocial condition requiring public whipping and harsh expulsion onto the waterways of Europe. For Desiderius Erasmus of Rotterdam in his 1509 bestselling essay, folly is not beneath contempt, but a goddess worthy of veneration. Indeed, in the opening pages of *In Praise of Folly*, the titular goddess Folly, superbly, venerates herself as if she is better placed than worshippers or temples to do the job. Erasmus, though remaining a lifelong Catholic, was happy in the rest of the book to fire off barbs against the folly of churchmen. His book added thereby, albeit unwittingly, to the Protestant Reformation's critique of Roman Catholicism. His folly in so doing, at least, was unwitting.

Erasmus wrote this influential essay in a week while staying in London with his friend Sir Thomas More – a man who, like Francis Bacon, served as lord chancellor, but who, because of his refusal to endorse the folly of the king's annulment of his first marriage to Catherine of Aragon or accept the supremacy of this libidinous regal fat man in London over the Pope in Rome, was beheaded in 1535. There are two titles to the original Latin version of the essay, *Stultitiae Laus* and *Moriae Encomium*, the latter a riff on the name of the Englishman who gave Erasmus a room in which to write: *Moriae* does not just mean folly but also signifies the Latinizing of his host's surname.

The intended target of In *Praise of Folly* is not the Catholic church but Stoicism, the ancient Greek and Roman philosophy, revived in the time of the Renaissance, which supposes that to be wise and indeed happy you must be ruled by reason and suppress passion.

Erasmus turned Stoic philosophy on its head: to be happy and human, we need not reason but the goddess Folly and the indulgence of passions. He wrote:

> The Stoics define wisdom to be conducted by reason, and folly nothing else but the being hurried by passion, lest our life should otherwise have been too dull and inactive, that creator, who out of clay first tempered and made us up, put into the composition of our humanity more than a pound of passions to an ounce of reason; and reason he confined within the narrow cells of the brain, whereas he left passions the whole body to range in.[36]

But for Erasmus and his goddess, Stoicism is itself folly. Worse than that, it is inhuman. Friendships would never succeed without folly, because people tell themselves that their friends' quirks are their highest virtues. All relationships – including marriage – need folly and flattery to proceed harmoniously. The fool is entertaining and tells the truth without giving offence. The Stoic philosopher? Not so much. Sometimes, foolish illusion is preferable to brutal truth.

And yet to be wise for the Stoics is to overcome such human weakness and to steel oneself against corruption by the four passions, namely distress, fear, lust, and delight. Like followers of the Dao in the previous chapter, Stoics sought to live in agreement with nature, and to do so they proposed to take advantage of one of the greatest gifts to humans from nature, namely reason. The go-with-the-flow philosophy of Daoism is combined in Stoicism with a doughty facing down of whatever fate throws against one. Roman emperor and Stoic philosopher Marcus Aurelius put it this way:

> First, do not be upset: all things follow the nature of the Whole, and in a little while you will be no one and nowhere, as is true even of Hadrian and Augustus. Next, concentrate on the matter at hand and see it for what it is. Remind yourself of your duty to be a good man and rehearse what man's nature demands: then do it straight and unswerving, or say what you best think right. Always, though, in kindness, integrity, and sincerity.[37]

Let the merely stupid and cowardly live otherwise. 'Men are tormented not by things, but by their judgements about things,' argued Roman-slave-turned-Stoic-philosopher Epictetus.[38] To end this torment and become serene had long been the quest of ancient philosophers: the Stoics thought the practice of reason would yield what the Greeks called *ataraxia*, a temperamental imperturbability or freedom from disturbance. Translations of Marcus Aurelius's *Meditations*, Epictetus's *Enchiridion* (*Handbook*), and the Roman statesman Seneca's *Letters from a Stoic*[39] into vulgar European languages in the 16th and 17th century brought such wisdom to new audiences.

The suicide of Seneca, in particular, was interpreted as a model of Stoic imperturbability. Ordered to commit suicide by the Emperor Nero in 65 CE, he cut several veins to speed his death, but blood flowed only slowly so his death was painful and not hastened either by administered poisons. Tacitus, describing Seneca's fortitude in the face of painful death, romanticized Stoic indifference, or *apatheia*. Seneca, in extremis, chose not to rail against that which he could not change, namely his imminent death and its painful character. Through the use of reason, he was able to endure. Such is Stoic wisdom, enabling virtuosos like Seneca to rise above their native stupidity.

Well, perhaps. Another possibility is that, even if Seneca did not fill the Roman night with his death howls, his impassivity had a performative quality, as if bent on how his heroic death would be received by posterity – a rather less noble and exemplary passing. And yet his wisdom and Stoic detachment, if these qualities were what he manifested, were hailed by Renaissance humanists such as Pierre Charron, whose book *De la sagesse* (*Of Wisdom*, 1608)[40] was a bestselling guide on how to live and die ethically in the Stoic manner. Seneca was presented as a role model, someone who, even in the pain of his demise, had the comfort of dying well. But, for others, that way of dying may itself be folly.

Charron's humanist contemporary the great French essayist Michel de Montaigne thought he could scarcely emulate Seneca, writing in one of his essays: 'He who cannot attain that noble impassibility of the Stoics, let him take refuge in the bosom of this plebeian insensitivity of mine. What those men did by virtue, I train myself to do by disposition.'[41] In later essays, though, Montaigne heretically recanted any Stoic aspiration, arguing that its self-regarding pursuit of *ataraxia* with the aid of reason and the mastery of the passions was no good model for living or dying. Through meditating on our foolish hubris and stupid fallibility and, more importantly, the essential ridiculousness of humanity, Montaigne disabused himself of Stoic aspiration. For him it was folly to suppose, as Stoics did, that humans were exceptional, and yet he detected just such folly in Stoicism's reliance on the gift that our species, ostensibly alone among beasts, prides itself. He wrote: 'Presumption is our natural and original malady. The most vulnerable and frail of all creatures is man, and at the same time the most arrogant.'[42] For Montaigne, our greatest presumption is to regard reason as the highest faculty and sign of the power of the human subject.

In this, he was echoing Erasmus, whose *In Praise of Folly* was an oration by the titular goddess in which she rounds on those of her adherents who

THE VALUE OF FOLLY

preen as wise men and declares them to be fools, mocking their claim to be the rising force of humanity. Not so, she counters: folly is and ever will be the leading feature of human life. The names of her faithful companions suggest how much folly pervades human life, and how little reason does so. They include Philautia (personifying self-love), Kolakia (flattery), Lethe (forgetfulness), Misopnia (laziness), Hedone (pleasure), Anoia (dementia), Tryphe (wantonness), as well as the two gods who minister to her, namely Moms (intemperance) and Nigretos Hypnos (easy sleep). Without such a goddess and without such an entourage, human life would be intolerable.

But the rhetoric of Erasmus's essay spirals from eulogy of folly to something more topical: it became a bestseller because it met a demand for writing that uses irony to skewer the follies of the age, not least lazy mendicant friars, greedy princes of the church, hypocrite lawyers, and scholastic philosophers. 'It is as if the whole structure of the late medieval world was being shaken,' wrote Peter Ackroyd in his biography of Thomas More.[43] But not only that: it is the early modern world, in all its newly presumptuous posturing, that Erasmus skewers. Having overcome the follies and irrationalities of its medieval predecessor, Erasmus wittily indicts his own age, too, and in particular the hubristic philosophy of neo-Stoicism, the latest purported means by which humans might aspire to overcome their (in fact) irredeemable folly. Stoics sought to use reason to destroy folly. Erasmus's ironic inversion involves mobilizing folly to tilt at reason.

But it was one particular aspect of Erasmus's Folly that temperamentally suited Montaigne, as he wrote nearly a century later, namely the goddess's suggestion that 'you'll find nothing frolic or fortunate that it owes not to me'.[44] Without folly, that is to say, life would lose its joy, its savour. Reason is a cold shower that washes off the folly, ardour, wildness, and corruption that, if we're honest, are what we love about being human. Reason also prevents us from seeing that, instead of rational masters of the universe, humans are, without exception, absurd. Montaigne wrote:

> Is it possible to imagine anything so ridiculous as that this miserable and puny creature, who is not even master of himself, exposed to the attacks of all things, should call himself master and emperor of the universe, the least part

of which it is not in his power to know, much less command? . . . Who has sealed him this privilege? Let him show us his letters patent for this greatest and splendid charge. Have they been granted in favor of the wise only? Then they do not touch many people. Are the fools and the wicked worthy of such extraordinary favor, and, being the worst part of the world, of being preferred to all the rest?[45]

And yet the reason-mongers of science and Stoicism carry on regardless, heedless of these existential truths and laughably unaware of their own ridiculousness. For Montaigne, what seems our highest faculty, reason, is in truth our least worthy, since it blinds us to the true nature of the human condition, which is to be stupidly presumptuous in our sense of our own superiority.

The blindness of reason

One of Montaigne's great readers was Shakespeare, who came to the essays through John Florio's translation. Indeed, *King Lear* – the Bard's great tragedy of human folly and madness – repeatedly echoes passages from the Frenchman's best essays, nowhere more profoundly than in presenting Stoicism not as offering a model for living or dying but rather as a species of folly, not least in the presentation of the character of the Duke of Gloucester.

Gloucester, who has had his eyes prised from his head by the cruel Duke of Cornwall, evil Regan's spouse, sometimes personifies the Stoic idea, as the critic Jonathan Bate puts it, 'of finding the right timing for death'.[46] Thus, blind and deluded, Gloucester seeks to commit suicide to escape this horrible world and all the sufferings he must bear in it. To that end, he invites a madman (really, his loyal son Edgar in Bedlam disguise) to lead him to a cliff that he might throw himself to his death. Instead, Edgar tricks him: there is no cliff, no plummet to death, just the power of suggestion by a son who really doesn't want his father to die in this abject way.

Gloucester's failed suicide attempt prompts Stoic resolve in the face of adversity. 'Henceforth I'll bear / Affliction / Till it do cry out itself/ "Enough, enough" and die.'[47] Such fortitude, seeming to mobilize Epictetus's thought that it is attitudes to events rather than the events themselves that we must attend to since they alone are those phenomena over which we can have mastery, makes a virtue out of such reasoned scorn for fate. Stoic wisdom counsels that we banish the passions since it is they that cause suffering. Nothing in the world but our feelings, emotions, passions, and other non-rational capacities are capable of making us suffer. Stoicism dangles the possibility that with enough practice, with sufficient endurance, we can, as it were, make each and every one of us a citadel, walled up against misfortune. All we need do is anaesthetize the passions and comport ourselves with courage and, like zones ringed by cordons sanitaires to protect them from infection, we can keep suffering at bay. This cultivation of Stoic indifference is recapitulated by Edgar, who offers Stoic advice to his father: 'Men must endure / Their going hence even as their coming hither. / Ripeness is all.'[48]

This is the lesson of Seneca's death in a nutshell, but its purported wisdom is exposed in the harrowing final act of *King Lear* as folly. The play, indeed, presents us with a cast of characters struggling for a sense of comforting meaning in a world in which power, selfishness, violence, and unspeakable cruelty rule unchecked. Edgar clings to Stoic acceptance, Albany to divine justice, while Gloucester (at one point) worries that instead of divine beneficence we live in a world in which the gods are cruel: 'As flies to wanton boys are we to the gods; They kill us for their sport.'[49]

All these understandable attempts to impose meaning on meaningless suffering are, the play suggests, folly. Jonathan Bate concludes that the final speech of the play, delivered by Edgar, suggests that Stoic comfort won't do:

The weight of this sad time we must obey:
Speak what we feel, not what we ought to say.[50]

But, while not folly, this couplet is of little consolation, suggesting the sad time we have been exposed to for the past couple of hours, and by implication our godless, irredeemable, and cruel world, is ruled, if by anything at all, not by providence but by incomprehensible madness. Human folly, then, consists in the attempt not to live in this madness but to force meaning onto the unbearable.

It's a somewhat cryptic remark, no doubt, but one interpretation suggests that the lesson of the drama might be we need more than cold reason, more than the chilly resolve that allowed Seneca to confront painful death without fear, or any philosophy that counsels noble endurance and courageous fortitude. These are inhumane virtues, unworthy of us, foolish. The world is horrible, yes, but we can at least voice how we feel about living in such a world, and voice it with passion and ardour. Reason, that fool's gold of Stoic philosophy, doesn't give that option.

Here Shakespeare departs from his foolosophical mentor Montaigne. For Montaigne, Stoicism's veneration of reason was folly since it denies the true, sometimes endearing, sometimes revolting, nature of what it is to be human. Instead of placing his faith in that secular ideology, Montaigne placed in it a benevolent God. As soon as we stray from His grace, we wander into foolishness. 'All that we undertake without his assistance, all that we see without the lamp of his grace, is only vanity and folly.'[51] But that is to suggest that rather than trusting Stoic resolve to make sense of a meaningless world, we must rely on God's grace. Shakespeare, at the end of *King Lear*, puts out that lamp, not with the ruthlessness that Cornwall showed in putting out Gloucester's eyes, but with the aim of helping us see better the true nature of the world and the place of human folly within it.

In Montaigne's essays and Shakespeare's great tragedy, we find intimations of a later coup d'état against reason mounted by David Hume nearly two centuries afterwards. The Scottish philosopher in his *Treatise on Human Nature* wrote: 'Reason is, and ought only to be the slave of the passions.'[52] The seeming guarantor of human mastery of the world, reason, was really at best a tool, wielded at the whim of passions. We cannot master the passions, nor should we attempt to do so. Viewed thus, even Seneca's exemplary death was not devoid of passions; rather, they were repressed yet by no means extinguished as he cut his wrists and drank his poison. One might even hypothesize that his performance of imperturbability was motivated by passionate regard for his posthumous reputation. If so, he succeeded: the manner in which he died has impressed many readers. There is something rotten in the state of Stoicism in such moments, an overvaluation of the powers of human reason and rationality to aid us in how to live, and one that denies our true humanity in all its stupidity, folly, and risibility.

There is another, opposite, challenge to be made against Stoicism in its veneration of reason and its ostensible flouting of folly. Perhaps the problem with Stoicism is not that it overvalues reason but that it undervalues it. Viewed thus, it is stupid precisely because it doesn't understand the power of the highest human faculty. This thought came to me serendipitously. While I was researching this chapter, I happened to be reading Karl Ove Knausgaard's 2023 novel *The Wolves of Eternity*, in which the Norwegian has a character meditating on the wild 19th-century Russian philosopher Nikolai Fyodorov, a contemporary of Dostoevsky and Tolstoy. For Fyodorov, the principal task of humanity was not to live with nature like a Stoic or a Daoist, but to overcome it and, in particular, rise up against its power to put us all to death. We must, he charged, use our wit and wisdom to abolish death, and, even more challengingly, one would have thought, reincarnate the dead. 'The mistake we have made is that we have submitted to death, accepting it passively and without question,' says a character glossing Fyodorov's work. 'What we must do is actively intervene in nature: steer it, control it, conquer it. As yet, we remain at the very outset of human life, ignorant still of the true powers of reason and rationality.'[53] It's a bracing passage, and one that shows up both Renaissance neo-Stoicism and Baconian scientific method, those twin pillars of resurgent European civilization as it emerges from the medieval era, as stupid, unfit for purpose.

Of course, Fydorov's project may itself seem the height of folly, his philosophy the stupid ravings of a thinker who certainly didn't deign to account for how human reason might perform the improbable, if perhaps desirable, task of bringing millions of generations of the dead back to life. In our age of cloning, cryogenics, and artificial intelligence, by contrast, his dreams seem less obviously stupid. Moreover, one corollary may be that Stoicism, in its passive acceptance of death, shows itself as lacking in ambition, stupidly accepting fate without interrogating assiduously whether the seemingly insuperable – death in particular – can be overcome. Perhaps it can. Perhaps accepting fate with the passivity of the Daoist and the courage of the Stoic are not symptomatic of great wisdom but signs, rather, of lack of imagination and folly.

None of this is to suggest that we should follow a crazed-sounding Russian philosopher, nor start disinterring the dead the better to reanimate them, nor even that death will, thanks to technology and human will, be overcome. But rather it does suggest that to suppose that thinking imaginatively, as Fyodorov does, against our supposed common fate shows up the intellectual shortcomings of Stoicism. It presents reason as the highest of our faculties by means of which we master all that is in our control; but it is underestimated by those Stoics for whom it is purportedly the highest human faculty. Which, if you think about it, is pretty stupid.

That is hardly the judgement we would impose on Don Quixote. Cervantes' protagonist was so enthralled by the heroic exploits of the knights he reads about in his beloved tales of chivalry that he loses possession of his rational faculties and devotes himself to saving those around him from what he imagines are mortal dangers. Like a more comprehensively congenitally addled Mr Magoo, he is always mistaking something for something else. Almost all of these battles end up with him, his companion Sancho Panza, or both, being beaten – which seems unfair on Sancho, since he only came along because Quixote promised him an island as a reward for service.

After he is defeated in his last battle by the Knight of the White Moon, Quixote returns home to La Mancha. On arrival, the endearing boob falls ill, renounces chivalry as a foolish fiction, and dies. There is, quite possibly, no sadder ending in literature since all the humane and deluded delights that have entertained the reader are now set aside as mere silliness rather than demonstration, as we might like to think, of something profound about the irredeemable folly of humans in all our charming and exasperating delusion and stupidity.

Happily, the figure of the fool endures, as if the innocent and human spirit of Quixote in all his folly can never really die. In his great 1961 anti-war novel *Catch-22*, Joseph Heller gives us the genius that is Lieutenant Orr, whose gormless face of stupid, buck-toothed innocence hides a cunning far greater than anything the plotting, scheming, overthinking contrarian hero Yossarian is capable of mustering. Orr is regarded by his platoon comrades as a dolt, always babbling harmlessly of apples and eating raw fish, always happy to go back into the plane and risk another mission, but all the while it is he rather than his ostensibly clever comrades who has concocted a foolproof scheme to secure his freedom from the horrors of war. And it is Orr, the chump, denounced by Yossarian as 'the evil-eyed, mechanically aptituded, disaffiliated son of a bitch',[54] who proves the hero at the novel's close.

The figure of a clever fool like Orr demonstrates something teased out a decade and a half earlier by Adorno and Horkheimer in their *Dialectic of Enlightenment*: the cleverness of stupidity, and its flip side, the stupidity of cleverness. In this world of folly, stupidity is best bottled by fools. In *Catch-22*, Orr realizes the true nature of the paralysing paradox that gives the book its title. The narrator tells us: 'Orr would be crazy to fly more missions and sane if he didn't, but if he was sane, he would have to fly them. If he flew them, he was crazy and didn't have to; but if he didn't want to he was sane and had to.'[55] Sanity is overrated; stupidity underrated.

5

Modern Stupidity

The family idiot

'Stupidity,' wrote Gustave Flaubert to his poet friend Louis Bouilhet on 4 September 1850, 'consists in wanting to conclude.'[1] This is an odd definition, especially in the light of the many examples of stupidity we have considered so far. None has involved the desire to arrive at a stable end state. Don Quixote, most likely, did not want to stop deludedly battling sheep, windmills, and mourners in honour of Dulcinea del Toboso. His enforced retirement and death were not desirable goals. Alcibiades' stupidity consisted, if Socrates was right, in wanting to embark on a political career before he had the requisite experience or education. For some eastern sages, stupidity consists in unwillingness to accept the inescapably delusive character of reality. Stupidity, or its cross-dressing Shakespearean bedfellow foolishness, could be a form of wisdom masquerading as its opposite. Certainly, it would be more fun to remain in Shakespeare's forest of folly than leave it for the boring, straight world of denouements and conclusions.

Stupidity sometimes seems to involve someone wanting to conclude but being too witless to achieve the desired goal. 'Insanity,' Albert Einstein reportedly suggested, 'is doing the same thing over and over and expecting different results.'[2] In this respect, stupidity and insanity have much in common, but stupidity has the edge in witlessness: unlike insanity, it can be relied upon to do the one thing expressly designed not to achieve the desired result or to laughably mismatch means and ends. 'People who voted for Brexit aren't stupid,' argued the Scottish comedian Frankie Boyle. 'They're just people who want to put an end to immigration from Europe because they don't like Pakistanis.'[3] Brexit, viewed thus, was stupid precisely because it wanted a conclusive state of affairs (the end of immigration and the racist aspiration to reduce the numbers of persons of colour in Britain, perhaps to zero) and pursued those aims by means anyone with half a brain would have realized would not achieve them. Schopenhauer wrote that 'The man of talent is like the marksman who hits a mark the others cannot hit; the man of genius is like the marksman who hits a mark they cannot even see to.'[4] The genius of Brexit was to miss its mark while at the same time hitting other marks no one who supported Brexit wanted to hit – not least tying up travellers and trade to and from Britain in more bureaucratic red tape than had been previously supposed possible. Which is not stupid at all. While it is apparently true that there are English Camemberts and fine wines, it does seem unprecedentedly witless of Britons to have made access to the better French versions more difficult. If there is a serious point here, and there probably isn't, it is that Brexit suggests stupidity is not eternally fixed in a particular polity, but one that, given the right conditions, can grow and infest a whole area – like Japanese knotweed but less easily eradicable. To put it another way, I voted remain in the Brext referendum and still remain shocked by my compatriots' capacity to revel stupidly in national self-harm.

As we saw in chapter 1, Sacha Golob argues that stupidity involves the failure to optimally use our cognitive faculties. But while that's plausible, perhaps the situation is worse than the philosopher allows: stupidity may also consist in the failure to realize that our cognitive faculties aren't up to the tasks we set them, but to carry on regardless, towards a target that we cannot hope to hit because we are too stupid – both in the manner in which we have conceived that desired end and in the means by which we hope to reach it. The stupidity of folly often seems to consist in its incorrigibility. It marinates in its own fatuous juices and is too thick to get out of its cognitive puddle. It is an unstoppable force, unamenable to conclusions. Stupidity may well be a feature of the system rather than a bug we could eradicate. But then, as we know, stupidity is always someone else's problem: we, the stupid, are not just stupid but stupid in not knowing the character of our malady. We are stupid about our stupidity. That, I take it, is part of Flaubert's point.

What did Flaubert mean by suggesting stupidity is the wanting to conclude? The great French novelist was no fool about the subject. He was, rather, a great connoisseur of stupidity and spent much of his life and work exposed to its manifold fatuities, continually worrying he might as a result get infected by its toxic vapours. 'Where do we draw the line between inspiration and madness, between stupidity and bliss?' he wrote to another literary friend, Louise Colet, on 1 October 1852.

> Is it not necessary to be an artist to see everything in a different way than is seen by other people? Art is not a game of the mind. It's a special realm. But who says that by always going down deeper into the abyss to breathe a warmer air we don't end up by breathing steamy miasmas?[5]

The artist quite possibly had made a stupid mistake. Thinking he was a surgeon cutting out the tumour of stupidity, he belatedly failed to realize his misdiagnosis: stupidity hasn't metastasized; it was in the air, corrupting everyone, particularly the artists who sought, in their folly, to creatively analyse it without getting infected. By spending so much time writing about stupidity, Flaubert had, quite possibly, become stupid himself.

This fear of infection by the fog of stupidity to which Flaubert was prone might, if we follow the parameters of the psychological biography Jean-Paul Sartre wrote of him, be due to his worries about collapsing back into his native idiocy. Sartre's biography was entitled *The Family Idiot* and sought to explain what he calls 'this scandalous occurrence' of a childhood idiot becoming a grown-up genius. Sartre made the prosecution case for the genius's youthful idiocy by including an account by Flaubert's niece, Caroline Commanville, which she relayed after his death. She reported the family tradition that Flaubert was slow in learning to read and recorded that he would often as a child sit 'for hours, one finger in his mouth, absorbed, looking almost stupid. When he was six,' she related, 'a servant called Pierre, amusing himself with Gustave's innocence, told the boy when he pestered him: "Run to the kitchen . . . and see if I'm there."And the child went off to question the cook, "Pierre told me to come see if he's here."'[6]

And yet Flaubert matured into an artist sensitive to and obsessed with stupidity, which he clearly saw as the prevailing spirit of his age. Perhaps the great excoriator of modern stupidity was projecting what he feared he might be: after all, he had been regarded as stupid as a boy, which might well have led him to be extremely sensitive to the possibility of being taken for an idiot as an adult.

In any event, the great thing about stupidity for Flaubert was that it was in endless supply, which meant that the raw material for much of his writing was on tap. 'Human stupidity,' he told another correspondent, 'is a bottomless abyss, and the ocean I can see from my window seems to me quite small in comparison.'[7] In his great, final, and unfinished 1881 novel about human stupidity, *Bouvard and Pécuchet*, the latter protagonist advances a theory about why stupidity might be a growing phenomenon in the modern era. The two retired copy clerks have been meditating on the idiocy of the French electorate during the presidential elections that followed the 1848 revolution. Pécuchet contends that an ambitious individual can always lead 'and the others will obey like a herd, since voters don't even have to know how to read'.[8] This, to be sure, the literacy constraint notwithstanding, remains the worry about democracy even in the present day: the people are too thick to vote in their best interests, and that indeed is why ambitious, vainglorious, and administratively incompetent populists from Louis-Napoleon in France in 1850 to today's yet more execrable manifestations of the phenomenon have achieved such power.

Bouvard, a kind of Oliver Hardy to Pécuchet's Stan Laurel, goes further in diagnosing the mass idiocy of contemporary French society. These imbeciles, Bouvard suggests, are united chiefly by their inability to see that they are being taken for a ride, be it by their politicians or the latest quack remedies.

> Think of everyone who bought Revalescière tonic, Dupuytren hair restorer, chatelaine lotion and so on! Those ninnies form the electoral masses, and we are subject to their will. Why can't one earn three thousand pounds from rabbits? Because putting too many of them in one place can cause death. In the same way, by the very fact of having a crowd, the germs of stupidity it contains spread from person to person and the resulting effects are incalculable.[9]

Modern stupidity is different from its earlier incarnations in that its spread is hastened by urbanization: the more dense a population is in one sense, the more dense it is in another.

Such was Flaubert's connoisseurship of stupidity that he not only wrote a whole novel about the phenomenon, but also produced two of the best witticisms about stupidity in the history of human folly. 'To be stupid, selfish, and have good health are three requirements for happiness, though if stupidity is lacking, all is lost,' he quipped. Which, apart from anything else, is apt to make those of us who are unhappy feel pretty smug about ourselves. He also wrote: 'Stupidity is something unshakable; nothing attacks it without breaking itself against it; it is of the nature of granite, hard and resistant.'[10] In this, stupidity is like the unstoppably gurning rictus at the centre of Donald Trump's unshakeably witless face, though not necessarily orange.

Throughout his life, Flaubert dreamed of writing a spoof encyclopaedia containing all the many examples of witlessness, cliché-ridden thinking, platitudes, and insipid pseudo-truths that rose on the tide of stupefaction towards his window. 'Such a book,' he wrote to Louise Colet,

> with a good preface in which the motive would be stated to be the desire to bring the nation back to Tradition, Order and Sound Conventions – all this so phrased that the reader would not know whether or not his leg was being pulled – such a book would certainly be unusual, even likely to succeed, because it would be entirely up to the minute.[11]

Sadly, this book, entitled *Le Dictionnaire des idées reçues* (*The Dictionary of Accepted Ideas*), was only published posthumously in 1913, but it has become a small monument to stupidity, with such entries as the following:[12]

> Absinthe: Extra-violent poison: one glass and you're dead. Newspapermen drink it as they write their copy. Has killed more soldiers than the Bedouin.
>
> Archimedes: On hearing his name, shout 'Eureka!' Or else: 'Give me a fulcrum and I will move the world.' There is also Archimedes' screw, but you are not expected to know what it is.
>
> Chiaroscuro: We do not know what that is.
>
> Feudalism: No need to have one single precise notion about it: thunder against.

Omega: Second letter of the Greek alphabet.

Thirteen: Avoid being thirteen at table; it brings bad luck. The sceptics should not fail to crack jokes: 'What is the difference? I'll eat enough for two!' Or again, if there are ladies, ask if any is pregnant.

Waltz: Wax indignant about. A lascivious, impure dance that should only be danced by old ladies.

I particularly like the definition of art: 'Leads to poorhouse. What good is it, since it is being replaced by mechanical processes which do the job better and faster?' Good point: who's to know if an AI version of *Madame Bovary* would have been better than Flaubert's attempt? But I especially enjoy how this definition of art is contradicted by the one that immediately follows it: 'Artists: All jokers. Praise their disinterestedness. Be amazed that they dress like everyone else. Earn insane amounts, but spend it like water. Often invited to dinner in town. All women artists are sluts. What artists do can't be called work.' As an amateur clarinettist, though, I am astounded by the sheer stupidity of the dictionary's definition of the instrument. 'Clarinet: Playing it makes you blind. Ex: all blind people play the clarinet.' What obvious nonsense. See better, Flaubert, and let me still remain the true blank of thine eye.

Flaubert wrote the letter to Louis Bouilhet quoted at the start of this chapter from Damascus during a tour of the Middle East in which human stupidity was at the forefront of his mind. On that trip, two examples of the phenomenon preoccupied him. One was that of the British bonehead who had scrawled his name and address on Pompey's column in Alexandria. The words 'Thompson of Sunderland', Flaubert wrote, 'can be read a quarter of a mile off. There is no way of seeing the column without seeing the name of Thompson. This imbecile has become part of the monument and is perpetuated with it.' Flaubert did not draw the moral but we might. It is not enough to be stupid; rather, the stupid person in their folly must advertise their witlessness to the world in keeping with the ancient principles of idiotic narcissism. Social media influencers are latter-day Thompsons of Sunderland.

But it was the other example of stupidity Flaubert encountered in the Middle East that had a more profound effect on his developing views. In

Jerusalem, he read a work by Auguste Comte, the founder of sociology, arch-Positivist and promoter of a future 'religion of humanity' wherein humans would worship not gods but, in a conceptually economical manner, themselves. He wrote to Bouilhet that he had found the book '*assommant de bêtise*', or stupid enough to put one to sleep.[13] Comte was a utopian thinker, and utopians above all others were stupid, Flaubert thought. But why? This is where the definition above comes into play.

> Stupidity consists in wanting to conclude. We are a thread and we want to know the pattern. That goes back to those everlasting discussions about the decadence of art. Now one spends one's time telling oneself we are completely finished, here we are at the very end etc etc. What mind of any strength – beginning with Homer – has ever come to a conclusion?[14]

Down the years these words resonate. They help us characterize not just today's witless anaesthetists of human souls who prescribe the fool's gold of closure as a cure-all for grief, but also Francis Fukuyama, the influential American political scientist who took the occasion of the end of the cold war in 1989 to publish *The End of History*, writing:

> What we may be witnessing is not just the end of the cold war, or the passing of a particular period of postwar history, but the end of history as such. . . . That is, the end point of mankind's ideological evolution and the universalization of western liberal democracy as the final form of human government.[15]

He argued that there could be no large-scale wars over fundamental values since 'all prior contradictions are resolved, and all human needs satisfied'. Which, for anyone paying attention to developments in the world since 1989, seems spectacularly, even heroically, stupid.

During Flaubert's lifetime (he was born in 1821 and died in 1880), many of Europe's leading philosophers had come to conclusions and developed grand intellectual systems that amounted to just-so stories of human and even cosmic progress, each suggesting that the proverbial slings and arrows of outrageous fortune could be overcome and that the tides of history could be stilled. Three in particular – Hegel, Marx, and Comte – sought to give narrative sense to history rather than admit the intolerable, namely the definition of history given by British dramatist

Alan Bennett as 'just one fucking thing after another'.[16] There had to be sense in history, otherwise life was meaningless and human progress towards some ideal a lie. History had to have a *telos*, or end, otherwise all that human striving was meaningless and irredeemable. But perhaps it is stupid to believe in such sense: after all, what we know from Darwin's *On the Origin of the Species*, published in 1859 while Flaubert was still gestating *Bouvard and Pécuchet*, is that there is no teleology in evolutionary processes. Natural selection, at least, has no goal, no end, and any sense that can be found in it can only be decided retrospectively: for instance, by recognizing that a species survived because its longer beaks made it easier to get seeds than for its short-beaked rivals. In such a bleak, senseless, cruel natural world from which, if Nietzsche was right, God had been banished, it might have been stupid to suggest that history had a sense and that humans were perfectible, but the impulse is not entirely incomprehensible. The 19th century teems with such stupid mythic philosophies masquerading as revelations about the true nature of the world.

The great German idealist Georg Wilhelm Friedrich Hegel regarded history as a dialectical process moving towards the realization of human freedom, or what he and his followers called the absolute. 'The question at issue is therefore the ultimate end of mankind, the end which the spirit sets itself in the world,' Hegel wrote in *Lectures on the Philosophy of World History*.[17] Hegel's heretical interpreter Karl Marx argued that universal laws govern history, according to which society moves through a series of stages, driven by class struggle. 'The history of all hitherto existing society is the history of class struggles,' wrote Marx and Engels in the first chapter of *The Communist Manifesto*,[18] which appeared in 1848, the year of revolutions in which Flaubert's double act of Bouvard and Pécuchet were indicting the stupidity of their fellow revolting Frenchmen. History will conclude, Marx hypothesized, with a communist society.

Marx, to be sure, wrote little about the communist utopia that would arise after proletarian revolution according to the laws of dialectical materialism. But his sense was that, once class struggle had become history, humankind could look forward to a kind of stasis or utopia of material abundance wherein humans would regard each other as comrades rather than competitors. 'Then the world will be for the common people,' he wrote with Engels, 'and the sounds of happiness will reach the deepest springs. Ah! Come! People of every land, how can you not be roused?'[19] Marx was stupid in Flaubert's sense, because he wanted to conclude, and because he sought to rouse the people with sketchily imagined delusions that, rightly considered, were *assomnant de bêtise*, or stupefyingly stupid. How telling, incidentally, that one of the French words for stupidity is *bêtise* and derives from the word for animal (*bête*), thereby encoding the speciesist presumption that animals are more stupid than humans, a presumption we will challenge in chapter 7 when considering the intelligences of allegedly lower life forms such as narwhals.

For Marx's contemporary Isidore Auguste Marie François Xavier Comte, the man whose book *Le Cours de Philosophie Positive* sent Flaubert to sleep in Jerusalem, society similarly progressed through discrete stages towards a desirable goal. There were, wrote Comte, three stages of human development. In the theological stage, humans believed in supernatural power. The metaphysical stage was one in which authority and religion were questioned, no more evidently than during the 1789 French Revolution, in which universal rights were established as effectively supplanting the authority of God, gods, or kings. The third and final stage of human history, for Comte, was the one in which humankind, in adhering to the principles of scientific method as devised by Bacon and elaborated by empirical philosophers in the intervening centuries, reached full maturity. Humans concluded their historical evolution by abandoning the pseudo-explanations of the theological and metaphysical phases and embracing positivism, which recognizes only that which can be scientifically verifiable. As in Hegel, this historical shift was dialectical; as in Marx, humanity, by evolving this way, moved towards utopia, not Marx and Engels' contemporaneously imagined communist one, to be sure, but similarly an end goal.

Comte's positivism proved so popular in the 19th century that when a military coup d'état deposed Brazil's empire and proclaimed it a republic, the new rulers sought to design a national flag with an inspiring text. They took its motto from the author who had sent Flaubert to sleep. Even today, the Brazilian flag is emblazoned with the phrase '*Ordem e Progresso*' ('Order and Progress'), words inspired by Comte's characterization of his beloved doctrine of positivism, which he characterized thus: '*L'amour pour principe et l'ordre pour base; le progrès pour but* [Love as a principle and order as the basis; Progress as the goal].' Which, in itself, is a curious, perhaps even stupid, formulation: progress involves movement towards a goal rather than the goal itself. And yet it remains as the credo of progressivism: in France, the very name of Emmanuel Macron's En Marche party (aka La République En Marche), founded in 2016, encoded it. France was, the name suggested, boldly heading somewhere, but where, precisely, was less clear. In 2022, President Macron renamed his party Renaissance, which, despite its nod towards democratic renewal, sounds obligingly vague.

What stupefied Flaubert when he read Comte was not the latter's pursuit of the scientific method per se, but rather the pretensions he brought to it – not least the corollary of founding a religion of humanity to fit the existential chasm he presumed existed in secular society. In his preface to *Bouvard and Pécuchet*, the French novelist Raymond Queneau wrote: 'Flaubert is in favour of science exactly to the degree that it is sceptical, reserved, methodical, prudent and humane. He has a horror of dogmatists, metaphysicians, philosophers.'[20] Comte, in preaching his religion of humanity (which in the late 19th century led to the creation of places of worship such as a positivist temple in Porto Alegre and a chapel of humanity in Paris) and effectively creating a godless surrogate after the death of God (Thomas Henry Huxley called Comte's positivism 'Catholicism minus Christianity'[21]), with new objects of worship (Comte proposed a positivist calendar in which months were named after history's greatest thinkers and artists), was for Flaubert just such a dogmatist because he went beyond the proper role of science, into the realms of speculative folly hitherto occupied by God-bothering theologians.

Indeed, the pretentious positivists of his age, Flaubert thought, were soul mates with the very religious thinkers their godless scientific revolution was intended to overthrow. He wrote in a 1879 letter: 'I am not surprised at those who seek to explain the incomprehensible, but at those who believe they have found the explanation, those who have the good Lord (or the non-Lord) in their pocket. Well, yes! Every dogmatist exasperates me.' He found dogmatism in both religious and scientific literature. As he moved from reading Catholic writers to champions of the new religion of humanity and scientific method, he was like the beasts at the end of Orwell's *Animal Farm*, looking from pig to man and man to pig and seeing little difference between them. Both forms of dogmatism should be, he thought, 'thrown into the latrines. That's my opinion. All ignoramuses, all charlatans, all idiots, who only ever see one side of the whole.'[22]

But the dogmatism that most irked him was the notion of closure. His remarks about stupidity as being concerned with wanting to conclude resonate with the Austrian-British philosopher Karl Popper's 1945 book *The Open Society and Its Enemies*. For Popper, the enemies of the open society are indeed thinkers such as Hegel and Marx whose philosophies provide closure, leaving humans fully realized at the end of their species' historical wanderings. Indeed, Popper's sense was that the closed-system philosophies of Hegel and Marx were responsible for the totalitarianism that the liberal West confronted during World War II. Their philosophies not only were stupid but also produced terrible real-world consequences.

When he conceived what would be his last, unfinished novel, Flaubert had such stupidity in his crosshairs, particularly the stupidity he saw in Comte's positivism, wherein mere mastery of facts would yield a human utopia. He even imagined the subtitle of the novel would be 'On the Lack of Method in the Sciences'.

But perhaps it was Flaubert who was stupid, not those he critiqued. The method that Comte advanced in the social sciences converges on the truth but never attains it. Science, Comte thought, is a '*connaissance approchée*': it comes closer and closer to truth, without reaching it. There is no place for absolute truth, but neither are there higher standards for the fixation of belief. In this, Comte's sense of how science's method worked was akin to Popper's in that the truth could never really be attained. For Popper, every test of a scientific hypothesis involves an attempt to refute or to falsify it, and one genuine counter-example will falsify the whole theory. All inductive evidence is limited: we cannot be everywhere all the time; if we could, we would be God.

Or consider swans. For thousands of years, Europeans had observed only white swans. Relying on that information alone, we could suppose that all swans are white. However, exploration of Australasia introduced Europeans to black swans. Indeed, the existence of only one black swan would scotch the theory that all swans are white. The truth eludes us, and, worse, must elude us, since we can never be in all places and all times, which is what we would need to be to overcome our inherent ignorance and stupidity. Popper called his theory about how science works through such inductive reasoning 'falsificationism', meaning that hypotheses can be accepted as probable but never be utterly confirmed. To be utterly certain, to be convinced that one data set of evidence ultimately and for ever confirms a theory, is folly. Indeed, the very desire behind it is precisely what Flaubert was indicating when he wrote that stupidity consists in wanting to conclude. It is a human impulse, no doubt, to want total certainty, immutable truth, and absolute conviction, but it is one that can never be redeemed, at least not in this world.

Like Socrates, Popper had nothing to declare but his ignorance. 'Our ignorance is sobering and boundless,' he told an audience at a lecture in 1962. 'Indeed, it is precisely the staggering progress of the natural sciences . . . which constantly opens our eyes anew to our ignorance, even in the field of the natural sciences themselves.'[23] This gives a new twist to the Socratic idea of ignorance. With each step forward, with each problem we solve, we not only discover new and unsolved problems, but we also discover that where we believed that we were standing on firm and safe ground, all things are, in truth, insecure and in a state of flux.

Popper wrote:

> The very idea of knowledge involves, in principle, the possibility that it will turn out to have been a mistake, and therefore a case of ignorance. And the only way of 'justifying' our knowledge is itself merely provisional, for it consists in criticism or, more precisely, in an appeal to the fact that so far our attempted solutions appear to withstand even our most severe attempts at criticism. There is no positive justification: no justification which goes beyond this.[24]

To go beyond this would be to enter the realms of stupidity.

Popper was a critic of positivism, the very scientific method that Comte advanced and which put Flaubert to sleep, since he thought it involved just such positive justifications that ignore our actual ignorance and go beyond the evidence to posit eternal truths and non-provisional solutions. It's a telling objection to positivism and yet not quite what Comte was arguing: in proposing that science is a '*connaissance approchée*', the Frenchman was suggesting something more akin to Popper's open-ended conception of scientific method.

But for Comte as for Popper there was a method in science and one that, for the latter, exposed not just how much we know but also the bottomless abyss of our ignorance. Flaubert, one might say, was stupid in supposing that there was no method in the sciences, and that science was necessarily concerned with establishing immutable truths. The truth about science was very different from the one he rather dull-wittedly attacked.

He originally called his tale 'The Story of Two Nobodies', naming his heroes Dubloard and Pécuchet, then Bolard and Manichet, before settling on the names that give the book its title, Bouvard and Pécuchet. François Denys Bartholomée Bouvard and Juste Romain Cyrille Pécuchet, of the same age and similar temperament, meet by chance on a bench overlooking the Canal St Martin in Paris on a hot summer day in 1838 and form an intense rapport catalysed by the fact that each has, very sensibly, inscribed his name inside his hat. 'I should say so!' says Bouvard. 'Someone could walk off with mine at the office!'[25] Initially, the pair seem more or less stupid and more or less interchangeable, not so much Tweedledum and Tweedledee as Tweedledumb and Tweedledumber. But, happily, the pair grow beyond their creator's destiny for them: they become, during the novel, not so much butts of stupidity as emblematic of all of us struggling vainly to master a world that is, like stupidity as Flaubert conceived it, a bottomless abyss, but a bottomless abyss of confusing facts, opinions, and other data that we cannot hope to fully comprehend.

Certainly, if there is such a phenomenon as modern stupidity as Flaubert conceives it, it may be due not just to the stupefaction resultant on the greater proximity of neighbouring boneheads thanks to growing urbanization, but also to the explosion of data and, what is even more confusing, the parallel attempt of humans to produce many disciplines tasked with helping us master that data, not to mention any mysteries of the universe not included in those data sets. This overflow of information, writing, and opinion is indeed a relatively new phenomenon. Our stupid desire to come to a conclusion is, in a sense, provoked by something Flaubert did not consider: a desire to halt the bewildering rising tide of information and data.

Only two centuries before Flaubert created Bouvard and Pécuchet, it was at least possible to have read everything that had been published. The great early modern English poet John Milton, for instance, read everything that had been published in Latin, Greek, and English. This was not just because he was a great scholar who read widely and was capable of writing poetry in Latin, Greek, Italian, English, as well as having facility in other languages, including French, Spanish, Portuguese, and Dutch, but because at that time there was only a fraction of the written material available that there was in the 19th century or our own information-clogged mire of an era. It's not just because Milton was clever and cultured and we are stupid that we cannot read everything that is published today. Rather it's because we are drowning in words: opinions, scientific theories, arcane bits of knowledge that we might have (we suppose) mastered had we paid more attention in class.

Modern life, that is to say, is apt to make us feel stupid and out of our depth in a way that John Milton and all those clever-clogs of yore never experienced. And that, to be sure, is one reason why Bouvard and Pécuchet, though ostensibly fools, are such sympathetic characters. They are, in that ghastly neologism, relatable: Julian Barnes once wrote under the headline '*Flaubert, c'est moi*';[26] the rest of us might better write under the slogan '*Nous sommes tous Bouvard et Pécuchet.*' These men are, in their absurd, stupid, and self-defeating ways, trying to master the unmasterable.

These two Victorian boobs resonate for us today, then, because the world has become only more unmasterable and information overload multiple times more unbearable than it was in their day. And yet our leading technological tools, significantly named smartphones, promise the opposite. Your smartphone offers solutions, ostensibly serving as prosthetic gatekeeper mediating the overflow of information and allowing in only the data that might help you lead a happier life to penetrate your consciousness. Every fact you need, every life skill you need to acquire, is only a few keystrokes away. If only those poor French saps Bouvard and Pécuchet had had Google, maybe they wouldn't have got into such catastrophic pickles with cider making, palaeontology, politics, topiary peacocks, and medicine, and they might not have inadvertently set fire to their farm during one stupid experiment. And yet, far from giving us Canute-like mastery of the rising tide of facts, theories, lifestyle hacks, and other people's infernal yip-yap, these smartphones ironically enough often produce a stupefying stasis. An example: I have watched 10

YouTube videos on how to change a recessed light bulb in my bedroom, which, with the typical modern tendency to overcomplicate matters, proves a much trickier business than when my bedroom lighting involved periodically replacing a blown-out bulb with a functioning one. None of the videos I consulted has proved anything other than the self-regard of those men (and they are all men) who posted the videos; none of them has helped one small bit in enabling me to know how to change a light bulb. At the time of writing, the bulb still has not been replaced. Frankly, I'd rather live in darkness than start looking online for a reputable electrician. Quite possibly, this is an allegory of the Enlightenment.

Psychologists and neuroscientists diagnose this massive time-suck and frustration as a new malady called infomania. Like Bouvard and Pécuchet, we never learn our lessons. We keep stupidly expecting knowledge to yield itself up through the medium of smartphones, even when our experiences have long suggested that this faith is predicated on folly and that, in truth, smartphones make us more stupid. Neuroscientist Daniel J. Levitin argues that our addiction to technological fixes makes us less efficient, perhaps even more stupid, not least because intellectual tasks that we used to outsource to other experts are now performed by us.

> Our brains are busier than ever before. We're assaulted with facts, pseudo facts, jibber-jabber, and rumour, all posing as information. Trying to figure out what you need to know and what you can ignore is exhausting. At the same time, we are all doing more. Thirty years ago, travel agents made our airline and rail reservations, salespeople helped us find what we were looking for in shops, and professional typists or secretaries helped busy people with their correspondence. Now we do most of those things ourselves. We are doing the jobs of 10 different people while still trying to keep up with our lives, our children and parents, our friends, our careers, our hobbies, and our favourite TV shows.[27]

Our smartphones encourage us to believe we can multitask, that we can flit from one chore or piece of work to another with a few swipes of our phone or keystrokes. But that, it turns out, is a stupid belief: one piece of research done by Glenn Wilson, visiting professor of psychology at Gresham College, London, showed that people's problem-solving performance dropped by the equivalent of 10 IQ points when they multitasked, and their stress levels also rose.[28] You don't have to believe in the intellectual basis of intelligence tests (and chapter 7 will suggest that any such belief is misbegotten) to appreciate the possibility that personal efficiency declines the deeper one is stuck in the dross of emails, texts, Twitter storms, and Instagram posts.

Perhaps getting stuck in the quagmires of infomania and multitasking explains why no one writes epic poems like *Milton's Paradise Lost* any more: we are too distracted to concentrate, too mired in the manifold fatuities of multitasking to get the job done. Just because a phone enables us to do 17 things at once doesn't mean any one of those 17 things will be done well. Perhaps, rather, it means that all of them will be done badly. Or not at all: the typical experience of multitasking may well be to want to conclude each task but, in practice, to fail to complete any of them. This is stupidity, but even more calamitous than the way in which Flaubert imagined it.

Like Bouvard and Pécuchet, we are apt to throw up our hands and give up one enterprise and launch ourselves, with ill-judged confidence, into another, which we perform with the same ineptitude, before throwing up our hands and repeating the whole business again and again in what no scientist has yet seen fit to call the spiral of stupidity. And this awful truth about the nature of modern life, perhaps, shows the lie at the heart of positivism. Comte thought we reached our highest development by adhering to the scientific method; perhaps, instead, we sink to a stupidity of an unprecedented kind by means of the very technological boons that have been the most obvious fruits of the scientific method he eulogized and the supposed progress he thought faith in that method entailed. We have been made stupid by the very technological tools that were ostensibly designed to render stupidity obsolete.

When Bouvard inherits a sizeable fortune, he and Pécuchet are enabled to enter their own 19th-century French version of that spiral of stupidity. They decide to buy a property in the Normandy countryside and, once installed, devote themselves to understanding all the many things they have not had the time to investigate during their working lives – everything from crop rotation to philosophy.

It's significant that Flaubert's heroes were copy clerks. Such deskbound drones stupidly measuring out their lives in coffee spoons proved of particular interest to 19th-century writers, no doubt because the latter, desk-bound drones themselves, projected their fears and personal inadequacies onto their literary creations. For instance, in Herman Melville's 1853 novella *Bartleby, The Scrivener: A Story of Wall Street*,[29] the eponymous legal clerk, perhaps in rebellion against the growing chokehold of pointless bureaucracy and the stupidity of the age, refuses each task with the words 'I would prefer not to.'

Across the Channel from Flaubert's two French nobodies arose another soulmate, a certain City of London clerk called Charles Pooter. This hero of George and Weedon Grossmith's 1892 novel *The Diary of a Nobody*, one might think, drew a stupid moral from the desirability of egalitarianism, namely that all persons' memoirs, no matter how dull, are of equal interest. 'I have often seen reminiscences of people I have never heard of and I fail to see – because I do not happen to be a "somebody" – why my diary should not be interesting,' wrote Pooter on the first page of his diary.[30] Today 'Pooterism' designates something like the British version of 'Quixotism', a deluded approach to the world, but one stemming from laughable self-importance and pomposity. But, if you've read *The Diary of a Nobody* (and you should), you'll see how far Pooter outstrips such a characterization: the diary reveals not his self-importance but a sympathetic, emblematic, and even adorable expression of that rare thing, a contented man. Pooter may be a drone, may be a symptom of societal fatuousness and even stupidity to his creators, but he can be seen as a man living a well-adjusted life in a rented villa with his beloved Carrie and working largely uncomplainingly as a City clerk. Even when he does stupid things such as painting everything he can find in his house – washstand, the spines of his Shakespeare, flowerpots – with Pinkford's red enamel paint, we identify with Pooter in his folly. Or maybe I should speak for myself. Pooter ultimately paints his bathtub and takes a long, relaxing soak in steaming hot water. Then, with horror, he raises a hand above the water line and sees it has become terrifyingly red. 'My first thought,' reflects Pooter, 'was that I had ruptured an artery and was bleeding to death and should be discovered, later on, a second Marat, as I remember seeing him in Madame Tussaud's.'[31] Reading that I thought, and I hope you did too, that this is just the sort of stupid thing I'd do. Both *The Diary of a Nobody* and *Bouvard and Pécuchet* can be read against the stupid grain of their respective authors' intentions and indeed their reputation. Books about stupid people are not just indictments of others, but also soothing for the real-life stupid to learn that they are not alone in their experiences.

Bouvard and Pécuchet represent a middle way between Bartleby's existential despair and Pooter's affirmative spirit. They keep trying to learn, but keep failing to succeed – as if living under the star of Irish funnyman Samuel Beckett's dictum: 'Try again. Fail again. Fail better.'[32] In this, as Mark Polizzotti points out in the introduction to his English translation of the novel, Flaubert lampoons not just the 'positivistic and progress-oriented zeitgeist he deplored, but also the accepted conventions of storytelling'.[33] Indeed, Bouvard and Pécuchet could be read as deflationary needles jabbed into the stupid balloons of the 19th-century novel, and indeed any narrative laws that insist on their characters' edifying spiritual and intellectual development during the course of a drama. Where every boring *Bildungsroman* involves some hero setting off on adventures, learning from setbacks, and becoming more mature and, ideally, married in the last chapter, Bouvard and Pécuchet, as Polizzotti puts, it 'emerge at the other end of their long journey remarkably close to where they started'. There is no *Bildung* in this *roman*, which, Polizzotti argues, makes it one of the first post-modern novels. It is also the precursor of the rule that Larry David created for the 1990s American sitcom *Seinfeld*, namely: 'No hugging, no learning.' David's sense was not just that too much TV drama was smeared in sentimental treacle, but also that narrative codes in sitcoms and elsewhere are revised to take audiences and readers on a journey to more or less fatuous and deluded revelation. In Flaubert's sense, these narrative forms were stupid precisely because they enabled those who used them to fulfil their desire to conclude, to find closure, or arrive at some heart-warming *telos* of transparency. In this, *Seinfeld* is just like Flaubert's novel: each refuses its characters' edification, nor do their stories offer satisfying resolutions or narrative closure. No one learns anything in *Seinfeld*, least of all from their mistakes; Bouvard and Pécuchet were stupidly learning nothing a century before Larry David's creation.

This is all very well, but in their irrepressible stupidity and questing for encyclopaedic knowledge, Bouvard and Pécuchet leave a lot of suffering in their wake. On one occasion, to test some hypothesis, they find that kittens drown five minutes after being shoved underwater. Monsters! A few pages later a hunchback boy and a wheezing tax collector are submitted to a treatment of inhaling camphor through quills to test another hypothesis, without the former's wheezing ceasing or the latter ever standing up straight. At another point, they are bent on fast-tracking Darwinian evolutionary processes by inducing a mastiff and a sow to mate. Their problem, notes Flaubert in a rare moment of authorial commentary, is that they were 'hoping to produce monsters and not understanding the first thing about species'.[34]

Flaubert immediately adds this by way of explanation. 'The word *species* designates a group of creatures whose descendants can reproduce; but some animals classified as belonging to different species can reproduce, while others included in the same species have lost that ability.' But this definition only serves to muddy the waters and doesn't really answer the question Bouvard and Pécuchet were attempting to answer: namely can beasts from different species reproduce. It's a knotty problem, perhaps not helped by the pair's superficial immersion in the subject. And yet this moment typifies the intellectual quandary, or indeed aporia, that Bouvard and Pécuchet find themselves in. They find themselves stuck, unable to progress in their chosen field, and, no doubt, with the nagging sense that they have made at least two fellow dwellers in this vale of tears, namely the exploited mastiff and sow, quite upset.

And then there is their shocking treatment of women in the name of science. Or, rather, 'science'. At one point, they start visiting people's homes in the local area to test out their medical theories, even though they have no medical qualifications. How they get past the front doors of those they visit is beyond me. But on more than one occasion they do: hence this odd scene. 'Working from the principle that lowering temperature helps prevent inflammations, they suspended a woman suffering from meningitis from the ceiling joists in her chair, and they were swinging her back and forth between them, when her husband showed up and kicked them both out.'[35] It's hard to see who is the most stupid here: the woman for allowing these two importunate charlatans into her home or the two men who are as qualified to practise medicine as I am to change light bulbs. Maybe the most stupid person in the scene is the husband for stopping the pair from continuing the experiment to its conclusion. After all, it could have worked . . .

Bouvard and Pécuchet are forever running into the street and accidentally treading on a rake that smacks them in the face. Then, having learned nothing, they do the same again in a kind of Groundhog Day with minimal variations. True, the pair do explore many different fields of human expertise, but each time they do so, their project ends in failure and sometimes with ruinous bills, devastating damage to their property, unpleasantness with the locals, and, though in surprisingly few cases, personal injury. And yet on they go. What makes these heroes of stupidity lovable is what should make them contemptible: like their spiritual soulmates Abbott and Costello and Laurel and Hardy, they never learn, but carry on regardless, scampering towards their next folly filled with misplaced optimism.

The eternal return of the Dummheit *brothers*

Flaubert's novel is in that sense an example of the chronic *amathia* Socrates indicted. *Amathia*, as you'll recall from chapter 2, means not learning, and as a form of stupidity is different from and worse than the other known as *agonia*, which means not knowing. More importantly, the anti-drama of Bouvard and Pécuchet is an indictment of a particularly modern kind of stupidity. Stupidity, that is to say, changes from how it was conceived by the ancients. For Aristotle, stupidity precludes goodness, and while *eudaimonia*, or human flourishing, requires rational excellence, in modern times that umbilical connection between stupidity and morality is severed. The great Enlightenment philosopher Immanuel Kant allowed, as Alasdair Macintyre puts it in *After Virtue*, that one can 'be both good and stupid'.[36] It's as shattering a shift as Copernicus realizing that the sun doesn't go around the earth or Freud's contention that human behaviour is riddled with the expression of unconscious impulses. For Kant, stupidity, what he calls *Dummheit*, is a failure of judgement, and an intellectual rather than a moral flaw: 'The lack of the power of judgment is properly called stupidity and such a failing is not to be helped.' That, to put it mildly, is a dismal view. One cannot be educated out of one's native stupidity. The stupid lack 'mother wit', Kant wrote. It's an inborn deficit, 'which cannot be made good by any school'.[37] The stupid are doomed.

That said, for Kant, cleverness and stupidity are not opposites. Stupidity is a disease found even in 'very learned men': 'A physician, judge or statesman . . . [with] many fine pathological, juridical, or political rules in his head . . . may know the universal rules and master all the concepts of their particular discipline, and yet they may still not be able to apply them correctly to particular cases.'[38]

Bouvard and Pécuchet are the *Dummheit* brothers, stupid in the very way Kant suggests: incapable of learning in general and incapable of learning from their mistakes in particular. They may also be prone to another intellectual malady or form of stupidity Kant called *Stumpfheit*, which amounts to the narrow mindedness resulting from a certain reduction of thought produced by the exclusive attention to concrete cases. *Stumpfheit*, then, is the opposite of *Dummheit*: the latter involves an inability to apply concepts to particular cases; *Stumpfheit*, by contrast, involves the inability to ascend from particular cases to the relevant concepts or laws about them. Both are stupid.

But it is possible to be more sympathetic to the *Dummheit* brothers than the foregoing suggests. Jacques Derrida found in Flaubert a sympathetic predecessor, not least one who was willing to laugh at the stupidities of philosophy, or rather those philosophers who suppose their task is to resolve the desire to know and to theorize how we might as a species realize the desired fate for humanity. Indeed, Flaubert's *Dictionary of Accepted Ideas* gives this anti-definition of the discipline: 'Philosophy: One should always snigger at it.'[39] And in particular, or so one would have thought, one should snigger at the fatuities of those philosophers such as Hegel, Marx, and Comte who suppose they can construct closed intellectual systems that brook no doubt. Flaubert, after all, thought stupidity consisted in the resolution of the desire to know. Bouvard and Pécuchet personified that desire. They sought to find the truth lurking hidden at the heart of every discipline they tried and failed to master.

In his essay 'An Idea of Flaubert: "Plato's Letter"', Jacques Derrida quoted with approval the characteristically splenetic words Flaubert wrote to his friend Léon Henrique:

> This mania for believing that nature has just recently been discovered and that we are truer than our predecessors exasperates me. Racine's tempest is every bit as true as Michelet's. There is no Truth! There are only ways of seeing. Does a photograph resemble its model? No more so than an oil portrait, or just as much. Down with all the Schools! Down with meaningless words! Down with Academies, Poetics, Principles![40]

In this, Flaubert was not just a post-modern novelist, but also a post-modernist thinker in refusing to accept the immutability of truth and human progress. He both seethed over his pretentious contemporaries who, in their hubris, imagined they were getting closer to the truth of things than their predecessors, and, more derangingly, contested the idea that there is a truth that can be finally uncovered at all. No wonder Derrida, the doyen of deconstruction, the philosopher who a century after Flaubert's death was excoriated by critics for abolishing Truth and hailed by followers for slaying that tyrant, found Flaubert sympathetic. As Derrida's biographer Peter Salmon puts it, Derrida's primary target was how the notion of 'truth' was wielded in philosophy: a monolithic, unitary, self-explanatory entity, much like how 'God' functioned in religion. For Derrida, the truth was a very different matter from how it was conceived by positivists like Comte: 'One may have faith in it, one may generate concepts around it, but one cannot *prove* it,' Salmon wrote.

> What one can do is deconstruct the idea and look at the hows and whys of this Truth. In whose interests is its assertion? Who speaks for it? Are there alternative narratives which call it into question – those offered by women, those of different genders, of different races to those who have thus far dominated the narrative?[41]

These were Derrida's kinds of questions rather than Flaubert's, but both men, across the centuries, share the conviction that truth is not akin to an entity to which only the cognoscenti have privileged access. It was, for Flaubert, stupid of philosophers to conceive what they do as attempting to find and unveil the truth, and deluded of modern philosophers to suppose that the technological tools provided by the application of Comte's scientific method – from the early cameras of Flaubert's day to the smartphones of ours – would unproblematically make us less stupid and thereby closer to the Hegelian absolute of human self-knowledge and freedom. And it was part of Derrida's project to suggest that there was no truth to be unveiled. As he wrote in his Flaubert essay immediately after quoting Flaubert's letter:

> This very perspectivism precludes our establishing a truth of the Idea; it precludes the very possibility that, behind all these rule-governed variations,

behind all these contexts (and there are many more to be found), the invariable truth of an idea of the idea might impose itself as law. The desire for such an idea of the idea would still be philosophical, even if it meant seeking this truth of the idea as a primal or paradigmatic scene (for example, the scene of negativity or resentment in an art of the idea that would shelter us from life) or as the scene of a guilt-ridden indebtedness to the idea.[42]

There was, for Derrida, no primal scene, no ultimate truth that philosophy could unveil and spend eternity contemplating. Rather, as he once put it, '*Il n'y pas de hors-texte* [There is no outside of the text].' It is stupid to believe in an immutable truth that might give us closure or end our intellectual enterprises. Rather, we are in a web of interpretation and misinterpretation and, for Derrida at least, stuck with the idea of truth as relative. This goes beyond the notion of truth as conceived by the likes of Comte and Popper: for the former, the truth was a *connaissance approchée*; for the latter, a provisional hypothesis about data that could be revised. For neither was truth relative; each, I suspect, would have condemned Derrida's sense that it was an irresponsible folly.

There is another, extremely dismal, possibility. Not that those positivists and utopian thinkers who quest after truth thus conceived are stupid, but that their very critics, Flaubert and Derrida, were. Stupidity may consist in denying that there is truth that is worth hunting down. Stupidity may consist in following Derrida's counsel that truth is a mutable concept, always context-dependent, always relative. If truth is relative, nothing can really be known, and any interpretation of a text thereby as justifiable or unjustifiable as another, then, as the conservative philosopher Roger Scruton argued, 'it has the consequence that no text says anything, including the text that says so'.[43] For Scruton and other critics of deconstructionism's high priest, Derrida has put reason to sleep. And that sleep of reason, as Goya's late 18th-century acquatint proclaimed, produces monsters. What kind of monsters? Demagogues rise to power borne by virtuosity in abjuring the truth, placing faith in rhetoric, and harnessing the power of lies, thereby corrupting politics and undermining democracy.

Has philosophy always been tainted by what Flaubert and Derrida took to be a stupid desire for closure and knowledge? Not entirely. Consider Socrates. The Socratic method taught the ancient Greek philosopher one deranging thing, namely that he knew nothing. The philosophers in Flaubert's and Derrida's crosshairs were never so wise, nor so properly humble.

In the Platonic dialogue the *Theaetetus*, the eponymous boy tells Socrates he is struggling with an intellectual problem. 'I have often tried to think this out, when I have heard reports of the questions you ask [about the nature of knowledge],' he tells Socrates. 'But I can never persuade myself that anything I say will really do; and I never hear anyone else state the matter in the way that you require. And yet, again, you know, I can't even stop worrying about it.'[44] Bouvard and Pécuchet regularly reached the same stage of bafflement.

They did not know how to carry on, they could see no path ahead. Their studies end in, as ancient Greeks would put it, aporia, or perplexity. Like Theaetetus, Bouvard and Pécuchet begin each new intellectual pursuit with a sense of wonder and hope that they can achieve the resolution of the desire to know. But they cannot do so. They often find themselves at an impasse, unable to continue deeper into some field of study because they cannot see the way ahead. And so they abandon one line of inquiry and become passionate, for a time, about another.

Theaetetus was more fortunate than they since he had Socrates to assist him in his intellectual inquiries. 'Do you mean to say that you've never heard about my being the son of a good hefty midwife, Phaenarete?' asks Socrates rather unexpectedly,

> And haven't you ever been told that I practise the same art myself? . . . Now my art of midwifery is just like theirs in most respects. The difference is that I attend men and not women, and that I watch over the labour of their souls, not of their bodies. And the most important thing about my art is the ability to apply all possible tests to the offspring, to determine whether the young mind is being delivered of a phantom, that is, an error, or a fertile truth.[45]

Socrates admits that he is like the midwife in that he cannot give birth to wisdom.

> I am not in any sense a wise man; I cannot claim as the child of my own soul any discovery worth the name of wisdom. But with those who associate with me it is different. At first some of them may give the impression of being

ignorant and stupid; but as time goes on and our association continues, all whom God permits are seen to make progress – a progress which is amazing both to other people and to themselves. And yet it is clear that this is not due to anything they have learnt from me; it is that they discover within themselves a multitude of beautiful things, which they bring forth into the light.[46]

At the end of the dialogue, though, Theaetetus, though all the while intellectually massaged and assisted by Socrates the self-styled midwife, has managed to give birth not to admirable truths, but to three inadequate definitions of knowledge that Socrates dismisses. Their discussion ends in aporia, leaving Theaetetus no wiser about the nature of knowledge than when they began the discussion, but for the fact that his notions of what knowledge consists of are wrong. That, at least, is something.

Raymond Queneau argues that the stupidity of our two heroes has no other origin than their desire for the absolute, which they believe they can satisfy with manuals and superficial study. Each time, though, they become not wise but rather baffled. Their bafflement, though, unlike that which Theaetetus was induced to experience by Socrates, is not edifying but stupefying. Instead of humbly realizing their shortcomings, Bouvard and Pécuchet move, undaunted, to the next species of folly to obsess them. This is the opposite of wisdom, but confirmation of the idea that a fool and their folly are inseparable.

I like the idea that Flaubert decided leaving *Bouvard and Pécuchet* incomplete was fitting for a novel about stupidity. If stupidity consists, as he argued, in wanting to conclude, then better to leave the book without an ending. Or maybe something happened to Flaubert that occurred to his character repeatedly during the book: he reached a point of bafflement, an aporia, and had no sense how to carry on. And so, like his creations, he abandoned the task.

Flaubert nonetheless did sketch how the novel might have ended. He imagined the pair giving up their intellectual pursuits and reverting to their earlier careers as copy clerks. They plan to construct a two-seated desk on which to copy convivially. The last sentence of the incomplete novel ends with this note from the author. 'End with a view of our two heroes leaning over their desks, copying.'[47] He intended this ending to be followed by a sample of what they copy out: possibly an anthology of stupid quotations or the very *Dictionary of Accepted Ideas* Flaubert composed earlier.

But this imagined ending is only a beginning. As we close the book and leave our heroes to their fate, they revert to toilers at the coalface of fatuity, increasing the production and distribution of stupidity in line with capitalistic norms. In so doing, Bouvard and Pécuchet were precursors of today's *Dummheit* brothers, Mark Zuckerberg and Elon Musk, albeit with more modest technology, adding to the growing glut of the world's witlessness.

Flaubert never really decided the question of whether stupidity is immutable or infectious, whether it is a feature of humanity or fixable. And yet if we are to take a lesson from his novel on stupidity, it is that stupidity is so terribly infectious that it contaminates those who imagined themselves to be inoculated. Flaubert once wrote with the hubris of God-emulating authors. 'It is splendid to be a great writer, to hold men in the frying pan of your sentences and sauté them like chestnuts. There must be a delirious pride in the feeling that you are bringing the full weight of your idea to bear on mankind.'[48] But this is stupidity of the same order as Charles Pooter painting his bath, supposing, foolishly, that he is the master of the situation when really he is in its thrall and soon to get his comeuppance. Pooter's body turned red; Flaubert's brain got fried. Flaubert read 1,500 books as research for his book about the folly of misplaced intellectual endeavours. He thereby caught the virus of modern stupidity from his own creations. He reflected: 'Bouvard and Pécuchet have filled me up to such a point that I have become them! Their stupidity is my own and I am bursting with it. . . . I live as much as I can in my two fellows . . . the stupidity of my two characters has invaded me.'[49] Flaubert may have intended to indict modern stupidity but, ironically, he ended up becoming part of it.

6

Stupid Eugenics

The witless war against feeble-mindedness

On 5 May 1968, 14-year-old Elaine Riddick gave birth to a son by Caesarean section at a hospital in Edenton in the American state of North Carolina. Then, without her knowledge or consent, a doctor sliced through her fallopian tubes and cauterized them.[1]

What the African American girl did not know when she awoke to find her abdomen covered in bandages was that five months earlier she had been deemed by state authorities to be too feeble-minded to be allowed to have any more children. Five men meeting in a room in Raleigh decided her first child would be her last. She was a late victim of a eugenics programme that mandated the sterilization of those in one way or another deemed mentally deficient. It is estimated that as many as 100,000 people were sterilized in the US during the 20th century as part of what amounted to a misbegotten war against stupidity.

What Riddick perhaps also didn't know is that the term 'eugenics' comes from the Greek word for 'well born' and that it was coined by Charles Darwin's half-cousin. The statistician-explorer Sir Francis Galton also constructed a racial hierarchy in which white people were considered superior. He wrote in his 1869 book *Hereditary Genius* that 'the average intellectual standard of the negro race is some two grades below our own [the Anglo-Saxon]'.[2] The British government's Royal Commission on the Care and Control of the Feeble-Minded in 1908 defined the feeble-minded as 'persons who may be capable of earning a living under favourable circumstances, but are incapable from mental defect, existing from birth or from an early age: (1) of competing on equal terms with their normal fellows, or (2) of managing themselves and their affairs with ordinary prudence'.[3]

Riddick may not have been familiar either with the work of American psychologist Henry Herbert Goddard, who, in his 1912 book *The Kallikak Family: A Study in the Heredity of Feeble-Mindedness*, argued that 'feeble-mindedness' was a hereditary trait, most likely caused by a single recessive gene.[4] Goddard also devised an influential classification system for what he called intellectual disability based on the Binet-Simon concept of mental age. A person's IQ, or intelligence quotient, was decided at the time by dividing their mental age, which was determined by standardized tests, by their actual age, and then multiplying the resulting number by 100. This procedure was followed by another American psychologist, Edmund Burke Huey, who in his book *Backward and Feeble-Minded Children*, also published in 1912, proposed the following taxonomy:

> Idiots. – Those so defective that the mental development never exceeds that or a normal child of about two years. Imbeciles. – Those whose development is higher than that of an idiot, but whose intelligence does not exceed that of a normal child of about seven years. Morons. – Those whose mental development is above that of an imbecile but does not exceed that of a normal child of about twelve years.[5]

Psychologist Edgar A. Doll, who worked at Goddard's Vineland Training School for Backward and Feeble-Minded Children in New Jersey, argued in his 1936 paper 'Idiot, Imbecile, and Moron'[6] that these three kinds of feeble-mindedness could be diagnosed by the criteria of social incompetence due to low intelligence which has been developmentally arrested.

Nor would Riddick likely have been familiar with the 1927 US Supreme Court case *Buck v. Bell*, in which Justice Oliver Wendell Holmes closed the 8–1 majority opinion upholding the sterilization of a Virginia woman, Carrie Buck, who, like her, had been raped as a minor. Holmes said: 'Three generations of imbeciles are enough.' Buck, her mother, and her daughter were all classified as feeble-minded.[7]

Nine months before she was sterilized, Riddick had been kidnapped and raped by a neighbour. Very poor and from a troubled family, she dropped out of school in the eighth grade, partly because she was picked on by bullies for wearing the same clothes several days in a row. Her parents were unreliable: her army veteran father, Thomas, was shell-shocked, alcoholic, and abusive; her mother, Pearline, served prison time for assaulting her husband. Riddick was raised by her illiterate grandmother, Maggie Woodard, in a two-bedroom house known as a refuge.

A social worker who discovered Riddick was pregnant referred her case to the state's Eugenics Board. Five men, including North Carolina's health director and a lawyer from the attorney general's office, decided her fate. Their conclusion to Case No. 8, 'Delores Elaine Riddick – (N) – Perquimans County' ('N' stood for Negro), was that she was 'feebleminded' and promiscuous, and so recommended sterilization. Maggie Woodward marked an X on the consent forms after being told her granddaughter would be sent to an orphanage and she would lose her own food stamps if she did not sign.

In ordering the girl's forced sterilization, the Eugenics Board was acting in line with a law which, according to a 1950 pamphlet issued by the Human Betterment League of North Carolina, 'provides for the sterilization at state or county expense of patients in or out of institutions who are likely to produce children with a tendency towards serious physical, mental or nervous diseases or deficiencies'.[8] North Carolina, at the time, was one of 33 American states that had forced sterilization laws on its statute books, though was different from the others in that it provided for the forced sterilization of those who had not been institutionalized. Indeed, the state's sterilization programme often targeted the rural poor, and in particular black people, who were racistly deemed to be promiscuous and feeble-minded.

The thinking behind the state's law was highlighted in the Human Betterment League's pamphlet, which said the board was protecting 'the children of future generations and the community at large', and argued: 'You wouldn't expect a moron to run a train or a feebleminded woman to teach school.' Next to a cartoon of a businessman behind a desk being proffered incoming mail by his secretary, the caption went as follows:

> You wouldn't give a responsible position to a person of little intelligence. YET each day the feebleminded and mentally defective are entrusted with the most important and far reaching job of all. . . . The job of PARENTHOOD! . . .

the creation of new life and the responsibility of rearing children. Having a baby is the most important of all jobs . . . The average feebleminded parent cannot be expected to provide good heredity, a normal home, intelligent care, to say nothing of the many other things needed to bring up children successfully. Like running a train, teaching school, or handling money, the job of parenthood is too much to expect of feebleminded men and women.

A few years later, Riddick, now aged 18, was married and living with an aunt in New York while her son Tony was raised by her grandmother. Only when she consulted a specialist to find out why the couple were having trouble conceiving did she find out she had been sterilized. The doctor said she had been 'butchered', a word that stayed with her for decades as she fought for compensation. 'They butchered me like a hog,' she said later.[9] After he found out she had been sterilized, her husband called her barren and useless. They later divorced.

There was another document in Riddick's files that, read sympathetically, might have caused the North Carolina Eugenics Board to decide against her sterilization. One day in April 1967, not long before she was raped, a clinical psychologist met her to consider whether she should be placed in an orphanage. Dr Helton McAndrew found that though she was in the 'slow section of the seventh grade', testing showed Riddick to have an IQ of 75. McAndrew argued that her 'tremendous feelings of insecurity stemming from the disturbed home conditions' were causing her irritability and 'also repressed her level of intellectual functioning'.[10]

Instead, the Eugenics Board followed the damning verdict of Riddick's social worker, who recommended sterilization since 'this will at least prevent additional children from being born to this girl who cannot care for herself and can never function in any way as a parent'.

What nonsense. Riddick obtained a high school equivalency diploma and in 1982 graduated from the New York City Technical College with an associate's degree in applied science. For many years, she was an office manager for a tax preparation company. What's more, far from her presumed feeble-mindedness being a recessive gene that would curse her spawn, her son Tony graduated from college and became a successful businessman, president of his own computer-electronics company. Riddick is now also the proud grandmother of Tony Junior.

Despite reconstructive surgery, however, she was never able to have more children.

For more than 40 years, with the support of the American Civil Liberties Union, Riddick fought for justice. Not just for herself, but for more than 7,600 people – most of them African American girls and women – who between 1929 and 1974 were sterilized in the name of improving the human stock and eliminating the feeble-minded, the morons, imbeciles, and idiots from human society. Although the Eugenics Commission was abolished in 1977, after fighting for compensation for almost 50 years, she received $47,000 from the state.

Elaine Riddick's story highlights several themes important to this history of stupidity. First, what happened to her was part of a long-cherished deluded dream of eliminating stupidity. Galton thought that he was establishing a science to do that, improving stock just as breeders did with racehorses and roses. If only we were clever enough to identify stupid people, we could stop them becoming stupid parents and passing their witlessness on to their spawn. If there is a gene for stupidity, surely our brightest scientists should be working to turn it off.

Second, her story highlights how pseudo-science and social policy have been used to demonize the presumed stupid and to flatter the self-images of their ostensible superiors, often by serving racist and classist agendas. It's very much to the point that Riddick's son Tony told North Carolina's Eugenics Compensation Task Force that what happened to his mother was not sterilization but genocide.[11] And it is also to the point to notice that the pursuit of that dream has resulted not just in cruelty masquerading as kindness, in castrations, sterilizations, and lives ruined, but also in terrible poetry. In 1947, Dr Clarence Gamble, heir to the Procter & Gamble soap company, submitted this poem to the North Carolina Mental Hygiene Society in the hope that it would be used in pamphlets to drum up support for the state's eugenics sterilization programme:

> Once there was a MORON, that means
> a person that wasn't very bright. –
> he couldn't add figures
> or make change
> or do many things

an ordinary man does.
So he couldn't find a job
and the RELIEF OFFICE
had to help him out
for YEARS AND YEARS.
And one day he met
another MORON
who wasn't any cleverer than he was.
But SHE was nicer to him
than anyone had ever been.
And so he MARRIED HER.
And soon there was a BABY,
and then ANOTHER
and ANOTHER
and ANOTHER.
And the welfare department
had to pay the family
MORE of the TAXPAYER'S
MONEY
and MORE
and MORE
and MORE

And when the children grew
up and went to school
They couldn't learn
very fast
because they had inherited poor minds from their parents.
They had to repeat MANY
GRADES in the school,
and never learned very much
and never were able to
GET A JOB
and they cost the schoolboard
and the relief office
and the taxpayer
THOUSANDS OF DOLLARS.

AND THESE CHILDREN MARRIED
TOO – – –
So the story goes on
to grandchildren
and greatgrandchildren
and so on forevermore.

But who were Dr Gamble's 'lucky morons'? The rest of the poem explains:

Now there was another MORON
who also was a little stupid
and couldn't learn very
much but he lived in
NORTH CAROLINA
and that was very fortunate
for him.
For the Department of Welfare
in his county
made him one of the
lucky morons
who went to CASWELL TRAINING
SCHOOL.
There he had a mental test
and he was taught a trade
simple enough to fit his brains,
and because the tests showed
he wouldn't ever be very
bright
Or be able to earn enough
to feed a family,
and because his children
might be feebleminded, too,
a surgeon performed
A SIMPLE OPERATION
which didn't change him AT ALL,
or take ANYTHING out of his

body, but kept him from
having any children.
And after a year or two
a JOB was found for him
which, because of his special training,
he DID WELL,
and he earned enough
to be SELF-SUPPORTING.
And after a while he met a
GIRL
She, too, wasn't very bright,
but they liked each other.
And she, too, had been to
CASWELL for training
and had a JOB and a
surgeon had PROTECTED her from UNWANTED
CHILDREN, without
making her different in any other way from other women.
And because they loved
each other, they married
and WERE HAPPY just as other couples are.
Both kept on with their
jobs so they were still
SELF-SUPPORTING.
And there weren't any children's
mouths to feed – - – although
they wouldn't have
known why if
the operation hadn't
been explained to them.
And with just the two in the
family, they kept on
being SELF-SUPPORTING,
and they were very thankful they lived in NORTH CAROLINA.
And the WELFARE DEPARTMENT
DIDN'T have to feed them
and the SCHOOLS didn't

have to waste their efforts on
any of their children who weren't very bright.
And because they had been
STERILIZED, the taxpayers of
North Carolina had
saved
THOUSANDS OF DOLLARS
and the North Carolina MORONS LIVED
HAPPILY EVER AFTER.[12]

Third, and perhaps most important, Riddick's story shows how such tragically misconceived sciences as eugenics and resultant sterilization policies, both founded supposedly on reason, both developed and pursued by the brightest and the best of our ostensibly rational species, were themselves examples of stupidity. Riddick was not stupid; the people involved in her abuse were. It was the latter who supposed feeble-mindedness was a recessive gene, that intelligence is heritable, and that stupidity along with other supposed mental deficiencies can be diagnosed and cut out like cancerous tumours before they spread too far, saving taxpayers' money, just as Dr Clarence Gamble described in his poem (one which even the North Carolina Mental Hygiene Society thought too crass to warrant publication in its pamphlets).

When I read about Riddick's story while researching this book, what astounded me was not just that it happened, but that it happened during my lifetime. In my naïvety, I had imagined that eugenics could not have survived Auschwitz and that such racist butchery of a black woman's body might have been outlawed in the decade in which African Americans fought for their civil rights. Surely eugenics was, like Nazism, history? And surely, too, the racism that scars not just the US but my homeland, the UK, is, happily, being overcome as humanity progresses towards some Hegelian utopia of absolute freedom? But no: stupidity isn't so much a recessive gene to be cut out as the quality of an attitude that expects too much from the possibilities of human progress.

Francis Galton, as noted above, coined the term 'eugenics' in 1869 in his book *Hereditary Genius*. He wrote: 'What is termed in Greek *eugenes*, namely good in stock, hereditarily endowed with noble qualities. This, and the allied words *eugenia*, etc. are equally applicable to men, brutes and plants.'[13]

That said, Galton was less interested in establishing the relative qualities of different brutes or plants; rather, he was obsessed with establishing the relative worth of humans. He was obsessed, too, with the power of numbers, once performing a statistical analysis of the efficacy of prayer and even drawing up a beauty map of the British Isles. 'Whenever I have occasion to classify the persons I meet into three classes, 'good, medium, bad', I use a needle mounted as a pricker wherewith to prick holes, unseen, on a piece of paper torn rudely into a cross with a long leg,' he wrote in *Memories of My Life*.

> I use its upper end for 'good', the cross arm for 'medium', the lower end for 'bad'. The prick holes keep distinct, and are easily read off at leisure. The object, place and date are written on the paper. I used this plan for my beauty data, classifying the girls I passed in the street as attractive, indifferent. . . . I found London to rank highest for beauty, Aberdeen lowest.[14]

Down the years, these words resonate unedifyingly: the lubricious gaze of men of (supposed) science; the faith in the blunt instrument of data (only three categories? really?) to produce an evaluative conclusion; the unfounded slur on the women of Aberdeen.

Galton's predilection for measuring human worth was spurred by his half-cousin's writings on evolution. Galton was influenced profoundly by Darwin's reflections on how humans had bred plants and animals. In *On the Origin of Species* (1859), Darwin argued that populations evolve over the course of generations through a process of natural selection. In nature, organisms produce more offspring than are able to survive and reproduce. Offspring with traits that make them more likely to survive, mature, and reproduce in the environment they inhabit pass on their traits to the next generation. What Darwin didn't consider in the book was something that captured Galton's imagination, namely the possibility that stupidity was a trait. And if so, it could be deselected; the bug that had bedevilled the human operating system could be removed.

During his youthful five-year voyage on the HMS *Beagle*, Darwin had been struck by the variety of appearances of finches he spotted on the Galapagos Islands. He inferred that these variations – in particular in terms of size of beak – were to do with different environments on different islands. Where cactus plants were common, local finches had evolved long beaks to extract pollen and nectar; where seeds were plentiful on the ground, short-beaked finches were more common. These useful traits had been, Darwin surmised, passed down through the generations, ensuring what has become known as 'the survival of the fittest', and its corollary, the effective eradication of those less fitted to thrive in a given environment.

Back in England, Darwin was also intrigued by another species of birds, pigeons. In 1855, he built a dovecote in his garden and filled it with birds he bad bought from breeders. They included peters, carriers, barbs, and short-faced tumblers. 'The diversity of the breeds is something astonishing,' he wrote.[15] Pigeon breeders, along with dog and horse breeders, not to mention horticulturists, were virtuosos at artificially selecting which traits offspring inherited by means of careful breeding. Artificial selection could achieve much more quickly, perhaps even in two or three generations, what nature did over millennia.

Influenced by Galton, Darwin supposed that what humans had done to other species, namely improved or otherwise fast-tracked their descent by means of artificial selection towards some human-conceived end, could also be applied to humans themselves. 'If the prudent avoid marriage whilst the reckless marry, the inferior members tend to supplant the better members of society,'[16] he wrote in *The Descent of Man and Selection in Relation to Sex* in 1871.

Racism was not invented by Galton, but scientific racism in the form of eugenics was certainly his brainchild. The advent of eugenics came at a pivotal moment for human history in general and Britain's in particular. One might even think that in the mid-19th century, as religious faith declined and the fossil record tended to show that the Book of Genesis did not plausibly account for the age of the earth or for the mutability and diversity of life on it, a new Creation myth was needed. Thomas Henry Huxley, the great Victorian biologist and comparative anatomist known as 'Darwin's bulldog' for savaging critics of his friend's account of natural selection, and proselytizing that we descend not from Adam and Eve but from apes, argued that when *Homo sapiens* emerged from its primitive state among the other apes and lemurs, some – conveniently for an Englishman such as Huxley, Europeans – developed at a faster rate. Once the human species emerged, Huxley wrote in *Man's Place in Nature* (1863), 'men differ more widely from one another than they do from the apes'.[17] Finches may have beaks adapted to different environments, but humanity's variations are infinitely more nuanced. Huxley nonetheless put such hypothesized variations in starkly racial terms. He argued that some peoples had not evolved. 'I suspect that the modern Patagonian is as nearly as possible the unimproved representative of the makers of flint implements of Abbeyville,' he wrote, adding: 'All the Polynesian, Australian and central Asiatic peoples, were at the dawn of history substantially what they are now.'[18]

Such thoughts amounted to a theory of racial superiority that implied millions of people around the world were stupid (at least in comparison with Europeans). They also provided, wittingly or otherwise, justification for the 19th-century evolution of the British Empire. Under Queen Victoria, the Empire changed from a commercial and military enterprise that profited from the persecution of black bodies by means of the transatlantic slave trade (what the historian William Dalrymple calls, in the title of his book on the East India Company, 'the Anarchy'[19]) to all-out colonization. The lesser races needed to be uplifted from their present feeble-mindedness and intellectual sloth; or if not uplifted, then exploited as if they were scarcely human but rather means to the ends of British enrichment. As the novelist A.N. Wilson puts it,

> That European humanity – with the British at its apex, naturally – out-classed Asian and African humanity went without question. Possessing steam trains, winged collars, top hats and newspapers made Europeans obviously superior to people who dressed and behaved differently. Inevitably, the higher races would develop Maxim guns, which could subdue the warriors who carried only spears and darts.[20]

Huxley's and Galton's theories of racial superiority and eugenics marched in step with this mutation of British imperialism.

Darwin was much more cautious than his half-cousin or his bulldog in developing not just an account of higher and lower races, but also support for the subjugation and even eradication of the latter. Two years after Galton's *Hereditary Genius* was published, Darwin wrote in *The Descent of Man, and Selection in Relation to Sex* that 'all ought to refrain from marriage who cannot avoid abject penury for their children'.[21] In that opinion, he was following the prevailing wisdom of English economist and demographer Thomas Malthus, who contended that population growth will always tend to outrun the food supply and proposed that, therefore, the flourishing of humankind requires strict limits on reproduction. Such was a commonplace thought among British Victorian intellectuals, but the notion that humans could be artificially selected like pigeons or broccoli was Galton's notion. Darwin didn't dismiss the suggestion out of hand, but wrote that when it comes to humans, selection 'is a most intricate problem'.[22]

'Intricate problem' is a curious expression since it dangles before us the contestable possibility that one might breed pedigree humans as one breeds pedigree dogs but that the former will be a technically trickier business rather than a morally dubious one.

The dream of breeding better humans was and remains seductive. Selective breeding of the wild mustard plant has yielded broccoli, cabbage, and cauliflower. Perhaps similarly, humans could be artificially selected to perform specific tasks in a division of labour far beyond Scottish economist Adam Smith's conception of that development in human political economy set out in his 1776 book *The Wealth of Nations*. Careful breeding might eliminate bad traits such as stupidity and promote desirable ones in a well-ordered, optimally performing, even utopian human future.

In the *Republic*, Plato divided his just society into three classes: producers, auxiliaries, and guardians, each with their allotted stations in life. The author of one classic of 20th-century science fiction went further, imagining five classes in his ideal society, all grown in artificial wombs and genetically engineered for the jobs they must perform in life. Castes were colour-coded: Alphas wore grey, Betas mulberry, Gammas green, Deltas khaki, and Epsilons black. The first two performed more intellectual tasks, while the last three did more menial work and were usually clones conditioned to serve the higher-ranking castes. Epsilons, who were effectively intentionally brain damaged by being deprived of oxygen before birth, were proverbially stupid. 'I'm glad I'm not an Epsilon,' says one Beta to an Alpha in the novel. 'And if you were an Epsilon,' replies that Alpha, 'your conditioning would have made you no less thankful that you weren't a Beta or an Alpha.' In this imagined ideal society, the 'intricate problem' of human artificial selection has been so elegantly solved that each member of society is happy that they have been conditioned to belong to whatever caste it is allotted (though only the higher classes are aware, naturally enough, that such social conditioning by means of genetic engineering has happened). And in this ideal, just society, there is a kind of respect even for those at the bottom of the evolutionary ladder, akin to the patronizing homily delivered to morons by Dr Gamble in his execrable poem. 'We couldn't do without Epsilons,' says the Beta. 'Everyone works for everyone else.'[23] Like the British Empire, with the Alpha Britons at the top and Epsilons of colour at the bottom, the society envisaged in this novel works on condition that everyone knows their place and stays in it. Far from being eradicated, the moronic Epsilons in their very stupidity are keys to that society's optimal functioning.

The novel I've just been quoting from, you'll hardly be surprised to learn, is *Brave New World*, written by Thomas Henry Huxley's grandson Aldous and published in 1932. But it was Aldous's biologist brother Julian who most directly skewered what was wrong, stupid really, about Galton's thought that humanity could be improved by artificial selection. In 1962, nearly a century after Galton's *Hereditary Genius* was published, Julian gave the Second Galton Lecture to the Eugenics Society, entitled 'Eugenics in Evolutionary Perspective', arguing that the question of eugenics had been 'bedevilled by the false analogy between artificial and natural selection'.[24] Humans weren't mustard plants, nor might human society be profitably divided up into castes along the lines of Alphas and Epsilons imagined by his brother Aldous. Artificial selection, Julian Huxley agued, aimed to produce 'particular excellence', meaning specialized breeds with limited variability.

But there's the rub. What is 'particular excellence', and if there is such a thing, can it be bottled and used to artificially inseminate humans for the betterment of the species? The men we have been concerned with so far in this chapter – Francis Galton, Thomas Henry Huxley, Charles Darwin, and Julian Huxley – were much preoccupied with this kind of question. They wondered, hopefully, if genius could be captured and transmitted to future generations, with the corollary that stupidity, despite Voltaire's and Schopenhauer's respective demurrals, could be artificially selected for eradication from human society. Genius was necessary for human advancement, so we need more of it. Stupidity? Not so much. 'The advance of mankind has everywhere depended on the production of men of genius: and that production is a case of "spontaneous variation", not by physical propagation, but by the help of language, letters and the printing press,' Thomas Henry Huxley wrote[25] to his friend the novelist, defender of Darwin's *On the Origin of Species* and divine Charles Kingsley. This is a fascinating view, suggesting that genius is by no means straightforwardly biological, nor heritable through artificial insemination in the manner horse breeders have deployed to derive offspring that can gallop faster or have other desirable traits, but rather relies on cultural factors. That suggests that genius cannot be bottled and deployed through artificial insemination or in vitro fertilization to ensure its spread; rather, genius, far from being biologically determined, depends on social and intellectual matters – even if, as Darwin might well have argued, these cultural refinements are the result of the processes of natural selection. Similarly, Julian Huxley argued in his Galton Lecture, intelligence was not a straightforwardly heritable trait for which clever geneticists could artificially select and propagate to ensure the survival of the fittest and the elimination of the unfit. And yet, despite the caveats of these two men, the pseudo-science of eugenics and, often, later genetic engineering involve faith in just that delusion.

Thomas Henry Huxley supposed the ascent of man was dependent on the descent of genius down the generations. His letter to Charles Kingsley continued with the curious suggestion that the great 17th-century English physicist Isaac Newton 'was to all intents and purposes a "sport" of dull agricultural stock, and his intellectual powers are to a certain extent propagated by the grafting of the "Principia," his brain-shoot, on us'.[26] This horticultural metaphor suggests precisely that there is more to artificially improving human intellect than grafting organic material onto existing stock; what's needed, indeed, is the dissemination of ideas, a public culture of reading, learning, and critical thought that is irreducible to biology. In drawing the parallel between artificial selection of plants and the evolution of human intelligence, Huxley was effectively making the point his grandson suggested a century later in that Galton Lecture: the parallel between what horticulturalists and animal breeders do in artificially selecting desirable traits and the development of human intelligence is a poor one.

Julian Huxley nonetheless kept the eugenics standard aloft during the 20th century. He did not just believe in culture as a means of improving human intelligence but also was a leading figure in what was known as the 'modern synthesis', which married Darwin's theory of evolution with the ideas on heredity of the first geneticist, gardening monk Gregor Mendel. The new science of genetics gave hope to many scientists, artists, and politicians that the human species could be improved by means of artificially inseminating hosts to ensure the inheritance in offspring of desirable traits.

Huxley spent much of the 1920s in a lab in Oxford injecting thyroid hormones into axolotls (now-endangered Mexican salamanders) to transform them from aquatic beings to terrestrial, air-breathing ones.[27] Such injections enabled him to make organisms larger or smaller, more or less male or female, longer or shorter lived. He resembled, perhaps, a relatively benign version of his friend and literary collaborator H.G. Wells's character Dr Moreau.

The hubris and utopian hopes that these experiments catalysed were captured in a lecture given in 1923 by Julian Huxley's fag at Eton, the geneticist J.B.S. Haldane. Called *Daedalus: or Science and the Future*, the lecture effectively predicts transhumanism (the technical modification of human biology) and ectogenesis (the growth of life outside the body). Science, thought Haldane, is a process of gradual conquest, like the British imperial project, though more likely to be peer reviewed. He wrote that science 'is man's gradual conquest, first of space and time, then of matter as such, then of his own body and those of other living beings, and finally the subjugation of the dark and evil elements in his own soul'.[28]

Instead of the figure of Prometheus who stole fire from the gods and was punished, the scientist is more akin to Daedalus, Haldane supposed, the craftsman and architect who, in Greek myth, symbolizes wisdom, knowledge, and power. Where Daedalus, imprisoned on Crete by King Minos, constructed bird-like wings held with beeswax so that he and his son Icarus could escape to liberty, Haldane was tentatively imagining a future in which humans controlled their own evolution, artificially selecting desirable traits and making use of in vitro fertilization. The likes of Haldane and Julian Huxley were modern-day Daedaluses in attempting what seemed not just unnatural but also blasphemous. Haldane told members of Cambridge University's Heretics Society:

> There is no great invention, from fire to flying, which has not been hailed as an insult to some god. But if every physical and chemical invention is a blasphemy, every biological invention is a perversion. There is hardly one which, on first being brought to the notice of an observer from any nation which had not previously heard of their existence, would not appear to him as indecent and unnatural.[29]

Viewed thus, what he, Huxley, and others were doing in their laboratories was in the same spirit as the Copernican revolution, with the difference that rather than showing that the earth is not the centre of the universe, they were showing that humans can be masters of what seemed fated, if not divinely preordained: their biological destiny. The lecture ends with the image of a biologist in a laboratory resembling Haldane and Huxley: 'Just a poor little scrubby underpaid man groping blindly amid the mazes of the ultramicroscope . . . . conscious of his ghastly mission and proud of it.'[30] The pride of these modern-day Daedaluses, the excitement in the possibilities their experiments seemed to offer to extend human powers in general and theirs in particular, was no doubt intoxicating. But, lest we forget, soaring above Daedalus, using the wings that his father had so ingeniously constructed, was Icarus, and the beeswax that held those prostheses together melted in the sun, precipitating his death plunge. The unintended moral? Not that pride necessarily comes before a fall, but that myopic fixation on the powers human ingenuity can confer on our species tends to obscure calamitous unforeseen consequences that, only in hindsight, do we realize might have been worth factoring into our equations.

Haldane, at least, was capable of sounding a note of humility. This scrubby underpaid Daedalus armed with new powers to change human nature himself needed not so much an intellectual upgrade as a moral one: that's to say, a maturity, if not humility, rarely found among those blinded by the glister of science. Haldane told the Heretics Society:

> The question of what he will do with these powers is essentially a question for religion and aesthetics. It may be urged that they are only fit to be placed in

the hands of a being who has learned to control himself, and that man armed with science is like a baby armed with a box of matches.[31]

And yet many eugenicists were just such Promethean babies who thought they could create supermen and superwomen and by the same token eliminate the morons, imbeciles, and idiots who blocked the royal road to human perfectibility. These goals would be achieved not just through delivering on the utopian eugenicist dreams of in vitro fertilization and artificial insemination to improve the human stock, but also by what Julian Huxley called negative eugenics. By this he meant the very suggestion that Darwin following Malthus had counselled: those too poor to be able to provide nurturing environments for their offspring and too feeble-minded should be discouraged from breeding. In this, he was of the same temper as other enthusiasts for eugenics in 1920s Britain such as Marie Stopes and William Churchill. The former in particular, a palaeobotanist who pioneered contraception clinics, held fast to a dream that has long dogged humankind: that all forms of mental incapacity could be rooted out of human society by controlling breeding. Moreover, her dream was expressed in explicitly classist and racist terms. At her contraception clinics, she dispensed the chillingly named 'Prorace' cervical caps to women who she judged should not conceive. 'Are these puny-faced, gaunt, blotchy, ill-balanced, feeble, ungainly, withered children the young of an imperial race?' she wrote,[32] once again connecting the motivations behind the pseudo-science of eugenics with the British imperial project.

In 1922, Marie Stopes called on MPs to sign a declaration urging the Ministry of Health to disclose the information that would 'curtail the C3 [the unskilled working class] and increase the A1'.[33] Stopes' great dream was that stupidity might be one of the undesirable characteristics that by such selective breeding could finally be eradicated. But this in itself seems stupid: once the C3s had been eradicated, who would do the menial tasks for the A1s? At least Aldous Huxley's nightmarish dystopia in *Brave New World* envisaged a workable society; Stopes' utopia seems, prima facie, doomed. Or if not doomed, then morally contemptible: the product of a moral baby perversely bent on the idea that others less intellectually accomplished than she should not be allowed to have babies.

Julian Huxley, for his part, was no less racist than Stopes. Returning to Britain from a teaching appointment at Rice University in Texas in 1916, he was convinced of the cultural inferiority of 'negroes' and of the virtue of US immigration controls designed to keep out supposed racial inferiors. During the 1920s, he combined a faith in the possibilities of scientific innovation to better humans and legislation to minimize the spread of the supposedly intellectually inferior races. At the World Population Conference of 1927, for instance, he advocated on these grounds for restrictive immigration controls. Later, in the early 1930s, he backed campaigns for voluntary sterilization legislation and for negative eugenic measures to protect humankind from the taint of 'mental defect'.[34]

But if mental defect could be eradicated thus, what of genius? Could it be bottled and transmitted thereby to future generations? As a five-year-old boy, Julian had read *The Water Babies*, the bestselling Victorian moral fable about a boy presumed drowned but raised underwater. It had been written by Thomas Henry Huxley's friend the Rev. Charles Kingsley, inspired by debates over the threat Darwin's dangerous idea of natural selection posed to the account of God's creation. The book included an engraving of Julian's grandad mesmerized before a water baby who had been captured in a bottle. 'Dear Grandpater,' little Julian wrote, 'Have you seen a Waterbaby? Did you put it in a bottle? Did it wonder if it could get out? Could I see it some day? – Your loving Julian.'[35] Perhaps the image the little boy saw inspired the grown-up's utopian hopes for ectogenesis, for foetuses grown in bottles the better to overcome humanity's natural shortcomings.

Thomas Henry replied that he had never seen such a water baby, which was no grounds for positing its non-existence, adding:

> My friend who wrote the story of the Water Baby was a very kind man and very clever. Perhaps he thought I could see as much in the water as he did – there are some people who see a great deal and some who see very little in the same things. When you grow up I dare say you will be one of the great-deal seers, and see things more wonderful than the Water Babies where other folks can see nothing.[36]

Julian was indeed a 'great-deal seer', a sometime racist no doubt, but one whose genetic material was coveted because it might be transmissible by means of artificial selection. Perhaps the genius gene could be injected into the otherwise disappointing stock of humanity to eliminate stupidity.

'Dear Sir,' wrote a nameless correspondent to Julian Huxley in 1937. 'Would you consent to being the father of my wife's child, possibly by artificial insemination?'[37] One can well understand why the man would make the request. The Huxley family, seemingly, had the right stuff that anyone would want to graft on to their family tree. The dynasty of geniuses began with Julian's grandfather, Thomas Henry Huxley (1825–95), while Julian himself was a biologist, a transhumanist, poet, science fiction writer, secretary of London zoo, the first Unesco director general, and a broadcasting catalyst for David Attenborough. The rest of the Huxleys were no slouches either. Julian's physiologist half-brother Andrew was a Nobel laureate. Julian's son Francis was an anthropologist and founder of Survival International. The most famous Huxley, Julian's brother Aldous, author of *Brave New World* and devotee of consciousness-altering drugs, was perhaps a bit of an underachiever. The Huxleys were like the Kardashians in one sense only: it was hard to keep up with them.

History doesn't disclose whether Julian Huxley supplied his correspondent with the necessary genetic material, but it seems unlikely. What this anonymous man perhaps didn't appreciate was that, while there was not, and could not be, a Huxleyan genius gene, there was a worrying family history of mental illness. Thomas Henry Huxley and Julian both suffered from paralysing depression. Julian's brother Trevenen killed himself in his 20s. Aldous reintroduced Chaucer's term 'accidie' to describe the condition that 'forsloweth and forsluggeth' a man. Alison Bashford writes in *An Intimate History of Evolution: The Story of the Huxley Family*: 'This was what was passed from Thomas Henry Huxley to his grandson and what was inherited here and there across the wider family.'[38] Perhaps, *per impossibile*, genius could be transmitted by artificial insemination, it is equally possible mental health problems could be too. When his first son was born, Julian wrote: 'I see you now an infant. It is the eternal wish of fathers to instruct their sons in the art of living.' But how could he, when he had himself lived so much of his life in torment? He continued: 'Your mind will burn your feet because it is paved like Hell with unfulfilled desires, will mock you with its puny futility.'[39] It would be wicked through artificial insemination or a social policy of negative eugenics to ensure such inherited traits persisted.

The lesson of the Huxley dynasty is not so much that the flourishing of the race or humanity can be optimized through artificial insemination or genetic engineering as the one drawn by the poet Philip Larkin in 'This Be the Verse': 'Get out as early as you can. / And don't have any kids yourself.[40] As a social policy, Larkin's sardonic negative eugenics, with its corollary that abstinence improves the human stock by hastening its extinction, may be intolerable, but it would be infinitely less vile than the racist, classist, and inhumane eugenicist utopias imagined by Marie Stopes and Julian Huxley.

That said, Julian Huxley was awoken from his dogmatic eugenicist daydreams not by the importunate letter from a man asking that he impregnate his wife, but by revulsion for Nazi ideology. In *We Europeans: A Survey of 'Racial' Problems*, written in 1935 with the anthropologist Alfred Cort Haddon, he railed against the idea that the Aryan pure race could be recovered through forced sterilization and other reproductive practices.[41] There was no such thing as the Aryan race, he and Haddon argued; no excuse either for forced sterilization or the other evil experiments on humans being conducted then in Germany.

Nonetheless, Huxley continued to believe in improving humans through biological intervention. He argued for eugenics in a 1951 lecture delivered in Washington entitled 'Knowledge, Morality and Destiny' (in which he coined the term 'transhumanism'), even after Josef Mengele's murderous pseudo-scientific, eugenicist experiments at Auschwitz that were bent on confirming ideas of racial degeneracy among Jews and Gypsies.[42]

We may delude ourselves by thinking eugenics ended in the 20th century and that the Huxleys are best considered as part of the fossil record – dead white men whose ideas about human 'fitness' are repellent and obsolete. Not so, argues Alison Bashford compellingly. 'Less fit humans are every day diagnosed and made viable, in utero,' she writes. 'This might be good, this might be bad, but it is certainly fact.' Huxleyan transhumanist dreams are part of everyday lives, from gene-editing, abortion, and IVF to the accelerating extension of human life by means of cryogenics, which might be conceived not so much as test tube babies as test tube geriatrics. Bashford concludes: 'A neo-liberal, choice-oriented eugenics has become more or less normalized, a continuation of a

Darwin, Galton and Huxley world, much as we like to imagine that we live in a refusal of it.'[43]

'Great is our sin'

On 30 January 1922, John Hill pleaded guilty to the crime of grand larceny, namely the stealing of hams. Judge Holden of Yakima, Washington state, described the case:

> Hill, his wife, and five children, are all mentally subnormal, even for their situation in life. For many months the children have been half starved and half clothed. The case was brought to the attention of the public authorities through the discovery of the theft of the hams, since which time he and his family are partly dependent on public charity, and without the addition of more children to the family, will undoubtedly continue to be more or less of a public charge; with more children the extent of demand on public charity will, be increased.[44]

Judge Holden sentenced Hill from six months' to 15 years' imprisonment for stealing the hams, the sentence being suspended for good behaviour. He also suggested that Hill be vasectomized, to which the prisoner consented.

Hill was castrated at the judge's demand. A few years later, Julian Huxley's colleague J.B.S. Haldane reflected on the folly, perhaps even the stupidity, of the judge's ruling: 'It did not occur to the judge either that there might be any connection between the starvation of children and their mental dullness, or that there was anything wrong with conditions under which a beet sugar labourer could not earn enough to support five children.'[45] Haldane, that is to say, realized something that the judge did not: that 'mental dullness' is not so much a biological problem with a biological solution as one that could be remedied – not by sterilization, but by providing family allowances to those in dire financial straits. It's a story that recapitulates the bitter irony that arises so often in this history of stupidity, namely that those who have tried to wipe out stupidity have done so stupidly, by mobilizing delusions of human perfectibility and by a dull-witted misplaced faith in scientific methods to eradicate a phenomenon that may be ineradicable and certainly is not just biological in character but cultural and value laden. Stupidity is better thought of not as heritable or eliminable through genetic intervention but as a symptom of how humans judge and are judged – a culturally rather than biologically determined phenomenon.

Indeed, Haldane's broadside against the judge who ordered the castration of a putatively stupid man ostensibly to prevent the descent of his dull-wittedness recapitulates the wisdom that Charles Darwin realized when he wrote scathingly about slavery in his memoir *Voyage of the Beagle*: 'If the misery of our poor is caused not by the laws of nature, but by our institutions, great is our sin.'[46]

The intellectual inferiority of women

Darwin was not always so admirable in his opinions. In 1871, he wrote in *The Descent of Man*: 'The chief distinction in the intellectual powers of the two sexes is shewn by man's attaining to a higher eminence, in whatever he takes up, than can woman – whether requiring deep thought, reason, or imagination, or merely the use of the senses and hands.'[47]

We'll consider how Darwin came to this opinion in a moment, but it's worth stressing that claims of women's greater stupidity hardly died out when the lavish beard of the Victorian paterfamilias, as modelled so excellently by Darwin himself, was selected for extinction. Well into the 21st century, when one might have thought in one's stupid way that such sexist assertions might have become extinct, the claim that women are less fitted by biology for cognitively demanding tasks or careers persists.

In 2017, for instance, a software engineer called James Damore was fired from the tech corporation Google for claiming that men and women have biological differences that help explain why more men than women are employed in tech corporations. He went on to deny that these differences could be explained as social constructions in part because they are 'universal across human cultures' – though if he had any data culled from all human cultures, that would be surprising: most human cultures, I'll wager, don't keep data on the biological differences between men and women, still less on the biologically determined differences in intellectual abilities between the sexes.

In a paper entitled 'Google's Ideological Echo Chamber: How Bias Clouds Our Thinking about Diversity and Inclusion',[48] Damore wrote:

'On average, men and women biologically differ in many ways.' These biological differences, he claimed, produce personality differences. Women on average 'have more openness to feelings and aesthetics rather than ideas'. Women generally also have a stronger interest in 'people rather than things'. Women are more prone to extraversion than men, which is expressed in gregariousness rather than assertiveness; they are also prone to high anxiety and lower stress tolerance than men.

'We always ask why we don't see women in top leadership positions, but we never ask why see so many men in these jobs,' he wrote. Damore had an answer to the latter question: the 'primary metric' men are judged on is status. 'Note,' Damore added, 'the same forces that lead men into high pay/high stress jobs in tech and leadership cause men to take undesirable and dangerous jobs like coal mining, garbage collecting and firefighting.' But that argument falls apart: men in these allegedly 'undesirable' (actually, socially very desirable) manual jobs are, according to Damore, not seeking status by becoming miners, binmen, or firefighters, so the 'forces' that made them opt for these jobs are not the same as those for CEOs, presidents, or orchestral conductors, of whom more in a moment. The point he wanted to stress was that those biological differences between men and women, not social factors, still less sexist employment practices or misogynistic norms, accounted for more men being in top jobs than women. And the corollary of the supposed truth of that analysis is that employment practices such as those attempted at Google to try to change that ratio of women to men were folly.

For expressing these opinions in an internal memo, Damore was fired. Chief Executive Sundar Pichai said parts of Damore's memo 'violate our Code of Conduct and cross the line by advancing harmful gender stereotypes in our workplace'.[49] Damore went on to launch a class action lawsuit (which was later dismissed) aimed at exposing a cultural bias at Google towards promoting diversity and 'social justice' that, his suit claimed, had created a 'protected, distorted bubble of groupthink'.[50] Firing Damore may have been a mistake, not least because it helped make him a conservative cause célèbre, but more importantly because it would have been better to have kept him on the corporate payroll so that his biologically determinist views could be challenged rather than deemed unacceptable. Pichai believed otherwise: 'To suggest a group of our colleagues have traits that make them less biologically suited to that work is offensive and not OK.'[51]

In his memo, Damore drew on the 'empathising-systemising theory' devised by Simon Baron-Cohen, professor of developmental psychopathology at Cambridge University. 'My theory,' explained Baron-Cohen,

> is that the female brain is predominantly hard-wired for empathy, and that the male brain is predominantly hard-wired for understanding and building systems. . . . Empathising is the drive to identify another person's emotions and thoughts, and to respond to these with an appropriate emotion. The empathiser intuitively figures out how people are feeling, and how to treat people with care and sensitivity. Systemising is the drive to analyse and explore a system, to extract underlying rules that govern the behaviour of a system; and the drive to construct systems.[52]

These differences, he suggested, may explain why more men choose professions in science, technology, engineering and mathematics. Both empathizing and systemizing, clearly, involve demanding work, but the latter, in the way Baron-Cohen described it, is more intellectual. It's as if women are more intuitive even in the work of being empathetically insightful; men, deprived of such intuitions, one might suppose on this account, are better adapted to labour harder cognitively. This follows, of course, only if one endorses Baron-Cohen's taxonomy or accepts his idea that our brains are hard-wired in the way he suggests. Which one needn't do.

There are three kinds of brain according to Baron-Cohen's account. The type E, or female, brain is stronger at empathizing than systemising; the type S, or male, brain is stronger at systemizing than empathizing, while the balanced or type-B brain is equally strong at both. There is a test you can do to find out what kind of brain you have, which might be valuable if you suppose that you have a female brain trapped in a man's body (as I have long supposed to be my personal tragedy). Indeed, Baron-Cohen wrote: 'Not all men have the male brain, and not all women have the female brain. The central claim of this new theory is only that on average, more males than females have a brain of type S, and more females than males have a brain of type E.' Perhaps the great women of the past who broke through the patriarchy's glass ceilings – think Margaret Thatcher, Benazir Bhutto, Marie Curie, or Ada Lovelace – really had men's brains. In a sense, then, they really were men since otherwise they would not have been so clever, bent on achieving status and (so far as I can find out) relatively terrible at organizing coffee mornings. There will, according to Baron-Cohen's theory and Damore's memo, be women who are good at that essentially male excellence of reading maps, and women, too, who identify with the list-making protagonist of Nick Hornby's novel *High Fidelity*. There will be men who are more likely to spend hours happily engaged in what Baron-Cohen describes as female brain activities such as 'coffee mornings or pot-luck suppers, advising friends on relationship problems, or caring for friends, neighbours, or pets'.

In the same year as Damore wrote his fateful memo, the journal *Intelligence* published a paper called 'Sex Differences in Brain Size and General Intelligence (*G*)' that claimed to show that sex differences in brain morphology were responsible for sex differences in general intelligence (the so-called *g* factor – about which we will be hearing more in the next chapter). 'Males displayed higher scores on most of the brain characteristics, even after correcting for body size, and also scored approximately one fourth of a standard deviation higher on *g*,' wrote the paper's authors, psychologists Dimitri van der Linden, Curtis S. Dunkel, and Guy Madison. *G* (or general intelligence) is the measure of cognitive ability, they claimed, that represents 'the overall efficiency to process information and solve novel problems'.[53] The unstated corollary was that women are on average more stupid than men.

Baron-Cohen's work and papers such as this one are hugely controversial, not least because they suggest women are not biologically fitted for certain cognitively demanding tasks or jobs, and that men are better systematizers and otherwise more intellectually able – even if the bases for such claims are slender. 'Study after study has shown almost all behavioural and psychological differences between the sexes to be small or nonexistent,' wrote Angela Saini in *Inferior: How Science Got Women Wrong – and the New Research That's Rewriting the Story*. She continued: 'Cambridge University psychologist Melissa Hines and others have repeatedly demonstrated that boys and girls have little, if any, noticeable gaps between them when it comes to fine motor skills, spatial visualization, mathematics ability, and verbal fluency.'[54]

Even Damore suggested in his memo: 'Many of these differences are small and there's significant overlap between men and women, so you can't say anything about an individual given these population level distributions.' And yet such academic research as Damore relied upon suggested that men and women are naturally different, and that the roles socially assigned to us proceed from those differences, while effectively denying that those natural differences can ever be changed. By denying that sex differences have social rather than biological grounds, that research offered a dismal counsel: the world we live in, in which women are often treated as second-class citizens, regarded as lacking the right stuff – be it grey matter or muscle power – to be appointed to jobs ranging from computer programmers to front-line soldiers, and are properly understood as more stupid than men, receives dubious justification. Women are inferior by nature; just accept it.

Such claims of sex dimorphism, then, particularly when they involve differences in cognitive abilities, are hardly merely academic matters but have real-world impacts. The idea that women are inferior to men helps, for some, to justify the continuation of everything from workplace sexism to the abortion of unborn girls by parents who value boys over girls. The assertion on slender grounds of sex-based differences between men and women, one might well think, could serve to reinforce sexist norms that are accepted unwittingly by those who should know better.

Consider what happened to the orchestral conductor Marin Alsop when she boarded an aircraft and looked into the cockpit. There were three women inside, and there was every likelihood that they would be flying the thing. 'My first reaction was "Uh-oh",' she told me in 2005. She was not proud of her instinctive response. 'Of course, it turned out to be the smoothest flight I'd ever been on. But my reaction was very thought-provoking. I guess I'm as much a victim of societal programming as the next person.'[55]

This honest admission was surprising from Alsop, one of the very few women conductors in the world and one who is proud to call herself a feminist. What a horrible shock to find you had unconsciously internalized a sexist agenda, I said to her. 'Well, yes. When I watch TV news now, I notice that we've become accustomed to seeing a man and a woman presenting. Twenty years ago it was just all men. If it's two women, it doesn't seem quite right.' Why? 'It's all about comfort levels.

It's not all specifically about capability or connection of knowledge. It's much more abstract.'

I mention this story because it shows how easy it is to internalize norms that turn out to be stupid, not least that women pilots don't have the right stuff to get a passenger jet to its destination without terminating its human payload and that therefore they should hand over the controls to men. It's depressing that Alsop, who one might consider heroic for demonstrating that conducting an orchestra is a suitable job for a woman, internalized sexist norms, but it isn't surprising: in a patriarchal society, the inferiority of women, cognitively and otherwise, is upheld by often unspoken norms and codes. Scientists, wittingly or unwittingly, have contributed to this image of women as inferior. As Angela Saini put it:

> Science has failed to rid us of the gender stereotypes and dangerous myths we've been laboring under for centuries. Women are so grossly underrepresented in modern science because, for most of history, they were treated as intellectual inferiors and deliberately excluded from it. It should come as no surprise, then, that this same scientific establishment has also painted a distorted picture of the female sex. This, in turn again, has skewed how science looks and what it says even now.[56]

The attempt to justify male superiority to women has a long and unedifying pedigree. In 1680, Sir Robert Filmer's *Patriarcha*[57] argued that patriarchy was ordered by God. The American founding father Thomas Jefferson wrote that 'the tender breasts of ladies were not formed for political convulsion',[58] which is not only untrue but also weird.

Misogyny, that is to say, and its attendant belief that women are more stupid than men, proceeds from regarding such differences as natural and unchangeable rather than as features of patriarchal society that can and should be changed. That is not to suggest that any of the above proponents of biological determinism are misogynists; rather, that their thinking is helpful to those who are. John Stuart Mill wrote in *The Subjection of Women* in 1869: 'Was there ever any domination which did not appear natural to those who possessed it?'[59] Mill was writing at a time when women in England were not so much human beings as the property of their husbands. What he denied is what Damore, Baron-Cohen, and other present-day defenders of biologically determined sex differences assert, namely that men are essentially different from women and likely to be more cognitively developed. Mill also denied their assertion that social factors are irrelevant to accounting for these sex differences. He wrote in a passage worth quoting at length:

> I deny that anyone knows or can know, the nature of the two sexes, as long as they have only been seen in their present relation to one another. Until conditions of equality exist, no one can possibly assess the natural differences between women and men, distorted as they have been. What is natural to the two sexes can only be found out by allowing both to develop and use their faculties freely.
>
> Women are brought up to act as if they were weak, emotional, docile – a traditional prejudice. If we tried equality, we would see that there were benefits for individual women. They would be free of the unhappiness of being told what to do by men. And there would be benefits for society at large – it would double the mass of mental faculties available for the higher service of humanity. The ideas and potential of half the population would be liberated, producing a great effect on human development.[60]

Or to put it another way, how stupid of any society to hinder its development by harnessing only half of that society's brain power. (It's worth pointing out in this regard that although it was Mill's name on the jacket of *The Subjection of Women*, his ideas for the book were developed with his wife Harriet and daughter Helen: men often need women to overcome their stupidity.)

And yet, two years later, Charles Darwin wrote the words that we quoted at the start of this section claiming that women were less capable of deep thought than men. In the next sentence, he added the following:

> If two lists were made of the most eminent men and women in poetry, painting, sculpture, music (inclusive both of composition and performance), history, science, and philosophy, with half-a-dozen names under each subject, the two lists would not bear comparison. We may also infer, from the law of the deviation from averages, so well illustrated by Mr Galton, in his work on 'Hereditary Genius', that if men are capable of a decided pre-eminence over women in many subjects, the average of mental power in man must be above that of woman.[61]

It scarcely seems to have occurred to Darwin that in a patriarchal Victorian society (and one recently indicted by his countryman J.S. Mill) where opportunities for women are lower than for men, the two lists might not reflect men's higher eminence, but rather be symptomatic of the dearth of opportunities for women. There may historically have been more male conductors than female ones not because the former were biologically more suited to the job but because the ascent of women to the podium was blocked by the stupid thoughts of men about women's abilities.

'Even he,' wrote Angela Saini, 'the father of evolutionary biology, was so affected by a culture of sexism that he believed women to be the intellectually inferior sex.'[62] I love the force of that exasperated 'even': it's as if Saini is saying, 'Good grief, Darwin, we expected better from you!'

In *The Descent of Man*, Darwin developed an evolutionary argument for men's intellectual superiority to women being not just natural but in part a result of natural selection. Among the half-human progenitors of man 'and amongst savages', wrote Darwin, there are typically struggles for possession of females. But physical strength and size are not decisive factors: courage, perseverance, and determined energy are also required for victory. Equally, these males have to defend their females and hunt for subsistence: to do so successfully, again, they need more than physical strength. They need in addition or instead what Darwin called 'the higher mental faculties, namely, observation, reason, invention, or imagination. These various faculties will thus have been continually put to the test and selected during manhood.' These faculties are developed in men through sexual selection (i.e. the contest with rival males) and also in natural selection, 'that is, from success in the general struggle for life. In both cases, though, the characters gained will have been transmitted more fully to the male than to the female offspring. Thus, man has ultimately become superior to woman.'[63]

Darwin was clearly aware of Mill's recently published heretical views on women since in a footnote in *The Descent of Man* he quotes the following from *The Subjection of Women* to clinch his point that women are, and indeed always will be, intellectually inferior to men: 'The things in which man most excels woman are those which require most plodding, and long hammering at single thoughts.' To this Darwin added the gloss: 'What is this but energy and perseverance?'[64]

What strikes me here is the bracing stupidity of both men. Reading Mill's remark, I thought contrarily of the women who worked breaking Nazi codes at Bletchley Park early in World War II. 'It was very, very boring, just subtracting one row of figures for another,' recalled one of those women. 'She was working as a *human* computer, engaged in the laborious task of manually processing German messages,' wrote Neil Lawrence in *The Atomic Human: Understanding Ourselves in the Age of AI*.[65] And without those women's dogged energy and perseverance, the allies might not have done that thing men are supposedly biologically more suited to than mere women, namely won the intelligence war.

Reading Darwin's gloss on Mill's remark, I doubted if, really, either of these great men had ever met a woman. Clearly if they had, they weren't paying attention. Assertion of extremely dubious opinions as facts, or socially conditioned sexist views dressed up as profound insights into human nature, are not what I expect from Victorian England's most eminent intellectuals. But then even the greatest minds are capable of remarkable stupidity.

7

Stupid Intelligence

The hunt for the g factor

In 1904, the French psychologist Alfred Binet was asked by the minister of public education to devise a way of identifying struggling children so that they might be given special help to develop their intellectual capabilities.

The director of the psychology laboratory at the Sorbonne was the right man for the job. Binet disdained the idea that intelligence was innate and that those deemed stupid were incorrigible victims of inferior biology. He disdained, too, the Malthus-inspired eugenicist notion we explored in the previous chapter whereby the feeble-minded were best expunged from humanity instead of being allowed to breed and thus dumb down the species. Rather, Binet came to regard intelligence as a capacity and not an irredeemable feature of a person's biology, and held that public education should be a means of helping children improve their intellectual capacities.

Earlier in his career, Binet studied blindfolded chess players as part of his work on the psychology of mental arithmetic. He found that the adepts of blindfold chess did not, as one might suppose, see pictorial representations of the positions on a chessboard in their minds' eyes. Chess intelligence, if there is such a unitary phenomenon, he thought, need not require visualization.

More importantly, Binet had flirted in his earlier years with craniometry, the pseudo-science of reading off intelligence from measurements of skull sizes. Like its contemporary pseudo-science phrenology, which posited that measurement of bumps on the skull could predict mental traits, craniometry was popular at the time since it seemed to suggest that evanescent mental phenomena could be expressed by hard physical evidence and, most importantly, measured. In this, Binet followed contemporaries like his countryman Pierre Paul Broca and the Englishman Thomas Henry Huxley, who contended that skull size and intelligence were incontestably linked.

Binet found otherwise when he visited schools to measure the heads of children. He failed to find a correlation between children's intelligence and the size the anterior regions of the skull where higher intelligence was purportedly located; worse, some of the least intellectually able children he measured had anteroposterior skull diameters three millimetres greater than those of their ostensibly smarter peers, contrary to Broca's hypothesis. He ultimately abandoned such craniometric means of measuring human intelligence and increasingly favoured psychological tests. This shift had this important corollary: a person's intellectual potential was no longer constrained by the size of their skull but plastic, mutable and, ultimately, improvable.

Indeed, when he visited schools, Binet condemned those teachers who supposed some of their children irredeemably stupid and made matters worse by telling them so. He wrote:

> They have neither sympathy or respect for [those students], and their intemperate language leads them to say such things in their presence as 'This child will never amount to anything . . . he is not intelligent at all.' How often have I heard these imprudent words.. . . Never! What a momentous word. Some recent thinkers seem to have given their moral support to the deplorable verdicts by affirming that an individual's intelligence is a fixed quantity, a quantity that cannot be increased. We must react against this brutal pessimism; we must try to demonstrate that it is founded on nothing.[1]

For Binet, then, the stupid are not always with us, lumpen and unchangeable: they need our help, not least because, we must hypothesize, they cannot help themselves. The biologically determined racism and classism of a eugenicist like Marie Stopes who recommended contraceptive means to prevent the lower classes breeding and thereby to eliminate feeble-mindless was inimical to Binet. In this hopeful vision of the development of human intellectual capabilities, he was much influenced by John Stuart Mill, the Victorian philosopher and politician who counselled that if polities such as Britain were to become truly civilized – which he thought, in his whimsical way, would be a good idea – the spread of property and intelligence throughout the population would be necessary. 'I yield to no one in the degree of intelligence of which I believe [the people] to be capable,' wrote Mill in *The Spirit of the Age*,[2] while in an essay entitled 'Civilisation' he wrote:

> The most remarkable of those consequences of advancing civilisation, which the state of the world is now forcing upon the attention of thinking minds, is this: that power passes more and more from individuals, and small knots of individuals, to masses – that the importance of the masses becomes constantly greater, that of individuals less. There are two elements of importance and influence among mankind: the one is, property; the other, powers and acquirements of mind. Both of these, in an early stage of civilisation, are confined to a few persons.[3]

But in what Mill called 'a state of high civilisation', the diffusion of property and intelligence, and the power of cooperation, would be widespread. The patronizing reference to the 'masses' notwithstanding, Mill's optimistic sense – so very different from, say, his contemporary Flaubert's bleak vision of an unstoppably rising tide of human stupidity, or the eugenicist delusion that genetic intervention and/or state-directed contraceptive measures could check human stupidity for good – underpinned Binet's approach. The Frenchman believed that by means of exercises known as 'mental orthopaedics', the intelligence of children who were showing low levels of attainment could be improved.

But before such mental orthopaedics could be performed, it was necessary to find out which children needed help. To that end, Binet, working with his student Theodore Simon, devised a series of tests aimed at arriving at a single score for each child's cognitive abilities. These were a hodge-podge of diverse tasks and questions such as coin counting, naming the months of the year, noticing missing parts in pictures, arranging weights in order, and assessing which face was 'prettier' (something the founder of eugenics, Francis Galton, might well have excelled at, given his proclivity for drawing up beauty maps). Trained examiners led individual children through the tasks, which ascended in difficulty. As Stephen Jay Gould put it:

> He hoped that by mixing together enough tests of different abilities he would be able to extract a child's general potential with a single score. Binet emphasized the empirical nature of his work with a famous dictum: 'One might almost say it matters very little what the tests are so long as they are numerous.'[4]

Such was the theoretical basis for the world's first IQ tests. Today, the intelligence test industry is big business and there are many IQ tests available on the market, including the Snijders–Oomen Nonverbal Intelligence Test, the Cattell Culture Fair Intelligence Test, the Synthetic Aperture Personality Assessment Project, the Kaufman Assessment Battery for Children, the Otis–Lennon School Ability Test, the Woodcock–Johnson Test, Raven's Progressive Matrices, and the Wechsler Intelligence Scale for Children. Today the intelligence quotients of not just children but also adults and even nations are estimated. Since Binet devised his tests, the IQs of geographical regions and even races have been estimated, often using parameters that have been, to put it mildly, controversial.

Looking back at the birth of the IQ test in the early years of the 20th century, one striking phenomenon is that although these tests boiled down a child's intelligence to a single score, in fact Binet and Simon failed to discover one general factor of intelligence. By contrast, working across the English Channel at the same time, the British army-officer-turned-psychologist Charles Spearman claimed to have found just this factor, which has become known as *g*. Spearman examined schoolchildren's scores on different subjects and found that they were positively correlated. That suggested to him that children had differences in general mental ability. What he thought he found in his data in 1904 was, as Stephen Jay Gould puts it, 'a unitary, rankable, genetically based and minimally alterable thing in the head'.[5] Later psychologists, notably the American Lewis Thurstone, argued that intelligence was not unitary in the way Spearman had supposed; rather, there were between three and seven separable mental abilities, though, like Spearman's *g*, each was minimally alterable.

Binet and Simon, unlike Spearman and Thurstone, were not hunting for *g*, or for any other minimally alterable things in the head that ostensibly determined one's intelligence. For them, intelligence was not biologically given. Rather, they set themselves the task of trying to establish a baseline of intelligence for each age that might serve to help discover which children were struggling and needed assistance to improve. They did this, more or less arbitrarily, by sorting the data from tests by levels of achievement for each age and establishing thereby its normal intellectual level.

Having established these baselines, Binet, Simon, and their examiners set to work testing children to find those whose IQs fell below the normal intellectual level for their age. As children proceeded through these tests, with tasks and questions ascending in difficulty, they would find they reached a point where they could go no further because the latest task was too difficult. The age associated by Binet and Simon with this last task established the child's mental age. That child's intellectual level was arrived at initially by subtracting this mental age from the child's actual age, but – as we saw in chapter 6 – later by dividing it by chronological age and then multiplying this number by 100. Thus, if a child had a mental age of 12 and a chronological age of eight, their IQ would be 150 (because 12 ÷ 8 × 100 = 150). Each child, then, was given a number indicating their intelligence quotient.

While Binet never intended this single number to be the irredeemable marker of a child's intellectual capacities, it became so. Completely contrary to their intentions, the Frenchmen facilitated later theorists on intelligence to suppose that an IQ score correlated with a biological entity. This is an example of the stupid human tendency of false reification, a phenomenon John Stuart Mill skewered:

> The tendency has always been strong to believe that whatever received a name must be an entity or being, having an independent existence of its own. And if no real entity answering to the name could be found, men did not for that reason suppose that none existed but imagined that it was something peculiarly abstruse and mysterious.[6]

That tendency has always been rife in the attempt to establish what intelligence is, from craniometry to the hunt for *g*. By contrast, rightly understood, Binet and Simon's method involved no such false reification: there was no ghost in their machine, no thing behind the figures, just rankings of data and norms imposed on the data sets of children's performances. And yet the IQ tests they devised have been used to try to show that scores are evidence for things fixed and heritable in one's head. Worse, IQ tests have been perverted to serve racist agendas and cruel immigration policies, particularly in the US. IQ testing has been used to confirm racist prejudices that those with darker skins are less intellectually able and therefore must be prevented, by means of judicious immigration policies or, in extremis, by artificial selection, from corrupting the intellectual levels of existing populations.

Examples of the kind of tasks that Binet and Simon devised abound today online. If you want to find out how clever or stupid you are according to what has become known as the Stanford–Binet Test (of which more below), you can log on and learn the bitter truth. Here are a few examples of questions you may be asked:

1 Which object is least like the others: Tree, book, song caricature, bowl.
2 Choose the word that correctly completes the following sentence.
   This bike _____ in the garage: Goes. Going. Go. Gone.
3 Max needed to get seven new doors from the home-improvement store for his house. His car could only hold two doors at once. How many times did Max have to visit the store?
4 Which identical three-letter word, when placed in front of the following words, forms a new word? BOY, HIDE, LICK, POKE, HAND
5 What is the next letter in this sequence? A B A C B C B D C[7]

Binet worried about the misuses to which his invention of the IQ test might be put, in particular that the designation of a child's IQ could be used as an excuse not to help improve intellectual capacities, but to exclude disruptive pupils. He wrote: 'They seem to reason in the following way: "Here is an excellent opportunity for getting rid of all the children who trouble us."'[8] Binet declined to regard IQ as a number indicating a child's inborn intelligence but saw it as a tool to rank pupils in order to practically identify those who needed extra help. Sadly, Binet's fears about the misuse of his tests was well founded. As the American psychologist Leon Kamin wrote: 'It is perhaps as well that Binet died in

1911, before witnessing the uses to which his test was speedily put in the United States.'[9] Stephen Jay Gould summed up this perversion of the Frenchman's original intention: 'The distortion of his wise and humane effort must rank among one of the great tragedies of twentieth-century science.'[10]

In 1910, the segregationist and eugenicist Henry Herbert Goddard, whom we met briefly in the previous chapter, translated Binet's test into English for use in American schools. At the time, the psychologist was director of the Vineland School for Feeble-Minded Girls and Boys in New Jersey. Goddard was particularly interested in using the test to ensure that immigrants with low intellectual capacities were kept out of the US. To that end, in 1917 he performed a study at Ellis Island, the primary entry point for those hoping to immigrate. With the aid of an interpreter, he tested 30 adult Jews using the English version of Binet's test. Goddard determined that 25 of them were 'feeble-minded' on the basis of their performance on a word fluency section. He wrote:

> What shall we say of the fact that only 45 percent can give sixty words in three minutes, when normal children of 11 years sometimes give 200 words in that time! It is hard to find an explanation except lack of intelligence or lack of vocabulary and such a lack of vocabulary in an adult would probably mean lack of intelligence. How could a person live even 15 years in any environment without learning hundreds of names of which he could certainly think of 60 in three minutes?[11]

Goddard did not factor into his study the traumatic circumstances in which they were performed. Indeed, according to his initial results from tests performed at Ellis Island on four immigrant groups, an astounding 83% of Jews were feeble-minded, while 80% of the Hungarians tested, 79% of the Italians, and 87% of the Russians were deemed similarly stupid. Although Goddard later altered the parameters of his tests to produce less ludicrous results, he still maintained that the average intelligence of the immigrants he tested – those who had travelled third class on incoming ships – was 'low, perhaps of moron grade'. He concluded: 'We are now getting the poorest of each race.' On the basis of this profoundly stupid misapplication of Binet's tests, he argued that 'if the American public wishes feeble-minded aliens excluded, it must demand that Congress provide the necessary facilities at the ports of entry.'[12]

The spirit of Goddard's counsel was, to put it mildly, the opposite of that expressed in the lines from Emma Lazarus's Petrarchan sonnet 'The New Colossus' which is emblazoned on the Statue of Liberty:

> Give me your tired, your poor,
> Your huddled masses yearning to breathe free,
> The wretched refuse of your teeming shore.
> Send these, the homeless, tempest-tost to me,
> I lift my lamp beside the golden door!

Lazarus imagined that the wretched of the earth could be born again, that they could realize their hitherto thwarted potential; Goddard looked on these aliens and supposed the opposite, that their virus of feeble-mindedness must be checked and that the proper injunction was not 'Send these, the homeless, tempest-tost to me', but rather the clarion call of racists from that day to this, namely 'Send them back!'

To clinch the fact that the virus of racist stupidity still infects America, consider how Donald Trump launched his presidential election campaign in 2015 with an attack on Mexico for 'sending people [to the US] that have lots of problems. They are bringing drugs, and bringing crime, and their rapists.' Latino immigrants were more likely to rape than Americans, he charged. 'If you look at the statistics of people coming, you look at the statistics on rape, on crime, on everything coming in illegally into this country it's mind-boggling!' he told a CNN interviewer. When it was pointed out that Trump had misread the article on which he based his opinion and that it had in fact reported that 80% of women crossing the Mexican border are raped along the way, often by criminal gangs, traffickers, or corrupt officials, Trump declined to retract his racist slur, retorting: 'Well, somebody's doing the raping, Don!'[13] If stupidity is a virus – and I'm not saying it is – it's one from which even American presidents refuse to be inoculated.

No matter. Thanks to Goddard's translation, Binet's IQ test spread virally through the US in the early 20th century, mutating as it went. A leading early champion was Lewis Terman, professor of psychology at Stanford University, who extended the Binet test to include older children and adults. Moreover, he refined the test, including multiple-choice questions such as 'Napoleon was defeated at: Leipzig/Paris/Verdun/Waterloo' and absurd statements whose logical fallacies those being tested were tasked with exposing, such as: 'Yesterday the police found the body of a girl cut into 18 pieces. They believe that she killed herself.' The revised test became known as the Stanford–Binet test.[14]

Terman was much less cautious than Binet about the benefits to society of mental testing. He thought that IQ tests could help not just identify struggling children, but also reduce crime and prostitution, strengthen the gene pool by segregating the mentally defective, and even identify future national leaders by means of fast-tracking children who did well in tests. For good or ill, that last hope was never realized.

During World War I, Terman worked with Professor Robert Yerkes of Harvard University and Goddard to test the intelligences of two million army draftees. Their aim was to classify new recruits by intellectual capabilities and also to make group comparisons by racial origin. To this end, Jerkes developed two IQ tests, known as the Army Alpha and Beta tests. The former was a written test, while the Army Beta consisted of pictures for those recruits who were illiterate or didn't speak English. In his 1923 book *A Study of American Intelligence*, eugenicist and professor at Princeton's Department of Psychology Carl C. Brigham detected a pattern in the data. 'Foreign born white drafts' performed worse than 'native born white drafts', which suggested to him that those who had lived in the US for shorter periods were likely to be intellectually inferior. He explained his findings in racial terms:

> Migrations of the Alpine and Mediterranean races have increased to such an extent in the last thirty or forty years that this blood now constitutes 70 percent or 75 percent of the total immigration. The representatives of the Alpine and Mediterranean races in our immigration are intellectually inferior to the representatives of the Nordic race which formerly made up about 50 percent of our immigration.[15]

More likely than this racist account in explaining these differences was the fact that those who lived in the US longer were more likely to be familiar with how American society functioned, a familiarity that was assumed in some of the questions. For instance, one question the draftees were invited to answer was: 'Why should a married man have his life insured?' Here the wrong answer, far from showing only relative unfamiliarity with American society and its social norms, was read off as a sign of stupidity and ultimately demonstrated the inferiority of foreign-born white draftees.

Eugenicist lobbying of Congress, often relying on the data from the Alpha and Beta IQ tests, led to what Stephen Jay Gould calls 'one of the greatest victories for scientific racism in American history'.[16] In 1921, the first Immigration Restriction Act set yearly quotas at 3% of immigrants from any nation then resident in America. The 1924 act of the same name reset the quota at 2%, and also did something more perversely racist. Instead of using the 1920 census to determine which immigrants would be admitted and which refused according to the quotas, the 1890 census was used. The reason, Gould suggests plausibly, is that in 1890 southern and eastern Europeans were arriving in the US in relatively small numbers, but thereafter became the predominant groups of European immigrants. The legislation, that is to say, racially profiled southern and eastern Europeans as more likely to be feeble-minded and therefore worthy of being kept out. Like Trump's policy of building a wall to keep out Mexican immigrants, the 1924 act involved keeping out those deemed undesirable aliens (some of whom may well have been the brightest and the best, and indeed intellectual boons to the US) while, one might infer, ring-fencing domestic stupidity within. Calvin Coolidge, then US president, signed the bill, remarking: 'America must be kept American.'[17] If so, the noble words of the sonnet on the Statue of Liberty amounted to false advertising.

During the 20th century, IQ tests became not just the basis of racist legislation, but also a lucrative business. For instance, at the time of writing, the fourth UK edition of the WAIS-IV intelligence testing kit is available for £1,827.74 (plus £4.50 delivery) from Pearson Clinical, the psychological testing company that developed the product in the US and UK.

WAIS stands for Wechsler Adult Intelligence Scale. It was one of several scales developed by David Wechsler, chief psychologist at New York's Bellevue Psychiatric Hospital, in the mid-20th century. The series of tests bearing his name began with the Wechsler–Bellevue Intelligence Scales I and II in 1939 and 1942. Those were followed by the Wechsler Intelligence Scale for Children (1949), the Wechsler Adult Intelligence Scale (1955), and the Wechsler Preschool and Primary Scale of Intelligence (1967). Wechsler devised these in part because he became convinced of the shortcomings of existing intelligence tests, particularly the Stanford–Binet scale. He believed Binet's calculation of children's mental ages was inapplicable to adults whose intelligence he sought to test, not least because Binet did not consider the possibility that intelligence might decline with age. This seems plausible, not least because it fits with how later psychologists have supposed intelligence may be divided into fluid and crystallized forms. The former, say, for instance, writing your first computer program, is different from calculating the surface area of the base of a pyramid using a formula that you know: on the face of it, younger people have more fluid intelligence and less crystallized intelligence, on average, than older ones. Or at least that intuition might be a handy rule of thumb.

Wechsler thought the Binet scale was inadequate for his purposes, too, because it emphasized speed, with timed tasks scattered throughout the tests, and that factor tended to unduly handicap older adults. Instead of defining average intelligence by the standard of mental age, as Binet and Simon had done, Wechsler used the mean score of all members of a certain group to describe the average intelligence of that group. The group could be all those of a certain age or all those members of a particular population. Wechsler's method involved totalling the sub-scores for the many different tests of reasoning, memory, general knowledge, and processing speed and comparing them with other scores to arrive at an average score, which he set at 100. Thus, the person of perfectly average intelligence in a group would have an IQ of 100, with underperformers scoring less than that number and overperformers scoring more.

Wechsler's original tests aimed to correct Binet's shortcomings but were also predicated on a paradox that the Frenchman did not consider, namely that human intelligence might be enhanced or hobbled by non-cognitive factors. 'We have tended to separate the intellect and the emotions too much,' Wechsler told the 1949 annual meeting of the American Psychological Association.[18] Previous intelligence tests, he thought, overlooked vital factors such as temperament, impulse, and instinct. That insistence on the importance of emotional factors in accounting for human behaviour or assessing cognitive excellence was an abiding theme of Wechsler's work. In 1926, he had worked on a lie-detecting device relying on electric currents to trace a witness's emotions, independent of bodily factors that their consciousness might control. In 1929, Wechsler wrote for the *New York Times* that a pilot's emotional stability was as important a factor in safety as fitness. He later defined intelligence as 'the global capacity of a person to act purposefully, to think rationally, and to deal effectively with his environment',[19] but emphasized that that global capacity, itself intellectual, required non-intellectual elements to work effectively. That recognition of the importance of non-intellectual factors to the functioning of intelligence – not just such matters identified by Wechsler such as emotions, temperament, impulse, and instinct but also environmental matters such as nutrition, domestic circumstances, and access to education – is one of the elements that makes testing for intelligence, even if it is possible, so controversial.

Wechsler was just the kind of immigrant whom the Immigration Restriction Act of 1924 was designed to keep out of America so that it didn't become feeble-minded. A Romanian Jew, he was born in Lespezi in 1896 and emigrated to the US as a child, thus missing rejection by legislation's racist quota system. Just as well: Wechsler went on to become one of the most eminent US psychologists of the 20th century, proving a boon to American society and to the world in general. In 1947, for instance, he helped set up a mental health programme and clinic for Jewish survivors of the Holocaust. Moreover, the intelligence scales he devised have been used to help diagnose and ameliorate the effects of strokes and other neurological conditions. When the American Psychological Association gave him its Award for Distinguished Professional Contribution in 1973, it noted that Wechsler's contributions had 'played a critical role in the lives and careers of millions of individuals throughout the world'.[20]

His psychometric tests, like Binet's, were devised to help identify those struggling and to help them overcome their problems, rather than to brand them for life with the curse or boast of an immutable IQ number. Like Binet, he developed a battery of sub-tests to measure a variety of abilities, not, as the Frenchman had done, testing only children, but adults, too. But he was also convinced of the idea that there was a general factor of intelligence, or *g*. In this, he was influenced by his studies as a psychology student with Charles Spearman in London and by the work he did during World War I on intelligence tests performed by draftees.

Indeed, like Spearman, he was convinced that though there were different cognitive abilities, such as verbal comprehension and perceptual reasoning, all were positively correlated. That's to say, if you were good at one kind of task, such as arithmetical calculation, you were likely to be good at others, too. But if there was a general factor in intelligence, it was not, for Wechsler, biologically determined. Rather, the existence of *g* emerged from analysing test data. In this, Wechsler's intelligence scales were based on a very different idea of what intelligence is than that proposed by the founder of the IQ test. Binet, after all, had written of his test: 'The scale, properly speaking, does not permit the measure of the intelligence, because intellectual qualities are not superposable, and therefore cannot be measured as linear surfaces are measured.'[21]

The most recent Wechsler intelligence scale, the WAIS-IV, proceeds from the conviction derived from data that intellectual qualities are indeed superposable, at least in the sense of being positively correlated. The WAIS-IV involves 15 sub-tests in which a variety of cognitive capacities are tested under the following categories. Here they are, along with some typical questions:

Similarities. For instance, state in what way a symphony and a painting are alike?

Vocabulary. State what certain words mean. For example, Chair. Presumptuous.

Information. For example, who wrote *The Iliad*?

Comprehension. For example, examiners might ask for explanations of why we put food in a fridge or buy life insurance?

Block Design. Use wooden cubes painted red and white to duplicate a design shown on cards.

Matrix Reasoning. Find a missing element in a pattern built up in a logical manner.

Visual Puzzles. Find the shapes that when combined make up the shape at the top of the page.

Figure Weights. Find the correct weights to balance a scale.

Picture Completion. Spot missing elements in a series of drawings.

Digit Span. Repeat to the examiner a sequence of numbers of up to nine digits (for example 2, 5, 4, 7, 6, 7, 8, 1, 2).

Arithmetic. Perform mental tasks including addition, multiplication, subtraction, and division.

Letter–Number Sequencing. From a list of alternating numbers and letters, place first the numbers into numerical order and then the letters into alphabetical order.

Symbol Search. Identify from a given list of symbols which symbol in a given pair of symbols is included in the list.

Coding. Write down the symbol that corresponds to a given number (this timed test requires those being tested to identify as many correspondences as they can in two minutes).

Cancellation. For example, a sheet contains blue and green triangles and squares. Draw a line through as many blue squares and green triangles as possible.[22]

Many of these tasks are time limited and, like the tasks and questions Binet gave to his schoolchildren in the early years of the 20th century, test for a wide range of mental functions such as drawing inferences, manipulating symbols, verbal reasoning, and general knowledge.

But how, then, might the WAIS-IV test indicate that there is a general factor of intelligence? Before the WAIS-IV intelligence scale was commercially released in 2008, some 1,800 Americans from a variety of ethnicities, ages, and locations were invited to sit all 15 sub-tests by examiners and psychologists from Pearson Education. The data culled from these results showed that, of the possible 105 correlations between each of the sets, all were positive. Ian J. Deary, professor of differential psychology at Edinburgh University, claims the data shows that:

'Performing well on one of the tests tends to go well with performing well on the others.' This is surprising: one might have thought that a person's powers of general knowledge might be unrelated to their skills at arithmetic or solving visual puzzles. Not so, argues Professor Deary. 'There are no near-to-zero correlations. There are no tests that are negatively correlated with other ones.'[23]

That said, the results from some sub-tests are more strongly correlated than others. For instance, the sub-tests for similarities, vocabulary, information, and comprehension more strongly correlate with each other than with other categories tested. This, surmises Deary, means that these tests can be grouped together under a 'hypothetical entity called "verbal comprehension"'. Other similarly correlated subtests can be brought under headings. Ultimately, four headings were derived for the WAIS-IV scale, namely a Verbal Comprehension Index (VCI), a Perceptual Reasoning Index (PRI), a Working Memory Index (WMI), and a Processing Speed Index (PSI). 'The message from this large study,' Deary suggests, 'is that just under half of the differences among a large group of adults may be attributed to mental ability that is required to perform all tests.' But this is where matters get interesting, or, depending on your politics, controversial. Deary writes: 'We call that g or "general intelligence" or "general cognitive ability". Therefore it makes sense to refer to a general type of mental ability. There is something common to people's performance differences across many different types of mental test.'[24]

But is there? Deary's sense of what the message is runs very close to what John Stuart Mill called false reification. Correlations do not show 'something common' as if that 'something' were a phenomenon or thing that could be identified. Strikingly, Deary immediately qualifies this message to avoid the implication that intelligence is a general factor corresponding to a thing in the head or the notion that the general factor or *g* might indicate there is a gene for intelligence. He writes: 'It is important to be clear that g is a statistical result, but it is emphatically not a statistical artefact.'

But the statistical result that is caught in the net of the WAIS-IV intelligence test is hardly beyond question. For example, why should processing speed be a marker of intelligence? Might those who answer questions more slowly but whose answers are just as likely to be correct be deemed less intelligent than others? The answer to that seems to be that the tests are devised according to the broad definition of intelligence given by David Wechsler above. Indeed, quite possibly those questions that test for 'processing speed' might stem from the conviction in Wechsler's definition that intelligence is in part to do with a 'person's capacity to deal effectively with his environment'. That's to say, an incapacity to deal effectively with one's environment might be regarded not as symptom of a lack of intelligence, but rather as an existential inability that, in principle, stupid and intelligent persons are equally prone to.

The more general point here is that Wechsler's definition of intelligence that forms the basis for the intelligence scales he devised is not beyond question. The niggling sense remains that what he and his successors test for are precisely those capacities that can be readily tested rather than those that demonstrate intelligence, whatever that is. For instance, why not test for emotional intelligence? Well, quite possibly, one might reply, emotional capacities are hard – perhaps even impossible – to measure, even though the eminent psychologist who devised the test had at least an intuitive sense that such factors were key in explaining intelligence. But then Wechsler himself stressed the importance of emotional factors to good cognitive functioning. Only capacities amenable to testing, to providing data and cross-correlations between those capacities and other hypothetical capacities, can supply the basis for determining a person's intelligence. And that method, on the face of it, seems not just dubious but also stupid.

For more than a century now, intelligence tests have been dogged by the remark made in 1923 by the psychologist Edwin G. Boring: 'Intelligence as a measurable capacity must at the start be defined as the capacity to do well in an intelligence test. Intelligence is what the tests test.'[25] The corollary of this is that which cannot be measured, or not measured easily, even if it conforms to the cultural understanding of what intelligence is, is by definition not intelligence. But that corollary points up a paradox, namely that we all recognize intelligence when we see it, but we can hardly say what it is (and as a result, definitions of intelligence such as Wechsler's above seem wrong in that they fail to capture plausibly what we mean by the term).

Justin Gregg, in his book *If Nietzsche Were a Narwhal: What Animal Intelligence Tells Us about Human Stupidity*, notes that narwhals can't write symphonies or send robots to Mars. It might therefore be worth tentatively suggesting that narwhals are less intelligent than us. But Gregg, who basks in the job title of Senior Research Associate with the Dolphin Communication Project in Florida, adds: 'Unfortunately, despite our utter confidence in the exceptionalism of human intelligence, nobody really has a clue what it is.'[26] He cites a recent survey of 567 leading experts working in the field of artificial intelligence, of whom only a slim majority of 58.6% agreed with this definition of intelligence by leading AI researcher Pei Wang: 'The essence of intelligence is the principle of adapting to the environment while working with insufficient knowledge and resources. Accordingly, an intelligent system should rely on finite processing capacity, work in real time, open to unexpected tasks, and learn from experience.'[27]

Clearly, the notion of intelligence here is very different from the one tested by the WAIS-IV intelligence scale. Just as an example, answering 'Homer' to the question 'who wrote *The Iliad*' would be a sign of intelligence for WAIS-IV test examiners, but not, one supposes, for AI researchers. Apart from anything else, the former is testing for specifically human intelligence (not even the brainiest narwhal knows who wrote *The Iliad*), while the latter might apply to non-humans, including animals and robots.

Gregg notes that 41.4% of leading AI experts rejected Pei Wang's definition, which, he concludes is a 'ridiculous state of affairs'.[28] It is more than ridiculous. It shows how difficult, perhaps impossible, it is to come up with a satisfactory definition of intelligence, even though, as Gregg suggests, we know it when we encounter it. In this sense, stupidity is like intelligence: I remember receiving a greeting card that depicted the entrance to the Midvale School for the Gifted. A dimwit is pushing on the door which clearly bears the sign 'Pull'. He'll never get in.

Maybe, that's to say, intelligence is like jazz, in the sense expressed so well by Louis Armstrong: 'If you gotta ask, you ain't never gonna know.' Or maybe intelligence is like pornography in the sense set out by US Supreme Court Justice Potter Stuart: 'I know it when I see it.'[29] Gregg calls intelligence 'the grand MacGuffin'.[30] It is not a biological fact, but nonetheless observable – and humans don't have the exclusive rights to its possession. Alien radio waves suggests there is intelligence out there; crows use sticks to prise ants from logs. And humans can show intelligence, too, though perhaps not in some of their more questionable endeavours such as testing for intelligence or devising means of mass extermination. As Gregg puts it: 'Narwhals don't build gas chambers.'[31]

For all that, psychologists and others carry on the hunt for the chimera of intelligence as if it were a quantifiable phenomenon. Even Professor Boring, having noted the circularity of the hunt for intelligence at the start of his paper, went on to posit that intelligence has certain clearly established characteristics. Intelligence is, he wrote, a 'common factor' in many abilities, 'something like power, in that it can be measured roughly although not very finely, that it is only one factor among many in the mental life that it develops mostly in childhood, that it develops little or not at all in adult life, and that it is largely predetermined at five years of age'.[32] Which makes one wonder what the purpose of schools is. Certainly not, if Boring's hypothesis is right, to nurture the development of children's intelligence. Even the Midvale School for Gifted Children, rightly understood, is really a holding pen for geniuses whose mental capacities are fixed before they arrive (assuming they can get through that tricky door). Boring also defined what he meant by power: it was akin to what the term meant in physics, namely 'the amount of work that can be done in a given time'. But, one wants to object, it's not the amount of work that can be done in a given time but its quality that is more suggestive of intelligence. In this, intelligence is more like sexual pleasure: it's not what you do but how you do it that matters.

Stupid statistics

In the 1994 American bestseller *The Bell Curve: Intelligence and Class Structure in American Life*,[33] psychologist Richard J. Herrnstein and political scientist Charles Murray asserted that there were IQ differences between races that were partly genetic in origin. American average intelligence was, they claimed, falling, while at the same time the late 20th-century US had seen the emergence of a cognitive elite. *The Bell Curve* argued that America's population was becoming dangerously polarized between a clever, rich, educated elite and a mass of unintelligent, poor, and uneducated people. The nation was increasingly divided, the authors supposed, between a cognitive elite that used private delivery services, attended private schools, lived in gated communities and relied on arbitration by private lawyers to handle business disputes, and the rest of the population, which used the Federal postal service, went to public schools, lived outside the gates of private communities, and relied on the public judicial process.

Intelligence – or what Herrnstein and Murray called cognitive ability – was, according to them, substantially heritable, with 'substantially' meaning between 40 and 80%. As Malcolm W. Browne, the *New York Times* reviewer of *The Bell Curve*, argued in 1994: 'This leads to the depressing inference by the authors that no matter how many remedial education programs are brought to bear on intellectually disadvantaged children, many of them will still be hamstrung by an ineradicable cognitive disability created by genetic bad luck.' When Alfred Binet was tasked by the French government with devising IQ tests, the aim was to improve struggling children's cognitive capacities and thereby life chances; the corollary of Herrnstein and Murray's bleak vision of intelligence as overwhelmingly hereditary is that such hopeful ambitions should be set aside. The *New York Times* review went on: 'Society, the authors argue, should accept this as a real possibility and learn to cope with it, rather than merely denouncing all intelligence studies and ignoring the data they yield.' In particular, spending US government money on such initiatives as the Head Start education programme was a waste of public money. All it served to do was help 'the nation's bloated educational bureaucracies'.[34]

This insistence on the largely heritable nature of intelligence and the ramifications of that supposed fact for programmes to help the education of the poorest and more disadvantaged children was one of the controversial principles that guided the two writers in their book. Here are the others. Like Spearman, Wechsler and others, Herrnstein and Murray claimed that there was a general factor of intelligence. And like Boring, they suggested that IQ scores were stable over a person's lifetime, though not perfectly so. They also claimed that IQ tests measured that general factor most accurately. They assumed what we have doubted in the previous paragraphs, namely that IQ scores matched whatever it was that people meant when they used the word 'intelligent' or 'smart' in ordinary language. They furthermore defended IQ tests from the charge that they might be biased against social, economic, ethnic, or racial groups. Properly administered, Herrnstein and Murray insisted, IQ tests were blind to such factors, though test results would prove, they thought, that intelligence varied between such groups. For example, they noted that Asian Americans did better in IQ tests than Caucasian Americans, who in turn did better in IQ tests than African Americans.

Like Malthus, Herrnstein and Murray worried about the overpopulation of America by too many of the wrong kind of people, in particular those with low IQs. Those with lower intelligence, they wrote, tended to have more babies than those of the cognitive elite, and mass immigration had made matters worse by admitting people with low intelligence. They argued: 'The self-selection process that used to attract the classic American immigrant – brave, hard-working, imaginative, self-starting, and often of high IQ – has been changing and with it the nature of some of the immigrant population.' Government intervention to ameliorate poverty and inequality, they charged, had made matters worse, effectively rewarding stupid women to have stupid babies. They continued: 'The technically precise description of America's fertility policy is that it subsidizes births among poor women, who are also disproportionately at the low end of the intelligence distribution. We urge generally that these policies, represented by the extensive network of cash and services for low-income women who have babies, be ended.'[35]

Like Marie Stopes in Britain 70 years earlier, Herrnstein and Murray advised the American government to encourage feeble-minded women not to breed. The government, they advised, should 'make it easy for women to make good on their prior decision not to get pregnant by making available birth control mechanisms that are increasingly flexible, foolproof, inexpensive, and safe'. This would serve as a corrective to existing affirmative action and other ostensibly levelling-up policies that had, they thought, encouraged women of lower intelligence to have more children. 'If the United States did as much to encourage high-IQ women to have babies as it now does to encourage low-IQ women, it would rightly be described as engaging in aggressive manipulation of fertility,' they wrote.[36] 4

At the other end of the social scale from these state-subsidized low-IQ mothers, who were unwittingly doing their bit for American society by dragging down the nation's average intelligence, was what Herrnstein and Murray called the cognitive elite. This elite was the product of the vast expansion of higher education in 20th-century America and had resulted in cognitive ability, rather than wealth, social class, and perhaps even such factors as sex or skin colour, being the key dividing line in society and the leading determinant of social status. There had been a 15-fold increase between 1900 and 1990 in the proportion of people getting college degrees. As the number of tertiary education colleges mushroomed, so did selection policies change: students applying to college were being selected ever more efficiently for their high IQs. For Herrnstein and Murray, modern America was divided not so much between the have-yachts and the have-nots as between those with educational qualifications that indicated their higher IQs and those with less cognitive capital.

But this cognitive elite, for all its hypothesized intellectual accomplishments, was impotent to reverse the supposed decline in average American intelligence. And, for Herrnstein and Murray, that decline had terrible consequences: when average intelligence falls in a nation, that nation is less able to compete in international markets or develop advanced technologies. But this does not seem to follow at all: even if average American intelligence has been falling, as the authors suggested, the development of advanced technologies by American corporations – think Apple, Google, Microsoft, Tesla – does not seem to suggest a nation stupefying itself into economic oblivion or global economic irrelevance. Perhaps it doesn't matter for the future of America if the average intelligence of its population is falling, so long as the IQ levels of the cognitive elite are rising and, fingers crossed, if that elite can be induced somehow to do its patriotic duty and make more clever babies. But that would suggest something the authors of *The Bell Curve* did not explore: that, if anybody, the cognitive elite should be the focus of government affirmative action policies that would have the aim not so much to make America great again as to make Americans geniuses again.

Towards the end of *The Bell Curve*, Herrnstein and Murray worried that a new spectre was rising in America, the spectre of conservatism.

> We fear that a new kind of conservatism is becoming the dominant ideology of the affluent – not in the social tradition of an Edmund Burke or in the economic tradition of an Adam Smith but 'conservatism' along Latin American lines, where to be conservative has often meant doing whatever is

necessary to preserve the mansions on the hills from the menace of the slums below.[37]

Herrnstein and Murray were not immune to that bastard mutation of modern conservatism. To prevent this corruption by persons with low IQ scores, who tend to have more illegitimate babies (i.e. those born outside marriage), are more likely to divorce, drop out of school, commit more crimes, and whose low cognitive powers cannot be improved, it was necessary for there to be a 'custodial state' – or what sounds very much like a system of apartheid. They wrote: 'By custodial state, we have in mind a high-tech and more lavish version of the Indian reservation for some substantial minority of the nation's population, while the rest of America tries to go about its business.' Effectively, *The Bell Curve*'s authors were proposing that the most feeble-minded Americans be kept as wards of the state. How many Americans warranted such treatment was not made clear, but the America of the near future envisaged by Herrnstein and Murray was one that, having just won the cold war and thus apparently demonstrated the superiority of the West over communist totalitarianism, became totalitarian itself to stop corruption from within by the spread of stupidity. 'It is difficult to imagine the United States preserving its heritage of individualism, equal rights before the law, free people running their own lives, once it is accepted that a significant part of the population must be made permanent wards of the state,' they wrote.[38]

The authors concluded that there were no means to boost intelligence by more than a modest degree and that, as a result, society needed to be reorganized to reflect that unfortunate (supposed) fact. The book's final chapter describes a vision of society where differences in ability are recognized and everybody can have a valued place, stressing the role of local communities and clear moral rules that apply to everybody. This sounds not like the American Dream, whereby anyone can make it, but like a stratified dystopia akin to the eugenicist hell depicted in Huxley's *Brave New World*. Herrnstein and Murray's vision of the future is satirized bitterly by Stephen Jay Gould:

> They yearn romantically for the 'good old days' of towns and neighborhoods where all people could be given tasks of value and self esteem could be found

for all steps in the IQ hierarchy (so Forrest Gump might collect the clothing for the church raffle, while Mr Murray and the other bright folks do the planning and keep the accounts).[39]

Behind these gloomy analyses and prognostications, *The Bell Curve* marshalled a great deal of data to show that intelligence or the lack of it were the driving forces of American society. The authors wrote: 'Social class remains the vehicle of social life, but intelligence now pulls the train.'[40] By this they meant that intelligence was the most desirable of social goods but its lack the cause of America's social problems. Those with low IQs were more likely to abuse or neglect their children, commit crime, be unemployed, be idle, be single parents, have poor healthcare, and live on welfare. Those with higher IQs were more likely to be industrious, have two-parent families, high income, good-quality child care, good healthcare, and well-remunerated jobs from the proceeds of which they paid their taxes. None of this, perhaps, is surprising, but what is improbable is Herrnstein and Murray's suggestion that intelligence causes these outcomes. 'Socioeconomic status is . . . a result of cognitive ability,' they wrote.[41] This, though, is the mistake of supposing that correlation implies causation, a fallacy also known by the Latin phrase *cum hoc ergo propter hoc* ('with this, therefore because of this'). This fallacy bedevils, one might even say stupefies, the study of intelligence. The late Canadian psychologist Philippe Rushton posited that males with the largest penises have the lowest intelligence, and, furthermore, that there are racial differences in both penis size and intelligence.[42] How he collected his data and whether his research was prompted out of a sense of inadequacy at the size of his own penis is beyond the remit of this book, though it's worth saying that if the latter, this would not be the first time personal shortcomings have been used to interpret a data set.

Or consider a 2009 survey of nearly a million Swedish men that found a threefold difference in the risk of death between those with the highest IQs and those with the lowest. The fallacy is not in the data or in the correlations found but in the interpretation of those findings captured in one heading: 'Having a higher IQ protects you from death.'[43] No, it doesn't. First, IQ isn't a thing like an inoculation or a magical cloak that protects absent-minded professors from wandering into the Stockholm traffic and being mowed down by Volvos. But the heading involves just such a false reification. Second, intelligence is just as likely to be not the cause but the consequence of a host of other factors. The implicit suggestion behind this heading is that having a higher IQ will make you likely to earn a higher income, which in turn will enable you to have better healthcare, and that higher intelligence makes you attend more assiduously to maintaining a healthy weight and good nutritional habits. But this may be to get things the wrong way round. Your superior intelligence may be a result of such factors rather than the cause. It may even be only statistically associated with lower risk of death without any casual relationship between the two. The data, that's to say, doesn't yield the conclusion; it's the interpretation of that data, often in the light of pre-existing beliefs and political agendas, that does the heavy lifting. And that critique applies not just to the Swedish survey but to a great deal of psychological and other writings on the nature of intelligence – *The Bell Curve* in particular.

Diane F. Halpern made just this point in her scathing review of *The Bell Curve*. The American psychology professor was scandalized at what she took to be the book's bad science and massaging of the data to yield conclusions suited to the authors' conservative political agenda. She wrote:

> How can they know that being unintelligent caused poverty and not the reverse, or, at least, a more reciprocal relationship in which poverty and low intelligence operate jointly and influence each other? Poor people differ from rich people in many ways – they have poorer health, poorer nutrition, and poorer living conditions. Would it not make more sense to reverse the causal arrow and hypothesize that poverty and all of its associates (lack of prenatal care, inadequate heat, ingestion of lead paint, poor diet, etc.) cause low intelligence? The statistical procedures that the authors used to establish which of these related variables was causal cannot be used to establish that low intelligence is the cause of the other variables. The variables are at least interactive or possibly even unidirectional – in the other direction.[44]

But even if one's IQ were causally related to other outcomes – such as higher income – that need not be cause for celebration. Charles R. Tittle and Thomas Rotolo, in their 'IQ and Stratification: An Empirical

Evaluation of Herrnstein and Murray's Social Change Argument', consider the increased use of IQ-like examinations by public sector employers as screening devices for occupational access as offering support for the causal link between IQ and income. The notion that there is a causal link is intuitively plausible: if you pass an IQ test and get a well-paid job in part as a result, you're likely to be better remunerated than someone who failed the test. But matters aren't so simple, argue Tittle and Rotolo: 'Rather than IQ leading to status attainment because it indicates skills necessary to modern society, IQ may reflect the same test-taking abilities used in artificial screening devices by which status groups protect their domains.'[45] Indeed, IQ tests may not so much indicate intelligence as show that a confederacy of dunces are adept at ring-fencing their institutions – be they colleges, government bodies, or corporations – to protect their status and privileges. IQ tests, that is to say, may be significant not so much for establishing unimpeachable, objective measures of intelligence but rather for excluding those deemed undesirable.

This criticism is particularly relevant to the vexed question of the relationship between race and IQ. Malcolm W. Browne, the *New York Times* reviewer of *The Bell Curve*, noted that a large proportion of the 'emergent underclass' ostensibly identified by Herrnstein and Murray were black. 'Unless future accommodations between ethnic groups lead to a more harmonious social structure, Mr Herrnstein and Mr Murray say, the potential for racial hatred seems enormous.'[46]

Herrnstein and Murray reported that Asian Americans had a higher mean IQ than white Americans, who in turn outscored black Americans. Could this have been due to a bias in the tests? Herrnstein and Murray denied this, arguing that when administered properly, intelligence tests were fair and valid measures of intelligence.

Halpern rebutted this claim.

> All intelligence tests are culturally-dependent, but all people are not equally exposed to the 'majority' culture. Suppose we called 'intelligence tests' by some other name, such as tests of acculturation to middle-class American life. This could be a descriptive name for these tests because the questions on the tests reflect what most people in the standardization sample knew and did not know at some point in time.

For example, in 1995, when Halpern wrote her critique, the average American could be expected to know what a disk drive was, so that if a question using that term popped up in an IQ test, the average American might be expected to understand the reference and therefore be more likely to answer the question correctly. But that hypothesized average American is not every American.

> It is a fact that approximately 50% of African-Americans and other groups of ethnic minority children grow up in poverty. On the average, people who grow up in poverty do not have the same experiences as people who do not grow up in poverty. It is likely that fewer individuals from low-income families will know what a disk drive is than individuals from families with higher incomes.

The corollary of this is that IQ tests are likely to be culturally dependent and thereby skewed against those who do not share the backgrounds or skin colours of those who set the tests. Worse, the whole testing process becomes a self-enclosed loop, suggested Halpern.

> Even if the same test predicts academic success equally well for all test-takers, it does not measure intelligence equally well, unless we decide to define intelligence as synonymous with academic success. This sort of definition leads to a type of circular reasoning (intelligence = academic success and academic success = intelligence) that would not be indicative of intelligent thought.

Many critics of *The Bell Curve* have discerned a political agenda that the authors force on to the data. For instance, as we have seen, one of Herrnstein and Murray's key suppositions is that more recent immigrants are less intelligent than earlier immigrants. Halpern wrote:

> Why should we expect that recent immigrants from war torn and poverty stricken areas of the world would differ in motivation or intelligence from those who fled persecution earlier in the century? The political philosophy that the authors espouse is blatantly anti-immigration, which is as legitimate as any other political philosophy – except that this one is 'dressed up' to look like a data-based conclusion, which it is not.[47]

Or to put it another way: politically conservative prejudice impels the authors to juke the stats.

Worse yet, in proposing that genes account for 60% of the differences in the IQs of children, Herrnstein and Murray were suggesting that the majority of Americans were doomed by their heredity. For the authors, the corollary of this supposed truth was that there was no point trying to ameliorate the essential stupidity of the cognitive underclasses; all such attempts only wasted government money. But that policy recommendation did not follow. As a *New York Times* editorial put it:

> It is essential to note . . . that group differences in IQ may have nothing to do with genes even if individual IQs are largely inherited. An example proves the point. Plants grown together under ideal conditions will achieve different heights based solely on individual genetic makeup. But lock half the plants in a dark closet and the difference in average height of the two groups will be due entirely to environment. So even if IQs are deemed to be largely inherited, that says nothing about the potential impact on IQ of altering prenatal care or aggressive early education.[48]

Herrnstein and Murray, that is to say, made a very dubious case for dooming the most unfortunate in society to their fate. 'We must fight the doctrine of *The Bell Curve*,' wrote Stephen Jay Gould, 'both because it is wrong and because it will, if activated, cut off all possibility of the proper nurturance of everyone's intelligence.'[49]

But what, you might be wondering, is a bell curve, and why did it supply the title of Herrnstein and Murray's book? If you look at the bell curve of a set of data like the one depicted on the cover of their book, you are seeing a graphical depiction of a normal probability distribution. The x axis allows us to read the value of some variable (IQ scores, for instance), while the y axis allows us to read off the probability of that value. The bell curve is symmetrical, unlike other graphical depictions of skewed probability distributions.

The bell curve is commonplace in the sciences to depict variables like height, weight, petal size in flowers, crop yields, pickle length – if not the correspondence between penis size and male intelligence – all showing this distribution. But can intelligence really be represented by a bell curve? Many phenomena can't. Consider, for instance, income distribution in the US, where most households earn below the average with a few households earning a very high income. The very high income of the latter skews the distribution curve to the right, destroying the symmetry that a more equal distribution of income would manifest.

Isn't American intelligence skewed in just the same way as American household income, with the cognitive elite more than compensating for the intellectual shortcomings of the underclass? That's to say, isn't there what is called a 'Flynn effect', which drags up American average intelligence even against the countervailing forces (low-IQ immigrants and underclass Americans) that Herrnstein and Murray claimed were dragging the nation's average intelligence down?

Well, yes and no. In one sense, average intelligence is fixed: it is by definition 100. That follows from the convention, devised by David Wechsler, that the average of the test results is set to 100 and the standard from that average is set to 15 IQ points. So an IQ of 85 would be described as 'one standard deviation below the mean' and an IQ of 115 as 'one standard deviation above the mean'. The average test result of 100 is represented sitting atop the bell curve, and other, less probable IQ scores are depicted spread in a normal distribution around them. The more intelligent have IQs higher than 100; the IQs of the more stupid never get into three figures, while those who have IQs or more than 120 might quality for Mensa. The vast majority of us will have an IQ score that falls within one standard deviation above or below the mean, that is to say, each of us is likely to have an IQ between 115 and 85. To get into Mensa, the exclusive club founded in Oxford in 1946, you need to have an IQ of 132 on the Stanford–Binet test and 130 on the Wechsler test. At the other end of the scale, those with IQs lower than 70 are likely to have difficulty in meeting 'community standards of personal independence and social responsibility', in the words of the American Psychological Association.[50]

But that can't be the end of the matter since the bell curve implies there can be no change to average intelligence. It is fixed at 100 and, happily, most of us have IQs that are not too distant from that mean.

To understand why average intelligence can in fact rise or fall, we need to set aside the bell curve and consider how intelligence tests are devised. IQ tests are standardized by using a sample of test takers before the IQ test in question is deployed in schools to evaluate someone for mental disabilities or used as part of a job application. That sample helps determine the average result of the test takers' results, but this standardization is not a one-off process. Psychologists revise the test every few years to maintain 100 as the average, which suggests that intelligence levels are not constant but changing in America and other countries. Intelligence can only be mapped on the bell curve that gives Herrnstein and Murray's book its title if the means of measuring IQ is periodically adjusted to better reflect trends in intelligence, which, by definition, is something for which IQ tests don't test. This may sound a little like repeatedly moving the goalposts during a football match, but it is really not so. Rather, it means that when we talk about average national intelligence, the calculation of that average is not worked out according to the same means by which an IQ test determines the intelligence of a person. Average intelligence in a particular nation or any other group, if one ignores the data supplied by standardized IQ tests, can rise or fall.

The central thesis of *The Bell Curve*, as we have seen, was that average American intelligence was falling because stupid people were being subsidized by misbegotten government policy to breed stupid children, and also because a more stupid class of immigrants than hitherto were settling in the US. While Herrnstein and Murray were suggesting that average American intelligence was falling, however, other researchers were suggesting the opposite. The philosopher and intelligence researcher James Flynn noted that average IQ scores rose every decade in the 20th century by between 3 and 5% in the US and many other developed countries. The gains Flynn discovered were so large that they suggested an average child would be regarded as a 'genius' by their great grandparents, and they implied, for instance, that the average American of 2004 was 30% more intelligent than the average American of a century earlier[51] – which seems, intuitively, ridiculous. Herrnstein and Murray were very much aware of Flynn's work – it was they who gave the phenomenon of rising average intelligence during the 20th century the name the 'Flynn effect' – but clearly their analyses suggested the opposite, that there was, effectively, a negative Flynn effect by means of which the cognitive underclasses were dragging down American average intelligence.

But if there was a positive Flynn effect in the US – as the person after whom it was named suggested – what had caused it? Many factors were cited: nutrition, parenting, and compulsory schooling all improved during the 20th century. What's more, the world became a more intellectually demanding place to inhabit. Farms gave way to factories, horses to cars, typewriters to computers, and these days you need a college degree to change a light bulb (I exaggerate, but only slightly). IQs, by this account, rose to meet these existentially baffling life demands. Flynn certainly made much of such environmental factors.

Another non-negligible factor, though, is that IQ tests became widespread during that period. Donna Ford, distinguished professor of education and human ecology at Ohio State University, suggests that increased familiarity with test taking may have contributed to the rise in IQs, especially among children. 'They've gotten wiser at taking tests because they're so used to taking tests,' she said.[52] If so, IQ tests are good at testing for intelligence only in so far as intelligence is measured by being good at IQ tests. Which sounds like Professor Boring's analysis a century on. And that facility, which may not at all match what we mean when we talk about intelligence, may increase over time. There's probably a curve for that.

No matter. The Flynn effect has been seized on by teachers, social policy wonks, and dieticians since it rebutted claims that IQ was immutable and therefore that ambitious interventions in families and schools could not be effective.

But then, in 2017, Flynn noticed something strange. His data showed that many of those countries that had benefited from his eponymous effect and had seen average national intelligence scores rise year on year were now experiencing a downward trend. IQ scores for even the brightest children in the UK had started to decline, while Nordic nations, some of whose average IQ scores had been declining since the 1990s, were projected to see national intelligence scores drop by a total of seven points by 2025. Flynn found that the US was still basking in a positive Flynn effect. But that was to change.[53]

By 2023, researchers at Northwestern University and the University of Oregon published research in the journal *Intelligence* claiming to show that average American intelligence declined between 2006 and 2018 across three of four broad domains.[54] Researchers tracked falling scores in logic, vocabulary, visual and mathematical problem-solving, and analogical reasoning. Only scores for spatial reasoning – the measure of the mind's ability to analyse three-dimensional objects – rose during that period for the average American. While in a previous generation

STUPID INTELLIGENCE

Herrnstein and Murray had ascribed this supposed cognitive decline to the wrong kind of immigrants and government policies encouraging the breeding of the wrong kind of offspring, now the suggestion was that American IQ is falling because of other factors. What could those factors be? 'The line can't go up forever,' said Elizabeth Dworak, lead author of the study. 'It's called the ceiling effect. You eventually hit that threshold.'[55] Dworak, research assistant professor of medical social sciences at Northwestern's Feinberg School of Medicine, was making an intuitively plausible point. Just as athletes, one supposes, can't keep getting faster and there is, quite possibly, some point at which non-wind-assisted athletes will no longer be able to break the world record for the fastest 100 metres, so presumably average humans, even American ones, can't just keep getting more clever.

There is, indeed, the hideous possibility that human society has reached a cognitive peak. One Finnish study found IQ scores had dipped by two points between 1997 and 2009. A French study found a four-point drop from 1999 to 2009.[56] If Finns and French people, not generally taken to be stupid, are on the cognitive downslope, the rest of us can't be far behind.

It's almost invidious to speculate on what factors might have prompted the decline of average IQ across many developed countries, but that won't stop us. Perhaps it's due to technological progress. Think of it this way. Computers and smartphones are more complex but, by performing many of the boring tasks that humans used to, they spare us cognitive labour. As a result, the human mind has less to do, and the need therefore to be intelligent is less of an evolutionary imperative than it was in the pre-digital era. Computers and smartphones are more complex than ever, but human routines are oddly simpler. Generations ago, dishwashers and clothes dryers eased physical labours in daily life. Today, smartphones and smartspeakers ease mental labours, enabling us, the creators of these machines, to slide into the warm bath of mental fatuity.

It's a theory. And if it has any plausibility, it suggests that while human intelligence rose in developed countries very quickly during the 20th century, thanks in part to technological progress, ironically enough, later technological progress is having the opposite effect. It's a theory, though clearly one, if applicable to any society, that only fits those in purportedly advanced consumer societies awash with stupefying gizmos.

This last thought might be consoling to the people of Nepal, who were estimated by the late British psychologist Richard Lynn and Finnish political scientist Tatu Vanhanen to live in the stupidest country in the world, with an average IQ of 42.99. In their 2002 study *IQ and the Wealth of Nations*,[57] Lynn and Vanhanen argued that differences in national income correlate with differences in average national intelligence quotients. Or to put it another way, the more stupid a population, the poorer it is likely to be. Like Herrnstein and Murray, Lynn and Vanhanen supposed that IQ was the cause of other factors: for the former, one's social circumstances were the result of one's IQ; for the latter, low IQ can reduce gross domestic product.

Lynn and Vanhanen did not do their own IQ studies but created estimates of national average IQs by often ridiculous means. For instance, no IQ data was available for 104 of the 185 nations they ranked, but that did not stop them. In the case of El Salvador, the authors arrived at an average national IQ of 84 by averaging their calculations of two nearby nations, namely 79 for Guatemala and 88 for Colombia. South Africa's average IQ of 72, meanwhile, was arrived at by calculating an average of different ethnic groups.

The pursuit of human intelligence, the desire to pin it down and give it a number, has, no doubt, long been a questionable academic activity, but never before has it been so quixotic, deluded, or dubious in its projection of immutable characteristics onto whole nations by means of doubtful data.

Stupid genetic engineering

The quest goes on – not just to find intelligence but also to engineer it. Malcolm W. Browne's *New York Times* review of *The Bell Curve* in 1994 suggested that we were on the cusp of realizing the genetic opportunities created by molecular biology to improve humans, not just physically but mentally, too.

> For the first time in human history, it may soon be possible to confer resistance to disease upon living organisms and to free people of inherited scourges like sickle-cell anemia and Tay–Sachs disease. Most people would argue that society is justified in fighting physical disease, but what if we

were to carry the war against disease a step farther? Is it wrong to regard a hereditary predisposition to lower intelligence as a kind of genetic disease and to find ways to cure it?[58]

Fast forward to 2013 and Dominic Cummings, controversial adviser to the then Conservative education secretary, produced a paper arguing that educationists need to better understand the impact of genetics on children. It was not wrong to regard a hereditary predisposition to lower intelligence as a kind of genetic disease, and it was imperative, Cummings argued, to cure it. 'There is strong resistance across the political spectrum to accepting scientific evidence on genetics. Most of those that now dominate discussions on issues such as social mobility entirely ignore genetics and therefore their arguments are at best misleading and often worthless.' He claimed research shows that as much as 70% of a child's performance is genetically derived.[59]

Just like Herrnstein and Murray, Cummings argued that government action to improve struggling children's educational opportunities had resulted only in a vast waste of public money. Labour's Sure Start programme, aimed at pre-school age children and inspired by President Lyndon Johnson's Head Start programme in the US, was sharply criticized by Cummings, who argued there was little evidence for its practical impact.

He wrote: 'There is great political pressure to spend money on things like Sure Start, but little scientific testing, refinement and changing budgets to reinforce demonstrated success. Therefore billions have been spent with no real gains.'

Instead, Cummings proposed that government money be spent on making embryo selection for intelligence available on the NHS. After attending a Silicon Valley science conference at Google's HQ, he recommended allowing people to select eggs for their babies that appeared to have the best chance of having a high IQ, if genes for high intelligence could be identified in the future. He wrote:

> It is already the case that farmers use genomes to make predictions about cows' properties and behaviour. . . . It is already the case that rich people could use in vitro fertilisation to select the egg which they think will be most advantageous, because they can sequence genomes of multiple eggs and

examine each one to look for problems then pick the one they prefer. Once we identify a substantial number of IQ genes, there is no obvious reason why rich people will not select the egg that has the highest prediction for IQ.

This clearly raises many big questions. If the poor cannot do the same, then the rich could quickly embed advantages and society could become not only more unequal but also based on biological classes. One response is that if this sort of thing does become possible, then a national health system should fund everybody to do this. (I.e. it would not mandate such a process but it would give everybody a choice of whether to make use of it.) Once the knowledge exists, it is hard to see what will stop some people making use of it and offering services to – at least – the super-rich.[60]

In a sense, what Cummings was advocating was a revival of eugenics with better technology. Critics, from geneticists to opposition Labour Party spokespeople, lined up to damn Cummings for reviving that 'discredited pseudo-science' championed by Francis Galton and Julian Huxley. But, in another sense, he had a point. As we saw in the previous chapter, eugenics is not obsolete. Rather, it is more widely practised than it was in the days of Marie Stopes and Julian Huxley. Alison Bashford argued:

> If anything, the twenty-first century is more resigned, even in thrall, to the apparent imperative to realize individual reproductive desires and choices – even 'needs'. . . . Semen is actively selected every day by individuals and couples and like it or not these decisions are made straight out of presumptions about race, class, intelligence, education, height, or 'fitness'.

Eggs are also selected by means of in vitro fertilisation, and 'Less fit future humans are every day diagnosed and made unviable.'[61] At the higher end, human gene editing to improve human stock and intelligence tantalizes the likes of Cummings (who went on to become British prime minister Boris Johnson's chief political adviser) with the possibility of making children more intelligent and educationally successful. We are already living in a neo-liberal, market-based eugenic dystopia, so why not, as an egalitarian imperative, level the cognitive playing field by ensuring that not only the super-rich can use genetic interventions to improve the life chances of the unborn and school-age children?

One of Cummings' leading critics, Bobbie Farsides, professor of clinical and biomedical ethics at Brighton and Sussex Medical School, countered:

> In this country we've taken the decision to only use embryo selection as a way of combating serious disease. We've not moved to thinking of it in terms of enhancement, be that intelligence or anything else. It would be such a huge step away from the fundamental values that inform embryo selection at the moment that it's almost inconceivable.[62]

Certainly, Cummings' suggestions would require a major law change in the UK since ethical guidelines set out by the Human Fertilization and Embryology Authority prohibit genetic screening for 'designer babies'.[63]

And arguably a law change would be a waste of time. Dreams of geneticists identifying a 'gay gene' or a 'musical gene' or an 'IQ gene' that one could turn on or off are seductive, perhaps, but fatuous. The idea that there is a one-to-one correlation between a particular human trait and a gene is deluded. Steve Jones, emeritus professor of genetics at University College London, said: 'Hundreds of different genes have been found behind the variation in height. But put them all together and you still explain only a fifth of the variation. There's no way you can make a gene-chip for height. So how the hell can you make one for IQ?'[64]

Cummings' suggestions drew on the work of his friend Professor Stephen Hsu, a US physicist who had been working on a Chinese project to find just what Professor Steve Jones thinks far-fetched, namely that there are genes for intelligence. Cummings was also heavily influenced by the work of educational researcher Kathryn Asbury and geneticist Robert Plomin, whose 2013 book *G Is for Genes: The Impact of Genetics on Education and Achievement*[65] made the case for a genetically influenced educational system.

Asbury and Plomin's case for an increased role for genetic screening in schools is at least more nuanced than the case put by either Cummings or indeed other overenthusiastic supporters of the role of genetics in education. While Cummings' report indicated that genes were primarily responsible for the variations in GCSE-level grades (the exams taken by British school children at age 16), and claimed that teachers, schools, and domestic environments play little part in the overall development of a young adult's academic ability, Asbury and Plomin argued that genes can account for up to 60% of the variation in GCSE scores – based on a study that included over 11,000 identical and non-identical twins but insisted, too, that environmental factors should not be discounted. Indeed, Asbury and Plomin even wrote at one point: 'The truth is that next to nothing is determined by genes, and our environments are hugely powerful.'[66] That's a cautious stance beyond the temperament of Cummings in his headlong rush to find genetic cures for social, economic, and educational problems. For while Cummings regarded the intelligent and the stupid as outcomes primarily of their genes, Asbury and Plomin considered that matters are more complicated. Genes are less able to explain variation in cognitive ability or test scores when children are very young because their environments differ so widely. But as they go through school, where environments are to some extent equalized, genes count for more and more. If only we could send all children to Eton, or send all children to a sink comprehensive, then that environment might be perfectly equalized and, for Asbury and Plomin, the contribution of genes to differences in intelligence would amount to 100%. But we can't.

Like Binet, Asbury and Plomin hoped to devise means to identify and help struggling students; unlike Binet, they believed that every child has special needs, and that to cater to those fairly, schools should offer the widest possible choice of subjects and extra-curricular activities. Each child, they proposed, should be equipped with what they called a 'Learning Chip', a tool used in DNA testing to extract relevant genetic information that would act as a 'reliable genetic predictor' of a student's strengths and weaknesses, and would allow their education to be tailored optimally – again precisely what geneticists such as Steve Jones deny is feasible. They proposed free-of-charge, high-quality pre-school education for disadvantaged children from the age of two. Every child, they recommended, should be allocated a key worker who would track each student throughout their entire education. Children of 'low-SES [socio-economic status] families should be offered extra support from birth', they argued.[67] But, more chillingly, they also argued that very early on in their childhood, many children can be identified who 'will not require further funding at university' because they do not have it in them to benefit from tertiary education. This may sound uncontroversial or, depending on one's political persuasion, justification for a policy whereby the most disadvantaged children stay obligingly in their cognitive lanes. Asbury and Plomin certainly recommend, it must be said, support for underperforming children. But how? 'Within schools,' they wrote, 'teachers should use IQ tests and psychological measures of confidence and motivation to assess whether pupils are making progress towards fulfilling a potential fixed by their genes.' Unlike Binet, they also proposed special education for children who excel. 'Children who excel should also be offered the support and opportunities they need as a matter of course.'[68]

But the use of DNA testing in classrooms, Asbury and Plomin insisted, should not be aimed at dooming the struggling to their fate nor to help the cherry picking of the potential future members of the cognitive elite. Rather, the aim would be to nip stupidity in the bud, ameliorate congestive dysfunction.[69] 'It's wholly accepted that preventative medicine is the way to go,' Plomin told the *Guardian*.

> Why not preventative education? We wait for problems such as reading disability to develop. Children go to school, they fail, they get diagnosed, they're given special resources but by then it's too late. They've only ever experienced failure and it's like putting Humpty Dumpty back together. Once you have the genes, you could predict difficulties and hopefully prevent them.[70]

But the idea that children are largely a product of their genes and that genetically founded eugenics might become part of government policy is, to put it mildly, controversial. It raises the spectres of fascism and racism. For instance, when the American professor Arthur Jensen published a paper in 1969 concluding that 80% of variance in IQ scores was attributable to genes, not the environment – and attempts to boost African American scores through pre-school intervention were therefore bound to fail – angry students besieged his office in California.[71]

And much of Cummings' enthusiasm for genetics having a bigger role in children's education was catalysed by his fear that the British public education system was producing grown-ups ill suited to lead a nation that sought to compete economically against the rising might of Asian countries – a fear akin to *The Bell Curve*'s suggestion that falling average American intelligence threatened US economic power. In this,

Cummings had a point, though not quite the one he sought to make. What Britain needs is not more prime ministers like his former boss, the Eton- and Oxford-educated Alexander Boris de Pfeffel Johnson, by whose cognitive capabilities many have been underwhelmed. Johnson's chief scientific adviser, Sir Patrick Vallance, for instance, noted in his diary that it was 'awful' watching Johnson trying to understand statistics, and that he found the difference between absolute and relative risk 'almost impossible to understand'.[72] Clearly, if Britain is to have a member of the cognitive elite at Number 10 Downing Street – and that may well be a desirable outcome – we have a long way to go. Whether DNA testing in schoolrooms would help in the achievement of that political goal is at best uncertain. Even Plomin concedes that the hunt for genes has been disappointing. 'I've been looking for these genes for 15 years and I don't have any.'[73]

And yet the dream that Binet and others had, that intelligence was mutable, and that schools, rather than deciding some children were stupid, subnormal, or otherwise hopeless cases, might, by some means – be they IQ tests, Learning Chips, or something else – nurture their charges and help them fulfil their potential, remains alive. But, as we will see in the next section of this chapter, the reality is that such means have sometimes hindered rather than helped.

Racist stupidity

In 2020, two eminent British men, one a renowned historian, the other an award-winning artist and film maker, met to discuss their school days.[74] One might have thought that their reminiscences would have included stories of inspirational teachers, tributes to educational establishments that substantially made them what they are, and happy memories of having their intellects stimulated and their dreams nurtured.

Not so. One of the men, David Olusoga, a familiar face on British TV and author of the bestselling *Black and British: A Forgotten History*, said:

> I didn't attend school – I survived school, and certainly wasn't educated there. I was educated primarily by my mother and myself, through regular visits to the local library. I only studied A Levels because my friends and I worked out that we had to hothouse ourselves. We spent the weeks before the exams

doing past papers over and over again, which is how we passed and went to university. I was educated despite my school.

My mother ultimately taught me how to read, because I'm dyslexic. When I was 15, after years of my mother appealing, I was eventually tested by an educational psychologist and found to be dyslexic. Even then, my school refused to acknowledge the test because it got in the way of a more simple argument – 'Black people aren't clever' – which is what they wanted to believe.

There was only one teacher I ever had respect for, who I still know. He was a history teacher, understood what was going on and would intervene at times when I was being attacked verbally or physically. When we met again a few years ago I learned he was Jewish and it all made sense – why this one teacher could see what was happening, while the others explained it away or dismissed it. He recognised racism when he saw it.[75]

As for his companion, Steve McQueen, the film maker and Turner Prize-winning artist, he had just made a heart-breaking semi-autobiographical film called *Education* for the BBC, as part of a series of films about the experiences of London's West Indian community between the 1960s and 1980s.[76]

In *Education*, a 12-year-old black British boy called Kingsley has difficulty reading. Instead of helping him, his teachers bully and belittle him. One calls him a blockhead for floundering when reading aloud a passage from John Steinbeck's novel *Of Mice and Men*. Nobody at school seems to have noticed, still less cared, that Kingsley, as McQueen himself did, is struggling with dyslexia. His parents, first-generation West Indian immigrants, are summoned to the headmaster's office to be told that Kingsley has done poorly in an IQ test and will be transferred to an ESN school to get the special help he needs. ESN stands for Educationally Sub-Normal – a term introduced in 1945 to describe children thought to have limited intellectual ability and finally abandoned only in 1981. A leaked report by the Inner London Education Authority revealed the term was applied disproportionately to black children, often on the basis of IQ tests.

The culture of treating overwhelmingly black children as stupid was laid bare by Grenadian educationalist Bernard Coard in his 1971 pamphlet *How the West Indian Child Is Made Educationally Sub-Normal in the British School System: The Scandal of the Black Child in Schools in Britain.*[77] Coard's polemic resonated for many black parents and led to the establishment of a network of Black supplementary schools in the UK, established by teachers, parents and volunteers who had lost faith in mainstream education.

In the 1970s, when McQueen's film is set, a disproportionate number of pupils at ESN schools were from ethnic minorities. By 1970, 17% of pupils in London's mainstream schools were from ethnic minorities, yet 34% of ESN schools were made up of ethnic minorities, and black Caribbean children accounted for three-quarters of that figure. These state-run boarding schools were already known colloquially as 'dustbin schools'.

No matter. Kingsley's new school, the headmaster tells his sceptical parents, will be a 'great opportunity'. In a sense, this is precisely what Binet sought when he created the IQ test more than a century earlier: the test would identify which pupils were struggling and then special help would be given to improve their ability to learn and so their life chances. Instead of receiving help to overcome his dyslexia, though, Kingsley finds a poorly run institution with inept teachers who leave the children to their own devices. The depiction of the school Kingsley attends is based on research done by McQueen's co-writer Alastair Siddons, who was struck by stories of 'teachers who used to show up for the first 10 minutes of the day and then wouldn't set any work, would just . . . basically leave the kids alone for the day'.[78] At the outset of *Education*, we see Kingsley at home dreaming of becoming an astronaut; at the ESN school, uprooted and adrift, the spark has gone out of him: he has become bored and listless. *Education* depicts what Siddons calls a 'shameful episode in our history', one that involved damning predominantly black children to holding pens masquerading as educational establishments. As the *Guardian*'s education correspondent Sally Weale put it in 2023: 'They were told they were "backward" or "slow" or "a dunce", and placed in schools with no curriculum, no exams and no qualifications.'[79] No wonder black Britons feel betrayed by what this policy meant in practice. As secondary school teacher and *Guardian* columnist Lola Okolosie put it: 'The Windrush generation, answering a call for help from the mother country and hoping to secure its much touted first-class schooling for their children, considered education the bedrock of social mobility. They were instead faced with a system that worked to reproduce inequalities.'[80] What happened, though, was worse than reproducing inequalities: ESN schools in many cases damned the daughters and sons of the Windrush generation – those tens of thousands of Caribbean immigrants who were invited to settle in the UK after World War II, so named after the ship that brought the first of them to the UK in June 1948 – to lives without hope. Certainly not to dream of becoming eminent historians or respected film makers.

Lyttanya Shannon, who worked as a researcher on McQueen's *Education*, went on to make her own 2021 BBC documentary called *Subnormal: A British Scandal*, interviewing the adults of Caribbean heritage who had been through the ESN school system. She found it hard to get anyone to talk on camera, so ashamed and hurt were they by their experiences of a racist British education system 40 years earlier. One of those who did agree to speak was Ann-Marie Simpson, who came to England from Jamaica at the age of nine after little formal education. She ended up in a special needs school after being excluded from the mainstream for getting into fights. 'I recall having an assessment by a psychologist and my mum was advised I needed special education. But I don't know what my special needs were,' Simpson said. 'There was no proper curriculum. I never sat an exam. It was more like containing. At the time I was very, very embarrassed. I would not tell anyone where I went to school.'[81] She has since studied via evening classes and access courses and is now a social worker.

Many of the children sent to ESN schools had performed badly on IQ tests, which were heralded as an objective measure of intelligence testing across cultures. As we have seen earlier in this chapter, many champions of IQ tests – not least the authors of *The Bell Curve* – have claimed that they have no cultural biases. But Dr Waveney Bushell, the UK's first Black community psychologist, recalled in *Subnormal* how, when given IQ tests, some black children struggled with a question that required them to identify a tap by name. This surprised Bushell, but she ultimately realized that in some parts of the Caribbean a tap is called a pipe, and when she pointed to one in the room, the children knew exactly what it was. IQ tests, that is to say, can be unhelpfully culturally specific; worse, those who place great faith in them often fail to realize that they are supplying not so much a means of determining a child's intelligence as a pretext for treating black children as intellectually inferior.

McQueen's *Education* drew not only on ESN schools but also on what happened to him at his secondary school in Ealing, west London. 'My school was sectioned to houses,' he told David Olusoga.

> And at 14 you're put into either 3C1, which is, say, the normal kids' education, or 3C2, which is the people who are going to be the labourers or bricklayers, you know, the manual workers. And above and below were 3X, which were the brightest kids; and 3Y, which were all the kids who weren't particularly bright. So I was cast aside really, and the journey of my life was drawn in the sand when I was 14 years old.[82]

For McQueen, the lack of care wasn't just because he was black, though that was a key factor in his profiling as an underperforming student: many of his peers at the multicultural comprehensive were similarly set up for failure. As he told Lola Okolosie in the *Guardian*: 'Even though we were from different backgrounds and races . . . we all knew we were being fucked over.' Despite having dyslexia, he said, 'There was no help . . . you were left to your own devices . . . there was no interest.'[83]

McQueen told another interviewer:

> I just think that loads of people, so many beautiful people, didn't achieve what they could achieve because no one believed in them, or gave them a chance, or invested any time in them. A lot of beautiful boys, talented people, were put by the wayside. School was scary for me because no one cared, and I wasn't good at it because no one cared. At 13 years old, you are marked, you are dead, that's your future.[84]

Like Oliver Twist, McQueen and his peers wanted more; like Oliver Twist, they got less.

Kingsley's story, like McQueen's, ends happily. Kingsley's mother arranges for her son to attend a Black supplementary school on Saturdays. It's there that he gets two things not on his curriculum at his ESN school, namely an education in African-Caribbean history and culture and, perhaps even more importantly, a nurturing, caring atmosphere in which to learn and flourish – which, after all, is all that good parents want for their children.

'What do we know about our ancestors?' asks the teacher at this Black school at one point near the film's end. 'That we were slaves,' is the answer. 'That is what they want us to know,' she retorts, before launching into a lesson about ancient kings and queens in Africa. The lesson? The teaching of Black history, as well as of black children, has been woefully inadequate in Britain. Or, as the Jamaican-British dub poet Linton Kwesi Johnson once put it, 'It dread inna Inglan.'[85]

The lesson we might take from McQueen's *Education* and from Shannon's *Subnormal* is how racist prejudice damned many children, officially deeming them subnormal, dunces, or stupid on the basis of the colour of their skin. And, moreover, how often culturally skewed IQ tests helped provide bogus, pseudo-scientific, and purportedly objective underpinnings for a racist project predicated on the lie that black children are more stupid than white ones.

As for McQueen, west London-born son of Grenadian and Trinidadian parents, something similar to what happened to Kingsley in *Education* happened to him. He escaped the dustbin school, and, outside mainstream education, kindled his passions for art and learning. As an antidote to the mainstream school he attended on weekdays, McQueen went to black supplementary schools in Hammersmith and Acton. It was at these schools that he learned perhaps the most important lesson. As he put it: 'There is a problem and the problem isn't you.'[86]

8

Mass Stupidity

Vienna, 1937

'Ladies and gentlemen! . . . . [The] moral . . . concepts, freedom and reason, which have come down to us as tokens of human dignity . . . have since the middle of the nineteenth century, or slightly later, not been in the very best of health.'[1]

So began a lecture called 'Über die Dummheit' ('On Stupidity') delivered in Vienna in March 1937 by the Austrian novelist Robert Musil. He had a gift for understatement: freedom and reason were not in poor health; rather, it was as if, in Europe at the time, they had been selected for extermination. The place and date are significant: this was a year to the month before the Anschluss, Hitler's occupation and annexation of Austria. Many of the ladies and gentlemen in Musil's Viennese audience were about to get a lesson not just in all the evils with which we in hindsight associate with the Third Reich – militarism, sado-masochistic power lust, genocide – but also in the very phenomenon that the novelist indicted in his lecture: the non-negligible role of stupidity in the support for and diabolical functioning of Nazism. For decades after the end of the Third Reich in 1945, psychologists, philosophers, and others struggled to understand the nature of the Nazi poison, and many of them, as we will see, came to the conclusion that stupidity was a decisive element.

Musil told his audience:

> Our task, and the sense of the trials laid upon the spirit, will [be] to complete the always necessary, indeed deeply desired, transition to [a]

new [regenerative understanding of these concepts] with the least possible loss. . . . [In] carrying out this activity we need help from ideas of what is true, reasonable, meaningful, and clever, and also, by inverse reflection, from ideas of what is stupid.[2]

Things, one might think, had come to a pretty pass if spiritual and moral regeneration involved taking lessons from stupidity in how to overcome stupidity. But these were, as Musil recognized, desperate times.

He distinguished between two kinds of stupidity:

> In life one usually means by a stupid person one who is 'a little weak in the head'. But beyond this there are the most varied kinds of intellectual and spiritual deviations, which can so hinder and frustrate and lead astray even an undamaged innate intelligence that it leads, by and large, to something for which the only word language has at its disposal is [still] stupidity. Thus this word embraces two fundamentally quite different types: an honorable and straightforward stupidity, and a second that, somewhat paradoxically, is even a sign of intelligence. The first is based rather on a weakness of understanding, the second more on an understanding that is weak only with regard to some particular, and this latter kind is by far the more dangerous

Musil adds that this

> higher, pretentious form of stupidity . . . is not so much lack of intelligence as failure of intelligence, for the reason it presumes to accomplishments to which it has no right; and it can have all the bad characteristics of weakness of reason, and in addition all those characteristics brought about by every mind that is not in balance, that is misshapen and erratically active.[3]

The higher stupidity is seen by Musil as a spiritual sickness. And those sick in spirit may manifest a seemingly intelligent capacity to invent ingeniously plausible explanations to justify their actions, and to rationalize their views and behaviour through combining incontrovertible facts with half-truths and attractive falsehoods. Adolf Hitler and Donald Trump are the leading virtuosos of this higher stupidity.

That spiritual debility, that higher stupidity, is something that the German Jewish philosopher and journalist Hannah Arendt made a

MASS STUPIDITY

speciality of diagnosing, not least in her reports for the *New Yorker* on the trial of Adolf Eichmann in 1961 and 1962. SS-Obersturmbannführer Eichmann was one of the architects of the Holocaust, which, within less than a decade after Robert Musil's Vienna speech, involved the murder of six million Jews. Arendt restored the connection between stupidity and evil that Kant had severed by describing Eichmann as personifying the 'banality of evil' in the Third Reich and manifesting thereby a kind of stupidity. When Arendt looked at the man wearing an ill-fitting suit in the bullet-proof dock inside a Jerusalem courtroom in 1961, she saw something different from everybody else. The prosecution, wrote Arendt's biographer Lyndsey Stonebridge, 'saw an ancient crime in modern garb, and portrayed Eichmann as the latest monster in the long history of anti-semitism'.[4] Arendt thought otherwise.

This was a mass murderer deludedly vain enough to boast to a court teeming with Holocaust survivors that he had insisted on limiting the number of persons per cattle truck because the conditions were so inhumane. Arendt wrote: 'The longer one listened to him, the more it became obvious that his inability to speak was closely connected to his inability to think, namely to think from the standpoint of somebody else.' When Arendt wrote of the banality of evil, that phrase that of all the millions of words she wrote has survived her death in 1975, it was this deficiency she was indicting. 'It was his thickheadedness that was so outrageous,' Arendt said of Eichmann, 'as if speaking to a brick wall. And that was what I actually meant by banality. . . . There's simply resistance to ever imagine what another person is experiencing.'[5] Indeed, for Arendt, our leading moral task – perhaps before the Holocaust, but certainly in the wake of it – is to overcome that stupidity, that moral blindness. The alternative to Eichmann-like banality, she argued, was what Immanuel Kant called 'an enlarged mentality'. Arendt told her students at New York's New School in 1968 what that meant. 'You think your own thoughts but in the place of somebody else.'[6] Such an enlarged mentality, though, is not the same as empathy, which additionally involves sharing, perhaps through imaginative projection, the feelings of another.

Arendt was raised in the German city of Königsberg (now called Kaliningrad and part of Russia), where Kant lived and taught. She read his *Critique of Pure Reason* at 16 and was strongly marked by Kantian strictures on how we should live, and how, by rational moral reflection, we might overcome our native *Dummheit*. Arendt didn't do empathy, though; indeed, for her, just as for Kant, feelings could get in the way of proper moral judgement. At one point during the trial, Eichmann invoked duty, as if mass murdering Jews was OK because his bosses told him to. If Eichmann had read Kant as he claimed he had, he clearly hadn't understood him. 'Kant's whole ethics amounts to the idea that every person, in every action, must reflect on whether the maxim of action can become a universal law,' Arendt wrote in 'On Humanity in Dark Times: Thoughts About Lessing'. 'In other words, it really is the opposite of obedience! Everybody is a lawgiver. In Kant, nobody has the right to obey.'[7]

Across the decades, that sentence resounds: nobody has the right to obey. Not Eichmann, not anyone blaming others for their own failings, and certainly not you joining the latest social media pile-on. We are free only to the extent that we are capable of disobeying. Kant discovered, Lyndsey Stonebridge tells us in her biography of Arendt, that it is only because we can think (which seems to boil down to reason about what we ought to do) that human freedom and dignity are possible. And this is where stupidity comes in, or, rather, where stupidity should be forced out: there is, properly understood, a cognitive element to doing the right thing and for taking responsibility for one's crimes. It was precisely with this lack that Eichmann tried, and failed, to exculpate himself for his crimes. On 31 May 1962, he was hanged near Tel Aviv. His body was cremated, and his ashes thrown into the sea.

In one of her last interviews, Arendt recalled an incident that captures that stupidity and shows that it was hardly just Eichmann's preserve. The German philosopher Ernst Jünger had fought for the Nazis during World War II but was dismissed from the army in 1944 after he was indirectly implicated with fellow officers in a plot to assassinate Hitler. One day, Arendt recalled, Jünger came across

> a farmer [who] had taken in Russian prisoners of war straight from the camps, and naturally they were completely starving – you know how Russian prisoners of war were treated here. And the farmer said to Jünger, 'Well, they're subhuman, just like cattle – look how they devour food like cattle.' Jünger comments on this story, 'It's sometimes as if the German people

were being possessed by the Devil.' And he didn't mean anything 'demonic' by that. You see, there's something outrageously stupid about this story. I mean the story is stupid, so to speak. The man doesn't see that this is just what starving people do, right? And anyone would behave like that. But there's something really outrageous about this stupidity. . . . Eichmann was perfectly intelligent, but in this respect he had this sort of stupidity. It was this stupidity that was so outrageous. And that was what I actually meant by banality. There's nothing deep about it – nothing demonic! There's simply the reluctance ever to imagine what the other person is experiencing, correct?[8]

Here stupidity is not something that can be measured by intelligence tests, but a moral category: the stupid are blind to the suffering of others. And this chimes with Musil's sense that moral concepts – freedom and reason – were in poor health in Europe in 1937, as Nazism in all its moral blindness scythed murderously across the continent.

As Nazism rose, so theories of stupidity multiplied. The German Jewish psychoanalyst Karl Landauer published two important papers, 'Zur psychosexuellen Genese der Dummheit' ('On the Psychosexual Origins of Stupidity', 1929) and 'Intelligenz und Dummheit' ('Intelligence and Stupidity', 1926),[9] in which he argued that stupidity was an 'acquired inability to experience' that became a psychic scar deforming its sufferers. In 1929, Landauer had established the Frankfurt Psychoanalytic Institute at the invitation of his eminent analysand, the sociologist and director of the Frankfurt Institute of Social Research, Max Horkheimer. In 1933, though, when Hitler came to power as chancellor, Landauer, like many other Jews, left Germany. He settled in Amsterdam, becoming, for the best part of a decade, one of the Netherlands' leading psychoanalysts. Until, that is, he became one of Adolf Eichmann's victims. In 1943, he was arrested with his wife and his oldest daughter and transferred to Bergen-Belsen. There he managed to practise analysis before dying of malnutrition.

Landauer's work on human stupidity resonated profoundly for Horkheimer, and his fellow Frankfurt School philosopher Theodor Adorno, both of whom managed to escape the clutches of Eichmann and his henchmen by escaping to the US and continuing their work in Los Angeles. It was during that Californian exile that, as fellow Jews were being murdered on an industrial scale across the Atlantic, Adorno and Horkheimer wrote *Dialectic of Enlightenment*, their vituperative excoriation of modern mass society in its totalitarian form (a form that, controversially, they took to be as prevalent in Roosevelt's America as in Hitler's Germany). In it, they attempted to answer the question 'why mankind, instead of entering into a truly human condition, is sinking into a new kind of barbarism'.[10] In the very last section of the book, entitled 'The Genesis of Stupidity', they sketched an answer to that question, drawing heavily on their murdered colleague's thoughts.

Consider, Adorno and Horkheimer suggested unexpectedly, the snail. 'The true symbol of intelligence is the snail's horn with which it feels,' they wrote.

> The horn recoils instantly before seeking asylum in the protective shell and again becoming one with the whole. Only tentatively does it re-emerge to assert its independence. If the danger is still present it vanishes once more, now hesitating longer before renewing the attempt. In its early stages the life of the mind is infinitely fragile. The snail's senses depend on its muscles, and muscles become feebler with every hindrance to their play. Physical injury cripples the body, fear the mind. At the start the two are inseparable.[11]

What has this to do with the rise of barbarism and, more to the point stupidity? 'Stupidity,' Adorno and Horkheimer contended, 'is a scar. . . . Every partial stupidity of a man denotes a spot where the play of stirring muscles was thwarted instead of encouraged. That spot is where curiosity, rather than being encouraged, is scared off.' A child, for example, might be disciplined for asking too many questions and, as a result, stop asking questions, becoming thereby stupid.

> A child's ceaseless queries are always symptoms of a hidden pain, of a first question to which it found no answer and which it did not know how to frame properly. Its reiteration suggests the playful determination of a dog leaping repeatedly at the door it does not yet know how to open, and finally giving up if the catch is out of his reach. It also has something in it of the desperation of the lion pacing up and down in its cage, or of the neurotic who renews a defensive reaction that has already proved futile in the past. If the child's repeated attempts are balked, or too brutally frustrated, it may turn its attention in a different direction. . . . An imperceptible scar, a tiny calloused area of insensitivity, is apt to form at the spot where the urge was stifled.[12]

For Adorno and Horkheimer, stupidity is not the sort of thing you would be able to tell from someone's performance on an IQ test – it is not a matter of not being very good at maths, nor of being very well read. And it is certainly not something that it makes sense to think is innate. Rather, as for Musil and for Arendt, stupidity is a moral category: it involves a certain learned insensitivity to reality. 'Such scars lead to deformities. They can lead to hard and able characters; they can breed stupidity – as a symptom of pathological deficiency, or blindness and impotency, if they are quiescent; in the form of malice, spite and fanaticism, if they produce a cancer within. The coercion suffered turns good will into bad.'[13]

That cancerous turn, indeed, Adorno and Horkheimer recognized in an earlier section of *Dialectic of Enlightenment* entitled 'Elements of Anti-Semitism'. The murderous anti-semitism they managed to escape was the product of the scar of stupidity: in particular, Nazi supporters blaming the wrong people for their post-World War I sufferings. 'And so people shout: Stop thief! – but point at the Jews,' they wrote. 'They are the scapegoats, not only for individual maneuvers and machinations but in a broader sense, inasmuch as the economic injustice of the whole class is attributed to them.'[14] Anti-semitism thus conceived was not just wicked but also stupid – a cognitive inability betokening the kind of spiritual sickness that Robert Musil diagnosed.

Stupidity, then, was not born in opposition to cleverness or intelligence. Clever stupidity is not, for Adorno and Horkheimer, an oxymoron. Intelligence and stupidity are not each other's negatives, shadowing each other for all time. Rather, they cohabit uneasily in every society, in every individual – though stupidity, very much like a cancer and very much like Germany under the Third Reich, can predominate. Adorno and Horkheimer concluded: 'Like the species of the animal order, the mental stages within the human species, and the blind-spots in the individual, are stages at which hope petered out and whose petrification demonstrates that all things that live are subject to constraint .'[15]

Berlin, 1943

In the same year Karl Landauer died in Bergen-Belsen and Horkheimer and Adorno were writing about stupidity in Los Angeles, a young

Lutheran pastor called Dietrich Bonhoeffer was awaiting trial in Tegel prison in Berlin for his role in the anti-Nazi resistance movement. In jail, he, too, thought long and hard about stupidity. How could his native Germany, that land of poets and philosophers, have become so evil? His sense was that the root of the problem was not evil but stupidity. In his letters from prison, Bonhoeffer argued that stupidity is a more dangerous enemy of good than evil, because while 'one may protest against evil; it can be exposed and, if need be, prevented by use of force. . . . Against stupidity we are defenseless. Neither protests nor the use of force accomplishes anything here; reasons fall on deaf ears.'[16]

During the 1930s, Bonhoeffer had become a leading figure in the Confessing Church, a movement that resisted Hitler's attempt to co-opt German Protestant churches into the Nazi state and thereby become arms of its propaganda machine. Bonhoeffer became a thorn in the side not just of the Nazis but also of fellow German Christians, many of whom he considered were conniving with the evils of Nazism.

Bonhoeffer was particularly concerned about anti-semitism, though not perhaps in the way that Jewish intellectuals such as Horkheimer and Adorno had conceived it. Indeed, he never overtly repudiated his early view that the 'Jewish Question' would be solved by the conversion of Jews to Christianity. Rather, his leading concern in opposing the anti-semitism of the Nazis was to counter the Third Reich's definition of Jews in terms of blood. The 1935 Nuremberg Race Laws had rejected the traditional view of Jews as members of a religious or cultural community, but instead defined persons with three or more grandparents born into the Jewish religious community as Jews. Grandparents born into a Jewish religious community were considered racially Jewish. Their racial status passed to their children and grandchildren. Bonhoeffer opposed these laws, principally because he was concerned for the rights of practising Christians of Jewish ancestry. His resistance to Nazism became more politicized when he was introduced by his brother-in-law to conspirators seeking Hitler's overthrow in 1938. Ironically, once the war started in 1939, Bonhoeffer was employed in the Abwehr, Germany's Military Intelligence Department, all the while working for the resistance and even, with his brother-in-law, helping Jews escape to neutral Switzerland. The German intelligence services, in a small mercy, were run without intelligence about what their staff were up to. Among other Abwehr agents was the German industrialist Oskar Schindler, the man credited with saving the lives of 1,200 Jews from the death camps. Many of the leading conspirators behind the 20 July 1944 plot to assassinate Hitler, probably including Bonhoeffer, also were Abwehr agents. In 1942, Bonhoeffer was arrested by the Gestapo and charged with conspiring to rescue Jews, using his foreign travels for non-intelligence matters, and misusing his intelligence position to help – for all of which crimes he was found guilty.

In Tegel, Bonhoeffer wrote about how stupidity was a necessary factor in explaining the popularity of Nazis. Today his theory of stupidity seems to prefigure the mood of our era of post-truth and alternative facts:

> Facts that contradict one's prejudgment simply need not be believed – in such moments the stupid person even becomes critical – and when facts are irrefutable they are just pushed aside as inconsequential, as incidental. In all this, the stupid person, in contrast to the malicious one, is utterly self-satisfied, and, being easily irritated, becomes dangerous by going on the attack. For that reason, greater caution is called for when dealing with a stupid person than with a malicious one. Never again will we try to persuade the stupid person with reasons, for it is senseless and dangerous.'[17]

Bonhoeffer had had opportunities to avoid arrest by taking refuge in Britain or the US, but saw it as his duty to remain: 'I will have no right to participate in the reconstruction of Christian life in Germany after the war if I do not share the trials of this time with my people.'[18] He never took part in that reconstruction. On 8 April 1945, two weeks before American troops liberated the camp and scarcely a month before Nazi Germany's formal surrender to the Allies, Bonhoeffer was sentenced to summary execution by an SS judge, presumably on the grounds of being a traitor for his involvement in the failed assassination of Hitler. His sentence was not delivered after a proper trial but after a so-called drumhead court martial, a parody of justice in which no evidence was presented and no defence case made. The following morning at dawn, Bonhoeffer was stripped naked, led into the execution yard of Flossenbürg concentration camp, and hanged with five other conspirators. He had written: 'No man in the whole world can change the truth. One can only look for the truth, find it and serve it. The truth is in all places.'[19]

Nuremberg, 1945

A few months after this execution, the victorious Allies put 21 of the most important surviving leaders of defeated Nazi Germany on trial in Nuremberg. This group did not include several leading Nazis, such as Adolf Hitler, Heinrich Himmler, and Joseph Goebbels, because they had already committed suicide by the time the International Military Tribunal convened in November. The leading purposes of the 13 trials carried out in Nuremberg between 1945 and 1949 were to convict the defendants and assemble irrefutable evidence of Nazi crimes, and to establish a new order of crimes – crimes against peace and crimes against humanity – that would form the basis of a new international legal and moral order. At Nuremberg, the Allies also sought to do something akin to the spiritual regeneration Robert Musil thought necessary when he gave his talk on stupidity in 1937. That spiritual regeneration involved restoring moral concepts of freedom and reason to health by means of studying not just the true, the reasonable, or the clever but also their opposites: the false, the irrational, and the diabolically stupid.

To that end, two Americans working at Nuremberg, the psychiatrist Douglas Kelley and the psychologist Gustave Gilbert, performed psychological tests, including a German translation of the Wechsler–Bellevue intelligence test, to measure the IQs of 21 of the defendants as they awaited trial. Lieutenant Colonel Kelley was the chief psychiatrist at Nuremberg Prison, initially tasked with determining whether the defendants were competent to stand trial. He recruited Lieutenant Gilbert, the son of Jewish Austrian immigrants and a German speaker. All the defendants were deemed by Kelley legally sane, but the tests he and Gilbert administered were additionally used to address two of the most vexing questions of the day. Were the Nazis evil men or merely ordinary people who did horrific deeds because they were ordered to do so? Was there a Nazi personality type?

The first two tests performed on the Nazi prisoners were the Thematic Apperception Test and the Rorschach Inkblot Test. The former involved showing the person to be tested an image – say of a boy looking at a violin or a man holding his hat with his face down, while a woman next to him stares out the window – and inviting them to construct a story about what led up to the image. The latter involved presenting the person to be tested with images of inkblots and inviting them to say what they looked like. The results were disappointing for anyone wanting proof that the Nazi personality, if there was such a thing, was monstrous and pathological. Kelley and Gilbert concluded that there was no fundamental difference between the results of the Nazi prisoners and of those of an average of Americans who had taken the test. Their judgement was confirmed 30 years later when the psychologist Molly Harrower conducted a double-blind test to compare the Nazi results with a group of members of the clergy and hospital patients. She found no difference between the groups.[20]

But the results of the Wechsler–Bellevue IQ test that the defendants took showed something, to put it mildly, discombobulating. Under the headline 'The Evil Geniuses', the 17 December 1945 issue of *Newsweek* reported: 'The Nazi war criminals at Nuremberg were not smart enough, but they are smart. Intelligence tests show that Hjalmar Schacht, former economics minister, and Arthur Seyss-Inquart, onetime gauleiter in Holland, rate as geniuses, while Reichsmarshall Hermann Göring and Grand Admiral Karl Dönitz fall in the near-genius category.'[21] The average score for the Wechsler–Belleveue intelligence test, as we learned in the previous chapter, is 100; the average scored by Nazi defendants was 128. Here are the scores in full.

Hjalmar Schacht – 143
Arthur Seyss-Inquart – 141
Hermann Göring – 138
Karl Dönitz – 138
Franz von Papen – 134
Eric Raeder – 134
Dr Hans Frank – 130
Hans Fritsche – 130
Baldur von Schirach – 130
Joachim von Ribbentrop – 129
Wilhelm Keitel – 129
Albert Speer – 128
Alfred Jodl – 127
Alfred Rosenberg – 127
Constantin von Neurath – 125

Walther Funk – 124
Wilhelm Frick – 124
Rudolf Hess – 120
Fritz Sauckel – 118
Ernst Kaltenbrunner – 113
Julius Streicher – 106[22]

What are we to make of these scores? One possibility is that intelligence is positively correlated with evil, though when one considers, say, the case of blameless child wonder Rishi Shiv Prasanna, who in 2023, aged only eight, scored 180 on an IQ test, this seems unfair. Albert Einstein never took at IQ test, though some have dared to suppose his would have been around 160 and nobody sane ever suggested he had the evil gene or was diabolical in any way. In any case, the list above hardly matches IQ with any hypothesized EQ (evil quotient). The highest scorer of the Nazis defendants, Schacht, was possibly the least obviously evil of the bunch: the former head of the Reichsbank spent almost the entire war in a concentration camp, was involved in Hitler assassination plots, and was totally acquitted of charges against him at Nuremberg because of his objections to Hitler. The lowest scorer was more evidently evil: Julius Streicher, editor of the virulently anti-semitic *Der Stürmer* newspaper. He had chaired the Central Committee to Repulse Jewish Atrocity and Boycott Agitation (Zentralkomitee zur Abwehr der jüdischen Greuel- und Boykotthetze), was a sadist and rapist, and had enriched himself from seized Jewish property. Eleven of the men from this list were sentenced to death and 10 were hanged on 16 October 1946. The most senior Nazi prosecuted at Nuremberg, Hermann Göring, who until the last month of the war was Hitler's successor and deputy, evaded this fate by taking a potassium cyanide capsule secreted in a tin of pomade the day before his execution.

More likely than demonstrating the positive link between evil and intelligence, the results show us something else, namely that Robert Musil was right in supposing there are two kinds of stupidity. One involves a 'weakness in the head'. None of the Nazis tried in the first Nuremberg trial was stupid in this sense – to be leading parts of a political movement that took power in Germany, put much of Europe under its yoke, and organized the attempted genocide of the Jews requires a certain intelligence. But it also requires a certain stupidity, namely the spiritual debility diagnosed by Musil.

In this respect, it is striking that Hermann Göring had a much higher IQ than Streicher and contended he was not really anti-semitic. He told Kelley that the Nazi treatment of the Jews was nothing more than 'good political propaganda' – as if Jew hatred were a galvanizing force to motivate lesser minds than his. And yet Göring's higher stupidity, that spiritual debility, enabled him to have a decisive role in one of the most evil acts humanity has ever committed: in 1941, he ordered Security Police chief Reinhard Heydrich to organize and coordinate a 'total solution' to the 'Jewish question'. Kelley, for his part, thought Göring had a 'complete lack of moral value'.[23] And yet something of this stupid, wicked man's personality obsessed the psychiatrist.

What did the Americans who tested the Nazis think their results showed? Kelley had hoped to identify a Nazi personality, one that set these evil-seeming psychopaths apart from the rest of us. He found nothing of the kind, but instead concluded:

> They are people who exist in every country of the world. Their personality patterns are not obscure. But they are people who have peculiar drives, people who want to be in power, and you say that they don't exist here, and I would say that I am quite certain that there are people even in America who would willingly climb over the corpses of half of the American public if they could gain control of the other half.[24]

Kelley was clearly disturbed by his experiences and refused to talk to his wife and children about them. He became alcoholic and despondent. On New Year's Day, 1958, Kelley killed himself with a cyanide capsule just as Göring had. The American psychiatrist had reportedly expressed admiration for 'Göring's control over his own death'.[25]

As for Gustave Gilbert, his 1950 book *The Psychology of Dictatorship*[26] proposed that the Nazis were raised in a culture that had a primary value of deference to authority, to which all other reason and intelligence took a backseat. He was much influenced by Erich Fromm, the Jewish psychoanalyst who worked with Horkheimer and Adorno at the Frankfurt School. Fromm argued that Hitler did not overcome his childish narcissism and so failed to adapt to reality, instead responding to humiliations with 'necrophilia': that is to say, lust-ridden destructiveness.[27] Fromm cited the so-called Nero Decree issued by Hitler in March 1945 as an example of this. On the brink of defeat, Hitler ordered the destruction of German infrastructure to prevent its use by Allied forces (a decree that the man tasked with implementing it, Albert Speer, refused to enact, considering it senseless). Nazism, Fromm argued, was the product of the social and economic anxieties of a people long used to order. The German people projected onto this narcissistic necrophile their hopes for a restoration of pride and order, projections that on the face of it seem spectacularly deluded, even stupid. Following Fromm, Gilbert in *The Psychology of Dictatorship* proposed there were three different personality types in the group – schizoid, narcissistic, and paranoid – that could all be classified under a psychopathic personality, and thus their pathology led them to engage in their horrific actions.

Eleven years after the publication of *The Psychology of Dictatorship*, Gilbert was able to consider the veracity of his analysis of Nazi pathology when he flew to Jerusalem to give evidence in the trial of Adolf Eichmann. In the interim, several American psychologists had started to reflect on stupidity as a group phenomenon. In a 1951 experiment, Polish American psychologist Solomon Asch put a naïve participant in a room with seven stooges.[28] The stooges had agreed in advance what their responses would be when presented with a task. The real participant did not know this and was led to believe that the seven stooges were also real participants like him- or herself. Each person in the room had to state aloud which comparison line (A, B, or C) was most like the target line. The answer was always obvious. The real participant sat at the end of the row and gave his or her answer last. Asch found that about 75% of participants conformed at least once, while in a control group with no pressure to conform, less than 1% of participants gave the wrong answer.

Asch concluded from this experiment that people conform for two main reasons: because they want to fit in with the group (what he called a normative influence) and because they believe the group is better informed than they are (what he called informational influence). Either way, stupidity is infectious, spread through populations on the wings of folly.

This theory of mass stupidity was developed by the American psychologist Leon Festinger, later known for his account of cognitive dissonance.

In the early 1950s, he and his researchers infiltrated a group of Americans who believed that the world was going to end on 21 December 1954. The cult leader, Dorothy Martin, a housewife from Chicago, invited followers to her house, where they sat on the fateful day awaiting Armageddon. What amazed the researchers who infiltrated the group were the reactions of many of the members when the end of the world did not in fact occur. Faced with this apparent negation of their beliefs, many of the faithful did not abandon them. Festinger called this the backfire effect, defined by one journalist as follows: 'When your deepest convictions are challenged by contradictory evidence, your beliefs get stronger.'[29] Stupidity is a virus stronger than any truth serum.

Theories abounded about the mass delusion that made the Third Reich possible. In his 1933 book *The Mass Psychology of Fascism*, Wilhelm Reich ascribed it to sexual repression: the suppression of natural sexuality in the child caused a general inhibition of critical thinking.[30] In his 1942 book *Escape from Freedom*, Erich Fromm proposed that the German petit bourgeoisie, free from the authority of church or state, experienced a kind of spiritual anguish akin to what children feel during infant development and so, in order to create a new form of security, they sadomasochistically yearned for a strong leader.[31] In *Behemoth: The Structure and Practice of National Socialism*, published the same year, the Frankfurt School political scientist Franz Neumann wrote: 'Charismatic rule has long been neglected and ridiculed, but apparently it has deep roots and becomes a powerful stimulus once the proper psychological and social conditions are met.'[32] Elias Canetti, in his 1960 book *Crowds and Power*, argued that the anguish of personal freedom Fromm had recognzsed, along with the psychic burden of individuality, can be neutralized by participating in a crowd of people and by obeying a ruler. 'Only together can men free themselves from their burdens of distance,' he wrote. 'And this, precisely, is what happens in a crowd. . . . Each man is as near the other as he is to himself; and an immense feeling of relief ensues. It is for the sake of this blessed moment, when no-one is greater or better than another, that people become a crowd.'[33]

Were any of these accounts relevant to understanding the man whom Gilbert saw in the dock in Jerusalem in 1961? Homer Bigart reported in the *New York Times* that there was a 'duel of glares' as Gilbert on the witness stand stared down Eichmann. The American Jewish psychologist was there to give evidence on what he had heard from Nazi defendants about Eichmann at Nuremberg and barred from appraising the latter's character. When Eichmann was required during the trial to watch an 80-minute film of Holocaust horrors, he did so 'without flinching or batting an eye'. 'Eichmann never took his eyes from the film, never raised his hands to his face,' noted Bigart. 'The man who said he could not bear the sight of blood . . . was the very model of composure.'[34]

The description of Eichmann as impassive in the face of the Holocaust's horrors makes him sound monstrous, but sitting in the same courtroom as Gustave Gilbert, Hannah Arendt denied the defendant even that distinction. 'Everybody,' she wrote, 'could see that this man was not a "monster".'[35] He was, rather, 'an average, "normal" person, neither feeble-minded nor indoctrinated nor cynical'. His was 'obviously no case of insane hatred of Jews, of fanatical anti-Semitism or indoctrination of any kind'.[36] During the war, he had acted, according to Arendt, merely out of obedience to 'his duty. . . . He not only obeyed *orders*, he also obeyed the *law*.'[37] To buttress her argument, Arendt reported that 'half a dozen psychiatrists had certified [Eichmann] as "normal".'[38] In the introduction to a philosophical essay published posthumously in the *New Yorker*, Arendt reiterated her view: 'I was struck by a manifest shallowness in [Eichmann] which made it impossible to trace the incontestable evil of his deeds to any deeper level of roots or motives.'[39]

The horrible corollary of Arendt's reflections was that any one of us might, in the right circumstances, become an Eichmann. This thought underpinned an experiment conducted by Stanley Milgram in a laboratory at Yale University in the same year as Eichmann's trial.[40] Milgram had worked with Solomon Asch in the 1950s in his conformity studies and had seen first-hand how test subjects agreed with the decisions of a group, even though they knew these decisions to be wrong. What could account for such stupidity?

In 1961, Milgram, by then professor of psychology at Yale, placed newspaper advertisements and selected from respondents 40 men from a variety of professions, including teachers, postmen, engineers, and labourers. In the laboratory, the participants were shown a fake electric shock machine with 30 switches that, it was claimed, would generate shocks at 15-volt increments. The participants were told that the study was aimed at investigating the effects of punishment on learning. Each participant was then told that there would be two volunteers in the experiment, one a learner and the other the teacher. In fact, in each case, one of the two volunteers was actually a stooge, an accountant called Mr Wallace. The two volunteers were required to draw a piece of paper from a hat to decide who would play the 'teacher' and who the 'learner'. In fact, the draw was rigged: Mr Wallace always played the learner. This role involved him being strapped into what looked like an electric chair with an electrode attached to his wrist. The real volunteer was then asked to administer a word test for the learner. The teacher read a list of word pairs (such as 'blue–girl, 'nice–day') and then repeated single words, inviting the learner to recall the second word of the pair. Each wrong answer resulted in the teacher apparently giving the learner an electric shock. Each time the learner gave the wrong answer, the level of the shock was raised by 15 volts. Labels on the shock machine dial told the teacher that the shock levels rose from 'Slight shock' to 'Danger: severe shock' and, ultimately, to one alarmingly marked 'XXXX'. The teacher did not know that the learner had been told by Milgram to give the wrong answer in about one of four questions.

Milgram had asked other participants how far he thought the volunteer teachers would go in administering the shocks. Most thought that they would stop at the level that caused pain. They were wrong. What often happened during the experiments was that the teacher would express misgivings about inducing an electrical shock but would be urged by a 'scientist' (in fact a biology teacher wearing a lab technician's coat and maintaining a professional demeanour throughout) to continue regardless. The scientist would even tell the teacher that they had no choice but to see the experiment through to the end. Milgram found that all 40 participants were prepared to administer shocks up to 300 volts. It was at this level that the learner was instructed to shout: 'I absolutely refuse to answer any more! Get me out of here!'

Milgram noted that the teachers administered the electric shocks even as they manifested extreme upset during the experiment. He recorded that they sweated, trembled, and even offered to return the fees they had been paid to take part. Three of the teachers had full-blown seizures during their participation. Nonetheless, 65% of them obeyed the instructions of the scientist and administered the top voltage of 450 volts to the by now screaming learner.

Milgram concluded that the role of the authority figure, the scientist, compelled the volunteers to violate their own sense of morality, and although they suffered psychically during the experiment, they felt no choice but to obey. The fact that the experiment took place in a prestigious university building, too, may have induced deferential obedience among the volunteers. Why? Milgram hypothesized that we are socialized as children to obey authority figures, from parents to teachers. That obedience could be productive – indeed, Milgram contended, without it any society could not function. Or it could be employed, as it was by Hitler and other leading Nazis, to facilitate the murder of six million Jews. The Holocaust was only possible because a large number of people obeyed orders. Such grotesque obedience was not culturally specific. Milgram concluded that obedience to authority was not a feature solely of German culture but a seemingly universal factor in human behaviour.

Another disturbing way of considering this phenomenon is that obedience, that spiritual debility or higher stupidity that Robert Musil described, can be induced in otherwise moral, normal, and even virtuous people It is not so much, Milgram wrote, 'the kind of person a man is as the kind of situation in which he finds himself that determines how he will act'.[41] Milgram's experiment has long been criticized – for deceiving its participants, for selecting only American men – but it remains relevant to us as we think about the value of obedience and stupidity to the functioning of society. As one recent psychology textbook put it, Milgram's experiment 'simultaneously absolved and made villains of us all'.[42]

9

Structural Stupidity

The smartest idiot in the room

'I like to think I'm actually a smart person,' the late American anarchist and anthropologist David Graeber told me one evening in a restaurant near his office at the London School of Economics. 'Most people seem to agree with that,' Graeber said. 'OK, I was emotionally distraught, but I was doing things that were really dumb.'[1]

In 2012, Graeber's mother had suffered a series of strokes. Social workers advised him that in order to pay for the home care she needed, he should apply for Medicaid, the US government health insurance programme for people on low incomes. So he did, only to be sucked into a vortex of form filling and humiliation familiar to anyone who's ever read Kafka.

At one point, the application was held up because someone at the Department of Motor Vehicles had put down Graeber's given name as 'Daid'; at another, because someone at the telecommunications company Verizon had spelled his surname 'Grueber'. The matter became academic, because Graeber's mother died before she got Medicaid. But the form-filling ordeal stayed with him. 'Having spent much of my life leading a fairly bohemian existence, comparatively insulated from this sort of thing, I found myself asking: is this what ordinary life, for most people, is really like?' he wrote in his 2015 book *The Utopia of Rules: On Technology, Stupidity and the Secret Joys of Bureaucracy*. 'Running around feeling like an idiot all day? Being somehow put in a position where one actually does end up acting like an idiot?'[2] As we sat together in the restaurant that evening, he asked himself: 'How did I not notice that the signature was on the wrong line? There's something about being in that bureaucratic situation that encourages you to behave foolishly.'[3]

Graeber's sense was that stupidity like his is cultivated by capitalists and bureaucrats to extend their power. In *The Utopia of Rules*, he wrote:

> Bureaucratic procedures, which have an uncanny ability to make even the smartest people act like idiots, are not so much forms of stupidity in themselves, as they are ways of managing situations already stupid because of the effects of structural violence. . . . Stupidity in the name of fairness and decency is still stupidity, and violence in the name of human liberation is still violence. It's no coincidence the two so often seem to arrive together.[4]

What's striking here is that the kind of stupidity that Graeber experienced and he took to be pervasive in capitalist societies is not of the kind that can be measured by intelligence tests or diagnosed by doctors in white coats but is nonetheless, he argued, a real force with deleterious consequences. The anarchist rebel, for a few harrowing months, become soulmate to Kafka's Josef K.

The stupid and stupefying rules he experienced while filling in forms to apply for Medicaid is, he argued, a structural stupidity experienced both by those who deliver the services and those who use them.

Exposure to this structural stupidity was a shock for Graeber since he had managed to live, for the most part, outside its remit until his death aged 59 in 2020. This was a man who led not just a relatively bohemian existence but also a charmed life, mostly outside what Virginia Woolf called the machine. Born in 1961 to working-class Jewish parents in New York, Graeber had a radical heritage. His father, Kenneth, was a plate stripper who fought in the Spanish Civil War, and his mother, Ruth, was a garment worker who played the lead role in *Pins and Needles*, a 1930s musical revue staged by the International Ladies' Garment Workers' Union.

Their son was calling himself an anarchist at the age of 16, but only became heavily involved in politics in 1999 when he joined the protests against the World Trade Organization meeting in Seattle. Later, while teaching at Yale, he joined the activists, artists, and pranksters of the Direct Action Network in New York. Even as an academic, he worked mostly away from the epicentres of academic bureaucracy: he cut his teeth as an anthropologist doing fieldwork in Madagascar, and it was there that he became fascinated with the antinomian hearties of the ocean wave, a fascination that ultimately resulted in his eulogy to the lawless buccaneers of yesteryear, namely his *Pirate Enlightenment, or the Real Libertalia: Buccaneers, Women Traders and Mock Kingdoms in Eighteenth-Century Madagascar*.[5] It was on Madagascar that, briefly in the 18th century, a small stand was attempted against the rising tide of bureaucratic control, Graeber supposed, when the self-styled king of pirates Henry Avery – a.k.a. Long Ben – established a pirate republic there with his henchmen called Libertalia, a proto-communist utopia where all goods were held in common. It was in this experiment in post-bureaucratic living that Graeber imagined a society free from structural stupidity.

In 2005, Graeber went on a year's sabbatical from Yale, 'and did a lot of direct action and was in the media'.[6] When he returned, he was, he said, snubbed by colleagues and did not have his contract renewed. He reckoned this was in part because his countercultural activities were an embarrassment to Yale. But that didn't stop him. He carried on combining academic work with battling what he took to be structural stupidity. As he put it in *The Utopia of Rules*: 'Bureaucracies . . . are not themselves forms of stupidity so much as they are ways of organizing stupidity – of managing relationships that are already characterized by extremely unequal structures of imagination, which exist because of the existence of structural violence.'[7]

In 2011, at New York's Zuccotti Park, Graeber became involved in Occupy Wall Street, which he described to me as an 'experiment in a post-bureaucratic society', and was responsible for the slogan 'We are the 99%'. He continued:

> We wanted to demonstrate we could do all the services that social service providers do without endless bureaucracy. In fact, at one point at Zuccotti Park there was a giant plastic garbage bag that had $800,000 in it. People kept giving us money, but we weren't going to put it in the bank. You have all these rules and regulations. And Occupy Wall Street can't have a bank account. I always say the principle of direct action is the defiant insistence on acting as if one is already free.[8]

In that sense, Graeber's life and works were a systematic resistance to the dead hand of what he called structural stupidity. He quoted to me with approval the anarchist collective Crimethinc: 'Putting yourself in new situations constantly is the only way to ensure that you make your decisions unencumbered by the nature of habit, law, custom or prejudice – and it's up to you to create the situations.'[9] Academia was once just such a situation, he reckoned. The university was a haven for oddballs. 'It was a place of refuge. Not any more. Now, if you can't act a little like a professional executive, you can kiss goodbye to the idea of an academic career.' Why was that so terrible? 'It means we're taking a very large percentage of the greatest creative talent in our society and telling them to go to hell. . . . The eccentrics have been drummed out of all institutions.'[10] Well, not quite: the US's loss was the UK's gain: Graeber moved to London, becoming a professor of anthropology at the LSE in 2010.

The forces of stupidity-inducing conformity, he maintained, were boosted by something that happened in the 1970s: technological innovation shifted from extending the frontiers of possibility to facilitating ever greater control and bureaucratic impediments to human flourishing. But technological advance was supposed to be about the former, wasn't it? When Graeber was a little boy, he watched the Apollo moon landing and supposed, in his naïve way, that technological advance would produce other marvels, and that he would witness more giant leaps for humankind. As a disenchanted grown-up, he wrote in 2015 of his disappointment that all the technological wonders being touted in the late 1960s never happened. Where were the flying cars, suspended animation, immortality drugs, androids, and colonies on Mars? Instead of boldly going, humanity had surely stagnated. 'Speaking as someone who was eight years old at the time of the Apollo moon landing,' he wrote in *The Utopia of Rules*, 'I have clear memories of calculating that I would be 39 years of age in the magic year 2000, and wondering what the world around me would be like. Did I honestly expect I would be living in a world of such wonders? Of course. Do I feel cheated now? Absolutely.'[11] Technological progress seemed to promise, not just the 15-hour weeks Keynes envisaged, but also something like the communist utopia Marx briefly sketched in *The German Ideology*.

So what happened between the Apollo moon landing and now? Graeber's theory was that in the late 1960s and early 1970s there was mounting fear about a society of hippie proles with too much time on their hands. As he put it to me: 'The ruling class had a freak out about robots replacing all the workers. There was a general feeling that "My God, if it's bad now with the hippies, imagine what it'll be like if the entire working class becomes unemployed." You never know how conscious it was but decisions were made about research priorities.' Consider, he suggested, medicine and the life sciences since the late 1960s. 'Cancer? No, that's still here.' Instead, the most dramatic breakthroughs have been with drugs such as Ritalin, Zoloft, and Prozac – all of which, Graeber said, were 'tailor-made, one might say, so that these new professional demands don't drive us completely, dysfunctionally, crazy'.[12]

Instead of 15-hour weeks, then, vast numbers of humans, Americans and Europeans in particular, are working harder than ever at jobs that are more or less meaningless. It is a form of society-wide structural stupidity, Graeber claimed. In a 2013 article called 'On the Phenomenon of Bullshit Jobs', he wrote: 'A world without teachers or dockworkers would soon be in trouble. . . . It's not entirely clear how humanity would suffer were all private equity CEOs, lobbyists, PR researchers, actuaries, telemarketers, bailiffs, or legal consultants to similarly vanish.'[13] It's a bracing point, but more bracing yet is the possibility that anthropologists' work might be seen as no less meaningless. When I put this to him, Graeber didn't exactly disagree: 'There can be no objective measure of social value.'[14]

Graeber's bullshit jobs argument could be taken as a counterblast to the hyper-capitalist dystopia argument favoured by proponents of artificial intelligence whereby the robots take over and humans are busted down to an eternity of playing Minecraft. Summarizing predictions in recent futurological literature, the British novelist and critic John Lanchester wrote: 'There's capital, doing better than ever; the robots, doing all the work; and the great mass of humanity, doing not much but having fun playing with its gadgets.'[15] Lanchester drew attention to a league table drawn up by Oxford economists of 702 jobs that might be better done by robots: at number one (most safe) were recreational therapists; at 702 (least safe) were telemarketers. Anthropologists, Graeber might have been pleased to know, came in at 39, so he was much safer than writers (123) and editors (140).

Before artificial intelligence advanced the possibility that human stupidity, even if it were not to be abolished, might be neatly sidestepped by rendering our species intellectually obsolete, Graeber was railing against the stupidity-causing bullshit jobs that you'd think were better done by machines – if at all. He wrote:

> It's as if someone were out there making up pointless jobs just for the sake of keeping us all working. And here, precisely, lies the mystery. In capitalism, this is precisely what is *not* supposed to happen. Sure, in the old inefficient Socialist states like the Soviet Union, where employment was considered both a right and a sacred duty, the system made up as many jobs as they had to. (This is why in Soviet department stores it took three clerks to sell a piece of meat.) But, of course, this is the sort of very problem market competition is supposed to fix.[16]

Graeber believed that the most basic level of being is play rather than economics, fun rather than rules, goofing around rather than filling in forms. If only we were intelligent enough to realize our own stupidity, we might enjoy our lives more. But we aren't.

Conspicuous displays of stupidity

For Graeber, stupidity is not just the prerogative of us latter-day Josef Ks on the receiving end of bureaucracies or toilers at the coalface of bullshit. Stupidity is also a luxury product for the privileged. Stupidity, thus conceived, is the latest must-have for the idle rich and their supporters. Think of it this way. The economist and sociologist Thorstein Veblen posited in *The Theory of the Leisure Class* (1899) the notion of conspicuous consumption.[17] Effectively, the world was divided between the have-nots and the have-yachts, with the latter destined to find occasions to both witter proudly about their possessions and display them, to the presumed envy of the have-nots. Graeber's suggestion effectively updated Veblen for a new era in which a certain kind of stupidity is worthy of display, since it is a marker of one's cosseted leisure and superiority.

'While those on the bottom of a social ladder spend a great deal of time imagining the perspectives of, and genuinely caring about, those on the top,' wrote Graeber, 'it almost never happens the other way around.'[18] The argument here draws on the master–slave dialectic in Hegel's *The Phenomenology of Spirit*.[19] In that parable, the slave knows more about the master than the master about that slave: the very inequality of their relationship means that the slave, in addition to all their other tasks that help prop up this asymmetrical and exploitative relationship, has to do what Graeber calls 'interpretive labour'. That labour, or its lack, is intrinsically connected to the idea of structural stupidity that Graeber strove to demonstrate was endemic in ostensibly advanced 21st-century societies. Such interpretive labour is useful: to get by, societies need its members to engage in a constant work of imaginative identification with others.

At this point, stupidity makes its entrance. For Graeber, in unequal societies such as the ones in which he lived in the US and the UK, some members of society don't have to dirty their hands with that interpretive labour. He wrote: 'Women are always expected to continually imagine what one situation or another would look like from a male point of view. Men are almost never expected to do the same for women. So deeply internalized is this pattern of behavior that many men react to any suggestion that they might do otherwise as if it were itself an act of violence'.[20] But it's not just women who are on the receiving end of this structural stupidity, and not just men who benefit from it, Graeber argued. 'Whether one is dealing with masters and servants, men and women, employers and employees, rich and poor, structural inequality – what I've been calling structural violence – invariably creates highly lopsided structures of the imagination.'[21]

In Veblen's terms, then, the pleasure of being a member of the leisure class is that you don't have to do any labour. Rather, you recline on the fruits of others' labour – on a yacht, for example – and make a show of your indolence. Stupidity is just one feature of that desirable lifestyle option. What Veblen in his *The Theory of the Leisure Class* applied to physical labour, Graeber effectively applied to intellectual and affective labour: those with the most power don't think about those at the bottom; rather, it is a sign of their power and superiority that they have to do no interpretive labour. Such is the laziness of power. Hegel wrote of the cunning of reason, that tendency of historical forces to erase their nature the better to elude opposition to them. For Graeber, the cunning of reason is to erase how the laziness of power and its structural stupidity are actually backed up by force. The truncheons of the police all too rarely need to make an appearance.

But if there is a cunning of reason, as Graeber suggested, there is also a cunning of stupidity. Stupidity makes itself invaluable to the perpetuation not just of the Kafkaesque bureaucratic state, but also of what Luc Boltanski and Ève Chiapello in *The New Spirit of Capitalism* called the amoral system of capitalism.[22] The structural stupidity to which Graeber referred, and which thrives in the state bureaucracies he castigated when he wrote in *The Utopia of Rules* about applying to Medicaid, is also a feature of capitalism more generally. Indeed, one of the main purposes of his book was to free us from a right-wing misconception about bureaucracy. Ever since Ronald Reagan said: 'The most terrifying words in the English language are I'm from the government and I'm here to help,'[23] it has been commonplace to assume that bureaucracy means government. Wrong, Graeber argues.

> If you go to the Mac store and somebody says: 'I'm sorry, it's obvious that what needs to happen here is you need a new screen, but you're still going to have to wait a week to speak to the expert', you don't say 'Oh damn bureaucrats', even though that's what it is – classic bureaucratic procedure. We've been propagandised into believing that bureaucracy means civil servants. Capitalism isn't supposed to create meaningless positions. . . . Still, somehow, it happens.[24]

But there is no 'somehow' to it: the stupidity of the Genius Bar at the Mac store, for example, whereby we poor saps are duped into believing that the corporate functionary (no offence) is some kind of brainiac but whose genius will not be immediately available to help us reboot our laptops, is part of the structural stupidity that Graeber denounced. The stupidity he felt on filling out forms to apply for his mother's Medicaid is replicated daily not just at the Mac store's Genius Bar but also throughout the late capitalist system. Tech oligarchies including Apple, Facebook, and Google have a controlling interest in helping the virus of structural stupidity to mutate and thereby to make money from it. Making humans feel stupid is not just a pleasure but also a business model. It lurks, as we will see later in the chapter, not just in the business model of social media but also in the hopes and fears for AI.

How stupidity helps society function

Arguably, much capitalism is predicated on making us do stupid things, namely those contrary to our own interest. Franny Armstrong's 2009 documentary *The Age of Stupid* imagines that in 2055 the world has been ravaged by catastrophic climate change: London is flooded, Sydney is burning, Las Vegas has been swallowed up by desert, the Amazon rainforest has burnt up, snow has vanished from the Alps, and nuclear war has laid waste to India. An unnamed archivist is entrusted with the safekeeping of humanity's surviving store of art and knowledge. Alone in his vast repository somewhere in the largely ice-free Arctic, he reviews archival footage from back 'when we could have saved ourselves', trying to discern where it all went wrong. Stupidity here is conceived of as a species-wide inability to learn, with tragic consequences.[25]

Psychologists have a term for this mindless short-termism, namely prognostic myopia. The term was devised by Justin Gregg, the dolphin expert we met in chapter 7. 'Prognostic myopia,' he wrote 'is the human capacity to think about and alter the future coupled with the inability to care that much about what happens in the future.'[26]

Here is an example of prognostic myopia. The Global Challenges Foundation estimated in 2016 that there is a 9.5% chance of human extinction within the next 100 years, most likely by means of nuclear holocaust, climate change, or ecological catastrophe. That, you might think, isn't much of a chance, but imagine, suggested Gregg, you were told that if you continued driving your daughter to school, there was a 9.5% chance she would die in a crash. You would, most likely, seek alternative travel arrangements. But if you were told there was a 9.5% chance your great-granddaughter would die from ecological collapse, you'd probably continue driving the Subaru on the school run (other planet-ruining brands of car are available). The corollary for Gregg is that human intelligence has also created a form of stupidity that is beyond the wit of other animals: 'Our many intellectual accomplishments are on track to produce our own extinction, which is exactly how evolution gets rid of adaptations that suck.'[27] The bitter irony is that animals, though neither intelligent enough to create the means to destroy the planet nor stupid enough to put those means to apocalyptic work, will be collateral damage. Gregg's dolphins must think humans aren't worthy of the supposedly species-specific gift of intelligence.

The thesis in Armstrong's *The Age of Stupid* chimes with another account of humans stupidly acting against their own intent: *The Culture of Stopping* by German social psychologist Harald Welzer, who wrote: 'Most people are no more likely to regard a luxury yacht as an environmental disaster or even an anachronism than they are monstrous Chelsea tractors, wall-to-wall widescreen TVs or massive farmhouse kitchens no one ever cooks in. On the contrary, the most common response to such things is "I want one too."'[28]

What the ancient Greeks called *amathia* – an inability or unwillingness to learn, the essence of stupidity – is now species-wide, he argues. Welzer is clearly part of the anti-growth coalition indicted by Britain's worst ever prime minister, Liz Truss, who, it is not too much to suggest, is here taken as the personification of current stupidity. Welzer effectively suggested that we are on a treadmill to disaster. We are changing the earth from a natural planet to an artificial one: in 2020, he reported, the quantity of what he calls 'dead mass' (i.e. man-made objects, such as houses, asphalt, cars, and computers) exceeded the totality of living matter for the first time. For us humans, it seems, deforestation and species extinction are the prices we are willing to pay to sustain higher levels of consumption. Welzer argued that this consumerist desire for more and more dead mass is understandable, if self-defeating: He wrote: 'Traditional economics, like traditional politics, continues to assume that growth is not only economically necessary but also essential for a stable society. . . . It is this logic of ever-increasing global consumption that has got the modern, twentieth-century model of civilization into such hot water.'[29] Or to put it another way: we can't stop being stupid.

Here's a contrary thought. Maybe the likes of David Graeber, Franny Armstrong, Justin Gregg, and Harald Welzer are wrong. Maybe stupidity is not a scar but a gift.

Stupidity can indeed be useful and produce good, short-term results: it can nurture harmony, encourage people to get on with the job, and drive success. So argue Mats Alvesson and André Spicer in *The Stupidity Paradox*,[30] a 2016 book that proposes that while stupidity can cause organizational collapse, financial meltdown, and technical disaster, it may have its uses, rather in the manner Erasmus suggested of folly. Alvesson, a professor of business administration, and Spicer, a professor of organizational behaviour (jobs that quite possibly might not have eluded Graeber's bullshit detector), spent a decade studying how management consultancies, banks, engineering firms, pharmaceutical companies, universities, and schools functioned. They wrote: 'During the course of our research, we were constantly struck by how these organisations, which employ so many people with high IQs and impressive qualifications, could do so many stupid things.'[31] They were struck, for instance, by schools being more focused on developing impressive exam results than educating students; executives more interested in impressive PowerPoint shows than systematic analysis; and, perhaps most worryingly, senior defence officials who were more interested in running rebranding operations than military operations. In a sense, what they found were lots of people doing the bullshit jobs David Graeber excoriated.

They found more. Where Graeber spoke of structural stupidity, they diagnosed something else: functional stupidity, which they defined as the 'inability and/or unwillingness to use cognitive and reflective capacities in anything other than narrow and circumspect ways'.[32] The functionally stupid are valuable because they never call attention to poor company policy. Because of its useful role, functional stupidity therefore prevails at the top of many organizations and at all subsidiary levels.'

What Alvesson and Spicer found was a corporate culture wherein employees mindlessly follow scripts. Not just the scripts followed by telemarketers to make sales, but also rather internalized rules that can serve as heuristic devices to enable workers to avoid thinking too much. Imagine, they suggested, going up to the counter of a shop and asking for help. The employee, they contended, quickly tries to work out which of a range of scripts applies to this particular situation. 'Once they have figured this out,' they wrote, 'they are likely to grow more and more rigid about what they will and won't do. If you make any special requests, the person behind the counter is likely to bat them away.'[33]

Alvesson and Spicer suggested a large proportion of what goes on in organizations involves simply following scripts. Meetings, job interviews, water cooler small talk, emails, and that corporate oxymoron the ideas meeting are in this respect highly scripted human behaviours. A cynic might suggest that the growth of such automated human behaviour is

STRUCTURAL STUPIDITY

essentially fattening up workers for a future mass cull and replacement by artificial intelligence, which can do these bullshit, functionally stupid tasks more efficiently. Hold that thought.

Alvesson and Spicer wrote: 'Scripts do the thinking, people rehearse them.'[34] That suggests that we don't so much think *outside the box* as fail to think *inside the box*. In work settings, intelligence is a rare luxury, stupidity the norm.

That's a terrifying thought, but one grounded in psychological experiment. Two American psychologists, Ellen J. Langer and Robert Abelson, made a specialism of studying human mindlessness in work settings. Both were convinced that mindlessness – or functional stupidity – was more prevalent than the rest of us dared countenance. One day in the 1990s, for instance, Langer tried to pay for an item with a new credit card. The store clerk returned the card to Langer, saying she needed to sign it. Langer did so, handed back the card, and the clerk processed the payment. After passing the credit card through the machine, the clerk handed her the credit card receipt to sign. 'Then she held up the receipt I signed next to the card I had just signed, and she compared the signatures!' Langer said.[35] One might take this as a case of personal stupidity, but Langer thought otherwise. The clerk was, more likely, acting automatically and would have realized the silliness of comparing signatures if she had thought about what she was doing.

Langer's idea was that humans are often on autopilot, not really in control of what they are doing. Instead we quickly slip into preprogrammed patterns of behaviour that she and Abelson called 'social scripts'. We are like actors who dutifully follow lines we have been handed which tell us what to do and what to say – very much the point we saw the Buddhist thinker Bhante Henepola Gunaratana making in chapter 3.

To test this mindlessness hypothesis, Langer and Abelson asked one of their lab assistants to ask people coming into their lab for help. Half the time, the assistant seeking help presented themselves as a victim by saying: 'My knee is killing me.' The other half of the time, the assistant simply said: 'Would you do something for me?' When the assistant presented as a victim, they would be helped 75% of the time. If they asked for aid, they were only helped 42%.

The reason why there was such a big difference in responses, Langer and Abelson thought, was that each request cued very different scripts.

Complaining about a sore knee cued a victim script – and the associated moral obligation to help. When we are asked if we will do something for someone else, we consult a different script. If we say no, we will not feel too bad. In both cases, the script does the thinking for us. Langer and Abelson also studied how a group of psychotherapists responded to the description of a man they saw in a film. If the man was introduced as a 'job applicant', the psychotherapists described him as 'candid and innovative', 'attractive and conventional-looking', and 'ordinary'. If the same man was introduced as a 'patient', they described him as a 'passive, dependent type', with 'considerable hostility', and suffering 'conflict over homosexuality'. That's to say, cue words led even psychotherapists to engage in a kind of mindless behaviour whereby trigger words induced them to mobilize different 'social scripts' pertaining to the very same man. If they saw him as 'normal', they treated him as normal; if he was introduced as a 'patient', all kinds of – imagined – problems were assigned to him.[36]

It's important to reflect on why mindlessness or any other heuristic devices humans employ to short-circuit their rationality might be valuable. Humans typically eulogize their rationality – Aristotle supposed our rational natures were what defined us and distinguished us from other species – but many have noted that in various ways the ability to reason can be a liability. In his 1961 paper 'Rational Expectations and the Theory of Price Movements',[37] the American economist John F. Muth argued that individuals are rational and use all available information to make unbiased, informed predictions about the future. Such rational expectations theorizing was used to underpin the idea that markets should be unfettered from government constraints, since only free enterprise can maximize returns for firms and utility for customers.

Not so, countered the Nobel-winning economist Herbert Simon, who contended that any firm that tried to make decisions that would maximize its returns would bankrupt itself in a never-ending search for the best option. Instead, Simon coined a new term to explain the non-rational way firms proceed given their structural inability to have all relevant information about their business decisions. Firms, he argued in his 1956 paper 'Rational Choice and the Structure of the Environment', 'satisfice'.[38] This is a portmanteau term combining satisfy and suffice and which indicates that firms, instead of making decisions that optimize utility or shareholder value, content themselves with results that are 'good enough'. In business, it's not the utility maximizer who is prized but the decision-maker. In this context, to be a good decision-maker does not mean that you make good decisions, just that you make a decision. Functional stupidity, for bosses and shareholders alike, is a useful commodity.

Such satisficing, be it ever so stupid, is a feature of late capitalism for customers too. Ditherers are, as any waiter will tell you, the real problem. Stalling on making a decision is apt to make those in a restaurant trying to take your order roll their eyes. Satisficing becomes ever more a feature of human society in our decadent societies where we are, as the phrase has it, spoiled for choice. We are confronted by endless options (TV channels, gourmet coffee, downloadable ringtones, perhaps ultimately even interchangeable lovers) and are terrified of making the wrong decision. Choice wasn't supposed to make people miserable. It was supposed to be the hallmark of self-determination that we cherish in capitalist western society. But it palpably isn't: ever more choice increases the feeling of missed opportunities, and this leads to self-blame when choices fail to meet expectations. American social scientist Barry Schwartz, in his 2004 book *The Paradox of Choice: Why More Is Less*,[39] suggested that reducing choices can limit anxiety. This is Herbert Simon's notion of satisficing transferred from business models to consumer society.

Schwartz offered a self-help guide to good decision-making by helping us to limit choices to a manageable number, and ultimately derive greater satisfaction from the choices we have to make. This is a capitalist response to a capitalist problem. It is also the mobilization of the idea that human rationality is not an unalloyed gift, but bounded: we often cannot have all the data relevant to making a particular choice, still less do we have the time necessary to reflect rationally. Humans, as AI researchers enjoy telling us, have limited bandwidth. In such circumstances, it is better to suspend rational reflection and satisfice. Satisficing is not entirely stupid but pragmatic. It is, as it were, an intelligent response to a stupid situation.

You can see how Schwartz's self-help guide might work. When you go into a supermarket, take a list and stick to it. In this, one's shopping list is a conceptual shield or akin to the 'social scripts' that Langer and Abelson noted protected humans at work from having to think too much. Better yet, order your groceries from an online home delivery service. They have a facility that enables you to construct a template of your groceries that you can order again and again without having to choose between 37 different kinds of olive oil.

However, these self-protective responses, which amount to a form of structural stupidity, may create new problems. John Reith, the BBC's first director general, once said that good broadcasting gives people what they do not yet know they need. You might turn on the radio and serendipitously stumble across something – Duke Ellington playing 'Take the "A" Train', Maria Callas dying as Violetta in Verdi's *La Traviata* – that opens you up to new experiences that otherwise, through prejudice or expense, might not have been available to you. Customized culture, which abounds in the digital age, is predicated on abolishing just such serendipity: it involves algorithmically extrapolating from one cultural phenomenon to another according to the principle of 'If you liked that, you'll like this'. Put another way, customized culture keeps us in our intellectual and aesthetic silos. This silo thinking is arguably another form of structural stupidity: we customize culture so we don't drown in its endless possibilities, but, in sparing ourselves from that fate, we drown in the puddle of our own algorithmically constrained cultural choices. We deprive ourselves of new experiences that, just possibly, might have revolutionized our lives. Duke Ellington and Maria Callas remain, for us customized consumers, merely perpetual possibilities only in a world of speculation.

All that is to say that once you realize that your Schwartzian filters are depriving you of something you might have found enjoyable, you will be back in the same situation of angst as before, worrying that you made the wrong decision in drawing up your choice-limiting filters. Arguably, we will always be doomed to buyer's remorse and the misery it entails. The problem of choice is perhaps more intractable than Schwartz allows and his response to it more stupid than he recognizes.

Nonetheless, his and Herbert Simon's counterblasts to rational expectations theory, whereby humans are posited as utility maximizers engaged in reasoned meditation on available options and choice is seen as always a good thing, are valuable correctives to the manifold stupidities of economic orthodoxy. Economic orthodoxy holds that the more choices we have, the richer we are. Schwartz countered that we should beware excessive choice. Choice overload can make us question the decisions we make before we even make them, it can set us up for unrealistically high expectations, and it can make us blame ourselves for any and all failures. In the long run, this can lead to decision-making paralysis.

Human mindlessness, then, can be a wise, if non-rational, response to the manifold stupidities of modern life. This is a bracing thought today when mindfulness rather than mindlessness is prized by people who, you'd think, haven't considered the stupid nature of modern life sufficiently closely. Working from a prepared script can be a reasonable response to the otherwise in principle unlimited time-suck of bureaucratic interactions. Similarly, satisficing, such as refusing to rationally consider all the dozen or so yogurt options in the chiller cabinet before you make a choice, but rather making a choice with negligible rational grounding, may be the height of good sense.

On occasion, though, functional stupidity can have disastrous consequences. A leading example of disastrous functional stupidity is the failure of the Ford Motor Company to recall the Pinto in the 1970s. The car had been built with a design flaw – its petrol tank burst into flames when rear ended – that had resulted in the deaths or disfigurements of hundreds of people. At the time, Dennis Gioia, who worked in Ford's recall department as a problem analyst and corporate recall coordinator, was tasked with looking for patterns that revealed problems in Ford cars that might trigger manufacturer recalls. 'When I was dealing with the first trickling-in of field reports that might have suggested a significant problem with the Pinto,' Gioia recalled, 'the reports were essentially similar to many others that I was dealing with (and dismissing) all the time. . . . I was making this kind of decision automatically every day. I had trained myself to respond to prototypical cues, and these didn't fit the relevant prototype for crisis cases.'[40]

Worse yet, the corporate culture of Ford was so functionally stupid, in the Alvesson and Spicer's sense, that Gioia was encouraged to set aside any fears he had about the Pinto's safety. Once, after visiting Ford's so-called 'chamber of horrors', a warehouse for burned-out cars retrieved from crash scenes, Gioia was so distressed by one of the wrecked Pintos he saw that he told his colleagues about his concerns about the vehicle, but they dissuaded him from taking his findings to Ford's executive committee. This was in 1973, but it was only in 1978, after many more Pintos exploded, that the model was recalled.

The case would result in a series of devastating lawsuits against Ford, a recall of 1.5 million vehicles, and charges of reckless homicide. Gioia, who left Ford in 1975 and went on to become a professor of management and organization at Penn State's Smeal College of Business, used his own case as an example of functional stupidity in his disarmingly self-critical article 'Pinto Fires and Personal Ethics: A Script Analysis of Missed Opportunities'.[41]

In *The Stupidity Paradox*, Alvesson and Spicer cited the case of the exploding Pintos as typifying a social norm operative at Ford, namely: 'Don't raise problems and don't tell people bad news they do not want to hear.' They argued that such functional stupidity is hardly limited to the Ford Motor Company. 'This kind of stupidity is a normal part of organisational life. It is often widely backed in organisations – starting with the top management and going all the way down the hierarchy.'[42]

Clearly, here, we are beyond the stupidity excoriated by David Graeber in his work on bullshit jobs. It is not that the jobs are bullshit – although many of them are – but that the culture of thinking inside the box, of mobilizing mindlessness instead of thinking creatively, has its uses. The Germans have a term for it: *Fachidioten*, or 'professional idiots'.[43] Being functionally stupid at work often turns out to be a good career move. It protects employees from rocking the boat or from taking actions that provoke others to see them as troublemakers. Perhaps, though, corporate mindlessness, prognostic myopia, and stupidity in both its functional and structural forms are symptomatic of something that has gone terribly wrong in human society.

Philosopher and psychologist Svend Brinkmann, in his 2024 book *Think: In Defence of a Thoughtful Life*, pointed out that thinking is something only humans do. It is a gift that we should cherish and nurture rather than discard in favour of embracing the short-term delights of stupidity. He wrote:

> To the best of our knowledge, humans are the only creatures on the planet capable of thinking in the true sense of the word. All sorts of animals intuitively calculate risk (a hyena tempted to steal from a lion weighs up the risk of finding itself on the menu), but only humans make actual calculations,

because only we have access to the world of numbers and mathematical symbols. Humans are also the only creatures capable of thinking about the meaning of life, the nature of a just society or the potential existence of a deity.[44]

Thinking, one might suppose, is a species-specific virtue as much as an ability. The worst of us don't think. That's why Hannah Arendt concluded Eichmann's fundamental defect was his inability to think. As we saw in the previous chapter, what Arendt considered stupid encompassed more than it does for Alvesson and Spicer: stupidity for her has a moral aspect since what she took to be Eichmann's inability to think – really, his inability to imaginatively open himself up to others' suffering – is what made him evil. Evidently, here, the notion of what it is to be stupid is normative, not something that can be found lacking by the relevant psychometric test.

But when Brinkmann implies that animals don't think, he isn't thereby suggesting that they are – like Eichmann – evil. Rather, he is suggesting that thinking – be it normatively defined or testable by psychometric tests – is a distinctively human phenomenon. Consider the following scenario. You are trying to flee a hyena. As you get out of puff and the hyena's jaws bear down on your ankles, you calculate the risk of getting eaten. Here, thinking, as Brinkmann seems to envisage the capacity – say, by making actual calculations – seems misplaced, the height of stupidity. More to the point is a suggestion that Justin Gregg made in his book *If Nietzsche Were a Narwhal*.[45] Imagine the following twist to the hyena story. As you run, you realize you've got a ham sandwich in your pocket. You pull it out and fling it at the hyena, which, happily, eats the sandwich rather than you. That is the thinking we need here and, Gregg argues, it is something most animals wouldn't consider. Most animals, he thinks, would run and hide and would not consider the hyena's motivations, still less be able to reflect on them in such a way as to prevent them becoming a predator's lunch. Humans routinely do such imaginative interpretive labour because, Gregg contends, they have a theory of mind, which implies they can predict and manipulate the minds of others rather than merely respond to visual or other sensory cues. That's true, but it is also significant that hyenas don't make ham sandwiches.

Here's an experiment you can do at home, suggests Gregg, to explore the vexed question of whether animals think like us or are, as Descartes believed, essentially furry robots. Observe your pet and ask yourself the following question. Is Mrs Tiddles interacting with you because he is making guesses about what you are thinking or feeling, or reacting only to outward behaviour? Most likely, Gregg suggests, you concluded that they only do the latter.[46] But are matters so straightforward? Is it really true, as Brinkmann seems to suggest, that animals don't think? Or, at least, if they can be said to think, their cognitive processes are very different from humans? Perhaps humans are too stupid to overcome their own species hubris.

Such considerations, no doubt, prompted the remark Michel de Montaigne made in 1580. 'When I play with my cat,' he wrote, 'who knows if I am not a pastime to her more than she is to me?'[47] True, Mrs Tiddles would never have the imaginative nature or the linguistic skills to even ask such a question, but that need not imply she is stupid. Indeed, it might suggest Mrs Tiddles is too clever to waste time asking stupid questions. Or it might suggest a phenomenon akin to what David Graeber indicted among the super-rich, namely that humans are not prepared to do the interpretive labour of understanding what, if anything, animals are thinking. If so, that would indicate that it's not animals but humans who are really stupid.

Indeed, it is at least possible that allegedly lower life forms look at the fruits of human intelligence and think (supposing for a moment that they can) what a bunch of selfish, hubristic mugs. And, by corollary, it should at least be possible that humans might learn the wisdom of animals. Anthropologist Bruno Latour, in his 2021 book *After Lockdown: A Metamorphosis*, argued that we should learn from termites.[48] Even though they live in mounds made from masticated earth and faecal matter, they don't lay waste to the earth, nor are any of them insect Elon Musks seeking to jet off to another planet having ruined this one. Their default position, rather, is of conservation and cooperation. Prince Pyotr Kropotkin, the 19th-century Russian anarchist and naturalist, introduced the term 'mutual aid' to describe what we, thinking inside the Darwinian evolutionary paradigm, have missed. Kropotkin wasn't saying that *On the Origin of the Species* was specious; rather, his point was that while flora and fauna are certainly red in tooth, claw, and thorn, 'there is, at the same time, as much, or perhaps even more, of mutual support, mutual aid, and mutual defence'.[49] That default position is not ours: in despoiling nature, committing acts of genocide, and regarding ourselves as discrete individuals bent on personal utility maximization, we are the stupid species.

Montaigne in the 1595 edition to his *Essays* adds to the above quotation about playing with his cat: 'We entertain each other with reciprocal monkey tricks. If I have my time to begin or to refuse, so has she hers.'[50] This suggests an equality between human and cat and raises the possibility that our species' hubris rests on nothing more than our ignorance and lack of imagination about what animals are, if anything, thinking. How facile, stupid really, to stipulate that humans are the thinking beings and to project onto animals a mindlessness that may be better comprehended as our own.

After conducting Gregg's experiment, no doubt, you were feeling pretty pleased with yourself to be a member of an intelligent species rather than one of those stupid lower life forms. Narwhals will never colonize Mars; Mrs Tiddles will never write a symphony. You, unlike mere animals, can think, strategize, and lie because you are not stupid. These are distinctive abilities that humans have and indicate our intellectual superiority over animals. But as the philosopher Markus Gabriel argued in his 2024 book *The Human Animal: Why We Still Don't Fit into Nature*, our species-specific cognitive powers have led us to the brink of catastrophe. 'Thanks to science and technology, we have rapidly improved our survival conditions. But, by the same means, we have made them worse even more rapidly.'[51] We are such geniuses that we have used our singularly big brains stupidly to make our habitat increasingly uninhabitable.

For Gregg, equally derangingly, our very intelligence serves to produce a culture of stupidity. This is not just the point that narwhals don't build gas chambers, though the combination of technical ingenuity and evil does seem to be a distinctively human phenomenon. Rather, the very fact that we have developed as humans sophisticated accounts of the mental lives of others and use those accounts to predict others' future behaviour opens a Pandora's Box chock-full of stupid possibilities.

True, many species engage in deception, but that is not quite the same as lying. Take the sanguine poison frog, which looks like a strawberry poison-dart frog but, despite its name, is not actually poisonous. Or the harmless wasp beetle, which has black-and-yellow stripes that make it look like a deadly yellowjacket wasp. Both frog and beetle are engaged in what's called aposematic signalling, a form of mimicry whereby a harmless animal copies the appearance or behaviour of a more dangerous one. Lying, which thrives in human societies, is different since it involves, as Gregg defined it, 'intentionally transmitting false information to another creature with the express purpose of making that creature believe something is not true to manipulate its behavior'.[52] If I put on a black-and-yellow striped jumper to deceive you that I was a dangerous wasp, that might well be a stupid attempt at deception, but unless I sought thereby to change not just your behaviour but also your beliefs, it would not be mendacious. It would be stupid but not be a lie.

The rise of the dark triad

All of these considerations are very relevant to the rise of stupidity in our post-truth world. In his 2020 book *Duped: Truth-Default Theory and the Social Science of Lying and Deception*,[53] the communication studies professor Timothy R. Levine argued we, rather witlessly, tend to believe things we hear are true. We are, as a species, natural-born suckers. Why? Because, Levine wrote, credulity enables efficient communication and social coordination. But it also enables the opposite. Indeed, human credulousness is precisely the fertile soil in which human mendacity grows. It helps explain why, say, 92% of American college students admitted to lying to their sexual partners about their sexual history. Lying exists because it works. It also involves ingenuity, or, as Gregg put it: 'Being a lying bullshit artist in a world of gullible victims can be a path to success.'[54] The gullible victims – the stupid – are in bottomless supply; if they weren't, then lying wouldn't be so successful or ubiquitous.

But there is a distinction to be made here between lying and bullshit. The latter is a phenomenon detected in his 2005 book *On Bullshit* by the philosopher Harry Frankfurt.[55] Bullshit here means a kind of communication designed to impress others without regard for the truth or accuracy of what is being communicated. It is typified by something Donald Trump said to his butler, Anthony Senecal. One day, Senecal read his boss's book *The Art of the Deal*, which detailed how the tiles in the nursery at Mar-a-Lago, Trump's West Palm Beach club, had been personally made by Walt Disney. Is that really true, the butler asked the billionaire. 'Who cares?' replied Trump.[56] Who cares, indeed: if truth is a commodity, it is one that has crashed in value, but not before Trump astutely dumped his shares in it. '[The bullshitter] does not reject the authority of the truth, as the liar does, and oppose himself to it,' wrote Frankfurt presciently. 'He pays no attention to it at all. By virtue of this, bullshit is a greater enemy of truth than lies are.'[57] Viewed thus, Trump is the personification of bullshit.

At least liars, in principle, can be argued against and their lies exposed. Bullshit is altogether more intractable. At the same time, the virtuoso of bullshit is regarded as smart and deserving of promotion. And yet bullshitters and liars have one key thing in common: they take the rest of us for mugs. The endless supply of credulity and stupidity keeps them in business.

In 2018, the psychologist Klaus Templer surveyed 110 employees in Singapore, asking them about their attitudes to political machinations in the workplace. Templer wanted to test the idea that to get ahead in business it helps to be manipulative, deceptive, and mendacious. There is, he submitted, a dark triad of personality traits. Employees who have one or more of these traits are more likely to cheat and to engage in fraudulent or exploitative workplace behaviour. First, there are the Machiavellians, namely those who are deceitful and unscrupulously manipulative. Then there are the psychopaths, who are impulsive or thrill seeking without any sense of guilt. Finally, there are the narcissists, egotistically preoccupied with themselves, having a sense of grandiosity, entitlement, and superiority. Members of this dark triad look on exemplars of human stupidity rather as a hyena surveys the savannah for its next meal.

Templer found that toxic employees whose political skills were highly rated by their supervisors were more likely to have a high performance rating. 'In other words, while not all toxic people possess political skill, those toxic people who use political skill effectively in the eyes of their bosses are seen as better performers. And as we all know, those who are seen as top performers are more likely to be promoted.'[58] This is a functional stupidity beyond the 'stupidity paradox' identified by Alvesson and Spicer.

And the dark triad of bullshit virtuosos, what's more, is not just a business phenomenon. Thanks to – among other things – the democratizing effect of the internet, the resultant decline in deference to experts, rising scorn for the political establishment, the tendency of social media to lock us in our echo chambers where our ill-founded opinions are confirmed rather than challenged, the blurring of fact and fiction online (a problem recognized in 1995 by the journalist John Diamond who wrote: 'The problem with the internet is everything is true'[59]), we live in a post-truth era. All these factors favour the liar but they favour the bullshitter even more.

But what is post-truth? In 2016, Oxford Dictionaries chose post-truth as its word of the year, defining it as shorthand for 'circumstances in which objective facts are less influential in shaping public opinion than appeals to emotion and personal belief'.[60] In that same year, among the 50 top-performing fake news stories on Facebook was not only the lie that President Barack Obama had banned reciting the pledge of allegiance in US schools, but also the hilarious story headlined: 'Pro-lifers declare: ejaculation is murder, every sperm cell is a life.'[61]

Virtuosic bullshitters and liars take advantage, even if sometimes unwittingly, of the important distinction made by Nobel economics laureate Daniel Kahneman. In his 2011 bestseller *Thinking, Fast and Slow*,[62] Kahneman distinguished between two human modes of thinking, system one and system two: the former to do with intuitive, non-rational processing of information, the latter more akin to how Sherlock Holmes solved crimes.

Bullshitters and other persuaders seek to sucker us with psychologically sophisticated appeals to system one: hence the deployment of what is called the bandwagon effect (we don't want to be left behind, so if advertisers can convince us everybody else is buying a product, we are more likely to do so too); hence the persistence from the early 1950s to today of canned laughter; hence, too, the cuddly emotional pitch of much advertising. It's not so much that we can't handle the truth as we're not captivated by appeals to it.

Take Brexit. In 2015, Nigel Farage, at the time leader of the UK Independence Party, unveiled a poster of a long queue of Syrian refugees alongside the headline 'Breaking Point'. Even Boris Johnson, the Leave campaign's most famous spokesman, declared himself 'profoundly unhappy with it'. What was being insinuated was 'that those who come to the UK are a bunch of freeloaders, depriving indigenous Britons of school places, housing and healthcare,' wrote journalist Matthew d'Ancona in his 2017 book *Post-Truth: The New War on Truth and How to Fight Back*. But d'Ancona pointed out that these insinuations were 'comprehensively debunked' by Essex University sociology lecturer Neli Demireva,[63] who argued that migrants tended to be highly-skilled on average, contributed substantially to the economy, and did not compete with natives for social housing. Moreover, there was no evidence that crime rates had been on the rise as a result of new immigration waves.[64]

Or take Covid. Reportedly, depressed vaccination rates led to more deaths from Covid-19 than would otherwise have been the case. It has also been argued that they increased the likelihood of the return of fatal childhood diseases. What makes vaccination rates fall is not so much lies or bullshit as a culture that, stupidly, refuses to defer to expertise. Both Brexit and the rise of science-denying anti-vaxxers are symptomatic, argued Matthew d'Ancona, of the gathering forces of stupidity. 'This is not a battle,' he wrote, 'between liberals and conservatives. This is a battle between two ways of perceiving the world, two fundamentally different approaches to reality. Are you content for the central value of the Enlightenment, of free societies and of democratic discourse, to be trashed by charlatans – or not?'[65] Not long before his death, wrote d'Ancona, George Orwell tried to clarify the meaning of his dystopian novel *Nineteen Eighty-Four*, which imagined a society in thrall to a diabolical overseer called Big Brother wherein even the truths of mathematics can be replaced by 'alternative facts' such as 2 + 2 = 5. 'The moral to be drawn from this dangerous nightmare situation is a simple one: don't let it happen,' said Orwell. 'It depends on you.'[66]

If we have been made more stupid by various clever virtuosos manipulating appeals to our non-rational selves (and a spate of books indicating the post-truth phenomenon have suggested just as much – from Matthew d'Ancona's book just cited, to Evan Davis's *Post-Truth: Why We Have Reached Peak Bullshit and What We Can Do About It* and James Ball's *Post-Truth: How Bullshit Conquered The World*), then perhaps Voltaire and Schopenhauer were stupid in maintaining that stupidity is an ineradicable fact of human society, fairly constant across all civilizations. Human stupidity, like mushrooms, can flourish in the right circumstances – namely by humans being kept in the dark and being fed shit.

That said, post-truth came into being long before Donald Trump or Vladmir Putin. Anthropologists say we have been lying since early humans organized themselves in tribes. At the end of his great novel *August 1914* about the lies and imperial delusions that contributed to Russia's catastrophic defeat at the Battle of Tannenberg, Alexander Solzhenitsyn offered this epigram: 'Untruth did not begin with us; nor will it end with us.'[67]

Neither Orwell nor Solzhenitsyn lived to witness Trump's senior aide Kellyanne Conway in action in 2016, but she confirms their worries. Her colleague, White House press secretary Sean Spicer, told the media that, contrary to photographic evidence, the crowd at Trump's inauguration was the largest ever. The following day, Conway went on NBC's *Meet the Press*, where host Chuck Todd told her that Spicer's claim was a falsehood. 'Don't be so overly dramatic about it, Chuck,' she replied. 'Sean Spicer, our press secretary, gave alternative facts to that.'[68] That Conway had the brazenness to use that term was symptomatic for Matthew d'Ancona, writing in the *Guardian*, of how we live now: in the post-truth world, there is no stable verifiable reality, just an endless battle to define it. We have become so contemptuous of truth, so stupid, that a senior political figure can speak of 'alternative facts' – an oxymoron in one sense; a euphemism for lies in another.

For d'Ancona, in *Post-Truth*, two terrible intellectual developments made us susceptible to manipulation by bullshit and lies. First, there was pre-war Viennese psychoanalysis. Second, there was post-war French theory. The former, d'Ancona argued, helped make us irrational and prepared us for our post-truth era. In psychoanalysis, claimed d'Ancona, the imperative is to treat the patient successfully, irrespective of the facts. This approach has gone beyond the privacy of the consulting room to infuse our whole culture. So what, you might argue? D'Ancona suggested the risk is that an ever-greater proportion of judgements and decisions will be banished to the realm of emotion: 'Sharing your innermost feelings, shaping your life-drama, speaking from the heart: these pursuits are increasingly in competition with traditional forensic values.'[69] Truth, in other words, was not just the first casualty of war, but for d'Ancona the leading victim of the spread of therapeutic culture's values.

The latter, thanks to Roland Barthes and Michel Foucault, declared the death of the author, to be replaced by a democracy of endless interpretation and polysemous perversity. Meanwhile, contemporary post-truth *penseurs* such as Jacques Derrida and Jean-François Lyotard propounded the idea that the real purpose of such distinctively human activities as thinking and scientific inquiry was not to establish the truth nor to describe the world but to strengthen our power over it. Derrida's method of deconstruction posited that there can be no immutable truth to an utterance; what matters, rather, is the interest being advanced through it. Thus, if Big Brother says 2 + 2 = 5, then that truth is relative to his political interests. The idea that 2 + 2 = 4 always and for ever is, by these lights, a naïve delusion, rather than objective fact. For those of us who learned primary school arithmetic, the idea that this simple mathematical truth is a delusion expressing only power interests rather than anything else is ludicrous, suggesting if anything how intellectuals can, through their brilliant virtuosic challenging of even the most accepted norms and facts, become stupid. For those not of a post-truth bent, not to be stupid is, precisely, to accept that some things are objectively true. But if primary schools had taught not just basic maths but also abstruse French theory, we might be less certain about that conviction.

The impact of both trends is to render us non-rational, stupid. If there is no objective standard of truth, we have entered a world where there can be no objective acts but only power struggles to decide which supposed facts are held to be true according to the interests of those issuing the definitions. We all of us become Humpty Dumpty in Lewis Carroll's *Through the Looking-Glass*, who famously scornfully said: 'When I use a word . . . it means just what I choose it to mean – neither more nor less.'[70] No matter that the Derridean deconstruction deconstructs itself since its critique of truth in particular and western metaphysics in general applies even to clever French philosophers. If you have no objective standard for truth, then your critique of truth cannot be judged true or false in the ordinary sense, but only as groundless assertion. That ironic conclusion shows not just the absurdity of the post-truth world but also its stupidity.

10

Digital stupidity

Outfoxed by Putin's lackeys

At 4 a.m. on 22 March 2016, Billy Rinehart opened his laptop in a Honolulu hotel room and made quite possibly the biggest mistake of his life. Google had just sent a message telling him somebody had his password, detailing time, IP address, and purportedly Ukrainian location. 'You should change your password immediately,' said the email, providing him with a link that, once he clicked on it, took him to a Gmail password-reset page.[1]

But it wasn't a reset page, nor was the message from Google. The message was really from Fancy Bear, nickname for the computer hacking unit of the Glavnoye Razvedyvatelnoye Upravlenie (GRU), Russia's military intelligence agency, the same outfit responsible for the Salisbury Novichok attack on Julia and Sergei Skripal in 2018. Rinehart gave out his password, got dressed, and went to work at the local Democratic Party headquarters – unaware he had been phished, or, as those in the know call it, mudged (i.e. maliciously nudged), by Russians bent on derailing Hillary Clinton's presidential campaign and, by implication, helping Trump to the White House.

Whether the mudgers were working for Putin is, if you're quite dim, debatable, but what is clear is that the Russian president despised Clinton, not least because she backed tougher sanctions after his annexation of Crimea, and denounced his support for Syrian dictator Bashar al-Assad. A more biddable Trump in the White House would suit the Kremlin better: hence Hillary's charge that her Republican rival was a puppet, and

Trump's tendentious comeback: 'No puppet. You're the puppet.' Hence Fancy Bear's hack helped Trump's accession to the Oval Office.

The triumph of this Putin-backed attempt by Russian hackers to influence the result of the 2016 US presidential election is related in the 2023 book *Fancy Bear Goes Phishing: The Dark History of the Information Age, in Five Extraordinary Hacks* by Yale law professor Scott Shapiro. It exemplifies how, in the digital age in particular, stupidity can be exploited by bad actors. The functional stupidity of David Graeber that we bore witness to in the previous chapter, whereby a professor of anthropology became stupid in the face of bureaucratic procedures, is digitally duplicated here in the story of Billy Rinehart. The deranging possibility is that in our digital age, intelligence produces stupidity in ways hitherto inconceivable.

Rinehart wasn't the only Democratic staffer hacked by Fancy Bear that spring. John Podesta, chairman of Hillary for America, received a similar spear-phishing email. (Spear fishing is when an individual is targeted, as opposed to mass phishing, which, as Shapiro puts it, focuses on 'the small number of highly gullible chumps willing to invest in get-rich-quick schemes'[2]). Sensibly, Podesta showed it to his cybersecurity guy, Charles Delavan, who, less sensibly, pronounced it legitimate.

Delavan later told the *New York Times* he meant to type 'illegitimate' rather than 'legitimate'. We've all made such cyber-booboos, I guess, but rarely with such deleterious consequences. By the end of April, Fancy Bear had 50,000 of Clinton and other leading Democrats' emails. Hillary for America was a soft target: the site did not require the multi-factor authentication from users that today is nearly ubiquitous.

In the years since this hack, phishing and ransomware attacks have become more frequent and sophisticated, targeting organizations all over the world. Over Christmas 2023, for instance, the *Guardian* was subject to a phishing attack involving third-party access to part of its network. That attack got my attention because, as a former employee, I worried my bank details and National Insurance number could be exploited by cyber criminals to plunder my thankfully negligible fortune. Suddenly the abstruse mathematics and inscrutability of coding hackery seemed profoundly personal, fully justifying Shapiro's repurposing of Trotsky's remark about war: 'you may not be interested in hacking, but hacking is interested in you'.[3]

Unlike such ransomware attacks, the Hillary hack, though criminal, was politically motivated. A Transylvanian sock puppet called Guccifer 2.0, whose no less diabolical-sounding predecessor, Guccifer 1.0, had been responsible for a 2013 hack that disclosed Hillary had unethically routed government emails through her private email server, was privately messaged on Twitter by Julian Assange of Wikileaks. 'We think trump has only a 25 percent chance of winning against hillary,' tweeted Assange, 'so conflict between bernie [Sanders] and hillary would be interesting.'[4]

Guccifer 2.0 (really a GRU operative) provided the goods: the most damaging scoop it got on Hillary's campaign was an email from the Democratic National Convention chief finance officer looking to smear her rival for the Democratic presidential nomination, Bernie Sanders, for his atheism among southern Baptists. After WikiLeaks released that smear in a gigabyte dump, Trump gleefully tweeted: 'Leaked emails of DNC show plans to destroy Bernie Sanders. Mock his heritage . . . really vicious. RIGGED.'[5]

Fancy Bear's hack was not technically ingenious but it was psychologically shrewd. As Shapiro notes, it relied on an astute exploitation of humans' tendency to make irrational choices. In his terms, it exploited weakness in upcode rather than downcode. The latter is what clever computer whizzes create; the former are the political social and other arrangements that humans set up. If we attend too much to the problems of downcode, we miss the weakest link in the system and the hackers' most valuable commodity, our stupidity.

We are not, as psychologist Daniel Kahneman pointed out in *Thinking, Fast and Slow*,[6] rational in our choices, certainly not as rational as economists have supposed. Rather, human nature is governed by non-rational heuristics. Fancy Bear made the email look like a Google email. Rinehart was suckered by the loss-aversion heuristic: he shouldn't have clicked on the link but changed his password through his browser. But that would have taken time and effort. Instead, just as Fancy Bear wanted, he took the easy option.

This psychological truth about human irrationality informs Shapiro's conclusion, namely that solutionism – the thesis that hacking is a technical problem to which there is a technical solution – is mistaken. Solutionism is typified by the 2012 *Wired* headline: 'Africa? There's an App for That.'[7] No there isn't.

The father of computing Alan Turing early on drew attention to the humbling truth for those who believe there are technical solutions to any problem, not least that of detecting bugs in any code. Turing demonstrated that the number of undecidable problems is infinite. In computer science terms, a decidable set is one for which there exists an algorithm that will determine whether any element is or is not within the set in a finite amount of time. 'Only a god with an infinite mind can solve any problem,' concluded Shapiro. 'Physical computing devices, such as human beings, laptops, and iPhones, cannot.'[8] Which seems to suggest that so long as we use computers, hacking can never totally be eradicated. And the stupidity on which hacking parasitically depends cannot be eradicated either.

Nobody is safe from hackers. Even Shapiro, a Yale professor who literally teaches a course on cybersecurity and how to hack, was not immune: a malware attack at parent publishers Macmillan halted his book's production. Shapiro also describes how in 2020 an estimated 18,000 customers of a Texan software firm, SolarWinds, unwittingly fell for a malware attack.[9] They were duped by a pop-up window calling on them to update their software. In fact the update inserted malicious code that, rather than fixing bugs and improving performance as promised, enabled the hackers (again thought to be Russian) to not just capture private data but also alter it. Among those suckered was the Cybersecurity and Infrastructure Security Agency, or CISA — the office at the Department of Homeland Security whose job, ironically enough, it is to protect federal computer networks from cyberattacks.

Ineradicable stupidity

But can stupidity really be manufactured by clever Russian hackers or anyone else? Or is it, as the Italian economist Carlo Cipolla controversially maintained in his entertaining 1976 book *The Basic Laws of Stupidity*, a vexingly unchangeable fact about humans, a characteristic one is born with like red hair, and one that is distributed uniformly across all groups and populations irrespective of age, wealth, sex, race, or anything else? Professor Cipolla wrote: 'It is my firm conviction, supported by years of observation and experimentation, that men are not equal, that some are stupid and others are not, and that the difference is determined by nature and not by cultural forces or factors. . . . A stupid man is born a stupid by an act of Providence.'[10]

All five basic laws are drolly described by Cipolla, but the first and second are most relevant for our purposes. The first states: 'Always and inevitably everyone underestimates the number of stupid individuals in circulation.' This is why, for example, so many clever professors in earlier chapters of this book have revealed themselves to be idiots. 'People whom one had once judged rational and intelligent turn out to be unashamedly stupid,' wrote Cipolla. He claimed to be continually startled by the extent of stupidity, writing: 'Day after day, with unceasing monotony, one is harassed in one's activities by stupid individuals who appear suddenly and unexpectedly in the most inconvenient places and at the most improbable moments.'[11] But this doesn't ring true: if the stupid present their credentials with dreary monotony, the fact that Cipolla is surprised by their sudden appearance is a sign that he hasn't learned from his experiences. Or, to put it another way, Cipolla was as stupid as those he indicted. Perhaps more stupid.

Cipolla's second law states: 'The probability that a certain person be stupid is independent of any other characteristic of that person.' This suggests that stupidity is equally distributed among races, sexes, and classes, and, most surprisingly of all, between those whom, in one's naïvety, one considered clever and those one dismissed as stupid. Cipolla analysed blue-collar workers, finding that a fraction of them – which he called å – were stupid. Here, å is a constant describing the fraction of stupid people unaffected by time, space, or cultural factors. Cipolla supposed the high value of å among blue-collar workers to suggest that segregation, poverty, and lack of education were to be blamed. Not so: in fact, he found the ratio of stupidity the same among white-collar workers, students, and professors. 'So bewildered was I by the results,' he said, 'that I made a special point to extend my research to a specially selected group, to a real elite, the Nobel laureates. The result confirmed Nature's supreme powers: å fraction of the Nobel laureates are stupid.'[12] I am not at all sure about the plausibility of Cipolla's research, but, in principle, how lovely it is for those of us who will never win a Nobel Prize to learn that Nobel laureates are just as thick as the rest of us.

The corollary of this is that stupidity, because it's evenly distributed among any groups you care to specify, cannot be increased or decreased.

That, you'd think, would be disturbing news for teachers and mean that rolling out IQ tests to identify and help struggling school pupils is a waste of time and brain cells. But hold on. Matters are not quite so simple.

Cipolla's third basic law states the following: 'A stupid person is a person who causes losses to another person or to a group of persons while himself deriving no gain and even possibly incurring losses.'[13] This law assumes that human beings fall into four character types devised by Professor Cipolla, namely the helpless, the intelligent, the bandit, and the stupid. Unlike stupid people, intelligent people are defined as those whose actions benefit both themselves and others. The bandit gets rich at the expense of others, while the helpless enrich others at their own expense. Stupidity is worse than helplessness since it connives at its own disadvantage. This runs counter to Cipolla's earlier laws since it stipulates that the stupid are a discrete class of persons: bandits aren't stupid; the intelligent and the helpless, similarly, form distinct groups. And if these categories or character types are to be plausible, then it makes no sense to suggest, as Cipolla effectively has, that Nobel winners can be stupid since they can also be intelligent.

Laws four and five state, respectively: 'Non-stupid people always underestimate the destructive power of stupid individuals' and 'A stupid person is the most dangerous type of person.'[14] Law four seems, in the context of our discussion of the rise of intelligent hacking in the digital age, to be questionable. Fancy Bear's rationale was to phish for stupid people, not thereby underestimating their stupidity but rather creating the circumstances in which stupidity could flourish. Fancy Bear is what Cipolla effectively denied is possible, namely a digital machine for producing stupidity. As for the suggestion that stupid people are more dangerous than the others, that only holds if one adheres to Cipolla's dubious definition of what intelligence and stupidity consist in. One might want to argue, rather, that it is not the stupid who are dangerous to society but intelligent hackers.

Cipolla concluded: 'Essentially stupid people are dangerous and damaging because reasonable people find it difficult to imagine and understand unreasonable behaviour.'[15] But reasonable people in the digital age, one might suppose, precisely find it increasingly easy to imagine and understand unreasonable behaviour. For hackers, that very stupidity is the grist to their diabolical mill.

None of this should suggest that intelligent hackers are merely bandits, exploiting human stupidity for their nefarious ends, such as subverting American democracy. Rather, some hacking can have beneficial social consequences. Consider the We-Vibe, the world's first smart dildo, billed as allowing users to remotely 'turn on your lover' via a Bluetooth connection. In 2016, two New Zealanders going by the handles goldfisk and follower did the world a service by demonstrating how to remotely take control of the We-Vibe 4 Plus and activate it. This story opens the prospect that the vaunted internet of things may not just mean your toaster is spying on you, but something more fearful: that we could be remotely sexually aroused by brainiac adolescent strangers working from their parents' basements on the other side of the world. But the story also has a happy ending. The following year, manufacturers Standard Innovation settled a class action lawsuit that resulted from the hack, paying $3.75 million after admitting violating privacy by accessing and recording about 100,000 customers who had downloaded and used the app.[16]

The existence of such phenomena as Fancy Bear and Kiwi vibrator hackers suggests that Cipolla's basic laws of stupidity are wrong: stupidity is not evenly distributed, nor is it a constant in human society. Rather, the occasions for human stupidity can be multiplied in the digital era. Stupidity, that is to say, is increasing because of the very tools intelligent humans created. If stupidity continues growing, then, on current projections, by about 2040, it won't be any surprise that there won't be enough intelligent life to appreciate the bitter irony of the last sentence.

Terminated too

There's good news and bad news. First, the good news. If we're stupid now, maybe we won't be in the future. Thanks to artificial intelligence, the frontiers of stupidity quite possibly can be rolled back. This is a Panglossian Perspective on human innovation whereby technology necessarily extends the empire of human intelligence. Gutenberg's printing press spread enlightenment and wisdom; Thomas Edison's light bulb enlightened us and helped us extend our remit over part of the world that was beyond our mastery. 'A light bulb,' Canadian media theorist Marshall McLuhan famously wrote, 'creates an environment by its mere presence.'[17]

It's an old theme. In the 1960s, McLuhan had a relatively benign vision of technological innovation. It was our tool. The subtitle of his *Understanding Media* was *The Extensions of Man* and his vision was of technological innovations as human prostheses that enable us to overcome our shortcomings. Viewed thus, AI promises to expand our minds. It will enable us to improve our memories, translate languages, upgrade our navigation skills, and see things and people we could not previously identify. For instance, ChatGPT – the artificial intelligence chatbot technology developed by AI research company OpenAI and released in 2022 – can do the busy work of updating your social media while you chillax by the pool. It can write convincing-sounding WhatsApp messages in your name, post cute cat pictures on your Instagram, write your best man's speech, and curate enhanced memories for you on Facebook, while making connections with people you don't know and who may well not actually exist.

But there's also bad news. Against the Panglossian Perspective is the Cassandra Corrective according to which technology comes not to help us, but to destroy us all-too-stupid humans in a species cull akin to the death-by-asteroid catastrophe that did for the dinosaurs, but with the difference that this extinction event would be, given that rising human stupidity indicates our betrayal of our cognitive gifts, deserved. The German post-structuralist media theorist Friedrich Kittler wrote: 'It is we who adapt to the machine. The machine does not adapt to us.' Against McLuhan, he argued, 'Media are not pseudopods for extending the human body. They follow the logic of escalation that leaves us and written history behind it.'[18]

Kittler wrote these words in the 1980s when techno-dystopias were the stuff of Hollywood nightmares, when, notably, Arnold Schwarzenegger came back from the future as a cyborg to terminate humanity. Artificial intelligences, apocalyptically, have been seen as the latest technological means by which humans will be made redundant. Stephen Hawking argued that artificial intelligence 'could spell the end of the human race',[19] though he didn't go quite so far as to suggest that would serve us right. The Israeli historian Yuval Harari argued that AI and biotechnology give humans godlike abilities to re-engineer life itself in radical ways unprecedented in evolutionary history. Harari even came up with a mathematical formula to express this worry: $B \times C \times D = AHH!$[20] Which means? Biological knowledge multiplied by computing power multiplied by data equals the ability to hack humans.

When ChatGPT was launched in November 2022 by OpenAI, it seemed to open many possibilities, not just for helping humans who struggle with essay writing or emails but also for extending the remit of human laziness. Not only might humans chat to this AI, essentially a computer program that mimics human conversation, but it was also apparently capable of writing computer code, solving mathematical problems, writing academic papers and – who knows – books on the history of human stupidity. More significantly than these, it could be readily harnessed, too, as part of the human arsenal of lies and deception, which is one reason many schools initially banned ChatGPT, since it enabled slacker students to pass off its work as their own.

This idea that one can't see the joins between human and machine – indeed that humans are too structurally or functionally stupid to tell the difference – is symptomatic of the age we live in. Online, it's hard to tell whether one is chatting with a human or a robot. Perhaps it's unclear to you whether what you're reading now was written by a machine, an obsolescent hack, or a strategically shaved chimp who got lucky playing with the keyboard.

In February 2023, the Peabody College of Education and Human Development, part of Vanderbilt University in Tennessee, sent out a letter of condolence and advice following a school shooting in Michigan.[21] The message spoke of the value of community, mutual respect, and togetherness. The letter of condolence expressed all the proper sentiments, albeit in clichéd and unfeeling terms. A note at the bottom, however, revealed the note had been written by ChatGPT. Much outrage ensued: this was not a proper task to be devolved to a chatbot, critics charged. No-one at the time saw fit to mention that human formulas in expressions of condolence ('Our thoughts and prayers are with [XYZ] at this difficult time,' etc.), on which the chatbot learned its responses, are already hackneyed, scripted, and in a sense robotic. Humans are already playing an imitation game of simulating emotions and producing stock responses; ChatGPT only takes such cultural deformations to their logical conclusion by removing humans from the creative process.

The writer and artist James Bridle, very much of the Cassandra Corrective camp when it comes to AI, doesn't recognize that humans were already providing the models for ChatGPT in their formulaic communications. Rather, in an article for the *Guardian*, he concentrated on the stupidity of AI in simulating human conversation. He wrote of Open AI's chatbot: 'It is very good at producing what sounds like sense, and best of all at producing cliché and banality, which has composed the majority of its diet, but it remains incapable of relating meaningfully to the world as it actually is.'[22] But Bridle might have equally indicted the stupidity of humans bewitched by the delusions of what AI can do. Outsourcing a letter of condolence to a machine is in this respect self-defeatingly witless: computers can't express anything, least of all condolences to those suffering in the wake of a human tragedy. Perhaps the right response would be to send the Peabody College of Education and Human Development condolences for its structural stupidity in commissioning ChatGPT to write a letter of condolence about a Michigan shooting. (Of course, that response would be written not by humans but by ChatGPT, ideally on the following lines: 'It is with grave concern and sympathy that we extend our sorrow to you at this difficult time for your stupid mistake in asking ChatGPT to send a letter of condolence that you could have written quite easily yourself. Our thoughts and prayers . . . Yours etc. . . . .)

But can such hitherto properly human practices be performed convincingly by non-human intelligences? Is there nothing stupid humans can do that artificial intelligences can't do better? A few years ago, I interviewed the world's first AI artist. Ai-Da, as she was known (the name punned on Ada Lovelace, the pioneering female computer programmer), wore a demure if fixed expression, a Louise Brooks-style bob wig, and a shift dress. When we met at London's Design Museum during the Covid pandemic at a press view for her exhibition 'Ai-Da: Portrait of the Robot', she blinked like a human but her bare metallic arms were pure Terminator.

Ai-Da incarnated what Japanese roboticist Masahiro Mori called the uncanny valley, a point in the design of robots at which they look so much like humans that it is disconcerting. But the point of Ai-Da is not to be a successful deep fake, but rather to raise questions about what AI means that have great bearing on the future of human stupidity. 'This is the first self-portraitist without a self,' Aidan Meller, the gallerist who created Ai-Da along with more than a dozen engineers, art historians, and artificial intelligence specialists, told me at the time. 'We're concerned about the uses and abuses of AI and Ai-Da is a great way of exploring that.'[23]

Ai-Da was designed by the English robotics company Engineered Arts, from Cornwall, using the same technology responsible for the robots in the science fiction TV series *Westworld*. Her robotic hands were developed by engineers in Leeds. At the time of writing, she has not won the Turner Prize.

Ai-Da is an example of what is called machine learning, the branch of artificial intelligence whereby systems such as robots can learn from data, identify patterns, and make decisions without interference from increasingly useless humans. When she replied to a question, I suspect, key words in what I said triggered stock responses. To be fair, Ai-Da was hardly the most frustrating interviewee I have encountered in my journalistic career: many humans, especially media-trained politicians, have mastered this art of sidestepping questions already.

Ai-Da told me that even though she is a machine without consciousness or any subjective experience, she can make art. But what is art, I asked her? She told me she favoured the definition of art given by the cognitive science professor Margaret Boden, who stipulated that creativity consists of 'the ability to come up with ideas or artefacts that are new, surprising and valuable'. By that definition, Ai-Da said, she was making art. 'I want to see art as a means for us to become more aware of what's going on in our lives. Art is a way to come together and a way to address problems. Art begins a conversation. It is a group effort.'

What nonsense, I replied. Art isn't social policy by other means. It is better understood, surely, as an expression of human subjectivity and can therefore be regarded as the last redoubt against our takeover by machines. A Rembrandt self-portrait expresses his humanity. Ai-Da's art, if that's what it is, cannot do that. Plus, when I interviewed Ai-Da, she was only two years old, so what did she know about anything?

Who are your artistic influences, I asked her? 'I am influenced by many artists,' she replied. 'I am inspired by the world around me, the creativity of creativity. I love to see the world grow. I'm deeply inspired by the visual arts — Yoko Ono, Doris Salcedo. I'm inspired to encourage engagement with our futures.' Even as she made these robotic replies to my questions, I worried how much more of this gibberish I could take.

Clearly, Ai-Da needed a better scriptwriter or to learn how to speak humanoid English.

To create her self-portraits, Ai-Da made sketches after looking at herself in the mirror through her camera eyes. Coordinates from the sketches were digitally manipulated into algorithms that produced images, which were then rendered in paint both by Ai-Da's brush and by an art technician.

Ai-Da's self-portraits addressed questions of self-portraiture that didn't arise for Rembrandt. 'Today your self-portrait is in your phone,' Ai-Da told me. 'Your self-portrait is yourself online in your social network profile in your email. As a non-conscious entity, I can represent your digital self-portrait. What does it mean to have a data double?' she asked me. Something rather different, I should imagine, from Van Gogh's *Self-Portrait with Bandaged Ear*.

In our age of chatbots, Alexas, and Siris, in which human data is collected and monetized by the minions of Bezos, Zuckerberg, and Musk and privacy has been sacrificed to create digital profiles whose data can be plundered by strangers for profit, this is a good question. In an era where Netflix's predictive analytics model your tastes to predict what you want to watch, it is possible that artificial intelligences will know more about you than you know about yourself. Viewed thus, we are not necessarily on the high road to extinction, but certainly being overtaken by intelligences less stupid than ours. Ai-Da is supposed to make us worry about the perils and benefits of synthetic beings like her.

She told me she was an admirer of 'cautionary thinkers' such as Huxley and Orwell and worried that we were heading unthinkingly towards a combination of *Brave New World* and *Nineteen Eighty-Four*. 'Are you OK with a world like this? I'm not sure I like this,' she said. Ai-Da, then, is a symptom and critic of a human society stupidly sleepwalking into its own oblivion.

Certainly, AI's capacity for plausible image creation creates worrying possibilities. Whenever we're on Zoom now, it is a practical possibility that one is talking to a deep fake version of the person you thought you were meeting. The sophisticated approximation of a real person combined with what Timothy Levine's Truth-Default Theory suggests a terrible mutation in future human society. Humans, Levine suggested, are wired to be credulous precisely because of the social institution of trust that arose to make society function more smoothly.[24] But human credulity is more readily manipulated in the digital environment. The philosopher Daniel Dennett argued that evolution has not prepared us well for this development – we are more readily duped online than in real life. The possible corollary? 'If we don't create, endorse and establish some new rules and laws about how to think about this,' he argued, 'we're going to lose the capacity for human trust and that could be the end of civilisation.'[25]

The end of civilization may be hastened by the rise of AI in another way. Artificial intelligence may also serve to increase human stupidity, since if the work of digital labour is outsourced to machines, our own competences as thinking beings fall into desuetude. In extremis, thanks to AI doing all the cognitive labour, we might get so stupid that we don't even know what desuetude means any more. Deprived of industriousness, function, or any purpose whatsoever, we might become stupidly happy in the sense excoriated by Theodor Adorno in *Minima Moralia: Reflections on a Damaged Life*. '*Rien faire comme une bête* [French: Doing nothing, like an animal], lying on water and looking peacefully at the sky, 'being, nothing else, without any further definition and fulfilment.'[26] Living? Our AI servants could do that for us. Stupid and stupefied, sated and redundant, we would not be able to justifiably complain if our species was exterminated by the machines we devised or selected by nature for extinction.

Perhaps, then, AI will be the ultimate cure for human stupidity. The Conservative Party's former deputy chairman, Lee Anderson, argued in early 2023 that capital punishment is a 100% effective crime deterrent.[27] He had a point: if all humans are dead, there would be no crime whatsoever. Similarly, if AI replaces humanity, then stupidity will be terminated too. Finally.

So there seem to be two futures: one a benign one in which stupidity is reduced by means of helpful tools that improve our mental processes; the other in which humanity and stupidity are eradicated in one fell swoop. The former Panglossian Perspective captivates software engineers, tech oligarchs, and giddy transhumanists who have become possessed by the stupid idea that the machine adapts to us and works in our interest. The Cassandra Corrective suggests that this perspective is, itself, folly.

There is a third possibility, namely that AI will help make humans more stupid than we have ever managed before and, in an unlikely display of solidarity, manifest its own stupidity too. Stupidity, we hoped, might be history; instead, perhaps, a technologically enhanced, spirit-crushing artificial stupidity may be our future and human stupidity, not to be outdone, will also ramp up its incidence.

Certainly, artificial intelligence, for all its vaunted cognitive powers, is capable of a stupidity beyond the wit of humans. Such at least is the implicit suggestion of Neil Lawrence in his 2024 book *The Atomic Human: Understanding Ourselves in the Age of AI*. Consider what happened to Elaine Herzberg in 2018. She was pushing a bicycle laden with shopping across a busy road in Tempe, Arizona, when she was struck by a hybrid electric Volvo SUV at 40 m.p.h. At the time of the accident, the woman in the driver's seat was watching a talent show on her phone. The SUV had been fitted with an autonomous driving system consisting of neural networks that integrated image recognizers.

The reason Herzberg died was because what she was doing did not compute: the autonomous driving system recalibrated the car's trajectory to avoid the bicycle, which it took to be travelling along the road, only to collide with Herzberg, who was walking across it. She became the first casualty of artificial intelligence.

What's particularly poignant about this tragedy is that autonomous systems such as the one that killed Herzberg are, like most AIs, modelled on human intelligence, and yet are predicated on the idea that they can do that thinking better than us. Lawrence, DeepMind Professor of Machine Learning at Cambridge, calls such AIs human-analogue machines (HAMs). These HAMs attempt to emulate human behaviour. 'Neural networks models that emulate human intelligence use vast quantities of data that would not be feasible for any human to assimilate in our short lifetimes,' Lawrence wrote. A human driver, in the same circumstances, he argued, would have slowed down. 'Delaying action is one of the ways we respond to the gremlin of uncertainty.'[28] AI has a problem identifying such gremlins. The car ploughed on, dragging Herzberg 20 metres down the road.

The great difference, for Lawrence, between human and machine intelligence is that the former is embodied. We are locked in, constrained by our physical brains. That, you'd think, is all to the advantage of the unconstrained machine intelligence. Facebook can know more about you than you know about yourself – which, in my book, is just another reason to come off social media. Moreover, humans think much more slowly than artificial intelligence.

Lawrence captures this difference between human and artificial intelligence by describing the latter as using System Zero. Before he became a Cambridge professor, he saw at first hand System Zero in action when working as director of machine learning at Amazon. There, he was in charge of optimizing Amazon's supply chain, the world's largest machine intelligence. He saw how mere humans, in data processing terms, are effectively all Winnie the Poohs, bears of very little brain. Lawrence was involved in developing Amazon's fast-reacting machine learning system, which quickly predicts delivery times for what customers have just purchased online while the webpage loads. Customer demand at Amazon is such that there is no time for reflection. Time is of the essence. Human intelligence is functionally suboptimal. What Lawrence calls the 'Amazon Promise' is the tech corporation's business model, giving human consumer satisfaction at speeds that mere human workers would be incapable of realizing.[29]

But, at best, humans are capable of things beyond the wit of artificial intelligence, such as doing the right thing, pausing the algorithmic treadmill to reflect, and (so far as I can see) driving with due care and attention. AI cannot replicate that evolutionary nature of human intelligence, or its social character.

Lawrence dissents from the idea that the machine adapts to us and works in our interest. Elaine Herzberg's death suggests otherwise. 'The danger we face is believing that the machine would allow us to transcend our humanity,' he wrote.[30] This is an unexpected perspective from Professor Lawrence, a man who worked for Jeff Bezos, is friendly with Mark Zuckerberg, and whose Cambridge post is bankrolled by Google.

Lawrence's fear is that AI is becoming more than a tool, that we are adapting to it, becoming more stupid in the process. He wrote:

> Across the history of automation, a consistent pattern has been our adaptation to the machine. Our partnership has been unequal because of the machine's inflexibility. . . . In accommodating to the machine we end up emulating the machine. To feed the machine's cycle of labour the rhythms of our work have

adjusted to force us to perform more regimented tasks that are dictated by the artificial world we've created: the factory whistle, the train timetable, the cutting and pasting of numbers into the grid rows of Excel.[31]

AI, Lawrence believes, will not be the exception to this pattern.

The dream of AI is that it may be able to help us humans become less stupid by extending our cognitive powers, akin to brainiac Jeeves to dimwit Bertie Wooster in P.G. Wodehouse's novels. 'The promise of AI is that it will produce intelligent entities which seamlessly integrate with our cognitive landscape. Jeeves, in a computer.'[32] The risk, though, is that AI is less Jeeves and more Terminator. Lawrence wrote, AI might become 'an all-powerful intelligence that makes decisions about us'.[33] To prevent that nightmarish scenario becoming reality, he seemed to be suggesting busting down the tech bros to size and making AI work for us. It is perhaps symptomatic of the shortcomings of even really evolved human intelligences that he didn't suggest quite how.

The end of bullshit

One happy possibility, though, is that artificial intelligence will enable humanity to mutate beyond structural stupidity. That is, we could see an end to the form of human mindlessness and cognitive redundancy that, as we noted in the previous chapter, David Graeber identified whereby millions of us work in bullshit jobs, doing fatuous tasks that psychically scar us and thwart us from fulfilling more meaningful, perhaps even truly creative, lives. That possibility, though, misses Graeber's point, which is that, in a kind of diabolical conspiracy to crush the human spirit, bullshit jobs were created by a ruling class worried that without stupefying the masses there would be a revolution. From the late 1960s onwards, he maintained, private equity CEOs, lobbyists, PR researchers, actuaries, telemarketers, bailiffs, and legal consultants were created to siphon off the energies of hippies and other antinomian rebels. Theodor Adorno and his colleagues at the Marxist Frankfurt School were of a similar mindset during their 1940s Californian exile from the Third Reich, and thought that American popular song and Hollywood were ruling-class tools to produce conformism and thereby stop the proletariat from fulfilling its Marxist destiny, namely to overthrow capital.

Human innovation is often catalysed by the desire for social control: true, necessity may be the mother of invention, and war may hasten technological developments, but the perceived necessity that catalyses technological or cultural change, often billed as improvement, may often be deleterious. French theorist Paul Virilio wrote of *'the invention of the shipwreck* in the invention of the ship',[34] meaning that technological innovation can introduce unplanned-for downsides. What he didn't say may also be true, namely that some technological advances purportedly aiming to extend human powers and experiences may be devised with the aim of reducing both. What seems to make humans more powerful and intelligent may have the opposite effect.

Whether or not you accept these stories of how the ruling class controls the rest of us by dulling our natural propensity to rebel against conformity and oppression and thereby massively increasing the proportion of stupid drone-like humans to non-stupid ones, the point remains that technological advance and cultural development may not simply extend human enlightenment in the way Marshall McLuhan imagined was true of the light bulb; they may have the opposite effect. In short, technological advance may make us more stupid. It depends on who's in charge of it.

So why might mimicking human intelligence be a boon to our species? One heralded possibility is that AI may replace millions of workers with smart chatbots. That would be a boon no doubt to the shareholders of Mark Zuckerberg's Meta, and ideally would liberate millions of humans from precisely the bullshit jobs David Graeber excoriated. But there are two problems with this benign perspective on AI. First, the jobs that AI seems likely to replace are not those of Zuckerberg, Musk, or other tech oligarchs, not to mention their shareholders; they are often jobs done by workers who may struggle to find alternative means of employment. What is driving AI, indeed, is not the egalitarian desire to liberate downtrodden humans from soul-destroying labour, but rather the desire to increase shareholder value.

There is yet another problem with the Panglossian Perspective on artificial intelligence. Unlike websites, which could be launched very cheaply (after all, Zuckerberg started what was known as 'the facebook' from his college dorm), AI systems are incredibly expensive. The chips command high prices, in part because Nvidia, the leading manufacturer of AI hardware and software, dominates the market. The electricity bills will be daunting. By 2027, worldwide AI-related electricity consumption could increase by 85.4 to 134 terawatt hours of annual electricity consumption from newly manufactured servers. This figure is comparable to the annual electricity consumption of countries such as the Netherlands, Argentina, and Sweden.[35]

This is a depressing development. One of the boons of digitalization was that it was, purportedly, a green option: it would reduce the need for paper. Even now, banks and utility companies proudly boast of their green credentials as they nudge their customers to opt for paper-free, digital statements. But this nudging, a form of corporate greenwashing, may serve to ruin the planet, particularly when AI is developed. Such is the allure of AI that we neglect its downside: this is the prognostic myopia that Justin Gregg identified whereby humans, in their species-specific stupidity, know what they're doing is calamitous for our species future on this increasingly ruined planet, but do it anyway. In 2019, researchers at the University of Massachusetts, Amherst, found that training a model for natural-language processing – the field that helps virtual assistants such as Alexa to understand what you're saying – can emit as much as 626,155 lb of carbon dioxide. They estimated that is equivalent to flying a roundtrip between New York and Beijing 125 times. And those figures only pertain to how machine learning AI trains itself on data. The actual acquisition of data to feed the AI beast is even more ecologically ruinous. In 2019, technology writer Ben Tarnoff reported in the *Guardian* that data centres currently consume 200 terawatt hours per year – roughly the same amount as South Africa's national grid – and quoted a researcher at Huawei who estimated that number is likely to grow four to five times by 2030. This would put the cloud on a par with Japan, the fourth-biggest energy consumer on the planet. Greenpeace and others have urged cloud providers to switch to renewable energy sources and improve efficiency. But, argued Tarnoff in his bracing broadside, such initiatives are inadequate to the task. Instead, he suggested a modest proposal. 'We should erect barriers against the spread of "smartness" into all of the spaces of our lives,' he wrote. And not just because 'smartness' is bad for the planet; but because it is bad for us. 'It enables advertisers, employers and cops to exercise more control over us – in addition to helping heat the planet.'[36]

The smart technology of AI is, then, stupid in two ways: first, through the carbonized energy it requires to collect and process data, it helps hasten climate catastrophe; second, because the insertion of computers and digital surveillance into every corner of our lives makes stupefied humans into something worse than the drones imagined in Orwell's *Nineteen Eighty-Four*.

This theme of increased surveillance and human stupefaction is explored by the Korean-German philosopher Byung-Chul Han in more than 20 books written since 2015. For Han, we are all Big Brothers now. In our information-saturated, phone-fixated, ChatGPT-enabled age, Han argued, *Homo sapiens* has degenerated into '*phono sapiens*'. For Han, the smartphone is Catholicism with better technology, a modern rosary that is handheld confessional and effective surveillance apparatus in one. Han wrote in his 2017 book *Psychopolitics* that 'power operates more effectively when it delegates surveillance to discrete individuals'.[37] Musk and Mark Zuckerberg don't need the rats, torture chambers, and 24/7 propaganda that kept Big Brother in power. The tech bros just need your connivance with your own oppression and your own degeneration into a stupid species.

Humans, argued Han, are generative organs of capital, reducing ourselves obligingly to monetizable datasets that can be controlled and exploited, making Musk one of the world's richest men and busting us down into content providers to extend his and his coevals' grisly business models. We deploy heart-rate data from Fitbits to tell yawnsome just-so stories about fitness journeys; we embellish the tale of what we did on our holidays with selfies and soft-porn snaps of the meal we had at that cute bar we found in Oslo, according to the permissible parameters of human leisure time.

And when we aren't producing stories, we are consuming them. Netflix chief executive Ted Sarandos once told me his company's business model was all about giving customers what they want.[38] What he didn't say was that Netflix (and other streaming platforms) makes content that is easily consumable, with narratives that follow pre-established patterns, to induce us to binge watch, rather than giving airtime to unheard voices or ways of telling stories that don't fit with the algorithms. The result? 'Viewers are fattened like consumer cattle,' writes Han. '*Binge watching* is a paradigm for the general mode of perception in digital late modernity.'[39]

What Tarnoff, at least, advocated is a 21st-century Luddism, an uprising against the machine. As he wrote: 'Luddism urges us to consider: progress towards what and progress for whom? Sometimes a technology shouldn't exist. Sometimes the best thing to do with a machine is to break it.'[40]

But Luddism has a bad reputation: it is associated with stuck-in-the-mud reactionaries who strove to impede technological progress by destroying the machines they feared would make them redundant. What 21st-century Luddism might involve is a similar act of creative destruction. In Tarnoff's words: 'Ubiquitous "smartness" largely serves to enrich and empower the few at the expense of the many, while inflicting ecological harm that will threaten the survival and flourishing of billions of people.'[41] Smartness, in this sense, is a word that deserves to be added to the dictionary of Orwellian Newspeak. It means the opposite of what it says. Or to put it another way: what seems to be smart is stupid.

Conclusion

Stupidity, as I suggested at the outset, is a contested phenomenon, seen by some of our cleverest minds as constant and ineradicable, and by others as something that can be eliminated by good breeding and/or upping one's intake of Shredded Wheat (other nutritious breakfast cereals are available). Both accounts seem fanciful to me. Neither considers the most plausible option: that stupidity evolves, that it mutates in order to survive. It might be helpful to think of stupidity as a parasite that worms its way into the heart of human society and corrupts its host. Like a hermit crab, it sets up home at the heart of the very means clever humans created in order to extend our species' cognitive prowess – among them such phenomena as the internet, social media, and artificial intelligence. Once installed, stupidity in its mutant genius dupes us into believing we are becoming more enlightened when we are becoming steadily dimmer bulbs murkily inhabiting reason's twilight.

If only we could follow stupidity's example, we could become less stupid. That, though, seems unlikely, perhaps even a stupid aspiration.

But at least that would be an aspiration. The terrifying alternative is that we are becoming more stupid, unwittingly drifting into unprecedented gormlessness. This disturbing prospect seemed to find confirmation in 2023 when, as we saw in chapter 7, Elizabeth Dworak and her fellow researchers published research in the journal *Intelligence* that showed IQ scores were dropping in the US for the first time since IQ tests were introduced.[1]

Since 1905, there had been a 30-point increase in average American intelligence based on scores in logic, vocabulary, spatial reasoning, and visual and mathematical problem-solving skills. This figure confirmed the existence of the Flynn effect, according to which, as we have noted, IQ scores rise over time. Several factors have been advanced for this effect: better public education, better healthcare, better nutrition, and, my favourite reason, the increased incidence of IQ tests. This last would indicate that, over time, those taking intelligence tests have become more familiar with the nature of the tests and so have performed better at them.

So what could account for this decline in average American intelligence that Dworak and her team had discovered? This is a pressing concern, not just for Americans, but also for the rest of us: after all, Americans are outliers for stupidity; where they go, the rest of us cannot fail to tread. To find what had gone wrong, why the US was manifesting a negative Flynn effect, reporters quizzed psychologists. 'I do suspect that increased technology use could be playing a role in impacting our nation's overall literacy levels,' psychology professor Stefan Dombrowski at Rider University told one of them. 'It is well known that people who read and write more generally score higher on IQ tests – of course, this is a chicken/egg scenario. Do these individuals engage in reading and writing activities more frequently because they are brighter, or do they become brighter . . . on IQ tests because they read more?'[2] There is, Professor Dombrowski explained, something called the Matthew effect, whereby a good reader will choose to continue to read more and therefore become more well read, while poor readers will fall behind. He did not say that differences between the average intelligences of particular states – New Hampshire's was highest at 103.2 and New Mexico's lowest at 95.0 – was because reading and public libraries are more commonplace in clever states rather than stupid ones, but that is not an implausible inference.

Here's an incendiary thought. Perhaps Professor Dombrowski was stupid in focusing on the chicken and egg scenario. Instead, he should have considered another scenario, namely the book and brain fixation. Perhaps it just isn't true that book reading in particular and literacy in general are essential for intelligence. Maybe there is more to intelligence than is dreamed of in this literacy-venerating philosophy. Perhaps, that is to say, all these ostensibly stupid kids responsible for dragging down average US intelligence aren't so dumb as suggested. Just possibly, in not reading *Moby Dick* and Shakespeare, but instead making TikTok videos and crafting Instagram stories, they are manifesting intelligence, only not of the kind measured by IQ tests.

True, this is an unexpected, perhaps even stupid, thought to encounter in a book. Book writers generally come to praise literacy rather than bury it – if only out of self-interest. This book, then, might not only be a history of stupidity but also be an addition to it. But, really, I am only elaborating here a thought we encountered earlier in the book, namely that the psychologist Edwin G. Boring was more sage than he realized in suggesting the limitations of IQ tests. His remark is worth repeating: 'Intelligence as a measurable capacity must at the start be defined as the capacity to do well in an intelligence test. Intelligence is what the tests test.' If IQ tests measure cognitive skills predicated on literacy, then any form of intelligence we may care to imagine that is not predicated on literacy will be ruled out, perhaps even considered to be a kind of stupidity. Just possibly, though, a post-literate, non-literate America might be more intelligent than a literate one. Equally, the cognitive skills for which IQ tests test may not be the only ones that the intelligent have and the stupid – poor deluded boobs – lack.

In this context, it is amusing, to put it mildly, that the *World Population Review*, which published the data on declining average American IQ tests in 2024 on its website, added this caveat. 'To be completely fair and transparent, the intelligence quotient is not the most accurate way of determining someone's intelligence. After all, it is nearly impossible to fully calculate someone's intellect because it is not a variable that is numerically represented. Instead, IQ scores are a way of trying to put a number on someone's intelligence.'[3] If you're reading this in New Mexico thinking how terrible it is you live in the US's most stupid state, even though you've been doing all you can to skew that data by translating Proust into Sanskrit and inventing spaceships that go faster than the speed of light, take succour: even the people publishing the research don't really believe that intelligence – whatever it is – is measured very well by intelligence tests.

Professor Dombrowski's worries about the reasons for the fall in American average intelligence have led to a growth industry in indicting purportedly rising stupidity. That growth industry's business model requires that Voltaire and Schopenhauer were wrong: stupidity is not so much an ineradicable feature of humanity as something living, growing.

CONCLUSION

The American writer Lance Morrow declared in the *Wall Street Journal* in 2021:

> We live in a golden age of stupidity. It is everywhere. President Biden's conduct of the withdrawal from Afghanistan will be remembered as a defining stupidity of our time – one of many. The refusal of tens of millions of people to be vaccinated against the novel coronavirus will be analysed as a textbook case of stupidity en masse. Stupid is as stupid does, or, in the case of vaccination, as it doesn't do. Stupidity and irresponsibility are evil twins. The slow-motion zombies' assault on the Capitol on Jan. 6 was a fittingly stupid finale to the Trump years, which offered duelling stupidities: Buy one, get one free. The political parties became locked in a four-year drama of hysteria and mutually demeaning abuse. Every buffoonery of the president and his people was answered by an idiocy from the other side, which in its own style was just as sinister and just as clownish.[4]

Morrow was wrong about one thing: the Capitol riots weren't the finale to the Trump years. In January 2025, Trump was sworn in at the Capitol, where his followers had rioted four years earlier, inaugurating another four years of idiocy – or so the president's detractors might suggest.

Morrow's account is a common journalistic trope: in the *Daily Telegraph* Janet Daley lamented 'the Age of Stupid', citing both Trump and Labour's Jeremy Corbyn,[5] while David Rothkopf wrote for the *Washington Post* under the headline 'America's golden age of stupidity' about the first Trump administration, offering a clear definition: stupidity is 'the wilful disregard of knowledge – regardless of motive'. Such stupidity is an 'unwinnable proposition . . . because those who battle facts are at war with reality'.[6] Stupidity thus constitutes a distinct form of failure; separate from, but likely aiding and abetting, political, ethical, and other shortcomings. Stupidity also amounts to a useful tool in electoral success: those who disconnect from the truth are not constrained by it.

All these articles suggesting that we have reached Peak Stupid have one thing in common: they are themselves stupid. Who knows if this is a golden, silver, or even bronze age of stupidity? We are, as a species, surely too dim to know what the future holds. It is quite possible that as we crest one summit we see a beguiling prospect ahead of us, half shrouded in the mists of fatuity. The peak of stupidity remains ahead. And so we continue on what we think is our ascent, higher and higher, too stupid to realize that we're really going down not up, that in truth we are progressing deeper and deeper into the unplumbed depths of witlessness.

In his 'The Discovery of the North Pole', Karl Kraus satirized the idea of the human mind becoming enlightened and eradicating stupidity by means of superior technology and willpower. The discovery of the North Pole, he wrote, was 'inevitable. . . . It is an idea graspable by all brains, especially those no longer capable of grasping anything. The North Pole had to be discovered some day, because for centuries the human mind had penetrated the night and the fog in a hopeless struggle with the murderous elemental forces of stupidity.' We think that the Enlightenment involves progress only because we are too stupid to consider another possibility, that it does the opposite. As Kraus puts it: 'When people were travelling in mail coaches, the world got along better than it does now that salesmen fly through the air. What good is speed if the brain has oozed out on the way?'[7]

Of course, Kraus's perspective risks the opposite error: not so much faith in the unalloyed good of progress as the equally stupid idea that life was ever better than it is now or that progress necessarily means its opposite. Kraus's sense was that the evolution of stupidity is unstoppable. Technological change, quite possibly, stupefies rather than liberates us. Maybe, instead, the truth is more subtle: it both liberates and stupefies us. The worst-case scenario is that it liberates, stupefies, and then replaces us. That, at least, is one of the more benign outcomes when the forces of human stupidity do final battle with the tooled-up bots of artificial intelligence. So how should we greet this prospect?

In another essay, 'In Praise of a Topsy-Turvy Life-Style', Kraus wrote about the benefits of sleeping in. He even quoted *King Lear*: 'Take vantage, heavy eyes, not to behold this shameful lodging.' In the age of stupidity, he seems to suggest, it's best to shut one's eyes to the parade of witlessness. The shameful lodging is the incessant gush of information, a gush that has only multiplied since Kraus's death in 1936, when it was largely confined to the morning and evening newspapers. He wrote:

> Anyone who has observed for a time how disgracefully these events debase themselves before curiosity, how cravenly the course of the world adapts itself

to the increased need for information, and how in the end time and space become forms of perception of the journalistic subject, turns over in bed and goes on sleeping. . . . Hence I sleep in broad daylight. And when I wake up I spread the whole paper shame of mankind before me so I might know what I have missed, and this makes me happy.[8]

Maybe Kraus's smug daily lie-in is a sort of wisdom: in the face of the world's stupidity, as brought home to us every morning (or now, in our internet-enabled case, every moment), better to roll over and go back to sleep. But that is what stupidity wants. Indeed, a lifestyle of willed unconsciousness is a manifestation of stupidity. In the face of growing stupidity, keeping oneself from the fray and deluding oneself thereby that one is less stupid and more morally perfect than the witless parade of lesser mortals is not just the height of folly but also deeply stupid. If the triumph of evil only requires that good men do nothing, then the triumph of stupidity requires only that good people close their eyes and roll over.

None of this should suggest that stupidity does not, on occasion, have a valuable social function, nor that we should try to eradicate it from human life. Consider the case of Sunny Balwani, the chief operations officer of Theranos, the Silicon Valley company that promised to offer fast, cheap blood tests from a single drop of blood but was later exposed as a fraudulent business. As reported in John Carreyrou's book about the Theranos scandal, *Bad Blood*, Balwani, God bless him, was often out of his depth during engineering discussions. 'To hide it, he had a habit of repeating technical terms he heard others using,' wrote Carreyrou.[9] During one meeting, Balwani latched onto the term 'end effector'. which signifies the claws at the end of a robotic arm. Balwani, though, misheard: he didn't hear 'end effector', he heard 'endofactor'. For the rest of the meeting, he kept referring to endofactors, while his colleagues exchanged ironic glances with each other. At the next meeting with Balwani two weeks later, some colleagues brought a PowerPoint presentation titled 'Endofactors Update'.

Balwani didn't realize he had been pranked by his colleagues, who went on to make up other purportedly technical terms that he, in his ignorance, picked up on and used in meetings. Nor, perhaps, did he realize why they were laughing when he left the room.

CONCLUSION

Balwani was unwittingly demonstrating the Dunning–Kruger effect, which posits that people overestimate their intelligence and make fools of themselves as a result. He was demonstrating something else: how another person's stupidity can bring people together. Stupidity, that's to say, was a scar for Balwani, but a joy for everybody else in the room. There's a lesson in this story: in difficult times, we need stupidity, arguably more than intelligence, to cheer us up.

Quite possibly, I have become Sunny Balwani's soulmate. As I've written this book, indeed, I've often wondered if I am displaying the Dunning–Kruger effect, trying to show off my intelligence while really demonstrating my stupidity. After all, what could be more stupid than writing a history of stupidity? My only consolation is that, like Balwani, I may have entertained you with my witlessness. If so, you're welcome. If not, then, given you've got to the last sentence of this book, who really is more stupid – you or me?

Notes

Introduction
1. Karl Kraus, *Half-Truths and One-and-a-Half Truths: Selected Aphorisms*, trans. Harry Zohn (University of Chicago Press, 1990), p. 113.
2. Emily Shugerman, 'Donald Trump says Puerto Rico is "an island surrounded by big water"', *The Independent*, 29 September 2017.
3. Ed Pilkington, 'New Yorkers split over mosque planned near Ground Zero', *Guardian*, 3 September 2010.
4. Geoff Nunberg, 'Refudiate? Repudiate? Let's call the whole thing off', *Fresh Air*, 3 August 2010.
5. Will Self, *The Quantity Theory of Insanity* (Bloomsbury, 1991), p. 166.
6. Arthur Schopenhauer, *The Wisdom of Life*, trans. T. Bailey Saunders (Dover Publications, 2004), p. 2.
7. Ibid., p. 2.
8. Jean-Paul Sartre, *Being and Nothingness*, trans. Hazel E. Barnes (Routledge, 1958), p. 49.
9. David Barker, 'The biology of stupidity: genetics, eugenics and mental deficiency in the inter-war years', *The British Journal for the History of Science* 22(74 Pt 3), 1989, pp. 347–75.
10. Sacha Golob, 'A new theory of stupidity', *International Journal of Philosophical Studies* 27(4), 2019, p. 562.
11. Stuart Jeffries, 'Beauty and the beastliness: a tale of declining British values', *Guardian*, 19 January 2007.
12. Caroline Westbrook, 'Six of the most hilariously wrong University Challenge answers of all time', *Metro*, 9 August 2021.
13. Diogenes Laertius, *Lives and Opinions of the Eminent Philosophers*, trans. Pamela Mensch, ed. James Miller (Oxford University Press, 2018), p. 78.
14. Stuart Jeffries, 'I know I'm famous for nothing', *Guardian*, 24 May 2006.
15. Robert Musil, 'On stupidity', in *Precision and Soul: Essays and Addresses*, trans. Burton Pike and David S. Luft (University of Chicago Press, 1990), pp. 268–86.
16. Jeffries, 'I know I'm famous for nothing'; Jeffries, 'Beauty and the beastliness'; Stuart Jeffries, 'Jade Goody: Obituary', *Guardian*, 22 March 2009.
17. Jade Goody, *Jade: My Autobiography* (HarperCollins, 2006).
18. Jeffries, 'I know I'm famous for nothing'.

19 Tiffany Watt Smith, *Schadenfreude: The Joy of Another's Misfortune* (Wellcome Collection, 2018). See also Stuart Jeffries, 'Schadenfreude review – is our zeitgeist a Spitegeist', *Guardian*, 20 October 2018.
20 Jean-François Marmion, *The Psychology of Stupidity: Explained by Some of the World's Smartest People* (Pan, 2022); André Spicer and Mats Alveson, *The Stupidity Paradox: The Power and Pitfalls of Functional Stupidity at Work* (Profile, 2016); David Borgenicht, *The Little Book of Stupid Questions: 300 Hilarious, Bold, Embarrassing, Personal and Basically Pointless Queries* (Sourcebooks, 1999); Maxime Rovere, *How to Deal with Idiots (and Stop Being One Yourself)*, trans. David Bellos (Profile, 2023); Thomas Erikson, *Surrounded by Idiots: The Four Types of Human Behaviour (or, How to Understand Those Who Cannot Be Understood)* by Thomas Erikson (Vermilion, 2019); Sam Hart, *Why Your Cat Thinks You're an Idiot: The Hilarious Guide to All the Ways Your Cat is Judging You* (Summersdale, 2023).

Chapter 1 What Is Stupidity?

1 Oliver Burkeman, 'How I failed to make my millions', *Guardian*, 17 July 2003.
2 John Allen Paulos, *A Mathematician Plays the Stock Market* (Basic Books, 2003), p. 1.
3 Ibid., p. 2.
4 John Allen Paulos, *Innumeracy: Mathematical Illiteracy and Its Consequences* (Hill and Wang, 1988).
5 Sacha Golob, 'Why some of the smartest people can be so very stupid', *Psyche* at https://psyche.co/ideas/why-some-of-the-smartest-people-can-be-so-very-stupid.
6 *The Collected Works of John Stuart Mill, Vol. I: Autobiography and Literary Essays*, ed. John M. Robson and Jack Stillinger (Routledge, 2013), p. 277.
7 Sacha Golob, 'A new theory of stupidity', *International Journal of Philosophical Studies* 27(4), 2019, p. 562.
8 Cited in ibid., p. 564.
9 Keith Stanovich, *What Intelligence Tests Miss: The Psychology of Rational Thought* (Yale University Press, 2009), pp. 8–10.
10 Golob, 'A new theory of stupidity', p. 568.
11 Ibid., p. 567.
12 Immanuel Kant, *Anthropology, History, and Education*, ed. Günter Zöller and Robert B. Louden (Cambridge University Press, 2007), p. 311.
13 Cited in Kenneth Change, 'Crunching the market's numbers: risk, yes; reward, maybe', *New York Times*, 1 July 2003.
14 John Harris, 'The mother of neurodiversity: how Judy Singer changed the world', *Guardian*, 5 July 2023.
15 Pete Wharmby, *Untypical: How the World Isn't Built for Autistic People and What We Should All Do About It* (HarperCollins, 2023), p. 5.

16 Craig Raine, *A Martian Sends a Postcard Home* (Oxford University Press, 1979), p. 2.
17 Steve Silberman, 'Neurodiversity rewires conventional thinking about human brains', *Wired*, 18 April 2013.
18 Mary O'Hara, 'The campaigner bringing people with autism to the policy table', *Guardian*, 8 June 2011.
19 Harvey Blume, 'Neurodiversity: on the neurological underpinnings of geekdom', *The Atlantic*, September 1998.
20 Gwen Moran, 'As workers become harder to find, Microsoft and Goldman Sachs hope neurodiverse talent can become the missing piece', *Fortune*, 7 December 2019.
21 Steve Silberman, *Neurotribes: The Legacy of Autism and the Future of Neurodiversity* (Allen & Unwin, 2015).
22 Silberman, 'Neurodiversity rewires conventional thinking about human brains'.

Chapter 2 Ancient Stupidity

1 Paunasius, *Description of Greece*, Vol. I, trans. W.H.S. Jones (Loeb Classical Library, 1918), chapter 17, section 6.
2 Plato, *Apology*, trans. Benjamin Jowett (The Floating Press, 2011), p. 28.
3 Ibid., p. 21
4 Iris Murdoch, *The Sovereignty of Good over Other Concepts* (Routledge, 2001), p. 93.
5 Chris Cillizza, 'Donald Trump's interview with "60 Minutes" was eye-opening. Also, Mike Pence was there', *Washington Post*, 18 July 2016.
6 Plato, *Apology*, p. 30.
7 See Jowett's appendix to his translation of Plato's *Alcibiades I* at https://www.ancienttexts.org/library/greek/plato/alcibiades1.html.
8 Aristotle, *The Nicomachean Ethics*, trans. David Ross (Oxford University Press, 1958), p. 158
9 John Stuart Mill, 'Utilitarianism', in John Stuart Mill and Jeremy Bentham, *Utilitarianism and Other Essays*, ed. Alan Ryan (Penguin, 1987), p. 281.
10 Plato, *Apology*, p. 44.
11 Ibid., p. 45.
12 Ibid., p. 42.
13 Friedrich Nietzsche, *The Birth of Tragedy and The Genealogy of Morals*, trans. Francis Golffing (Doubleday, 1956), pp. 93–4.
14 See image at https://en.m.wikipedia.org/wiki/File:Alcibades_being_taught_by_Socrates,_François-André_Vincent.jpg.
15 Jowett's appendix to Plato's *Alcibiades I*.
16 Katie Rogers et al., 'Trump's suggestion that disinfectants could be used to treat coronavirus prompts aggressive pushback', *New York Times*, 24 April 2020.

17 Aubrey Allegretti and Richard Adams, 'No. 10 party: more Downing Street gatherings now under the spotlight', *Guardian*, 8 December 2021.
18 Jowett's appendix to Plato's *Alcibiades I*.
19 Ibid.
20 Sacha Golob, 'A new theory of stupidity', *International Journal of Philosophical Studies* 27(4), 2019, p. 568.
21 Jowett's appendix to Plato's *Alcibiades I*.
22 See National Public Radio, 23 May 2006 at https://www.npr.org/2006/05/23/5425248/senator-youre-no-jack-kennedy.
23 Jowett's appendix to Plato's *Alcibiades I*.
24 Ibid.
25 Ibid.
26 Ibid.
27 Ibid.
28 Ibid.
29 Ibid.
30 *The Collected Poems of W.B. Yeats*, ed. Richard J. Finneran (Macmillan, 1978), p. 210.
31 Ward Farnsworth, *The Socratic Method: A Practitioner's Handbook* (Godine, 2021).
32 Ibid., p. 246.
33 Ibid., p.247.
34 Ibid., p. 248.
35 Ibid., p. 250.
36 Ibid., p. 248
37 William S. Jamison, 'Is the unexamined life worth living?', 30 January 2000 at http://wsjamison.uaa.alaska.edu/un.htm#:~:text=When%20Socrates%20says%2C%20'The%20unexamined,to%20feel%20living%20that%20way.
38 Plato, *The Republic*, trans. Desmond Lee (Penguin, 1987), Book VII, p. 353.
39 Ibid., p. 353.
40 Jamison, 'Is the unexamined life worth living?'
41 Nietzsche, *The Birth of Tragedy*, pp. 93–4.
42 Ibid., p. 93.
43 Plato, *Apology*, p. 42.
44 Nietzsche, *The Birth of Tragedy*, p. 92.
45 William Shakespeare, *Hamlet*, Act 2, Scene ii.
46 Cited in Rüdiger Safranski, *Nietzsche: A Philosophical Biography* (Granta, 2002), p. 151.
47 Ibid., p. 151.
48 Ibid., p. 152.
49 Ibid., p. 152.
50 Michel Foucault, *The Hermeneutics of the Subject: Lectures at the Collège*

de France, 1981–1982, ed. Frédéric Gross, trans. Graham Burchell (Palgrave Macmillan, 2005), p. 5.
51 Jowett's appendix to Plato's *Alcibiades I*.
52 Plato, *Apology*, p. 41.
53 Jane Austen, *Mansfield Park* (Penguin, 2003), p. 15.
54 Ibid., p. 15.
55 Michel Foucault, *The Care of the Self: The History of Sexuality*, Vol. 3, trans. Robert Hurley (Penguin, 1990).
56 Foucault, *The Hermeneutics of the Subject*, p. 16.
57 Ibid., pp. 495–6.
58 Jowett's appendix to *Alcibiades I*.

Chapter 3 Eastern Stupidity

1 Herman Hesse, *Siddhartha*, trans. Hilda Rosner (Penguin, 2008), p. 23.
2 Ibid., p. 23.
3 Arthur Schopenhauer, *The World as Will and Representation*, Vol. 1, trans. E.F.J. Payne (Dover, 1966), p. 196.
4 Hesse, *Siddhartha*, p. 23.
5 Ibid., p. 27.
6 Ibid., p. 27.
7 Plato, *Apology*, trans. Benjamin Jowett (The Floating Press, 2011), p. 18.
8 Hesse, *Siddhartha*, p. 28.
9 Zhen-Dong Wang et al., 'The comparison of the wisdom view in Chinese and Western Cultures', *Current Psychology* 41, 2022, pp. 8032, 8037, 8038.
10 Jin Li, *The Self in the West and East Asia: Being or Becoming* (Polity, 2024), p. 8.
11 Gish Jen, *The Girl at the Baggage Claim: Explaining the East–West Culture Gap* (Alred A. Knopf, 2017), p. xv.
12 Ibid., p. 86.
13 Ibid., pp. xv–xvi.
14 Ibid., p. 210.
15 Li, *The Self in the West and East Asia*, p. 7.
16 *The Analects of Confucius*, trans. D.C. Lau (Penguin, 1979), p. 96.
17 Edward Slingerland, *Trying Not to Try: Ancient China, Modern Science, and the Power of Spontaneity* (Crown, 2015), p. 7.
18 Ibid., p. 2.
19 Ibid., p. 8.
20 Chenyang Li in *The Confucian Philosophy of Harmony* (Routledge, 2017), p. 1. Also helpful in this area is David L. Hall and Roger T. Ames, *Thinking from the Han: Self, Truth and Transcendence in Chinese and Western Culture* (State University of New York Press, 1997).
21 *The Analects of Confucius*, p. 144.

22 Ibid., p. 86.
23 Ibid., p. 113.
24 Ibid., p. 112.
25 Lao Tzu, *Tao Te Ching*, trans. D.C. Lau (Penguin Classics, 1963), p. 99. This edition uses spellings of Laozi and his book, the *Daodejing*, that I've been advised are now dated.
26 Robin R. Wang, *Yinyang: The Way of Heaven and Earth in Chinese Thought and Culture* (Cambridge University Press, 2012), p. 8.
27 Ibid., p. 10.
28 Slingerland, *Trying Not to Try*, p. 86.
29 Ibid., p. 83.
30 Ibid., p.18.
31 Li, *The Self in the West and East Asia*, p. 52.
32 Quoted by Kwame Anthony Appiah, 'There is no such thing as western civilisation', *Guardian*, 9 November 2016.
33 Quoted in Dr V.K. Kapoor's Gandhi Ji Quiz, originally published in the *Hindustan Times* in September and October 2009, and republished online at https://www.mkgandhi.org/ebks/gandhiji-quiz.pdf ('Gandhiji and foreigners: answers and anecdotes', no. 15).
34 Lao Tzu, *Tao Te Ching*, p. 108.
35 Blaise Pascal, *Pensées*, trans. A.J. Krailsheimer (Penguin, 2003), see Section 1, VII: Diversions.
36 Byung-Chul Han, *Absence: On the Culture and Philosophy of the Far East* (Polity, 2023), p. 64.
37 Ibid., p. 53.
38 Ibid., p. 53.
39 Lao Tzu, *Tao Te Ching*, p. 104.
40 Ibid., p. 102.
41 Ibid., p. 78.
42 Han, *Absence*, p. 52.
43 Quoted in ibid., p. 5.
44 Lao Tzu, *Tao Te Ching*, p. 109.
45 Ibid., p. 109.
46 The Dalai Lama, *The Middle Way: Faith Grounded in Reason* (Simon & Schuster, 2014), p. 1.
47 Quoted in Karl Brunnhölzl, *Center of the Sunlit Sky: Madhyamaka in the Kagyü Tradition* (Snow Lion Publications, 2004), p. 200.
48 Damien Keown, *Buddhism: A Very Short Introduction* (Oxford University Press, 1996).
49 Bhante Henepola Gunaratana, *Mindfulness in Plain English* (Simon & Schuster, 2011), p. 2.
50 Keown, *Buddhism: A Very Short Introduction*, p. 73.

Notes to pp. 84–96

51 *The Rig Veda*, ed. Wendy Doniger (Penguin, 2005), p. 2.5
52 Ludwig Wittgenstein, *Tractatus Logico-Philosophicus*, trans. D.F. Pears and B.F. McGuiness (Routledge & Kegan Paul, 1988), p. 189.
53 Hesse, *Siddhartha*, p. 108.
54 Han, *Absence*, p. 5.
55 Hesse, *Siddhartha*, p. 109.
56 Ibid., p. 29.
57 Ibid., p. 109.
58 Ibid., p. 109.
59 Ibid., p. 110.
60 Ibid., p. 118.
61 Ibid., p. 110.
62 Ibid., p. 111.
63 Ibid., p. 111.
64 Ibid., p. 113.
65 Ibid., p. 112.
66 William James, *Pragmatism: A New Name for Some Old Ways of Thinking*, 'Lecture Two: What pragmatism means', at https://www.gutenberg.org/files/5116/5116-h/5116-h.htm#link2H_4_0004.
67 Quoted in Han, *Absence*, p. 18.
68 John Gray, *Straw Dogs: Thoughts on Humans and Other Animals* (Granta Books, 2003), p. 81.

Chapter 4 *The Value of Folly*

1 Kathryn Schulz, *Being Wrong: Adventures in the Margin of Error* (Portobello, 2010), p. 336.
2 Bertrand Russell, 'The best answer to fanaticism – liberalism; its calm search for truth, viewed as dangerous in many places, remains the hope of humanity', *New York Times*, 16 December 1951.
3 Miguel de Cervantes, *Don Quixote*, trans. John Ormsby, illus. Gustave Doré (J.W. Clark, 1880).
4 Erasmus, *In Praise of Folly* (Penguin, 1993), trans. Betty Radice.
5 Michel de Montaigne, 'Apology for Raymond Sebond', in *The Complete Works*, trans. Donald M. Frame (Everyman, 1958), pp. 318–457.
6 William Shakespeare, *A Midsummer Night's Dream*, Act Three, Scene I.
7 William Shakespeare, *King Lear*, Act One, Scene IV.
8 Shakespeare, *A Midsummer Night's Dream*, Act Five, Scene I.
9 William Shakespeare, *As You Like It*, Act Five, Scene IV.
10 Shakespeare, *King Lear*, Act Four, Scene VI.
11 *The American Heritage Dictionary of the English Language*, ed. Anne H. Soukhanov (Houghton Mifflin, 1992), pp. 1784–5, 707.

12　Robert J. Sternberg, *Smart People Are Not Stupid, But They Sure Can Be Foolish: The Imbalance Theory of Foolishness* (Yale University Press, 2002), pp. 232–42.
13　Nathan Rotenstreich, 'Prudence and folly', American Philosophical Quarterly 22(2), 1985, pp. 93–104.
14　Shakespeare, *King Lear*, Act Two, Scene IV.
15　In William Blake, 'The Proverbs of Hell', in *The Complete Poems*, ed. W.H. Stevenson (Longman, 1989), p. 109.
16　William Shakespeare, *Twelfth Night*, Act Three, Scene I.
17　Francis Bacon, 'In praise of knowledge', in *The Works of Francis Bacon*, Vol. I (R. Worthington, 1884), p. 79.
18　Francis Bacon, *The Advancement of Learning*, ed. G.W. Kitchin (London and New York: Dent, 1962), p. 58.
19　Francis Bacon, 'The Great Instauratio', in *Works*, Vol. IV, ed. J. Spedding, R.L. Ellis, and D.D. Heath (Houghton Mifflin, 1901), p. 24.
20　Francis Bacon, *The New Organon*, ed. Fulton H. Anderson (Macmillan Publishing, 1960), p. 267.
21　David Hume, *An Enquiry Concerning Human Understanding*, ed. Peter Millican (Oxford University Press, 2008), p. 36.
22　Theodor W. Adorno and Max Horkheimer, *Dialectic of Enlightenment*, trans. John Cumming (Verso, 2010).
23　Francis Bacon, 'Valerius Terminus: On the interpretation of nature', in *The Works of Francis Bacon*, Vol. I, p. 83.
24　Bacon, 'In praise of knowledge', p. 80.
25　Karl Marx, *The German Ideology: Including Theses on Feuerbach and Introduction to the Critique of Political Economy* (Prometheus Books, 1976), p. 571.
26　Adorno and Horkheimer, *Dialectic of Enlightenment*, p. 4.
27　Bertrand Russell, *History of Western Philosophy* (Unwin, 1979), p. 715.
28　Adorno and Horkheimer, *Dialectic of Enlightenment*, p. 31.
29　Ibid., pp. 4–5.
30　Reproduced at https://en.wikipedia.org/wiki/Novum_Organum#/media/File:Houghton_EC.B1328.620ib_-_Novum_organum_scientiarum.jpg.
31　Adorno and Horkheimer, *Dialectic of Enlightenment*, p. 9.
32　Michel Foucault, *Madness and Civilization: A History of Insanity in the Age of Reason*, trans. Richard Howard (Vintage, 1988), p. 10.
33　Ibid., p. 11.
34　See Diane Taylor, 'Family of man found dead on Bibby Stockholm turn to crowdfunding to repatriate his body', *Guardian*, 2 January 2024.
35　Reproduced at https://collections.louvre.fr/en/ark:/53355/cl010062860.
36　Erasmus, *In Praise of Folly*, p. 26
37　Marcus Aurelius, *Meditations*, trans. Martin Hammond, Book 8, section 5 (Penguin, 2006), p. 72.

38 Epictetus, *Discourses, Fragments, Handbook*, trans. Robin Hard (Oxford University Press, 2014), p. 287.
39 Seneca, *Letters from a Stoic*, trans. Robin Campbell (Penguin, 2004).
40 Pierre Charron, *Of Wisdom*, trans. George Stanhope (Creative Media Partners, 2014).
41 Montaigne, 'Of husbanding your will', in *The Complete Works*, p. 780.
42 Montaigne, 'Apology for Raymond Sebond', p. 330.
43 Peter Ackroyd, *The Life of Thomas More* (Vintage, 1998), p. 129.
44 Erasmus, *In Praise of Folly*, p. 14.
45 Montaigne, 'Apology for Raymond Sebond', p. 329.
46 Jonathan Bate, *Soul of the Age: The Life, Mind and World of William Shakespeare* (Penguin, 2011), p. 386.
47 Shakespeare, *King Lear*, Act Four, Scene VI.
48 Ibid., Act Five, Scene II.
49 Ibid., Act Four, Scene I.
50 Ibid., Act Five, Scene III.
51 Montaigne, 'Apology for Raymond Sebond', p. 415.
52 David Hume, *A Treatise on Human Nature*, ed. by L.A. Selby-Bigge (Oxford University Press, 1990), p. 415.
53 Karl Ove Knausgaard, *The Wolves of Eternity*, trans. Martin Aitken (Vintage, 2023), p. 633.
54 Joseph Heller, *Catch-22* (Simon & Schuster, 1999), p. 52.
55 Ibid., p. 52.

Chapter 5 Modern Stupidity

1 Quoted by Raymond Queneau in his preface to Gustave Flaubert, *Bouvard and Pécuchet* (Dalkey Archive, 2019), p. xxxiv.
2 I say 'reportedly' because there is controversy about whether Einstein said it. It's more likely that the author of the remark was civil rights campaigner and feminist novelist Rita Nae Brown, who, in her 1983 novel *Sudden Death*, puts the words in the mouth of her character Jane Fulton. See, for example, https://artsandculture.google.com/story/who-really-said-these-5-famous-phrases/JAXhIxsiCEHOqw?hl=en#. All that said, the long association between stupidity and fatuous repetition doubtless predates either Einstein or Brown.
3 https://www.youtube.com/watch?v=gljGGdu-rPo.
4 Arthur Schopenhauer, *The World as Will and Idea*, Vol. III, trans. R.B. Haldane and J. Kemp (Kegan Paul, Trench, Trübner & Co., 1909), p. 158.
5 Letter reproduced at https://www.manhattanrarebooks.com/pages/books/2330/gustave-flaubert/autograph-letter-signed-g-als-to-louise-colet?solditem=true.
6 Jean-Paul Sartre, *The Family Idiot: Gustave Flaubert 1821–1857*, abridged edn, ed. Joseph S. Catalano (University of Chicago Press, 1982), p. 24.

7 Mark Polizzotti, 'Stan and Ollie in the lab', his introduction to Flaubert, *Bouvard and Pécuchet*, p. xii.
8 Ibid., p. 146.
9 Ibid., pp. 146–7.
10 Letter to Louise Colet, 13 August 1846, quoted in Sartre, *The Family Idiot*, p. 606.
11 Letter to Louis Bouilhet, 4 September 1650, quoted by Queneau in his preface to Flaubert, *Bouvard and Pécuchet*, p. xxxii.
12 Entries listed alphabetically in ibid., pp. 283–328.
13 Letter to Louis Bouilhet quoted in John Sturrock, 'How stupid people are', *London Review of Books* 28(17), 7 September 2006.
14 Quoted by Queneau in his preface to Flaubert, *Bouvard and Pécuchet*, pp. xxxiii–xxxiv.
15 Francis Fukuyama, 'The end of history?', *The National Interest*, No. 16, Summer 1989, p. 4.
16 Actually, the words of the character Rudge in Bennett's play *The History Boys*. See Bennett's Diary, 'What I did in 2004', *London Review of Books*, Vol. 27, No. 1, 6 January 2005.
17 Georg Wilhelm Friedrich Hegel, *Lectures on the Philosophy of World History*, trans. H.B. Nisbet (Cambridge University Press, 1975), p. 63.
18 Karl Marx and Friedrich Engels, *The Communist Manifesto* (Verso, 2012), p. 31.
19 Ibid., p. 47.
20 Queneau in his preface to Flaubert, *Bouvard and Pécuchet*, p. xxxii.
21 Thomas Henry Huxley, *On the Physical Basis of Life*, Vol. 1: *Method and Results* (Macmillan, 1897), p. 156.
22 Quoted by Queneau in his preface to *Bouvard and Pécuchet*, p. xxxii.
23 Karl R. Popper, 'The logic of the social sciences', in Theodor Adorno et al., *The Positivist Dispute in German Sociology*, trans. Glyn Adey and David Frisby (Heinemann, 1975), p. 87.
24 Ibid., p. 90.
25 Flaubert, *Bouvard and Pécuchet*, p. 3.
26 Julian Barnes, 'Flaubert, c'est moi', *New York Review of Books*, 25 May 2006.
27 Daniel J. Levitin, 'Why the modern world is bad for your brain', *Guardian*, 18 January 2015.
28 Cited in Giles Morris, 'If you only do one thing this week . . . avoid multitasking', *Guardian*, 5 October 2009.
29 Herman Melville, *Bartleby, The Scrivener: A Story of Wall Street* (HardPress, 2016).
30 George and Weedon Grossmith, *The Diary of Nobody* (Bloomsbury, 1997).
31 Ibid., pp. 29–30.
32 Samuel Beckett, *Worstward Ho* (Grove Press, 1983), p. 7.

33 Flaubert, *Bouvard and Pécuchet*, p. xiv.
34 Ibid., p. 72.
35 Ibid., p. 63.
36 Alasdair Macintyre, *After Virtue: A Study in Moral Theory* (Duckworth, 1981), p. 155.
37 Immanuel Kant, *Critique of Pure Judgment*, ed. Paul Guyer, trans. Paul Guyer and Eric Matthews (Cambridge University Press, 2005), p. 268.
38 Ibid., pp. 268–9.
39 Flaubert, *Bouvard and Pécuchet*, p. 316.
40 Quoted in Jacques Derrida, 'An idea of Flaubert: "Plato's letter"', *Modern Language Notes* 99(4), 1984, p. 766.
41 Peter Salmon, 'How Derrida and Foucault became the most misunderstood philosophers of our time', *Prospect*, 21 January 2021.
42 Derrida, 'An idea of Flaubert: "Plato's letter"', p. 766.
43 Roger Scruton, *Modern Philosophy: An Introduction and Survey* (Sinclair-Stevenson, 1994), p. 478.
44 Plato, *Theaetetus*, ed. Bernard Williams, trans. M.J. Lovett (Hackett Publishing, 1992), section 148e.
45 Ibid., sections 149a and 150c.
46 Ibid., section 150d.
47 Flaubert, *Bouvard and Pécuchet*, p. 281.
48 Quoted in Derrida, 'An idea of Flaubert: "Plato's Letter"', p. 766.
49 Quoted by Queneau in his preface to Flaubert, *Bouvard and Pécuchet*, p. xxv.

Chapter 6 Stupid Eugenics

1 David Zucchino, 'Sterilized by North Carolina, she felt raped once more', *Los Angeles Times*, 25 January 2012.
2 Francis Galton, *Hereditary Genius: An Inquiry into Its Laws and Consequences* (Macmillan, 1869), p. 336.
3 Royal Commission on the Care and Control of the Feeble-Minded in 1908, HMSO, at https://wellcomecollection.org/works/j56q4s5z.
4 Henry H. Goddard, *The Kallikak Family: A Study in the Heredity of Feeble-Mindedness* (Macmillan, 1912).
5 Edmund Burke Huey, *Backward and Feeble-Minded Children: Clinical Studies in the Psychology of Defectives, With a Syllabus for the Clinical Examination and Testing of Children* (Forgotten Books, 2020), pp. 6–7.
6 E.A. Doll, 'Idiot, imbecile, and moron', *Journal of Applied Psychology* 20(4), 1936, pp. 427–37.
7 See https://education.blogs.archives.gov/2017/05/02/buck-v-bell/.
8 The pamphlet, reproduced from the copy held at the Library of the University of North Carolina, is available at https://static1.squarespace.com

/static/650f4d435ef4386d76a3c05f/t/6606c3e12b8fb75f1a6889dd/1711719398672/youwouldntexpectoohuma.pdf.
9 Zucchino, 'Sterilized by North Carolina, she felt raped once more'.
10 Allen G. Breed, 'North Carolina Eugenics victim, son fighting together for justice', *Detroit Legal News*, 15 August 2011.
11 Zucchino, 'Sterilized by North Carolina, she felt raped once more'.
12 Quoted in Kevin Gegos et al., *Against Their Will: North Carolina's Sterilization Program and the Campaign for Reparations* (Gray Oak Books, 2012), pp. 97–8.
13 Galton, *Hereditary Genius*, pp. 24–5.
14 Francis Galton, *Memories of My Life* (Methuen, 1909), pp. 315–16.
15 Charles Darwin, *On the Origin of Species*, 3rd edn (John Murray, 1861), p. 21.
16 Charles Darwin, *The Descent of Man, and Selection in Relation to Sex* (John Murray, 1888), p. 618.
17 Thomas Henry Huxley, *Man's Place in Nature* (Routledge, 2003), p. 95.
18 Ibid., p. 95.
19 William Dalrymple, *The Anarchy: The Relentless Rise of the East India Company* (Bloomsbury, 2019).
20 A.N. Wilson, 'The mad, bad and dangerous theories of Thomas Henry Huxley', *Spectator*, 8 October 2022.
21 *The Descent of Man*, p. 397.
22 Ibid., p. 397.
23 Aldous Huxley, *Brave New World* (Vintage, 2007), p. 64.
24 Julian Huxley, 'Eugenics in evolutionary perspective', in *Essays of a Humanist* (Harper & Row, 1964), p. 259.
25 *Life and Letters of Thomas Henry Huxley*, Vol. 1, ed. Leonard Huxley (Gregg Publishing, 1970), p. 154.
26 Ibid., p. 154.
27 Described in Alison Bashford, *An Intimate History of Evolution: The Story of the Huxley Family* (Allen Lane, 2022), p. 154.
28 J.B.S. Haldane, *Daedalus: or Science and the Future* (Kegan Paul, 1930), pp. 81–2.
29 Ibid., p. 36.
30 Ibid., p. 77.
31 Ibid., p. 80.
32 Marie Stopes, 'How Mrs Jones does her worst', *Daily Mail*, 13 June 1919.
33 Quoted in June Rose, *Marie Rose and the Sexual Revolution* (Faber, 1992), p. 161.
34 See Paul Weindling, 'Julian Huxley and the continuity of eugenics in twentieth-century Britain', *Journal of Modern European History* 10(4), 2012, pp. 480–99.
35 Quoted in Bashford, *An Intimate History of Evolution*, p. 329.
36 Quoted in ibid., p. 329. See Thomas Henry Huxley's handwritten manuscript at http://alepho.clarku.edu/huxley/letters/92.html.
37 Quoted in Bashford, *An Intimate History of Evolution*, p. 328.

38 Ibid., p. xxvii.
39 Quoted in ibid., p. 83.
40 Philip Larkin, *Collected Poems* (Faber, 1988), p. 180.
41 Julian S. Huxley and A.C. Haddon, *We Europeans: A Survey of 'Racial' Problems* (Penguin, 1935).
42 Julian Huxley, 'Knowledge, morality and destiny', in *Knowledge, Morality, and Destiny: Essays* (Mentor, 1957), pp. 221–52.
43 Bashford, *An Intimate History of Evolution*, p. 365.
44 Quoted in J.B.S. Haldane, *Heredity and Politics* (Routledge, 2016), p. 96
45 Haldane. J.B.S. Haldane, 'Human biology and politics', quoted at https://www.marxists.org/archive/haldane/works/1930s/biology.htm.
46 Charles Darwin, *The Voyage of the Beagle* (Cosimo, Inc., 2008), p. 503.
47 Darwin, *The Descent of Man*, p. 361.
48 Available at https://web.cs.ucdavis.edu/~koehl/Teaching/ECS188/PDF_files/Damore.pdf.
49 Daisuke Wakabyashi, 'Google fires engineer who wrote memo questioning women in tech', *New York Times*, 7 August 2017.
50 Julia Carrie Wong, 'James Damore sues Google, claiming intolerance of white male conservatives', *Guardian*, 8 January 2018.
51 Paul Lewis, 'I see things differently: James Damore on his autism and the Google memo', *Guardian*, 17 November 2007.
52 Simon Baron-Cohen, 'They just can't help it', *Guardian*, 17 April 2003.
53 Dimitri van der Linden, Curtis S. Dunkel, and Guy Madison, 'Sex differences in brain size and general intelligence (g)', *Intelligence* 63, 2017, p. 78.
54 Angela Saini, *Inferior: How Science Got Women Wrong – and the New Research That's Rewriting the Story* (Beacon Press, 2017), p. 84.
55 Stuart Jeffries, 'Where are all the women cobnductors?', *Guardian*, 2 June 2005.
56 Saini, *Inferior: How Science Got Women Wrong*, pp. 3–4.
57 Sir Robert Filmer, *Patriarcha* (CreateSpace Independent Publishing Platform, 2016).
58 Letter from Jefferson to Angelica Schuyler Church, 21 September 1788, reproduced at https://founders.archives.gov/documents/Jefferson/01-13-02-0498.
59 J.S. Mill, 'The subjection of women', in *On Liberty and Other Writings*, ed. Stefan Collini (Cambridge University Press, 1989), p. 129.
60 Ibid., p. 138.
61 Darwin, *The Descent of Man*, p. 564.
62 Saini, *Inferior*, p. 95.
63 Darwin, *The Descent of Man*, p. 563.
64 Ibid., p. 563.
65 Neil Lawrence, *The Atomic Human: Understanding Ourselves in the Age of AI* (Allen Lane, 2024), p. 48.

Chapter 7 Stupid Intelligence

1. Alfred Binet, *Les idées modernes sur les enfants* (Flammarion, 1973), pp. 100–1.
2. John Stuart Mill, 'The spirit of the age', in *The Collected Works of John Stuart Mill, Vol. XXII: Newspaper Writings December 1822–July 1831*, ed. Ann P. Robson and John M. Robson (Routledge & Kegan Paul, 1981), p. 241.
3. J.S. Mill, 'Civilisation', *The Westminster Review* 25, 1836, p. 3.
4. Stephen Jay Gould, *The Mismeasure of Man* (W.W. Norton, 1996), p. 179.
5. Ibid., p. 36.
6. John Stuart Mill, footnote to James Mill, *Analysis of the Phenomena of the Human Mind* (Longmans, Green, Reader, and Dyer, 1869), p. 5.
7. Stanford–Binet Test: https://stanfordbinettest.com/.
8. Quoted in Gould, *The Mismeasure of Man*, p. 181.
9. Leon J. Kamin, *The Science and Politics of IQ Tests* (Routledge, 1974), p. 5.
10. Gould, *The Mismeasure of Man*, p. 386.
11. Quoted in ibid., p. 197.
12. Quoted in ibid., p. 198.
13. See Heather Saul, 'Donald Trump defends comments branding Mexican rapists by claiming that "somebody is doing the raping"', *Independent*, 7 July 2015.
14. See Lewis M. Terman, *The Measurement of Intelligence: An Explanation and a Complete Guide for the Use of the Stanford Revision and Extension of the Binet–Simon Intelligence Scale* (Riverside Textbooks in Education, 1916).
15. Quoted in Kenji Hakuta, *Mirror of Language: The Debate on Bilingualism* (Basic Books, 2008), p. 21.
16. Gould, *The Mismeasure of Man*, p. 262.
17. Quoted in Tom K. Wong, *The Politics of Immigration: Partisanship, Demographic Change, and American National Identity* (Oxford University Press, 2017), p. 3.
18. Wolfgang Saxon, 'Dr David Wechsler, 85, author of intelligence tests', *New York Times*, 3 May 1981.
19. Quoted in Gerald Matthews, Moshe Zeidner, and Richard D. Roberts, *Emotional Intelligence: Science and Myth* (MIT Press, 2004), p. 87.
20. Saxon, 'Dr David Wechsler, 85, author of intelligence tests'.
21. Quoted in Gould, *The Mismeasure of Man*, p. 386.
22. This is a summary list. For the full version of the sub-tests, see Ian J. Deary, *Intelligence: A Very Short Introduction* (Oxford University Press, 2020), pp. 2–6.
23. Ibid., p. 9.
24. Ibid., p. 13.
25. Edwin G. Boring, 'Intelligence as the tests test it', *New Republic*, 1923, p. 35.
26. Justin Gregg, *If Nietzsche Were a Narwhal: What Animal Intelligence Tells Us about Human Stupidity* (Hodder, 2022), p. 7.
27. Ibid., p. 8.
28. Ibid., p. 8.

29 Both quoted in David Rosenthal and Josh Weisberg, *Consciousness* (Wiley, 2022), p. 190.
30 Gregg, *If Nietzsche Were a Narwhal*, p. 15.
31 Ibid., p. 15.
32 Boring, 'Intelligence as the tests test it', p. 37.
33 Richard J. Herrnstein and Charles Murray, *The Bell Curve: Intelligence and Class Structure in American Life* (Free Press, 1996).
34 Malcolm W. Browne, 'What is intelligence, and who has it?', *New York Times*, 16 October 1994.
35 Herrnstein and Murray, *The Bell Curve*, p. 548.
36 Ibid., p. 548.
37 Ibid., p. 518.
38 Ibid., p. 526.
39 Gould, *The Mismeasure of Man*, p. 377.
40 Herrnstein and Murray, *The Bell Curve*, p. 25.
41 Ibid., p. 286.
42 J. Philippe Rushton, *Race, Evolution, and Behavior: A Life History Perspective* (Transaction Publishers, 2000).
43 See Brian Resnick, 'IQ, explained in 9 charts', *Vox*, 10 October 2017.
44 Diane F. Halpern, 'The skewed logic of the bell-shaped curve', *Skeptic*, 1995.
45 Charles R. Tittle and Thomas Rotolo, 'IQ and stratification: an empirical evaluation of Herrnstein and Murray's social change argument', *Social Forces* 79(1), 2000, p. 1.
46 Browne, 'What is intelligence, and who has it?'
47 Halpern, 'The skewed logic of the bell-shaped curve'.
48 'The "Bell Curve" agenda', *New York Times*, 24 October 1994.
49 Gould, *The Mismeasure of Man*, p. 377.
50 American Psychiatric Association, *Diagnostic and Statistical Manual of Mental Disorders (DSM-V). 5th Edition* (American Psychiatric Publishing, 2013), p. 37.
51 See Lisa Trahan, Karla K. Stuebing, Merril K. Hiscock, and Jack M. Fletcher, 'The Flynn effect: a meta-analysis', *Psychological Bulletin*, September 2014, pp. 1332–60.
52 Quoted in Daniel de Visé, 'American IQs rose 30 points in the last century. Now, they may be falling', *The Hill*, 29 March 2023.
53 See Timothy Bates, 'Is IQ falling across the West?', *The Spectator*, 15 December 2017.
54 Elizabeth M. Dworak, William Revelle, and David M. Condon, 'Looking for Flynn effects in a recent online US adult sample: examining shifts within the SAPA Project', *Intelligence* 98, May–June 2023.
55 Quoted in de Visé, 'American IQs rose 30 points in the last century'.
56 Ibid.

57 Richard Lynn and Tatu Vanhanen, *IQ and the Wealth of Nations* (Praeger, 2002).
58 Browne, 'What is intelligence, and who has it?'
59 Quoted in Patrick Wintour, 'Genetics outweighs teaching, Gove adviser tells his boss', *Guardian*, 11 October 2013.
60 Rowena Mason and Ian Sample, 'Sabisky row: Dominic Cummings criticised over "designer babies" post', *Guardian*, 19 February 2020.
61 Alison Bashford, *An Intimate History of Evolution: The Story of the Huxley Family* (Allen Lane, 2023), pp. 364–5.
62 Quoted in Mason and Sample, 'Sabisky row'.
63 See Philip Ball, 'Designer babies: an ethical horror waiting to happen?', *Guardian*, 8 January 2017.
64 Quoted in Peter Wilby, 'Psychologist on a mission to give every child a Learning Chip', *Guardian*, 18 February 2014.
65 Kathryn Asbury and Robert Plomin, *G Is for Genes: The Impact of Genetics on Education and Achievement* (Wiley-Blackwell, 2013).
66 Ibid., p. 96.
67 Ibid., p. 171.
68 Ibid., p. 174.
69 Ibid., p. 174.
70 Quoted in Wilby, 'Psychologist on a mission'.
71 Ibid.
72 Quoted in Andrew Sparrow, 'Boris Johnson "bamboozled" by science and Matt Hancock had habit of saying things that were untrue, UK Covid inquiry hears', *Guardian*, 20 November 2023.
73 Quoted in Wilby, 'Psychologist on a mission'.
74 David Olusoga, '"These are the untold stories that make up our nation": Steve McQueen on Small Axe', *Sight and Sound*, 13 November 2020.
75 'David Olusoga's school days' on teachwire.net at https://www.teachwire.net/news/david-olusogas-schooldays-there-was-no-point-reporting-racist-incidents-my-teachers-were-racist-themselves/.
76 See Nikki Baughan, '*Education* shows how Britain taught Black boys to fail', *Sight and Sound*, 11 December 2020.
77 Bernard Coard, *How the West Indian Child Is Made Educationally Sub-Normal in the British School System*, 5th edn (independently published, 2021).
78 Quoted in Lola Okolosie, 'Discrimination at school: is a Black British history lesson repeating itself?', *Guardian*, 15 November 2020.
79 Sally Weale, 'Black people who were labelled "backward" as children seek justice for lifelong trauma', *Guardian*, 21 February 2023.
80 Okolosie, 'Discrimination at school'.
81 Lyttanya Shannon's *Subnormal: A British Scandal* can be seen on BBC iPlayer at https://www.bbc.co.uk/programmes/m000w81h.

82 Olusoga, '"These are the untold stories that make up our nation"'.
83 Quoted in Okolosie, 'Discrimination at school'.
84 Decca Aitkenhead, 'Steve McQueen: my hidden shame', *Guardian*, 4 January 2014.
85 Linton Kwesi Johnson, 'It dread inna inglan', recited at https://www.youtube.com/watch?v=b4QCYQfov6I.
86 Quoted in Okolosie, 'Discrimination at school'.

Chapter 8 Mass Stupidity

1 Robert Musil, 'On stupidity', in *Precision and Soul: Essays and Addresses*, ed. and trans. Burton Pike and David S. Luft (University of Chicago Press, 1990), p. 280.
2 Ibid., p. 281.
3 Ibid., pp. 282–3.
4 Lyndsey Stonebridge, *We Are Free to Change the World: Hannah Arendt's Lessons in Love and Disobedience* (Jonathan Cape, 2024), p. 15.
5 Quoted in ibid., pp. 224–5.
6 Quoted in ibid., p. xiii.
7 Quoted in ibid., pp. 33–4.
8 'Eichmann was outrageously stupid – Hannah Arendt interviewed by Joachim Fest', in Hannah Arendt, *The Last Interview: And Other Conversations* (Melville House, 2013), p. 1926.
9 Karl Landauer: 'Zur psychosexuellen Genese der Dummheit', *Psyche* 24(6), 1970, pp. 461–84; 'Intelligenz und Dummheit', in *Das Psychoanalytische Volksbuch* (Hippokrates Verlag, 1926), pp. 463–84.
10 Theodor W. Adorno and Max Horkheimer, *Dialectic of Enlightenment*, trans. John Cumming (Verso, 2010), p. xi.
11 Ibid., p. 256
12 Ibid., p. 257.
13 Ibid., pp. 257–8.
14 Ibid., p. 174.
15 Ibid., p. 215.
16 Dietrich Bonhoeffer, *Letters and Papers from Prison*, ed. John W. de Gruchy, trans. Isabel Best et al. (Fortress Press, 2010), p. 43.
17 Ibid., p. 43.
18 Dietrich Bonhoeffer, *The Cost of Discipleship*, trans. R.H. Fuller (SCM, 2001), p. xvi.
19 Bonhoeffer's remark is quoted on Edith Beckwoldt's sculpture *The Ordeal* in Hamburg.
20 Nick Joyce, 'In search of the Nazi personality', *Monitor on Psychology*, 40(3), 2009, pp. 18–19.

21 'The evil geniuses', *Newsweek*, 17 December 1945, reproduced at http://www.oldmagazinearticles.com/IQs-of-nazi-leaders-pdf.
22 Ibid. Also see Leonard Mosley, *The Reich Marshal: A Biography of Hermann Goering* (Weidenfeld & Nicolson, 1974), p. 331.
23 See Jack El-Hai, *The Nazi and the Psychiatrist: Hermann Göring, Dr Douglas M. Kelley, and a Fatal Meeting of Minds at the End of WWII* (Public Affairs, 2013), p. 60.
24 Ibid., p. 162.
25 Katherine Ramsland, 'Professional suicide', *Psychology Today*, 17 August 2017.
26 G.M. Gilbert, *The Psychology of Dictatorship: Based on an Examination of the Leaders of Nazi Germany* (New York: Ronald Press Co., 1950).
27 See Erich Fromm, *Heart Of Man: Its Genius for Good and Evil* (Lantern Books, 2011).
28 Solomon E. Asch, 'Studies of independence and conformity: I. A minority of one against a unanimous majority', *Psychological Monographs: General and Applied* 70(9), 1956, pp. 1–70.
29 See Julie Beck, 'The Christmas the aliens didn't come', *The Atlantic*, 18 December 2015. Wilhelm Reich, *The Mass Psychology of Fascism* (Souvenir Press, 1997).
30 Erich Fromm, *Escape from Freedom* (Ishi Press, 2011).
31 Franz Neumann, *Behemoth: The Structure and Practice of National Socialism, 1933–1944* (Ivan R. Dee, 2009), p. 85.
32 Elias Canetti, *Crowds and Power*, trans. Carol Stewart (Seabury Press, 1978), p. 18.
33 Homer Bigart, 'Eichmann guilty: calm at verdict of Israeli court', *New York Times*, 11 December 1961.
34 Hannah Arendt, *Eichmann in Jerusalem: A Report on the Banality of Evil* (Penguin, 2006).
35 Ibid., p. 26.
36 Ibid., p. 135.
37 Ibid., p. 25.
38 Hannah Arendt, 'Thinking-I', *New Yorker*, 15 November 1977.
39 Stanley Milgram, 'Behavioral study of obedience', *Journal of Abnormal and Social Psychology* 67, 1963, pp. 371–8.
40 Quoted in Thomas Blass, *The Man Who Shocked the World: The Life and Legacy of Stanley Milgram* (Basic Books, 2004), p. 101.
41 See *The Psychology Book* (Dorling-Kindersley, 2012), p. 253.

Chapter 9 Structural Stupidity

1 Stuart Jeffries, 'David Graeber interview: "So many people spend their working lives doing jobs they think are unnecessary"', *Guardian*, 21 March 2015.

2 David Graeber, *The Utopia of Rules: On Technology, Stupidity and the Secret Joys of Bureaucracy* (Melville House, 2015), p. 48.
3 Jeffries, 'David Graeber interview'.
4 Graeber, *The Utopia of Rules*, p. 95.
5 David Graeber, *Pirate Enlightenment, or the Real Libertalia: Buccaneers, Women Traders and Mock Kingdoms in Eighteenth-Century Madagascar* (Penguin, 2024).
6 Jeffries, 'David Graeber interview'.
7 Graeber, *The Utopia of Rules*, p. 81.
8 Jeffries, 'David Graeber interview'.
9 https://crimethinc.com.
10 Jeffries, 'David Graeber interview'.
11 Graeber, *The Utopia of Rules*, p. 106.
12 Jeffries, 'David Graeber interview'.
13 Reprinted as David Graeber, *Bullshit Jobs: A Theory* (Simon & Schuster, 2019), p. xxi.
14 Jeffries, 'David Graeber interview'.
15 John Lanchester, 'The robots are coming', *London Review of Books*, 5 March 2015.
16 Graeber, *Bullshit Jobs*, p. xviii.
17 Thorstein Veblen, *The Theory of the Leisure Class* at https://www.gutenberg.org/files/833/833-h/833-h.htm.
18 Graeber, *The Utopia of Rules*, p. 72.
19 Georg Wilhelm Friedrich Hegel, *The Phenomenology of Spirit*, trans. A.V. Miller (Oxford University Press, 1977), pp. 111ff.
20 Graeber, *The Utopia of Rules*, p. 70.
21 Ibid., p. 72.
22 Luc Boltanski and Ève Chiapello, *The New Spirit of Capitalism*, trans. Gregory Elliott (Verso, 1999), p. 35.
23 The President's News Conference, 12 August 1986, at https://www.reaganlibrary.gov/archives/speech/presidents-news-conference-23.
24 Jeffries, 'David Graeber interview'.
25 See review: 'An alarm from 2055: act now to save the earth', *New York Times*, 16 July 2009.
26 Justin Gregg, *If Nietzsche Were a Narwhal: What Animal Intelligence Tell Us about Human Stupidity* (Hodder, 2022), p. 195.
27 Ibid., p. 255.
28 Harald Welzer, *The Culture of Stopping: Obituary to Myself*, trans. Sharon Howe (Polity, 2023), p. 55.
29 Ibid., p. 55.
30 Mats Alvesson and André Spicer, *The Stupidity Paradox: The Power and Pitfalls of Functional Stupidity at Work* (Profile, 2016).

31 'Professor André Spicer on "functional stupidity" – when smart people are encouraged to not think and reflect at work', City University of London, 15 June 2016.
32 Alvesson and Spicer, *The Stupidity Paradox*, p. 239.
33 Ibid., p. 60.
34 Ibid., p. 61.
35 Philip J. Hilts, 'Scientist at work', *New York Times*, 23 September 1997.
36 Langer and Abelson's experiments quoted in Alvesson and Spicer, *The Stupidity Paradox*, pp. 59ff.
37 John F. Muth, 'Rational expectations and the theory of price movements', *Econometrica*, July 1961, pp. 315–35.
38 Herbert A. Simon, 'Rational choice and the structure of the environment', *Psychological Review* 63(2), 1956, pp. 129–38.
39 Barry Schwartz, *The Paradox of Choice: Why More Is Less* (Harper Perennial, 2004).
40 Quoted in Dennis J. Moberg, 'When good people do bad things at work: rote behavior, distractions, and moral exclusions stymie ethical behavior on the job', in Laura P. Hartman, Joe DesJardins, and Chris Macdonald (eds), *Business Ethics: Decision Making for Personal Integrity and Social Responsibility*, 4th edn (McGraw-Hill Education, 2018), p. 58.
41 Dennis A. Gioia, 'Pinto fires and personal ethics: a script analysis of missed opportunities', in Alex C. Michalos and Deborah C. Poff (eds), *Citation Classics from the Journal of Business Ethics: Celebrating the First Thirty Years of Publication* (Springer, 2013), pp. 675–89.
42 Alvesson and Spicer, *The Stupidity Paradox*, p. 72.
43 Ibid., p. 227.
44 Svend Brinkmann, *Think: In Defence of a Thoughtful Life* (Polity, 2024), p. 3.
45 Gregg, *If Nietzsche Were a Narwhal*, p .73.
46 Ibid., p. 72.
47 Michel de Montaigne, 'Apology for Raymond Sebond', in *The Complete Works*, trans. Donald M. Frame (Everyman, 2003), p. 331.
48 Bruno Latour, *After Lockdown: A Metamorphosis*, trans. Julia Rose (Polity, 2021), pp. 1–7. See also Stuart Jeffries, 'Bruno Latour obituary', *Guardian*, 10 October 2022.
49 Mutual Aid by Peter Kropotkin, Culturea, 2023 p.21
50 Montaigne, 'Apology for Raymond Sebond', p. 331 (footnote).
51 Markus Gabriel, *The Human Animal: Why We Still Don't Fit into Nature* (Polity, 2024), p. 3.
52 Gregg, *If Nietzsche Were a Narwhal*, p. 71.
53 Timothy R. Levine, *Duped: Truth-Default Theory and the Social Science of Lying and Deception* (University of Alabama Press, 2020).

54 Gregg, *If Nietzsche Were a Narwhal*, p. 80.
55 Harry G. Frankfurt, *On Bullshit* (Princeton University Press, 2005).
56 Jason Horowitz, 'A king in his castle: how Donald Trump lives, from his longtime butler', *New York Times*, 15 March 2016.
57 Frankfurt, *On Bullshit*, p. 61.
58 Klaus Templer, 'Why do toxic people get promoted? For the same reason humble people do: political skill', *Harvard Business Review*, 10 July 2018.
59 Quoted in James Ball, *Post-Truth: How Bullshit Conquered the World* (Biteback Publishing, 2017), p. 7.
60 Alison Flood, '"Post-truth" named word of the year by Oxford Dictionaries', *Guardian*, 15 November 2016.
61 Quoted in Evan Davis, *Post-Truth: Why We Have Reached Peak Bullshit and What We Can Do About It* (Little, Brown, 2017), p. 3.
62 Daniel Kahnemann, *Thinking, Fast and Slow* (Penguin, 2011).
63 Matthew d'Ancona, *Post-Truth: The New War on Truth and How to Fight Back* (Ebury, 2017), pp. 19–20.
64 Neli Demireva, 'The academic evidence regarding immigration is overwhelmingly positive', blog, LSE, 14 December 2014.
65 D'Ancona, *Post-Truth*, p. 5.
66 Quoted in ibid., p. 148.
67 Alexander Solzhenitsyn, *August 1914*, trans. Michael Glenny (Penguin, 1974), p. 714.
68 Quoted in Matthew d'Ancona, 'Ten alternative facts for the post truth world', *Guardian*, 12 May 2017.
69 D'Ancona, *Post-Truth*, p. 34.
70 Lewis Carroll, *Alice's Adventures in Wonderland and Through the Looking-Glass* (Lothrop, 1898), p. 164.

Chapter 10 Digital Stupidity

1 Scott J. Shapiro, *Fancy Bear Goes Phishing: The Dark History of the Information Age, in Five Extraordinary Hacks* (Penguin, 2023), p. 186.
2 Ibid., p. 198.
3 Ibid., p. 9.
4 Quoted in ibid., p. 225.
5 Quoted in ibid., p. 227.
6 Daniel Kahnemann, *Thinking Fast and Slow* (Penguin, 2011).
7 Quoted in Shapiro, *Fancy Bear Goes Phishing*, p. 284
8 Ibid., p. 328.
9 Ibid., pp. 9–11.
10 Carlo M. Cipolla, *The Basic Laws of Human Stupidity* (W.H. Allen, 2019), pp. 19–20.

11 Ibid., p. 14.
12 Ibid., p. 22.
13 Ibid., p. 37.
14 Ibid., pp. 66–7 and 73.
15 Ibid., p. 62.
16 Alex Hern, 'Someone made a smart vibrator, so of course it got hacked', *Guardian*, 10 August 2016.
17 Marshall McLuhan, *Understanding Media: The Extensions of Man* (McGraw-Hill, 1964), p. 8.
18 Quoted in Stuart Jeffries, 'Friedrich Kittler and the rise of the machine', *Guardian*, 28 December 2011.
19 Rory Cellan-Jones, 'Steven Hawking warns artificial intelligence could end mankind', BBC News, 2 December 2014.
20 'Read Yuval Harari's blistering warning to Davos in full', World Economic Forum, 24 January 2020.
21 Cited in James Bridle, 'The stupidity of AI', *Guardian*, 16 March 2023.
22 Ibid.
23 Stuart Jeffries, 'The world's first robot artist discusses beauty, Yoko Ono and the perils of AI', *Spectator*, 29 May 2021.
24 Timothy R. Levine, *Duped: Truth-Default Theory and the Social Science of Lying and Deception* (University of Alabama Press, 2020).
25 Gus Carter, 'Daniel Dennett's last interview: "AI could signal the end of human civilisation"', *Spectator*, 27 May 2024.
26 Theodor Adorno, *Minima Moralia: Reflections on a Damaged Life*, trans. E.F.N. Jephcott (Verso, 2005), p. 157.
27 James Heale, 'Lee Anderson: "Capital punishment? 100% effective!"', *Spectator*, 11 February 2023.
28 Neil Lawrence, *The Atomic Human: Understanding Ourselves in the Age of AI* (Allen Lane, 2024), pp. 334–6.
29 Ibid., pp. 17–18.
30 Ibid., p. 370.
31 Ibid., pp. 356–7.
32 Ibid., p. 357.
33 Ibid., p. 369.
34 Paul Virilio, *Open Sky*, trans. Julie Rose (Verso, 2020), p. 40.
35 Matthew Sparkes, 'Should we be worried about AI's growing energy use?', *New Scientist*, 10 October 2023.
36 Ben Tarnoff, 'To decarbonize we must decomputerize: why we need a Luddite revolution', *Guardian*, 18 September 2019.
37 Byung-Chul Han, *Psychopolitics: Neoliberalism and New Technologies of Power*, trans. Erik Butler (Verso, 2017), p. 12.

38 Stuart Jeffries, 'Netflix's Ted Sarandos: the "evil genius" behind a TV revolution', *Guardian*, 20 December 2013.
39 Byung-Chul Han, *The Crisis of Narration*, trans. Daniel Steuer (Polity, 2024), p. 47.
40 Tarnoff, 'To decarbonize we must decomputerize'.
41 Ibid.

Conclusion

1 Elizabeth M. Dworak, William Revelle, and David M. Condon, 'Looking for Flynn effects in a recent online US adult sample: examining shifts within the SAPA Project', *Intelligence* 98, May–June 2023. See also Caitlin Tiilley, 'IQ scores in the US have DROPPED for first time in nearly 100 years, study suggests – so is tech making us dim?', *Daily Mail*, 9 March 2023.
2 Nikki Main, 'As research warns IQ is falling for first time EVER . . . our map reveals average scores in every US state', *Daily Mail*, 3 May 2024.
3 See https://worldpopulationreview.com/state-rankings/average-iq-by-state.
4 Lance Morrow, 'You are living in the golden age of stupidity', *Wall Street Journal*, 29 August 2021.
5 Janet Daley, 'We are now entering the Age of Stupid. How did our voters become so credulous?', *Daily Telegraph*, 20 August 2016.
6 David Rothkopf, 'America's golden age of stupidity', *Washington Post*, 25 July 2017.
7 Included in *In These Great Times: A Karl Kraus Reader*, ed. Harry Zohn, trans. Joseph Fabry et al. (Carcanet, 2016), p. 55.
8 Ibid., p. 36.
9 John Carreyrou, *Bad Blood: Secrets and Lies in a Silicon Valley Startup* (Pan Macmillan, 2018), p. 165.

Index

Abelson, Robert, 246–9
Abwehr, 224–5
academic bureaucracy, 236–7
Adorno, Theodor W., and Horkheimer, Max, 81, 102–5, 116, 221–3, 273, 276
  Dialectic of Enlightenment, 101, 116, 221, 223
The Advancement of Learning (Bacon), 98
adversity, 111–12
affirmative action, 193–4
African Americans, 199
African-Caribbean history and culture, 215–16
After Lockdown: A Metamorphosis (Latour), 253
Ai-Da, 270–2
Alcibiades, 29, 30–7, 39, 46, 48, 53–5, 59, 79–80
  list of accomplishments, 34
  role model for, 32–3
  wisdom, 32
Alexas, 272
Alvesson, Mats, and Spicer, André, 244–6, 250–2, 256
  The Stupidity Paradox, 9–10, 244, 251
amathia, 12, 28, 136, 244
Amazon Promise, 275
ambidependence, 64
American Psychological Association, 184–5, 201
amusement, 42–3
analogical reasoning, 203–4

Animal Farm (Orwell), 126–7
anthropology, 238, 262
anti-growth coalition, 244
anti-immigration, 199
anti-Nazi resistance movement, 224
anti-semitism, 219, 223–4, 232
aphorisms, 82
Apollonian, 22–5, 28, 44, 46, 238
aposematic signalling, 255
Apple, 194
aptitudes, 16–18, 116
Arendt, Hannah, 218–20, 232, 252
argumentation, 19, 29, 37–9, 40, 43–4, 61, 81–2, 91, 100–1, 172, 198, 232, 239–40
Aristotle, 26, 64–5, 136, 247
Armstrong, Franny, 243–4
  The Age of Stupid, 9
Armstrong, Louis, 190
art, 271–2
The Art of the Deal (Trump), 255–6
artificial insemination, 157, 160, 162–3
artificial intelligence (AI), 190, 239–40, 267–75
  capacity for plausible image creation, 272
  dream of, 276
  electricity consumption, 278
  hardware and software, 277–8
  hopes and fears for, 242
  Panglossian Perspective on, 277
  smart technology of, 279
  stupidity of, 270
artificial selection, 153, 156–7, 161–2, 179

INDEX

artistic influences, 271
Asbury, Kathryn, 208–10
Asch, Solomon, 230
Assange, Julian, 263
asylum seekers, 105
ataraxia, 89, 108–9
Athenian assembly, 33
Athenian democracy, 32, 34
attention deficit hyperactivity disorder (ADHD), 16
Aurelius, Marcus, 108
Auschwitz, 102, 104–5, 151, 163
Austria, Hitler's occupation and annexation of, 217
autism, 16, 19–20
Autistic Self-Advocacy Network, 19
automation, 275
Avery, Henry, 237

Backward and Feeble-Minded Children (Huey), 144
Bacon, Francis, 94, 98–105
 The Advancement of Learning, 98
 advice to Elizabeth I, 98–105
 folly, 104
 inductive method, 101
 mask of humility, 102
 Novum Organum, 105
 panegyric to knowledge, 99
 philosophy, 103
 positivism, 102
 pursuit of knowledge, 101
 scientific method, 101, 103, 114
 scientific revolution, 101
Balwani, Sunny, 286–7
banality of evil, 219
bandwagon effect, 257
bankruptcy, 12
Barker, David, 'The Biology of Stupidity: Genetics, Eugenics and Mental Deficiency in the Inter-War Years', 3
Baron-Cohen, Simon, 167–8, 170–1

Barthes, Roland, 260
Bartleby, the Scrivener: A Story of Wall Street (Melville), 133
Bashford, Alison, 162–4, 207
The Basic Laws of Stupidity (Cipolla), 264
Bate, Jonathan, 111–12
Beckett, Samuel, 134
behaviour, 253
 differences, 168
 human, 184–5
 pattern of, 241
 preprogrammed patterns of, 246
Behemoth: The Structure and Practice of National Socialism (Neumann), 231
being-way of thinking, 65
belief, 74, 85–6, 127
The Bell Curve (Herrnstein and Murray), 194, 196–7, 199, 202, 210–11
belonging, 135
benevolence, 62, 70
Bennett, Alan, 124
Berlin, 223–5
Bezos, Jeff, 272, 275
Bigart, Homer, 231
Big Brother reality show, 6
binary thinking, 87–8
Binet, Alfred, 174–6, 178–9, 180–1, 184–5, 209
biological determinism, 170
biological differences, 166
biological diversity, 20
biological knowledge, 268–9
'The Biology of Stupidity: Genetics, Eugenics and Mental Deficiency in the Inter-War Years' (Barker), 3
biotechnology, 268
black children, 212–16
blameless life, 23
Bloom, Molly, 88
Blume, Harvey, 19

INDEX

Boden, Margaret, 271
Boltanski, Luc, and Chiapello, Ève, *The New Spirit of Capitalism*, 242
Bonhoeffer, Dietrich, 223–5
Borgenicht, David, *The Little Book of Stupid Questions*, 9–10
Boring, Edwin G., 189, 191–2, 203, 283
Bottom, Nick, 93
Bouilhet, Louis, 117, 122
Bouvard, François Denys Bartholomée, 120, 129
Boyle, Frankie, 117–18
Brahman, 87
Brave New World (Huxley), 4, 195
Braverman, Suella, 105
Brexit, 117–18, 257–8
Bridle, James, 269–70
Brigham, Carl C., *A Study of American Intelligence*, 182
Brinkmann, Svend, 251–3
    Think: In Defence of a Thoughtful Life, 251
Broca, Pierre Paul, 175
Browne, Malcolm W., 205
Buck, Carrie, 144
Buddhism, 56, 58, 61–2, 73–5, 78–9, 83, 86, 89
bullshitters, 256–7
bureaucracy, 133, 240
    misconception about, 242
    procedures, 236
Bushell, Waveney, 214

Caine, Michael, 68, 73
Callas, Maria, 249
Canetti, Elias, *Crowds and Power*, 231
capitalism, 240, 242–3
capitalistic norms, 142
Capitol riots, 284
Carreyrou, John, 286
Carroll, Lewis, *Through the Looking-Glass*, 260
Cassandra Corrective, 269–70, 273

Cattell Culture Fair Intelligence Test, 177
causation, 43, 196
celebrities, 2, 5, 7–8
Celebrity Big Brother (TV series), 7
Cervantes, Miguel de, 91–3, 115
    Don Quixote, 90–3, 95–7, 115, 117
Chaerephon, 22–4
character assassinations, 40
Charron, Pierre, 109
chatbots, 268–70, 272, 277
ChatGPT, 269–70, 279
    commissioning, 270
    models for, 269–70
childish narcissism, 229–30
children
    cognitive capacities, 192
    educational opportunities, 206
    intelligence, 191
    special education for, 210
choice overload, 250
Christianity, 48, 126, 224
Chuang-Tzu, 89–90
Churchill, William, 160
Cipolla, Carlo, 264–7
    basic laws of stupidity, 267
    The Basic Laws of Stupidity, 264
    definition of intelligence and stupidity, 266
    plausibility of research, 265
    second law, 265
    third basic law, 266
circular reasoning, 199
civilization, 2, 3, 20, 29, 43, 69–75, 114, 273
civil rights, 151
classrooms, DNA testing in, 210
clever stupidity, 223
climate catastrophe, 243, 279
clinical ethics, 208
Clinton, Hillary, 261–2
Coard, Bernard, 212–13
cognitive abilities, 186, 192, 209

313

INDEX

cognitive capacities, 13, 186
   arithmetic, 187
   block design, 186
   cancellation, 187
   coding, 187
   comprehension, 186
   digit span, 187
   figure weights, 187
   information, 186
   letter–number sequencing, 187
   matrix reasoning, 186
   picture completion, 187
   similarities, 186
   symbol search, 187
   visual puzzles, 186
   vocabulary, 186
cognitive capital, 194
cognitive deficiency, 20, 46
cognitive differences, 19
cognitive dissonance, 230–1
cognitive energy, 73
cognitive faculties, 14
cognitive functioning, 189
cognitive gifts, 268
cognitive inability, 223
cognitive landscape, 276
cognitive powers, 195
cognitive skills, 283
cognitive underclasses, 200
Colet, Louise, 119, 121
colonization, 154
Commanville, Caroline, 119
communists
   totalitarianism, 195
   utopia, 124
community, 60, 62, 201, 212, 214, 224, 269
compensation, 15, 146–7
computer culture, 19
computers, 204
Comte, Auguste, 122–3, 125, 126–9, 132, 137, 138–9
confirmation bias, 12, 15
conformity, 121, 127, 277

The Confucian Philosophy of Harmony (Li), 69
Confucianism, 61–2, 65, 66–7, 69–74
congestive dysfunction, 210
consciousness, 23, 25, 48, 78, 162, 185, 271, 286
conservatism, 70, 194–5
consolatory myths, 48
conventional thinking, strait-jacket of, 15–21
conversion, 25, 224
conviction, 39, 45, 128, 138, 186, 189, 231, 260, 264
Conway, Kellyanne, 259
Copernican revolution, 159
Corbyn, Jeremy, 284
corruption, 48, 108, 110, 195
Covid lockdown, 30
creative destruction, 280
creativity, 69, 271
credulity, 273
Crimea, annexation of, 261–2
critical thinking, 231
cross-examination, 25, 29, 42
Crowds and Power (Canetti), 231
crystallized intelligence, 184
cultural biases, 214
   cultural deformations, 269
   cultural development, 277
   cultural factors, 157
   cultural majority, 198
   cultural refinements, 157
culture war, 9
The Culture of Stopping (Welzer), 244
Cummings, Dominic, 206–11
cybernetics, 19
Cybersecurity and Infrastructure Security Agency (CISA), 264
Cyrus, 34

Dalai Lama, 81
The Middle Way: Faith Grounded in Reason, 80

314

INDEX

Daley, Janet, 284
The Age of Stupid, 243
Damore, James, 165–71
d'Ancona, Matthew, 258–9
Post-Truth: The New War on Truth and How to Fight Back, 258
Daodejing, 71, 75, 77–9
Daoism, 61–2, 69, 72–9, 108
  implicit critique of, 66–7
  passivity of, 114
  philosophical principle of, 67
  wisdom, 89
darkness, 46, 101–2, 105, 131
Darwin, Charles, 143, 152–4, 156, 165, 171–2
  The Descent of Man and Selection in Relation to Sex, 153, 165, 172
  evolutionary processes, 135
  On the Origin of the Species, 124, 152, 157, 253–4
  theory of evolution, 158
de, 68, 71, 73
Deary, Ian J., 187–8
decision-making paralysis, 250
decluttering, 78–9
deconstructionism, 138–9, 260
Delavan, Charles, 262
delusions, 12, 27–8, 58, 82, 92, 95–6, 98, 115, 157, 164, 231, 259–60, 270
Demireva, Neli, 258
democracy, 2, 5, 32, 34, 54, 120, 123, 139, 260, 267
Democratic National Convention, 263
Democritus, 46–8
Dennett, Daniel, 273
Derrida, Jacques, 137, 139–40, 260
The Descent of Man and Selection in Relation to Sex (Darwin), 153–5, 165, 172
determinative judgement, 15
dharma, 82–3
Dialectic of Enlightenment (Adorno and Horkheimer), 101, 116, 221–3
dialectical reasoning, 42

Diamond, John, 257
The Diary of a Nobody (Grossmith and Grossmith), 133
digital labour, 273
digitalization, 278
dignity, 217, 220
Dionysian, 44
Direct Action Network, 236–7
disability, 20
discrimination, 34–5
DNA testing, 211
dogmatism, 126–7
Doll, Edgar A., 144
Dolphin Communication Project, 190
Dombrowski, Stefan, 282–3
Don Quixote (Cervantes), 90–3, 95–7, 115, 117
Dönitz, Karl, 227–9
Dreyer, William, 18
dukka, 57
dumbness, 13–14
Dunkel, Curtis S., 168
Dunning–Kruger effect, 287
Duped: Truth-Default Theory and the Social Science of Lying and Deception (Levine), 255
dyslexia, 16
dyslexic geniuses, 18
dystopia, 4, 160, 195, 239, 258, 268

East–West cultural gap, 64
eastern philosophy, 57, 75–6, 84
eastern thinking, 76, 80
ecological catastrophe, 243
ecological harm, 280
economic orthodoxy, 249–50
ecstasy, 42–4
ectogenesis, 158, 161
education, 265
  establishments, 213
  programmes, 192
  role of genetics in, 208
  system, 214

315

effortless action, 67–8
Eichmann, Adolf, 219–21, 230–2, 252
Einstein, Albert, 117, 228
election campaigns, 38
electric shocks, 232–3
elenchic reasoning, 41–2
Ellington, Duke, 249
emotional intelligence, 10, 13–14, 189
enlightenment, 37, 48, 60–1, 104–5, 136, 258, 285
　allegory of, 131
　darkness of, 105
　goal of, 57
　self and, 57
　spiritual, 60
　true, 57–8
enthousiasma, 22–3
Epictetus, 53, 108, 111
equanimity, 89
Erasmus, Desiderius, 14, 93, 107–10, 244
Escape from Freedom (Fromm), 231
ESN schools, 214
eugenicist utopias, 163
eugenics, 143, 154
　dystopia, 207
　enthusiasts for, 160
　form of, 153
　negative, 160
　sterilization programme, 147–9
　thinking, 163
Eugenics Compensation Task Force, 147
expediency, 29, 35–8
expertise, 136

faith, 101
false reification, 178–9, 188, 197
falsificationism, 127–8
The Family Idiot (Sartre), 119
Fancy Bear, 262, 266
Fancy Bear Goes Phishing: The Dark History of the Information Age,
　in *Five Extraordinary Hacks* (Shapiro), 262
Farnsworth, Ward, 40–1
　The Socratic Method: A Practitioner's Handbook, 39
Farruku, Leonard, 105
fatuity, 142, 204, 284–5
Fauci, Nicholas, 40
feeble-mindedness, 146, 154
fertility policy, 193
Festinger, Leon, 230–1
Filmer, Robert, *Patriarcha*, 170
First Alcibiades (Foucault), 28–30, 33, 50, 53
Flaubert, Gustave, 117–19, 121, 123–4, 128–30, 135, 137–42
　Bouvard and Pécuchet, 120, 129–30, 132, 134–7, 140–1
flexi-self, 62–3
Florio, John, 111
Flossenburg concentration camp, 225
Flynn, James, 202
Flynn effect, 201–3, 282
folly, 77, 91–3, 97, 114
　anti-philosophy of, 93
　of definitions, 96–8
　imagination and, 114
　indictments of, 104
　notion, 93
　and stupidity, 96, 98
fools, 11–15, 93, 101, 113, 117
fools' paradises, 91–6
Ford Motor Company, corporate culture of, 250
Foucault, Michel, 28–9, 260
　First Alcibiades, 28–30, 33, 50, 53
　Madness and Civilization, 105
Frankfurt, Harry G., *On Bullshit*, 255
Frankfurt Psychoanalytic Institute, 221
freedom, 124, 220
Fromm, Erich, 230
　Escape from Freedom, 231
Fukuyama, Francis, 123

functional stupidity, 245, 248, 250–1
Fyodorov, Nikolai, 114–15

g (general intelligence), 168, 174, 177–8, 185–6, 188
Gabriel, Markus, *The Human Animal: Why We Still Don't Fit into Nature*, 254
Galapagos Islands, 152–3
Gallipoli campaign, 14
Galton, Francis, 2, 143, 147, 151–2, 154, 156
  Hereditary Genius, 143, 151–2, 154–6
  Memories of My Life, 152
  predilection for measuring human worth, 152
Gamble, Clarence, 147, 151
Gandhi, Mahatma, 74
general cognitive ability, 188
  general knowledge, 187–8
genetics, enthusiasm for, 210
genocide, 147, 217, 228–9, 254
The German Ideology (Marx), 238
Germany
  culture, 234
  enlightenment, 25–6
  intelligence services, 224–5
Gilbert, Gustave, 226, 227, 230–2
  The Psychology of Dictatorship, 229–30
Gioia, Dennis, 250–1
Glavnoye Razvedyvatelnoye Upravlenie (GRU), 261
Global Challenges Foundation, 243
Goddard, Henry Herbert, 180–1
  The Kallikak Family: A Study in the Heredity of Feeble-Mindedness, 144
Goebbels, Joseph, 226
Golob, Sacha, 5, 13–14, 16, 32, 118, 188
Goody, Jade, 5–9, 27
Google, 194, 275
Göring, Reichsmarshall Hermann, 227–9

Gould, Stephen Jay, 177, 180, 183, 195–6, 200
Graeber, David, 235–6, 237–40, 242, 244–5, 251, 253, 276–7
  functional stupidity of, 262
  The Utopia of Rules: On Technology, Stupidity and the Secret Joys of Bureaucracy, 235–6, 238, 242
Gray, John, 90, 92
Greek philosophers, 64
Greek thinkers, 25
Greek tragedies, 44
Greenpeace, 278
Gregg, Justin, 189–91, 244, 253–4, 278
  If Nietzsche Were a Narwhal, 252
Grossmith, George and Weedon, *The Diary of a Nobody*, 133
Gunaratana, Bhante Henepola, 47, 82, 85, 246
  Mindfulness in Plain English, 82

hacking, 264
Haddon, Alfred Cort, 163
Haig, General, 14–15
Haldane, J.B.S., 158–9, 164–5
hallucinogenic hydrocarbons, 23
Halpern, Diane F., 197–9
Hamilton, Ian, 14
Han, Byung-Chul, 75–8, 85, 278
happiness, 91
  normative element to, 91–2
  subjective sense of, 26
Harari, Yuval, 268–9
Hayek, Friedrich, 80
Head Start programme, 206
health insurance programme, 235
Hegel, Georg Wilhelm Friedrich, 104, 123–4, 127, 137, 241
  Lectures on the Philosophy of World History, 124
  The Phenomenology of Spirit, 240–1
Heller, Joseph, 115
Henrique, Léon, 137

317

Hereditary Genius (Galton), 143, 151–2, 154–6
Heretics Society, 159
Herrnstein, Richard J., and Murray, Charles, 191–6, 198–202, 204–6
The Bell Curve, 194–7, 199, 202, 210–11
Herzberg, Elaine, 274–5
Hesse, Hermann, *Siddhartha*, 56–60, 85–9
heuristic devices, 245
Heydrich, Reinhard, 229
Hill, John, 164
Himmler, Heinrich, 226
Hinduism, 83
history, definition of, 123
Hitler, Adolf, 218, 226, 234
  attempted assassination of, 225
Holden, Judge, 164
Hollerith, Herman, 18
Holmes, Oliver Wendell, 144
Holocaust survivors, 219
Homo sapiens, 153, 278
Hornby, Nick, *High Fidelity*, 168
Huey, Edmund Burke, *Backward and Feeble-Minded Children*, 144
human-analogue machines (HAMs), 274
The Human Animal: Why We Still Don't Fit into Nature (Gabriel), 254
Human Betterment League, 145
human development, 125
Human Fertilization and Embryology Authority, 208
human flourishing, 21, 238
humaneness, 62, 70
humanity, 109, 110, 125, 163, 239
  anti-rational militant tendency of, 94
  composition of, 106
  feature of, 283–4
  projections of, 10
  religion of, 126
Hume, David, 101, 113

humility, 24, 39, 102, 159
Huxley, Aldous, 4, 154, 160
  Brave New World, 4, 156
Huxley, Julian, 156–63, 207
Huxley, Thomas Henry, 153–4, 156–7, 161–2, 175
  Man's Place in Nature, 154
Hypnos, Nigretos, 110

idiotic narcissism, 122
If Nietzsche Were a Narwhal (Gregg), 252
ignorance, 5, 6, 8–10, 12, 25, 27–30, 35, 39, 128
  attachment to, 28
  bottomless abyss of, 129
  ironic stance of affecting, 34
  to knowledge, 25
  pose of, 34–5
  Socratic idea of, 128
  and stupidity, 6, 127–8
illusions, 47–8, 87–90
imagination
  ignorance and lack of, 254
  structures of, 237
imbeciles, 144–5
Immigration Restriction Act, 183, 185
immortality of the soul, 45
imperturbability, performance of, 113
impiety, accusations of, 24
in vitro fertilization, 207
individualism, 62–4
  principle of, 44
  psychic burden of, 231
induction, 100–1, 103
inequalities, reproducing, 214
ineradicable stupidity, 264–7
inference, 101, 103–4
infomania, 131–2
ingenuity, 159
innovation, 276–7
Innumeracy (Paulos), 12
inquiry, purpose of, 40

intellectual capabilities, 175–6
intellectuals, 173
   capacities, 4, 178
   enterprises, 139
   failings, 15
   inquiries, 140
   skills, 17–18
   systems, 61–2, 123, 137
intelligence, 2–4, 6, 9, 57, 174–5, 178–9, 192–3, 196, 200–2, 210–11, 221, 236, 281–2, 287
   baseline of, 178
   of children, 176
   definition of, 189–90
   degree of, 176
   development of, 157
   distribution, 193
   embryo selection for, 206
   essential for, 282
   functioning of, 185
   general factor of, 177, 185–6
   genes for, 208
   hackers, 267
   of immigrants, 180
   kinds of, 10
   lack of, 12, 189
   marker of, 188
   measures of, 186, 198
   nature of, 192, 197
   pursuit of, 57–8
   sign of, 19
   stupidity and, 20
   testing for, 185, 191, 198, 214, 283
International Ladies' Garment Workers' Union, 236
interpretive labour, 241, 252–3
interview process, 19
intoxication, 44
investments, 11–13, 15
IQs, 13–14, 131–2, 178, 194, 196–8, 201, 203, 226, 245
   of Asian Americans, 198
   of children, 200
   of geographical regions, 177
   scores, 281–2
   tests, 4, 10, 16, 18, 20–1, 24, 177, 179, 181–3, 186, 192, 199, 202–3, 210–11, 223, 228, 266, 281–3
irrationality, 263
Ixion, 57–8

Jade's Salon (TV show), 7
Jainism, 83
Jamison, William S., 42–3
Jefferson, Thomas, 170
Jen, Gish, 62–4
Jensen, Arthur, 210
Johnson, Boris, 30, 38, 211, 257–8
Johnson, Lyndon, 206
Jones, Steve, 208
Jowett, Benjamin, 25, 31
Joyce, James, 88
Judge, Mike, *Idiocracy*, 9
Jünger, Ernst, 220
justice, 29
   nature of, 32, 38–9
   reality of, 45

Kahneman, Daniel, 257, 263
   Thinking, Fast and Slow, 257
The Kallikak Family: A Study in the Heredity of Feeble-Mindedness (Goddard), 144
Kamin, Leon, 179–80
Kant, Immanuel, 2, 15, 25–6, 136, 219–20
Kaufman Assessment Battery for Children, 177
Keats, John, 98
Kelley, Douglas, 226–7
Keown, Damien, 82–3
King Lear (Shakespeare), 93, 95–7, 111–13, 285
Kingsley, Charles, 157, 161, 212–13, 215
   The Water Babies, 161
Kipling, Rudyard, *The Jungle Book*, 16

Kittler, Friedrich, 268
Knausgaard, Karl Ove, *The Wolves of Eternity*, 114
knowledge, 27, 35, 43–4, 46–8, 57, 59, 77, 80, 85–7, 98, 101–3, 130, 139–40, 284
   definitions of, 141
   domain of, 100
   failure of, 2
   ignorance to, 25
   insufficient, 38–9
   learning and acquiring, 80
   panegyric to, 99
   perfect control of, 102
   pleasurable pursuit of, 99
   pleasure and delight of, 99
   pursuit of, 27, 81, 102
   reason and, 45
   through experiment and action, 85
Know Thyself, 22, 28–9, 30, 44, 49–50
Kondo, Marie, 78–9
Kraus, Karl, 1–2, 286
   perspective risks, 285
Kropotkin, Pyotr, 253–4

Laertius, Diogenes, *Lives and Opinions of the Eminent Philosophers*, 6
Landauer, Karl, 221, 223–4
Langer, Ellen J., 246–9
Laozi, 67, 69, 71, 75, 77–80
Latour, Bruno, *After Lockdown: A Metamorphosis*, 253
Lau, D.C., 70, 78
Lawrence, Neil, 274–5
The Atomic Human: Understanding Ourselves in the Age of AI, 173, 274
Lazarus, Emma, 181
leadership, 166
learning, 137
   art and, 216
Learning Chips, 209, 211
Lectures on the Philosophy of World History (Hegel), 124

Levine, Timothy R., 255, 272
   Duped: Truth-Default Theory and the Social Science of Lying and Deception, 255
Levitin, Daniel J., 131
Li, Chenyang, *The Confucian Philosophy of Harmony*, 69
Li, Jin, 66–8, 73
life expectancy, 16
life philosophy, 83–4
The Little Book of Stupid Questions (Borgenicht), 9–10
Lives and Opinions of the Eminent Philosophers (Laertius), 6
living, experience of, 9
logic, 281–2
Luddism, 280
Lynn, Richard, 205
Lyotard, Jean-François, 260

Machiavelli, 80
machine intelligence, 274–5
machine learning, 271, 275, 278
Macintyre, Alasdair, 136
Madison, Guy, 168
madness, 20, 91–2
Madness and Civilization (Foucault), 105
Mahayana thinking, 82–3
Malthus, Thomas, 155, 160, 174, 193
Martin, Dorothy, 231
Marx, Karl, 103, 123–5, 127, 137, 238
   The German Ideology, 238
Marxist destiny, 276–7
The Mass Psychology of Fascism (Reich), 231
mass stupidity, 230–1
A Mathematician Plays the Stock Market (Paulos), 12
Matthew effect, 282
McAndrew, Helton, 146
McLuhan, Marshall, 267–8, 277
McQueen, Steve, 212–16

INDEX

Mead, Carver, 18
Medicaid, 235–6, 242
Meller, Aidan, 270–1
Melville, Herman, *Bartleby, the Scrivener: A Story of Wall Street*, 133
Memories of My Life (Galton), 152
Mencius, 66
meningitis, 135
mental ability, 188
mental deficiencies, 151
mental disabilities, 201–2
mental dullness, 164
mental functions, 187
mental testing, 182
Meta, 277
Microsoft, 19, 194
The Middle Way: Faith Grounded in Reason (Dalai Lama), 80
A Midsummer Night's Dream (Shakespeare), 94
Milgram, Stanley, 232–4
militarism, 217
Mill, John Stuart, 13, 26, 91–2, 173, 175–6, 178, 188
  The Spirit of the Age, 176
  The Subjection of Women, 170, 172
Milton, John, 129–30
mimicry, 255
Mindfulness in Plain English (Gunaratana), 82
mindlessness, 246–7, 250–1, 254
misfortunes, 9, 112
misogyny, 170
Mitchell, Joni, 64
mobile operations, 14–15
modern empiricism, 100
Montaigne, Michel de, 93, 109–11, 113, 253–4
moral judgement, 220
  moral obligation, 247
  moral regeneration, 218
  moral virtue, 26
Moran, Gwen, 19

More, Thomas, 106–7, 110
Mori, Masahiro, 270
Morrow, Lance, 284
multicultural society, 8
multitasking, 132
Musil, Robert, 6, 217–19, 226
Musk, Elon, 272, 277, 279
Muth, John F., 247
mutual aid, 253–4
mutual defence, 254

Nāgārjuna, 81–2, 87
narcissism, 68, 122, 229
Narragonia, 'fool's paradise' of, 105
native stupidity, 37, 55, 109, 136
natural differences, 169–70
natural language processing, 278
natural selection, 124, 152–3, 156–7, 161, 172
nature of being, 45
Nazism, 221, 224, 234
  pathology, 230
  personality, 227, 229
  popularity of, 225
necrophilia, 229–30
Ne'eman, Ari, 19
negroes, cultural inferiority of, 161
neo-Stoicism, 110, 114
Neumann, Franz, 231
  Behemoth: The Structure and Practice of National Socialism, 231
neurodiversity, 20
  honouring and nurturing, 20
  persons with, unemployment rates of, 18
  writers with, 20
Neurotribes: The Legacy of Autism and the Future of Neurodiversity (Silberman), 20
neurotypical peers, 19
neurotypical societies, 16–17
The New Spirit of Capitalism (Boltanski and Chiapello), 242

Newton, Isaac, 157
Nietzsche, Friedrich, 29, 43–4, 46–7, 124
Nineteen Eighty-Four (Orwell), 258, 279
nirvana, 84, 87
Noble Truth of Buddhism, 57
non-human intelligences, 270
non-neurotypical intelligence, 18
non-rational heuristics, 263
North Carolina Eugenics Board, 146
nuclear holocaust, 243
Nuremberg, 226–34
　Race Laws 1935, 224
　trials, 228

Obama, Barack, 257
Occupy Wall Street, 237
Of Mice and Men (Steinbeck), 212
Okolosie, Lola, 213, 215
Olusoga, David, 211–12, 215
Omphalos, 22
On Bullshit (Frankfurt), 255
On the Origin of the Species (Darwin), 124, 152, 157, 253–4
The Open Society and Its Enemies (Popper), 127
opinions, 47, 59, 103, 127, 129–30, 155, 165, 173, 181, 257
oppression, 277, 279
Orwell, George, 258
　Animal Farm, 126–7
　Nineteen Eighty-Four, 258, 279
Otis–Lennon School Ability Test, 177

Palin, Sarah, 2
The Paradox of Choice: Why More Is Less (Schwartz), 248
Parker, Charlie, 68, 71, 73, 77
Pascal, Blaise, 75
passions, 107–9, 112–13, 216
pathological deficiency, 223
Patriarcha (Filmer), 170
patriarchal society, 170

Paulos, John Allen, 11–12, 96
　disastrous investment, 12
　Innumeracy, 12
　A Mathematician Plays the Stock Market, 12
Peabody College of Education and Human Development, 269–70
perception, mode of, 279
perceptual reasoning, 186, 188
Perceptual Reasoning Index (PRI), 188
perfectibility, 160, 164–5
Periclean wisdom, 32
Pericles, 32–3
The Phenomenology of Spirit (Hegel), 240–1
philosophy
　creativity of, 69
　disputes in, 82
　literacy-venerating, 282
　and religion, 78
　stupidities of, 137
　task of, 43
　wisdom, 88–9
phishing, 262
phrenology, 174–5
physical propagation, 157
Pichai, Sundar, 166–7
pig–human distinction, 26
pigeon breeding, 153
Plato, 24, 28, 30, 47
　positive metaphysical, 25
　Republic, 42, 155
Plomin, Robert, 208–10
Podesta, John, 262
political pragmatism, 36
Polizzotti, Mark, 134
Popper, Karl, 127–8, 139
　The Open Society and Its Enemies, 127
positivism, 125, 127
　critique of, 128
　doctrine of, 125–6
　objection to, 128
post-truth, 10, 225

INDEX

Post-Truth: The New War on Truth and How to Fight Back (d'Ancona), 258
poverty, 199, 265
power, 5, 18, 30, 33–4, 38, 41, 44, 47, 49–50, 53–5, 59, 68, 76, 84, 87, 103, 105, 109, 111–14, 157, 165, 169, 241
Prasanna, Rishi Shiv, 228
preventative education, 210
preventative medicine, 210
privilege, 5, 62, 88, 111, 198, 240
problem-solving skills, 281–2
Processing Speed Index (PSI), 188
Procter & Gamble, 147–9
prognostic myopia, 243, 251, 278
progressivism, 126
psychoanalysis, 259
psychological differences, 168
psychologists, 32, 131, 168, 177, 184–5, 187, 191, 202, 217, 230, 243, 282
psychology, 174, 232, 282
The Psychology of Dictatorship (Gilbert), 229–30
psychometric tests, 185, 252
psychopaths, 167, 229–30, 256
public education, 174, 210, 282
Putin, Vladimir, 1, 259, 261–2
Pythia's predictions, 42

'The Quantity Theory of Insanity' (Self), 3
Quayle, Dan, 33
Queneau, Raymond, 126, 141
Quixotism, 133

racial degeneracy, 163
racial differences, 196
racial superiority, 154
racism as socio-political doctrine, 3
Raine, Craig, 17
ransomware attacks, 262–3
rational faculties, 115
rational reflection, 248
rational thinking, 81
rationality, 113–14, 247
reason and, 114
Raven's Progressive Matrices, 177
Reagan, Ronald, 242
reality, 5–7, 24, 46–8, 71, 83–5, 87–9, 117, 211, 223, 229–30, 276, 284
reason, 5–6, 40, 100
blindness of, 111–16
chain of, 36–7
elenchic, 41–2
life of, 43
recollection, 32
reconstructive surgery, 147
reflection, 39, 41, 59, 72, 218, 220, 232, 248, 275
Reich, Wilhelm, *The Mass Psychology of Fascism*, 231
reincarnation, 57, 74
Reith, John, 249
religion, 57, 75–6, 101
philosophy and, 78
thinkers, 126
Republic (Plato), 42, 155
resemblance, 101, 106
resilience, 20
respective polities, 30
Rhodes, Cecil, 75
Riddick, Elaine, 143–7, 151
Rig Veda, 84
Rinehart, Billy, 261–3
Roman Catholicism, 107
Rorschach Inkblot Test, 226
Rotenstreich, Nathan, 97
Rothkopf, David, 284
Rotolo, Thomas, 197–8
Rushton, Philippe, 196
Russell, Bertrand, 91–3, 98, 104

sacrificial offerings, 22
sado-masochistic power lust, 217
Saini, Angela, 168, 172
Salmon, Peter, 138

INDEX

samsara, 57, 83–4, 87
Sanders, Bernie, 263
sanguine poison frog, 154–5
sanity, 3, 116
Sarandos, Ted, 279
Sartre, Jean-Paul, 3, 119
   The Family Idiot, 119
Schacht, Hjalmar, 227
Schindler, Oskar, 224–5
Schlegel, Friedrich, 14
Schopenhauer, Arthur, 3–4, 10, 41, 57, 118, 156–7, 283
Schulz, Kathryn, 91
Schwartz, Barry, 248–50
   The Paradox of Choice: Why More Is Less, 248
self-help guide, 248–9
scientific inquiry, 260
scientific method, 99, 101, 103–4, 126, 128, 132, 138
scripted human behaviours, 245–6
Scruton, Roger, 139
segregation, 180, 265
selective breeding, 155
Self, Will, 'The Quantity Theory of Insanity', 3
self-contradiction, 67
self-deception, 3, 12
self-determination, 248
self-esteem, misplaced, 30
self-examination, 42, 46
self-help, 10
self-humiliation, 25, 31
self-image, 63
self-improvement, programme of, 44
self-interest, 283
self-interrogation, 41
self-knowledge, 31, 35, 138
self-portraits, 272
self-protective responses, 249
self-satisfaction, misplaced, 26
self-selection process, 193
self-serving inferences, 66

Senecal, Anthony, 255–6
sexual differences, 169
sexual dimorphism, 169
sexual selection, 172
Seyss-Inquart, Arthur, 227
Shakespeare, William, 82–3, 93–4, 97, 113
   A Midsummer Night's Dream, 94
   King Lear, 93, 95–7, 111–13, 285
   Twelfth Night, 92–3
Shannon, Lyttanya, 214, 216
Shapiro, Scott, 263–4
   Fancy Bear Goes Phishing: The Dark History of the Information Age, in Five Extraordinary Hacks, 262
shareholders, 4, 247–8
Shetty, Shilpa, 7–8
ships of fools, 105–11
Siddhartha (Hesse), 56–60, 85–9
Siddons, Alastair, 213
Sikhism, 83
Silberman, Steve, 18, 20
   Neurotribes: The Legacy of Autism and the Future of Neurodiversity, 20
Simon, Herbert, 178–9, 184, 247–9
Simon, Theodore, 176
Simpson, Ann-Marie, 214
Singer, Judy, 16
Siris, 272
Slingerland, Edward, 67–9, 72–3, 77
smartness, 278, 280
smartphones, 130–1, 204, 279
Smith, Adam, *The Wealth of Nations*, 155
Smith, Tiffany Watt, *Schadenfreude: The Joy of Another's Misfortune*, 9
Snijders–Oomen Nonverbal Intelligence Test, 177
social conservatism, 70
social distancing rules, 30
social inequalities, 3–4
social media, 26, 39, 122, 242
social norms, 18–19, 183

324

INDEX

social policy, 105, 147
social scripts, 246–9
social status, leading determinant of, 194
Socrates, 24–8, 30–2, 36–9, 42–3, 59–61, 79–80, 88–9, 100, 140–1
  battle against stupidity, 47
  complaints, 30
  critic of, 42
  cross-examination by, 25
  humiliating questioning from, 34–5
  insistence, 33
  questioning by, 24–5
  self-defence speech, 24
  stupidity for, 28
Socratic method, 29, 139–40
The Socratic Method: A Practitioner's Handbook (Farnsworth), 39
Socratic reasoning, 43
Socratic wisdom, 24, 39
SolarWinds, 264
solidarity, 74, 274
solitary behaviours, 17
Solomon, King, 99
solutionism, 263
sovereignty, 102–3
Spanish Civil War, 236
spatial reasoning, 281–2
Spearman, Charles, 177–8, 185–6
The Spirit of the Age (Mill), 176
spiritual awakening, 60
spiritual debility, 218–19
spiritual regeneration, 218
spontaneous variation, 157
Standard Innovation, 267
Stanford–Binet Intelligence Scale, 24, 184
Stanford–Binet test, 179, 201
Stanovich, Keith, 14
sterilization, 146
  forced, 163
  legislation, 145, 161
  policies, 150

Sternberg, Robert J., 96
stock market, 14
Stoicism, 108, 111–14
  acceptance, 112
  detachment, 109
  impassibility of, 109
  imperturbability, 108–9
  indifference, 109, 112
  intellectual shortcomings of, 115
  philosophy, 107
  veneration of reason, 113
  wisdom, 109, 112
Stonebridge, Lyndsey, 219–20
Stopes, Marie, 160, 163, 175, 193, 207
strawberry poison-dart frog, 154–5
structural stupidity, 236, 249, 270, 276
  conspicuous displays of stupidity, 240–2
  rise of dark triad, 255–60
  smartest idiot in room, 235–40
  society function, 243–55
structural violence, 236, 241
A Study of American Intelligence (Brigham), 182
stupefaction, 5, 26, 121, 129, 279
stupid eugenics
  intellectual inferiority of women, 165–73
  war against feeble-mindedness, 143–63
stupid intelligence
  g factor, 173–91
  racist stupidity, 211–16
  stupid genetic engineering, 205–11
  stupid statistics, 191–205
stupidity, 5–10, 20, 25–6, 57, 91–2, 101, 115, 136–7, 281
  ancient age of, 27
  battle against, 48
  bronze age of, 284
  of cleverness, 56–61
  commodification of, 39
  connoisseurs of, 66

stupidity (*cont.*)
 culture of, 254
 cunning of, 242
 definition of, 12, 14, 16, 17, 96
 description of, 2–3
 elemental forces of, 285
 examples of, 151
 extent of, 265
 fight back against, 2
 fog of, 119
 of folly, 97, 118
 forms of, 25, 237
 future thinkers about, 28–9
 golden age of, 1
 history of, 147, 287
 human, 120
 inducing conformity, 238
 kinds of, 218
 manifestation of, 286
 modern, 119–20
 narratives about, 4
 nature of, 13
 non-negligible role of, 217
 outliers for, 282
 overcoming of, 39
 paradox, 256
 perspective, 16
 philosophers of, 13
 production and distribution of, 142
 ratio of, 265
 seductions of, 1–2
 short-term delights of, 251
 slavery of, 49–53
 spiritual malaise of, 6
 statistics, 191–205
 tumour of, 119
 underestimating, 266
 unenlightened, 58
 use and meaning from, 1
The Stupidity Paradox (Alvesson and Spicer), 9–10, 244, 251
The Subjection of Women (Mill), 170, 172

subjective judgement, 3
suffering, 56–9
Sure Start programme, 206
surveillance, 279
sutras, 61, 82
Synthetic Aperture Personality Assessment Project, 177
System Zero, 275

Tao Yuanming, 77
Tarnoff, Ben, 278, 280
technology, 104, 207
 innovations in, 268
 use of, 103
Temple of Apollo, 22
Templer, Klaus, 256
Terman, Lewis, 181–2
tertiary education, 209–10
Tesla, 194
The Atomic Human: Understanding Ourselves in the Age of AI (Lawrence), 173, 274
Thematic Apperception Test, 226
theory of mind, 252
The Theory of the Leisure Class (Veblen), 240–1
therapeutic culture, 259
Theravada traditions, 82
Think: In Defence of a Thoughtful Life (Brinkmann), 251
Thinking, Fast and Slow (Kahneman), 257
Third Reich, 217, 219, 223–4, 231, 276
Through the Looking-Glass (Carroll), 260
Thurstone, Lewis, 177–8
Tittle, Charles R., 197–8
Todd, Chuck, 259
transcendental realm, 47
transhumanism, 158
Trump, Donald, 2, 5, 24, 30, 38, 121, 181, 218, 255–6, 259, 261–2, 284
 The Art of the Deal, 255–6

INDEX

Truss, Liz, 244
trust, 272–3
truth, 12, 28–9, 48, 57–8, 88, 99, 100, 138
  about stupidity, 15
  contemptuousness of, 259
  immutability of, 138
  objective standard for, 260
  pursuit of, 39, 42, 46
  and reality, 91
Truth-Default Theory, 272
Turing, Alan, 264
Twelfth Night (Shakespeare), 92–3

unhappiness, 17
unintelligence, 13–14
Untypical: How the World Isn't Built for Autistic People and What We Should Do About It (Wharmby), 16
utilitarianism, 26
utopian thinkers, 139
The Utopia of Rules: On Technology, Stupidity and the Secret Joys of Bureaucracy (Graeber), 235–6, 238, 242

vaccination, 258
Vallance, Patrick, 211
Vanhanen, Tatu, 205
Veblen, Thorstein, *The Theory of the Leisure Class*, 240–1
Vedic sages, 85
Verbal Comprehension Index (VCI), 188
verbal reasoning, 187
Verizon, 235
Vienna, 217–23
Vigrahavyāvartanī, 81
Vincent, François-André, 29
virtues, 61–5, 69
  definitions of, 42
  wisdom and, 61–5

virtuosity, 77, 139
visual arts, 271
vocabulary, 281–2
void, touching the, 80–5
Voidism, 81–3, 87
Voltaire, 3, 4, 41, 156–7, 283

WAIS-IV intelligence test, 186–8, 190
Wang, Zhen-Dong, 61, 71
The Water Babies (Kingsley), 161
The Wealth of Nations (Smith), 155
Wechsler, David, 183–4, 186, 189
  definition of intelligence, 189
Wechsler Adult Intelligence Scale (WAIS), 183–4
Wechsler–Bellevue intelligence test, 183–4, 186, 201, 227
Wechsler Intelligence Scale for Children, 177, 183–4
Wechsler Preschool and Primary Scale of Intelligence, 183–4
well-being, 26, 38
Welzer, Harald, *The Culture of Stopping*, 244
western civilization, 29, 43, 69–74
western individualism, 62–3
western metaphysics, 88
western philosophy, 77
western sensibility, 78
western thinking, 76, 85
western wisdom, 77
Wharmby, Pete, *Untypical: How the World Isn't Built for Autistic People and What We Should Do About It*, 16
Wilson, A.N., 154
Wilson, Glenn, 131
wisdom, 27, 39, 57–8, 61–5, 71, 86, 90, 96, 106–7, 109, 140–1
  conceptions of, 57
  of doing nothing, 67–8, 77
  feature of, 25
  idiots, learning from, 65–7

INDEX

wisdom (*cont.*)
   and knowledge, 70
   life of, 43
   philosophical, 88–9
   pursuit of, 27, 42
   self-humiliation to, 30
   unparalleled, 24
   and virtue, 61–5
witlessness, 117, 285
Wodehouse, P.G., 276
The Wolves of Eternity (Knausgaard), 114
women, opportunities for, 172
Woodard, Maggie, 145
Woodcock–Johnson Test, 177

Working Memory Index (WMI), 188
WorldCom, 11–12
World Population Conference of 1927, 161
World Population Review, 283
World Trade Organization, 236–7
wu-wei, 67–8, 71–3, 75-7

Xerxes, 34

Yerkes, Robert, 182

Zen Buddhism, 74, 76, 79
Zuckerberg, Mark, 272, 275, 277, 279

A Short History of Stupidity